International Series in Operations Research & Management Science

Volume 305

More information about this series at http://www.springer.com/series/6161

Fausto Pedro García Márquez • Benjamin Lev
Editors

Internet of Things

Cases and Studies

 Springer

Editors
Fausto Pedro García Márquez
Ingenium Research Group, ETSI
Industriales de Ciudad Real
University of Castilla-La Mancha
Ciudad Real, Spain

Benjamin Lev
LeBow College of Business
Drexel University, Decision Sciences and
MIS
Philadelphia, PA, USA

ISSN 0884-8289   ISSN 2214-7934   (electronic)
International Series in Operations Research & Management Science
ISBN 978-3-030-70477-3   ISBN 978-3-030-70478-0   (eBook)
https://doi.org/10.1007/978-3-030-70478-0

This Springer imprint is published by the registered company Springer Nature Switzerland AG
The registered company address is: Gewerbestrasse 11, 6330 Cham, Switzerland

Preface

Internet of Things (IoT) is a relatively new discipline, an emerging research field which utilizes tools and techniques taken from operations research and management science (OR/MS). IoT is a network of devices connected and capable of transferring information over the network. Devices on the network can include machine, equipment, human, animal, parking lot, or anything. It can transfer text, signals, media, and software. This book introduces the topic and its origin. It starts with basic concepts and present cases, applications, theory, and potential benefits as seen from OR/MS point of view, for example, advanced analytics and machine learning. Examples are from smart industry, city, transportation, home, and smart devices. The future applications, trends, and potential benefits of this new discipline are discussed. The book provides an interface among OR/MS, engineering/technology, organization and administration, and IoT. It is yet to be seen how OR/MS will influence the development, direction, and shape of IoT. The future of IoT is bright and strong. It will stay with us for decades, will be part of our daily life, will be almost everywhere, and will be extremely useful.

Ciudad Real, Spain   Fausto Pedro García Márquez

Philadelphia, PA, USA   Benjamin Lev

Introduction

Internet of Things (IoT) is a relatively new discipline, an emerging research field that requires the use and application of management science. This book introduces the topic and its origin. It starts with basic concepts and overview and then presents cases, applications, theories, and potentials. The chapters in this book cover a wide array of topics as space permits. Examples are smart industry, city, transportation, home, and smart devices. It also discusses future applications, trends, and potential of this new discipline.

IoT is a network of devices connected and capable of transferring information over the network. The network can be a group of machines, equipment, human, animal, parking lot, and so on. It could transfer text, signals, media, and software. To build and manage IoT, new disciplines in management science have emerged such as advanced analytics and machine learning. Specifically, this book provides an interface between the main disciplines of engineering/technology and the organizational, administrative, and planning capabilities of managing IoT.

This book provides relevant theoretical frameworks and the latest empirical research findings in IoT. It has been written for professionals to show their understanding of the strategic role of IoT at various levels of the information and knowledge organization, that is, IoT at the global economy level, at networks and organizations, at teams and work groups of information systems, and, finally, at the level of individuals as players in the networked environments.

This book is intended for professionals in the field of engineering, information science, mathematics, economists, and researchers who wish to develop new skills in IoT, or who employ the IoT discipline as part of their work. The authors who contributed to this book describe their original work in the area or provide material for cases and studies successfully applying the IoT discipline in real-life cases and theoretical approaches.

Blockchain is a new technology resulting from a continuous research on consensus mechanisms to ensure the integrity of a distributed shared replica. It represents a data structure built on a hash function and distributed among the various participants according to previously agreed consensus rules. Chapter 1 aims to carry out a comprehensive survey of the consensus mechanism that forms the heart of blockchain technology and its suitability for the IoT. It begins by explaining blockchain technology from a historical and technical point of view before approaching the different philosophical approaches within the consensus mechanism, their disadvantage, and their suitability for the IoT sector.

IoT implementation depends, to a large extent, on human and technological resources availability and cultural aspects and priorities of organizations. According to their state, the different factors can be enablers or inhibitors of IoT implementation. Since IoT implementation is a case of digitalization, main elements of digitalization and most typical enablers and inhibitors are presented in Chap. 2. Based on scientific and professional literature, the specific enablers and inhibitors of IoT are presented. They involve technological enablers (ability to provide power to the devices, connectivity, communication capability between elements, and data handling capacity), strategic enablers (IoT adoption as a strategic element, formulation of a global architecture of IoT), organizational enablers (digital talent and skills and digital culture), organizational barriers (need for standardization, security risks, privacy restrictions, cost, and regulatory issues), and cultural barriers (perception of complexity and lack of trust)

The use of the IoT in the healthcare sector has shown to be a promising solution to reduce the workload of doctors and provide better service to patients. However, shared data may be subject to theft or misuse due to the security issues on various devices. Moreover, transparency among stakeholders, confidentiality, and micropayments need to be addressed. The objective of Chap. 3 is to use federated learning over blockchain data generated from IoT devices with the usage of zero-knowledge proof or confidential transactions. The proposed architecture ensures the user a level of privacy set by them while making sure of sharing relevant insights with the concerned parties.

IoT has been undergoing a rapid development and has obtained increasing visibility. Many scientific research achievements have been published. Chapter 4 aims to provide a bibliometric review for highly cited papers in the field of IoT using the Essential Science Indicators, a widely used database to evaluate scientific outputs. Through the retrieval process, 388 papers were identified as highly cited papers. Based on these 388 papers, it analyzes their characteristics from four perspectives: annual and discipline distributions; productive players in terms of journals, countries, institutes, and authors; top-15 most-cited papers; and author keyword analysis. Interesting results are given after the analyses. Through author keyword analysis, the chapter also provides research trends of the IoT for future study.

In macroeconomics, "information" is a copiable product with no additional cost. Despite services on IoT consider the information, their scalabilities are smaller than other information products. Chapter 5 models IoT services as a composition of information, devices, and electricity, and points out that the existence of devices and electricity prevents reducing marginal costs of the services. It is mentioned that the informatization of the computer industry in the past was the replacement of accounting subjects. The chapter describes that design to scale IoT services is to develop incentives letting others shoulder the costs of devices and electricity

In Chap. 6, COVID-19 data are analyzed using the biclustering approach to gain insights such as which group of countries have similar epidemic trajectory patterns over the subset of COVID-19 pandemic outburst days (called bicluster). Countries within these groups (biclusters) are all in the same phase but with a slightly different trajectory. An approach based on the Greedy Two-Way K-Means biclustering algorithm is proposed to analyze COVID-19 epidemiological data, which identifies subgroups of countries that show a similar epidemic trajectory patterns over a specific period. It is the first time that the biclustering approach has been applied to analyze COVID-19 data. In fact, these COVID-19 epidemiological data are not a real count because not all data can be tracked properly, and there are other practical difficulties in collecting the data. Even in developed countries, it has huge practical problems. Therefore, if the IoT-based COVID-19 monitoring system can be used to detect the origin of the COVID-19 outbreak, then the real situation can be identified in each country. Results confirm that the proposed approach can alert and help the government authorities and healthcare professionals to know what to anticipate and which measures to implement to decelerate the spread of COVID-19.

Chapter 7 aims to review IoT applications in the healthcare domain that are representative and active in practice and research. The chapter introduces the existing IoT products in the healthcare market; reviews the studies on developing, using, and improving IoT healthcare applications; and presents and discusses the recent trend and focus of IoT healthcare applications. First, the chapter describes a general picture of IoT healthcare applications. Then, the chapter studies IoT healthcare applications in four scenarios: (1) acute disease care – three applications are introduced to show how IoT benefits acute care: vital sign monitoring, acute care telemedicine, and IoT-based detection and control of infectious diseases; (2) chronic disease care – the chapter focuses on remote health monitoring used for patients with chronic diseases, especially patients with Alzheimer's disease, diabetes, and heart failure; (3) self-health management – the chapter pays attention to the most common representative device for self-health management, smartwatches, and analyzes the two main functions of smartwatches on self-health management, sleep monitoring, and exercise monitoring; (4) hospital operations management – the chapter also discusses IoT application for hospital operation management including asset and automated hospital workflow management, since it can finally improve the efficiency and effect of healthcare delivery and then benefit patients and doctors.

Chapter 8 presents a use-case based on the development of an interactive, integrated, and adaptable visiting system for complex buildings and surrounding grounds (smart places). The system features a mobile application that allows the user to access information from several smart places in a single application, and an indoor location and tracking system that infers the user location during the smart place visit. The system calculates the tracking and location of the user based on the positioning of neighboring BLE devices sensed via Bluetooth on the user's mobile device. The approximate location, behavior, and interests, and hence the visiting profile of each user, can be inferred by the signals from multiple beacons installed on the building at specific pre-defined positions. The system also integrates a backend content management system to allow the creation and management of smart places information and supports information import from BIM tools.

Chapter 9 analyzes contemporary machine learning techniques for the computation of market and asset liquidity risk for multiple-assets portfolios. Furthermore, this chapter focuses on the theoretical aspects of asset liquidity risk and presents two critically robust machine learning processes to measuring the market liquidity risk for trading securities as well as for asset management objectives. To that end, this chapter extends research literature related to the computation of market and asset liquidity risks by providing generalized theoretical modeling algorithms that can assess both market and liquidity risks and integrate both risks into multiple-assets portfolios settings. The robust modeling algorithms can have practical applications for multiple-securities portfolios, and can have many uses and application in financial markets, particularly in light of the 2007–2009 global financial meltdown in issues related to machine learning for the policymaking process and machine learning techniques for the IoT data analytics. In addition, risk assessment algorithms can aid in advancing risk management practices and have important applications for financial technology (FinTech), artificial intelligence, and machine learning in big data environments.

The current IoT development involves ambient intelligence, which ensures that IoT applications provide services that are sensitive, adaptive, autonomous, and personalized to the needs of the users. A key issue of this adaptivity is context modeling and reasoning. Multiple proposals in the literature have tackled this problem according to various techniques and perspectives. Chapter 10 provides a review of context modeling approaches, with a focus on services offered in ambient assisted living (AAL) systems for persons in need of care. The chapter presents the characteristics of contextual information, services offered by AAL systems, as well as context and reasoning models that have been used to implement them. A discussion highlights the trends emerging from the scientific literature to select the most appropriate model to implement AAL systems according to the collected data and the services provided.

IoT is a platform governed by information and communication technologies that facilitates affordable data communication among heterogeneous devices in large scale. However, computation rich applications running on IoT need specific considerations as user response plays key role in critical situations particularly in transportation, healthcare and smart cities. In this view, Chap. 11 explains in details characteristics of various software components that are in use in IoT over existing communication networks, and presents various problems solving techniques for IoT applications in intelligent transport systems. Further, the role of algorithms and computational structures for development of efficient IoT application is illustrated in detail with three real time case studies in transportation domain.

Chapter 12 considers the "Mobile Kukan Toukei™" (mobile spatial statistics) to examine characteristics of the and spatial movement patterns in specific tourist destinations in Nagoya City (Japan). This chapter also attempts to estimate visitor volume and flow using movement data acquired by Wi-Fi tracking sensors installed widely in tourism destinations. A Wi-Fi tracking sensor is a device that acquires a media access control (MAC) address unique to communication devices such as smartphones. By installing sensors in a tourism area, the same MAC address is acquired between them, and a movement information of the visitor can be collected. This chapter examines wide-area travel routes of visitors in the northern part of the Kyoto Prefecture (Japan) and combines data obtained through sensors with other survey data to clarify movement patterns of visitors for each attribute within the area.

One of the greatest needs today in road safety and its conservation work is to obtain traffic data in real time to predict traffic and increase safety of people. In Chap. 13, a camera embedded in an unmanned aerial vehicle in static flight has been used to get information about traffic in a roundabout. These infrastructures are key since they are considered conflictive points in the circulation flow, which is complex to analyze. A system has been developed to analyze images online and that obtains vehicle behavior data in real time. It offers information such as vehicle count, their instantaneous speed at each moment, average speed of each one, individual trajectory, traffic density, and lane changes and trouble spots. The information provided by this system allows a better decision making, security, traffic flow, and scheduling maintenance tasks.

Finally, many thanks to our families for their moral support, encouragement, and patience. My son Ron (M.D.) and his wife Melitza, my daughter Nurit (J.D., Lieutenant Colonel, Retired) and her husband James (Colonel, Retired), and my five beautiful grandchildren: Hannah (senior, Carnegie Mellon University), Jimmy (freshman, Virginia Polytechnic Institute), Veronica, Sebastian, and Arya.

This book is dedicated to my beloved father, Faustino García Rodríguez, 1931–2020, who overcame many challenges, but sadly succumbed to complications related to COVID-19 recently.

Ciudad Real, Spain   Fausto Pedro García Márquez

Philadelphia, PA, USA   Benjamin Lev

Contents

About the Editors

Fausto Pedro García Márquez works at the University of Castilla-La Mancha, Spain, as full professor (accredited as full professor since 2013). He is an honorary senior research fellow at Birmingham University, UK, and lecturer at the Postgraduate European Institute, and he has been senior manager at Accenture (2013–2014). Prof. Fausto obtained his European PhD with the highest distinction. He has been awarded with the following prizes: Runner Prize for Management Science and Engineering Management Nominated Prize (2020), and Advancement Prize (2018), First International Business Ideas Competition 2017 Award (2017); Runner (2015), Advancement (2013), and Silver (2012) by the International Society of Management Science and Engineering Management (ICMSEM); Best Paper Award by the *International Journal of Renewable Energy* (impact factor 3.5) (2015). He has published more than 150 papers (65 % International Scientific Indexing, 30% Journal Citation Reports, and 92% internationals), some recognized as: "Applied Energy" (Q1, as "Best Paper 2020"), "Renewable Energy" (Q1, as "Best Paper 2014"); "ICMSEM" (as "excellent"), "Int. J. of Automation and Computing," and "IMechE Part F: J. of Rail and Rapid Transit" (most downloaded). He is author and editor of 25 books (Elsevier, Springer, Pearson, Mc-Graw Hill, Intech, IGI, Marcombo, AlfaOmega) and holds 5 patents. Prof. Fausto is editor of 5 international journals and committee member of more than 40 international conferences. He has been principal investigator in 4 European projects, 6 national projects, and more than 150 projects for universities and companies. His main interests are: artificial intelligence, maintenance, management, renewable energy, transport, advanced analytics, and data science. He is an expert of the European Union in AI4People (EISMD) and ESF. Prof. Fausto is the director of www.ingeniumgroup.eu. More information in https://blog.uclm.es/faustopedrogarcia.

Benjamin Lev is the University Trustee Professor at LeBow College of Business, Drexel University, Philadelphia, Pennsylvania, USA. He holds a PhD in operations research from Case Western Reserve University. Prior to joining Drexel University, Dr. Lev held academic and administrative positions at Temple University, University of Michigan-Dearborn, and Worcester Polytechnic Institute. He is the editor-in-chief of *OMEGA – The International Journal of Management Science* www.OmegaJournal.org; co-editor-in-chief of *International Journal of Management Science and Engineering Management*; and serves on several other journal editorial boards (INFORMS *JAA* (formerly *Interfaces*), *IAOR*, *ORPJ*, *Financial Innovation*, *OPSEARCH*, *IDIM*, *IIE-Transactions*, *ERRJ*, INFORMS *JOR*). He currently holds faculty appointments at seven Chinese Universities (Beijing Jiaotong University, Chengdu University, Nanjing University of Aeronautics and Astronautics, Nanjing University of Information Science and Technology, Nanjing Audit University, Xidian University, Tianjin University). Dr. Lev is the former TIMS VP – Meetings and INFORMS VP – Meetings. He has been INFORMS fellow since 2003. He has published 16 books as well as numerous articles and organized many national and international conferences including ORSA/TIMS Philadelphia, INFORMS Israel, IFORS Scotland, ALIO-INFORMS Buenos Aires, and ICMSEM Philadelphia. https://en.wikipedia.org/wiki/Benjamin_Lev.

Chapter 1
Blockchain as a Complementary Technology for the Internet of Things: A Survey

Mohamed Ikbal Nacer, Simant Prakoonwit, and Ismail Alarab

Abstract Blockchain is a new technology resulting from a continuous research on consensus mechanisms to ensure the integrity of a distributed shared replica. It represents a data structure built on a hash function and distributed among the various participants according to previously agreed consensus rules. This work aims to carry out a comprehensive survey of the consensus mechanism that forms the heart of blockchain technology and its suitability for the Internet of Things. It begins by explaining blockchain technology from a historical and technical point of view before approaching the different philosophical approaches within the consensus mechanism, their disadvantage, and their suitability for the IoT sector.

Keywords Blockchain · Consensus · Internet of things · Proof of work · Proof of stake · Tangle · Deep learning · Soft computing · Hybrid consensus · Byzantine fault tolerance

1.1 Introduction

The growing interest in smart cities, roads, and universities has highlighted the impressive impact that the Internet of Things (IoT) may have on the world. The IoT is a set of devices that share information within the network or with an end storage framework. This shared information is intended to allow devices to act collaboratively or to perform a desired functionality. As a result, the IoT network generates a huge number of transactions between different sensors and devices that are passed to the cloud database for analysis and monitoring. However, security is an issue within the IoT infrastructure, since the storage of personal data in the cloud raises numerous security concerns. The rapid adoption of the IoT technology has

M. I. Nacer (✉) · S. Prakoonwit · I. Alarab
Bournemouth University, Bournemouth, UK
e-mail: mnacer@bournemouth.ac.uk; sprakoonwit@bournemouth.ac.uk;
ialarab@bournemouth.ac.uk

© Springer Nature Switzerland AG 2021
F. P. García Márquez, B. Lev (eds.), *Internet of Things*, International Series in
Operations Research & Management Science 305,
https://doi.org/10.1007/978-3-030-70478-0_1

1

made the use of a centralised approach infeasible [74]. The use of a peer-to-peer network with a distributed registry is a promising solution to eliminate failure and cyberattacks, respond to privacy issues, and handle micropayments.

Blockchain is based on the coupling of cryptographic techniques with distributed algorithms to give the world's first software prototype that has eliminated the need for a trusted third party in transaction processing. The heart of the blockchain architecture lies in its consensus and coming from transaction data, which depends on previous streaming data, based on this. The mechanism can be divided into two stages: the agreement between the various nodes of the community on the validity of the data and the organisation of the relevant information. It builds a chain of blocks that are linked together through hash values and organised internally using a Merkle tree [57]. The chain of trust was previously in use within the field of computing security and certificate chains in the Java platform; however, the condition of adding a block to the chain made the essential difference. On the other hand, Google's search algorithm is based on distributed computing, with nodes working together to generate the relevant page for a query; it is a more of collaboration than a consensus. Thus, the statement that consensus generally depends on the context to which the additional block is a subject of validation is very important.

The problem of distributed consensus is hard, and yet it is an essential step within the blockchain technology. Consensus has been a topic of intense research interest in recent years and has been the subject of significant research in distributed systems since the development of event ordering and the logical clock [51]. In a coordinator attack, there is no way to ensure consensus within a network where an unknown number of messages may be undetectably lost [17]. Blockchain has to deal with specific problems related to its context, such as selfish, defective, or malicious nodes, and to try to eliminate their impact in order to secure the validity of the ledger [77]. The consensus is always subject to the three primary criteria, which are safety, liveness, and fault tolerance. Different proposals have favoured certain of these criteria over others to suit the context in which the scheme will be applied; for example, the Paxos [49] and Raft [60] algorithms favour fault tolerance and safety, leading eventually to a single state of the ledger. In contrast, Bitcoin [59] and other cryptocurrencies favour safety and liveness to secure for each node its own copy of the ledger [76].

As noted above, blockchain technology relies on a hash function to resist any change in the ordering of the ledger content, and the heart of the technology is consensus. This technique has led to the success of the cryptocurrency, and the adoption of the same technique in other domains is very promising. However, throughput and latency can be a problem in terms of coupling it with other technologies. Consensus also suffers from issues related to resource consumption, monopoly, and malicious behaviour. Furthermore, the validity of new information arises from a data structure that may take various forms. Several works have been proposed to solve this problem using a linear chain, a tree chain, and a graphic chain before applying incentive mechanisms such as proof of work (PoW), proof of stake (PoS), or a traceability mechanism.

This work reviews the mechanisms of consensus within blockchain technology and identifies the disadvantages of each approach in the context of the IoT. The next section is an introduction of the blockchain technology from a technical/historical point of view in order to provide the reader with a good background. The third section presents a brief discussion of the different works related to the IoT and what the blockchain can offer. The fourth section is devoted to the types of consensus, which are classified into the different approaches adopted by researchers in the literature. The fifth section discusses the data structure based on which the consensus operates to ensure its validity and integrity and raises the need for a consensus dedicated to the IoT. The final section is the conclusion, which summarises the contributions of this work.

1.2   Blockchain Technology

Blockchain technology was born from combining several concepts in order to introduce Bitcoin [59]. The hash function forms the basis of this technology, and it is believed to be infeasible to find the original message x from the image y. The drawback of this technique lies in the criterion that the original message is mapped to a fixed size. MD5 and SHA1 functions, introduced in the mid-1990s, were identified as having weaknesses before the rise of cryptanalysis, and this led to significant research by the American standardisation institute NIST to introduce SHA2 and SHA3. However, all cryptographic functions have the following main characteristics [71]:

- Collision resistance: This ensures that it is very difficult to find two messages that generate the same message digest.
- Preimage resistance: This means that it is very difficult to get the source message from the hashed value of an unknown message.
- Second resistance to the preimage: For a given message, it is difficult to find a different message that maps to the same message.

A Merkle tree is a critical part of each block and is used to fix the order of the transactions and link them to the previous block. Merkle [57] discussed the use of different cryptographical techniques such as digital signatures and proposed the use of tree authentication, which can solve many problems of communication for which the digital signature is not a suitable conceptual fit. The process of hashing involves repeatedly applying a function that takes an input of a fixed size and gives a random output.

Blockchain is a chain of blocks, and the first proposal for the use of this type of chain was to ensure the integrity of a document. It was an alternative approach to the digital safety deposit box, which suffers from issues related to privacy, bandwidth storage, incompetence, and trust [37]. This approach used a hashed chain of blocks to keep records of each access to a document for security. A later work proposed optimisation through the use of a Merkle tree [8].

PoW is a protocol proof that depends on making the miner do extensive work; for example, it has been used to discourage spam emails in Hashcash [4]. PoW is used in the validation of transactions within blockchain technology [14, 59]. The Bitcoin protocol depends on extensive queries of the hash function with an incrementable nonce number, timestamp, and transaction contents. The mining is complete when the output has the required leading zero. This was intended to create a race between different participants to find a suitable nonce, unlike Hashcash, which simply discourages malicious senders from using a service.

The above-stated concepts were combined to produce the blockchain network for the Bitcoin protocol. Although the system has shown impressive performance in terms of eliminating double-spending without the need for a trusted third party, it has many drawbacks that have launched searches for different forms of block organisation and consensus validation. Szabo [73] discussed previous work by Wei Dai with additional usage of cryptographic techniques. The work aimed to automate the contractual relations based on the ability to virtualise the organisation and the intellectual and physical properties as entities within a distributed system. A smart contract takes a completely different approach from the consensual mechanism by forcing the rules to be validated periodically by miners; the Ethereum platform has introduced smart contracts within the blockchain transaction of values, acting as a proxy interface within the distributed system. This was an initiation of the idea of the autonomous distributed corporation that exchanges values based on different conditions.

1.3 Blockchain for IoT

The goal of the blockchain is to eliminate the need for a trusted third party by ending the manual verification of information. It can be used to optimise various processes such as facilitating trade, expediting cross-border money payments, providing identity verification, securing diamond grading, and tracking shipments around the world [25]. The rapid development of this technology has highlighted the different ways in which it can make daily life easier. Since the first proposal of the blockchain network, including the way in which all the nodes came to consensus on the validity of a financial transaction, it was clear that this technique could ensure privacy, transparency, accountability, traceability, and identity management. Singh et al. [70] discussed the security issues that made the blockchain a game-changer within the IoT sector by providing a peer-to-peer implementation instead of depending on a central server, thus providing transparency to the different stakeholders and users. Moreover, it introduced an architecture that separated the user and the miner in order to keep a record of the validity of the ledger. Fakhri and Mutijarsa [30] carried out a comparison test of a blockchain system and a non-blockchain implementation dedicated to data storage by IoT devices and concluded that the blockchain would be a very secure method of communication among the different devices.

Buccafurri et al. [13] studied the suitability of the blockchain within the context of the IoT. They claimed that the advantages of the network, such as record-keeping, coordination among stakeholders, transparency, and irrevocability of transactions, are characteristics that are also desirable within the IoT sector. Pankaj and Mendki [56] proposed an architecture to enable the use of the blockchain within a fog system to secure communication between a user and the fog end server, taking into consideration the limitations on horizontal scalability. Ali et al. [2] studied the possible impacts on the Internet from the integration of the blockchain as a backbone communicative mechanism. They found that cyberattacks such as the denial of service arise from the centralisation of the different services offered by the network. El Kafhali et al. [27] introduced a raw data stream within the fog and cloud base by proposing the use of different blockchains network for each part of the platform.

The various works in the literature show that the integration of the blockchain within the IoT can provide the following advantages:

- Non-central failure: Due to the distributed nature of the technology, the data will be subject of a duplicative distributed ledger among the participants with non-reversible order.
- Security in two respects: Secure communication that ensures privacy by attaching information to a public key identifier can provide a level of secret communication among users. In addition, the functioning of the system is more secure since it will not be prone to central management-oriented attacks.
- Transparency: Both the stakeholders and the users of the service will benefit from shared knowledge, which provides transparency in the generated bill of payment.

Blockchain has robust features that can be integrated into IoT services, for example:

- Micropayments: A user may be more interested in the micro-usage of service, yielding a micropayment that is easily handled with the blockchain.
- Data tracking: The different stakeholders need to keep track of the different types of data generated by their users in order to provide the best monitoring and analysis and to ensure transparency between each other.
- Decentralisation of services: Services such as DNS, which can be subject to attacks, can be decentralised with the use of the blockchain to provide users with a better service.

1.4 The Blockchain Consensus

Consensus is the core of blockchain technology. The adoption of the solution on a horizontal level led to the introduction of a different approach at each step, such as mining incentives or block organisation using a linear linked chain, tree of block, or directed acyclic graph [43]. Consensus is driven by a ledger;

therefore, this work starts by introducing several radically different approaches to the blockchain consensus between the nodes before examining the different data structures that have been proposed as solutions for the ledger above which the consensus mechanism operates.

1.4.1 Proof of Work

PoW involves solving a mathematical puzzle in exchange for a reward, thus maintaining the validity of the ledger by disincentivising sibling attacks. The scheme proposed by Nakamoto et al. [59] was the first well-performing distributed ledger for a cryptocurrency. Digital signatures and PoW are two concepts that are used to build a reliable consensus mechanism, based on securing the authenticity of the sender using a digital signature. The robustness of the system is secured by making the validation subject to latency, with a resource consumption mechanism to eliminate double-spending and sibling attacks. It is based on extensive querying of the hash function to fill a specific requirement of a leading zero, creating a race among participants, each of which has a certain probability of getting the reward described with his resources over the whole network resources.

$$P_i = \frac{W_i}{\sum_{j=1}^{n} W_j} \tag{1.1}$$

where P is the probability of winning the race described on the resource dedicated by miner i over the resource dedicated by the whole network, j goes over each node in the network up to n, and W stands for hardware resources.

The Nakamoto consensus functions by validating the rules, transactions, and puzzle. Figure 1.1 shows the basic functioning of the miner, including cloning the ledger, getting new transactions from the pool, and starting to mine by querying the hash function, and the first miner to find the hash will broadcast the block to be appended by others. Although the process of validating the rules and the transaction can be carried out internally within each node, the solution to the puzzle must be broadcast to the community, and the mining algorithm used to find a suitable nonce is described in Algorithm *1.1* [81].

Algorithm 1.1 Proof of Work Mining

```
input: blockContent
output: digest
leadingZero←0;
nonce←0;
digest←"";
whileTruedo
      digest =SHA-256(blockContent, timestamp, nonce);
      Leadingzero= calculate_leading_zeros(digest);
ifleadingZero ≥ di f f icultythen
      block = createBlock(blockContent,digest,nonce,timestamp);
```

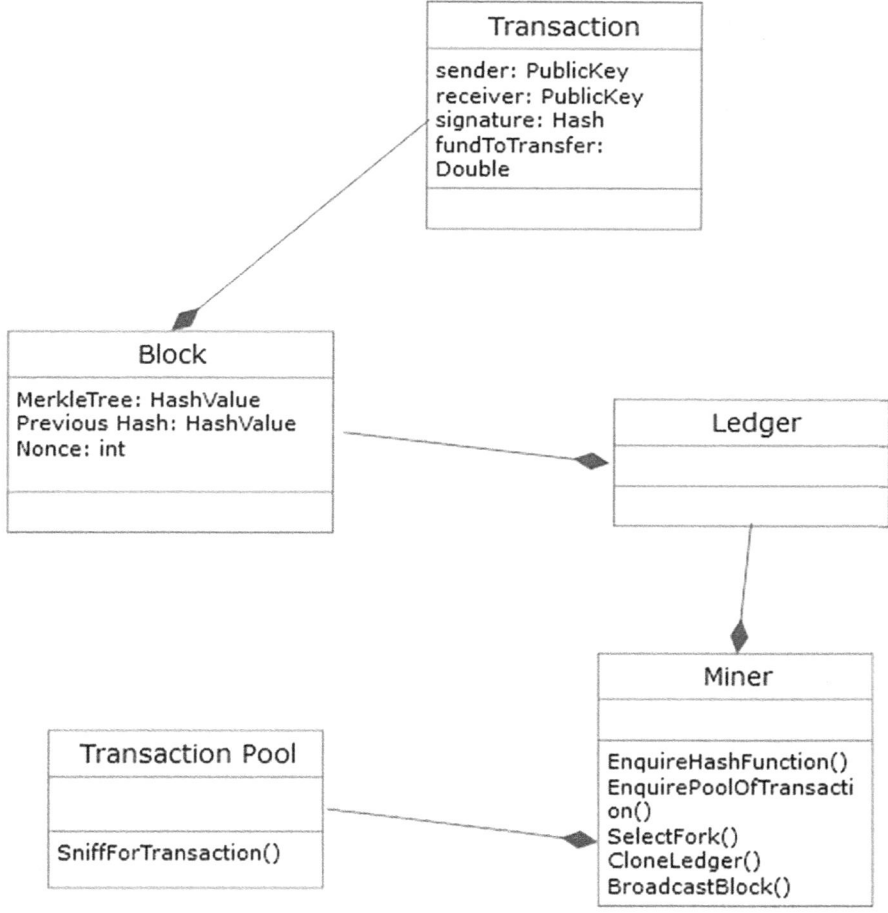

Fig. 1.1 Miners functioning

```
        Broadcast(block);
        break;
else
        increment(nonce,1)
end
end
```

The vulnerability of the PoW lies in the coordination between validators after the process of electing a leader in the race to find the solution to the puzzle. The race game introduces a competency that leads to mining cartels that intend to maximise the benefit to the group in honest or dishonest ways [11]. Each chance of winning by a miner or pool of miners is proportional to the resources that they invest in the whole network. However, selfishness by miners leads to the introduction of various malicious activities to increase their gains. Selfish mining attacks involve keeping an internal chain private to secure an advantage over a public one by investing in the longest chain rule [29]. Block withholding takes advantage of the splitting of computational power among the participants in the pool and mining dishonestly within another pool in order to sabotage it; an analysis is given by Bag et al. [5]. Lie in wait [66] raises the personal gain of a miner by making use of the vulnerability related to dividing the rewards among pool members based on their finished hashed queries. It involves hiding a found block and investing specifically in that pool to gain the highest proportion of the historical hashing power of the pool, thus gaining an advantage. Pool hopping [9] involves spying on other pools and deciding on the next step of the search to solve the NP-complete problem based on the results of other pools. Usually, it appears at the time out of block hash value search set by the network. Nakahara and Inaba [58] solved the issue of fairness among miners by calculating two parameters derived from three other variables: the mining computing power, the number of blocks generated, and the participating term for mining. The two generated parameters will adjust to each miner or pool of mining it appropriate difficulty number.

Liu et al. [54] discussed different game theory papers and analysed the incentive mechanism within the blockchain technology, claiming that comparable to different optimisation approach that does not consider the interaction among the actors; game theory is the mathematical study of rational behaviour among nodes. Eyal [28] introduced the miner's dilemma and offered a mathematical analysis of block withholding by modelling the scenario to determine the infiltration rate and giving a full analysis of how these types of attackers behave within the network by assuming a non-cooperative game. Liao and Katz [53] studied bribery transactions within the Bitcoin ledger and how attackers try to double-spend by initiating a whale transaction (Wt). A Wt is a transaction with a high validation fee that aims to fork the chain. They analysed it by assuming a non-cooperative game and tried to determine the selection of the block and fork. Kroll et al. [48] discussed the technical functioning of Bitcoin before introducing the Goldfinger attack, in which the attacker is not interested in selfish gain but aims to devalue the Bitcoin network, and modelled the game using a non-cooperative model with two players.

PoW is a technique that relies on the impracticality of overcoming a problem rather than being a conceptual technique to deal with malicious behaviour. Nevertheless, different proposals have been made to optimise or replace the Nakamoto PoW by investing in its vulnerability, such as fairness in [58] or HashCore [34] which used a new function for general-purpose processes. Hazari and Mahmoud [38] put forward a parallel treatment of transactions through a PoW by introducing a manager to generate the hashed block and nonce for the fellow miners. Several solutions have been proposed to optimise the cost of computation power by adopting another *NP-complete* problem such as proof of prestige [47], proof of useful work [7]. Werner et al. [78] discussed the vulnerability of the uncle block in the Ethereum platform, the equivalent to the stale block or orphaned block in linear ledgers such as Bitcoin [59], and proposed a policy to eliminate this issue via a discrete event.

The sharing of knowledge within the IoT infrastructure has always raised concerns over privacy. However, the use of a zero-knowledge proof combined with PoW to hide the shared knowledge among the participants is possible, such as in zero cash [67]. The computational power invested in the validation of a transaction is massive due to the limited computational power of each IoT device, and even if there is a dedicated server for computation power, it still vulnerable to a 51% attack. Moreover, the throughput limitations on the number of transaction validations lead to a finality delay in addition to the transaction fee that motivates the miners to maintain the ledger, which is a disadvantage in a highly communicative platform. Thus, PoW is not suitable for a platform that depends on rapid communication, such as a network connecting cars or smart houses. Nevertheless, the implementation of this type of robust proof for smart cities within a high-level component abstraction is the first option and with a data structure based on a graph instead of a linear ledger, which means it is subject to the continuous updating and removing of legacy data.

1.4.2 Byzantine Fault Tolerance

Lamport et al. [52] introduced the Byzantine consensus. Its application within blockchain technology was explored by [36], who developed a secure algorithm based on the properties of a shared replica, which are agreement, termination, and validity. This author also identified the issues with different forms of consensus before discussing the advantages of the Byzantine consensus within the consortium blockchain. The property of randomness within Byzantine fault tolerance (BFT) was discussed by Rabin [64] with the aim of investigating the impact of a probabilistic finality over a deterministic one. The Monte Carlo Byzantine consensus is another variant of BFT that prioritises termination over agreement and validity and where either or both of the latter two proprieties are implemented using a probabilistic approach.

Lamport [49] proposed the Paxos algorithm to mimic the mathematical communication protocol between legislators within an ancient civilisation and used it to solve an ordering consensus problem. The protocol offered a solution to fail-stop tolerance based on prioritising safety and liveliness over fault tolerance. At the beginning of the process, a leader or leaders are elected within each cluster of acceptors to decide on one or many rounds a chosen value that stands for the order of an event and secures the safety propriety. A randomised time delay is used to secure the liveliness property, and the concept of the quorum was first proposed within that paper. BFT is a particular case of failure tolerance within a distributed system. Thus, the work to adjust Paxos within the context of 1/3 malicious nodes was called *the process of Byzantising*, and Lamport [50] discussed how to *Byzantise* with two variants of the Paxos family of algorithms, the Castro-Liskov algorithm [16] and Pcon.

Castro et al. [16] proposed the practical BFT (PBFT) and claimed normal functioning within asynchronous communication, or more precisely with a partial synchrony model. The process of agreement on the validity of a message broadcast from a client to the acceptor community involves four steps. Firstly, a 'pre-prepare' message to build a collaborative consensus among the acceptors. The primary replica ensures that all the members of the validation community are aware of the new request due to a 'pre-prepare' message that contains the client's message, a digital signature, a sequence number, and the view of the message. Secondly, a 'prepare' message ensures the validity of the later consensus among all the nodes and consequently ensures the overall order of the participants. Thirdly, the 'commit' message is initiated within a local circle, leading to the final step by replying to the client, which must receive a message from 1/3 of the community member plus one to learn the new information. It can be observed in Fig. 1.2. The high number of messages exchanged is one of the disadvantages of this approach, giving a complexity of $O(N)^2$; this means that the consensus is not scalable and its use within a permissionless peer-to-peer network is not practical. Jiang and Lian [42] reported the development of a highly scalable and faster version of PBFT [16], where the optimisation focused on the exchange of messages by making the primary replica a leader within the validation process. The reply messages to the pre-prepare collect-prepare which replace respectively prepare and commit will be communicated only to the leader, and after the leader broadcast commits to validating the decision, the entire community will send a reply message to the client at the collect-commit stage. Dahlia et al. [55] discussed the gravity of alive-but-corrupt attacks, in which the malicious behaviour of the attacker aims to maintain liveness but not safety. These authors claimed that this type of attack was more severe than the existence of Byzantised participants.

Moreover, it supports diversity with a communication model, rapid recovery if a client fails. On the discussion of quorum deconstruction by proposing the execution within the different shared beliefs, the flexibility of the quorum lies in its ability to adjust the assumed third community of Byzantised members by continuously observing the community. Although the proposed algorithm synchronises only at the commit stage, it assumes the same time clock in each machine, which is practically impossible. Moreover, Byzantising the environment can lead to the manipulation of the logic clock. In contrast, Kotla et al. [46] proposed the use of a speculative approach to minimise the cost of PBFT. In the Zyzzyva protocol, replicas reply directly to the client, and the client has the authority to help them adjust their ordering number in the case of inconsistency. Consequently, Rong et al. [65] claimed that the optimisation arising from Zyzzyva was more suitable as a basis for blockchain technology than PBFT. Zyzzyva functioning is described in Fig. 1.3.

Malkhi et al. [55] discussed the alive-but-corrupt behaviour within BFT that supports liveness but attacks safety and proposed a solution involving a flexible quorum that continuously observes the behaviour of a number of active nodes before switching to a synchronised mode. Continuous observation functions have been previously proposed, such as the approach of Dubois et al. [26], who built a self-stabiliser with BFT. Amir et al. [3] discussed the operation of a transparent leader election approach, which opened the way for several attacks, such as the pre-prepare delay attack, which aim to delay the broadcasting of a specific message

Fig. 1.2 Practical byzantine
fault tolerance

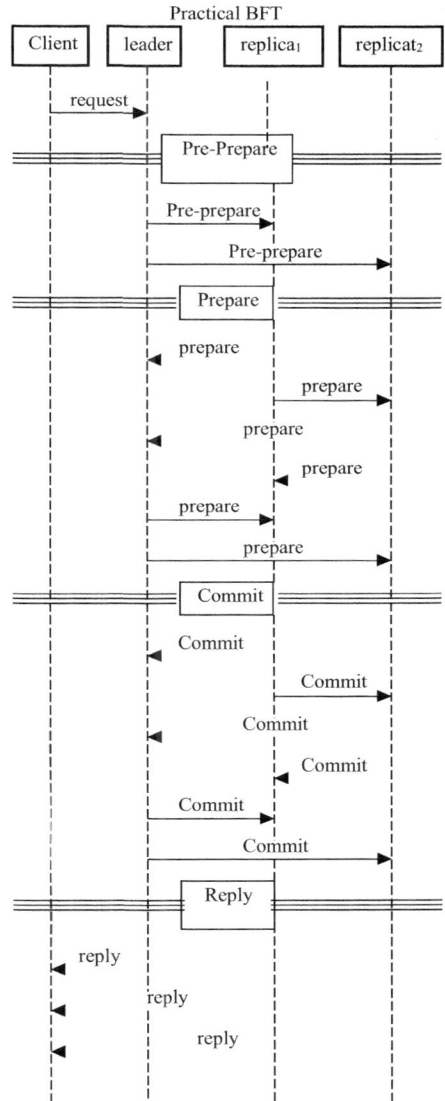

to the acceptors in order to retain the leadership position. Moreover, attacks such as denial of service can lead to time-out manipulation. Under the leadership of a malicious node, the system can experience long-term failure. The paper concluded by proposing a new performance-oriented correctness criterion for use with the BFT model.

The adoption of the BFT technique in blockchain technology applied to the IoT infrastructure is hard. The vulnerability lies in the leader-based approach, which

Fig. 1.3 Zyzzyva
(Speculative approach)

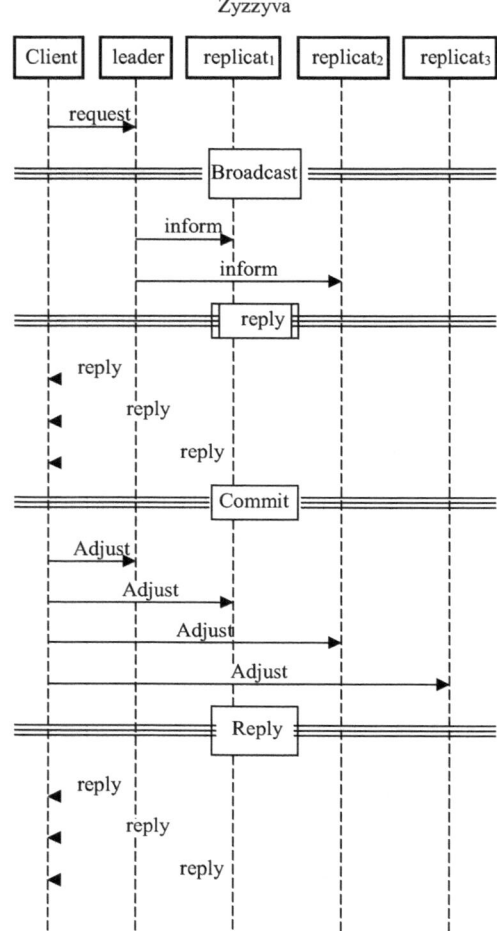

leads to targeted malicious behaviour and the manipulation of elections or retaining of positions. The central decision-making power makes the consensus suitable for a private blockchain, and the complexity of the message exchange is very high. Hence, its usage within the IoT model is limited to specific use cases such as smart houses.

1.4.3 Proof of Stake

The resource consumption of the PoW application within the cryptocurrency ecosystem led to the introduction of the PoS. PoS is based on a random selection in proportion to the number and/or age of coins attached to public keys. It is a working consensus for many cryptocurrencies such as BlackCoin [75], and Tezos [35]. The Ethereum foundation's attention to the PoS arose from its data structure, which was built in the form of a state transition account balance for each user. This approach uses follow The Satoshi (FtS) algorithm to select the leader, as explained by Bentov et al. [10]. The algorithm works by randomly choosing and then tracing a coin, investigating its minted block and identifying its current owner. All coins are indexed, and the coin is chosen as the result of a pseudo-random selection process. The algorithm adopted in many platforms such as BlackCoin functions by taking the header and outputting a token index and then finding the owner, which will be the leader of the consensus; consequently, the stake distribution in proportion to the others is the only factor considered in deciding the leader.

$$P_i = \frac{S_i}{\sum_{j=1}^{n} S_j} \tag{1.2}$$

where S is the stake of each participant, i stands for a particular node, and j for all the nodes in the network up to n. The algorithm will run over-indexed coins first, and this gives the entire mining community the opportunity to be chosen in proportion to their attached coins.

Autoboros [54] algorithm elects a leader dynamically from a committee based on the three-time epoch. The committee members participate in coin tossing to generate seeds to follow the Satoshi algorithm, and indexed coins are generated to identify the leader. The leader creates an empty block and the rest of the committee that acts as endorsers are responsible for filling it with different transactions. However, this proposal is still prone to 51% attacks.

On the other hand, Algorand [54] is based on the fact that the use of Autoboros to follow the Satoshi algorithm with a delayed time to lower the likelihood of corrupted participants in the voting circle is not secure. A corrupt participant can try to control the network via several different attacks. Consequently, in Algorand, the selection of participants is based on their balance, and the consensus is subject to BFT validation via a gossip algorithm to ensure the validation of transactions. This approach uses a verifiable random function (VRF) called cryptographic sortition, which starts by taking a private key from a node based on a randomly generated seed. As a result, it produces a hash value that leads to a selection based on a different margin of a hash value that is proportional to the community stake.

The PoS inherits the leader election process within a participant's community and is intended to maintain ledger validity while operating in a distributed environment. A pool attack on the PoS involves a pool withholding the broadcasting of blocks to another pool to diminish its ability to continue mining and thus force its members to immigrate to the attacker's pool [18]. Due to a lack of computational power and the complete dependency on the stockholders, many implementations of IoT solutions with PoS consensus have been proposed, such as those by Kang et al. [32, 44, 63]. Although this offers an alternative approach that can reduce the computational expense of the PoW, it still suffers from low throughput and high transaction finality delays. Moreover, centralisation of the decision among the stakeholders can introduce a vulnerability to malicious individuals or pool behaviour, such as forking and the injection of erroneous data. Several authors have discussed these attacks, for example, Gaz1, Kiayias, and Russell [33], who analysed stake-bleeding attacks; these can appear above long-range (LR) attacks. An LR attack is based on the ability of a minority to run the blockchain from the genesis block and generate an alternative history to the existing one by taking advantage of the non-resource consumption of the PoS. A study by Deirmentzoglou et al. [24] discussed concepts related to the PoS and the various attacks within the blockchain network, before focusing on LR attacks such as posterior corruption and stake bleeding. Moreover, several solutions for preventing these attacks are also discussed, such as key evolving cryptography, the longest chain rule, and moving checkpoints. One solution may be to centralise decisions but distribute computation in exchange for rewards.

To sum up, PoS suffer from attacks and monopoly, but due to its philosophy, several works have been proposed to build an IoT solution with this proof. Nevertheless, its application is limited to an environment with high trust.

1.4.4   Hybrid Consensus

The rise of a hybrid consensus as a way of exploiting each technique of consensus separately while taking into consideration the different characteristics of the running network comparable to the environment has led to the introduction of several proposals. The Peercoin white paper [45] proposed the initiation of the network with the use of PoW before replacing it with PoS. It assumes that the participant invested with resources at the initiation will be honest to maintain the network. However, the combination is separated, meaning that both techniques are subject to targeted attacks against them. Most of the proposals for PoS have considered BFT community management, such as Algorand, as stated in the previous section, which preserves the random selection of participants based on their stake. Casper, which was proposed by the Ethereum Foundation [15], aims to combine PoS with BFT. It introduces specific properties to BFT, such as accountability, in order to penalise malicious participants and prevent the nothing-at-stake attack. This approach aims to secure finality by introducing a checkpoint, which is an epoch of checking between the different validators at a certain height in the chain. The work by Pass and Shi [61] studied a combination of the PoW with BFT, finding that the PoW was inefficient, and aimed to increase responsiveness. The problem of consensus in a distributed setting is known to be impossible to solve; consequently, most of these proposals involve ways of making it practically impossible to break it, bearing in mind that the secret within the platform such as Bitcoin is within the hashing power of all the nodes that mine simultaneously and interested in the ledger validity.

Hybrid consensus may be an appropriate solution for the IoT but within the context of giving each topology a suitable consensus rather than the solutions currently available in the literature. Most of the existing solutions aim to address the problems of efficiency and latency and to speed up transaction finality. As a result, a proposal may involve implementing the PoW at a high level of component abstraction; PoS can be at the layer where there is inherited specific components that have a high level of trust, and BFT can be used within a closed setting.

1.4.5 Tangle IOTA

Tangle [62] was designed to address the need in the IoT for a no-fee micropayment; it is based on a directed acyclic graph (DAG) and the management of different weights between sites, which represent transactions. The concepts of blocks and miners are dropped, and each participant validates two previous injected trans-actions in order to submit one, running the PoW locally. The underlying idea is to allow the network to collaborate to ensure that the whole ledger is valid. The graph starts with the genesis transaction, which holds all the coins of the platform. The process of submitting a transaction involves making the initiator validate two previous transactions in addition to running a PoW with a low level of difficulty.

New transactions added to the pool are called tips and are dispersed over different leaves or end-paths of the DAG. The initiator of each transaction runs one of the three selection algorithms proposed by Popov [62]: a uniform random walk, an unweighted, random walk, or a weighted random walk.

The Tangle paper discussed the different properties of the function L (t), which returns the size of the tips pool at time t. It can be modelled using a Poisson process with rate λ, where H is the average time required by the participant node to process a transaction. However, the initiator will investigate the available tips, and based on the assumption that $\lambda \times H$ tips treated, the probability of choosing a tip is:

$$p = \frac{r}{(r + \lambda h)},$$
(1.3)

Where r is the number of tips at time t and h is the number of transactions that have been validated within a period of time but are not yet visible to the whole network. Moreover, for explanation purposes, it is assumed that h is received periodically, leading to the following function:

$$L_0 = r + \lambda h,$$
(1.4)

Bearing in mind that each transaction must validate two tips and based on the stationary assumption $2p$, it yields the following:

$$L_0 = 2\lambda h,$$
(1.5)

The Tangle IOTA algorithm was specifically proposed for the IoT, and several studies have discussed its implementation, such as those by Florea [31] and Shabandri and Maheshwari [69]. The drawbacks of this solution have also been addressed; for instance, Jiang et al. [43] raised concerns about the computational power consumed when the DAG becomes a massive network of sites. They proposed the usage of ReRam, a non-volatile memory that can execute memory calculations. Bu et al. [12] proposed a solution to introduce fairness involving a modified search algorithm that counters splitting attacks. Double-spending in IOTA takes advantage of the vulnerability of the tip selection algorithm by linking two conflicting tips to the same transaction; the algorithm will then choose exclusively between them, based on a Markov chain Monte Carlo (MCMC) approach which leads to the creation of two branches. The white paper that proposed Tangle also discussed double-spending attacks, the parasite chain, and network splitting attacks. The choice of a P-curl function was criticised by Heilman et al. [39], and its vulnerability to 34% attacks [68], replay attacks, and centralisation features were discussed by De Roode et al. [23].

The formal adoption of this solution by the IoT platform has been addressed in several papers [21], although it suffers from forking, leading to the need for an expensive searching algorithm when the graph grows to a very large size [43]. The solution relies on the use of PoW in a Hashcash approach to eliminate spam and flooding of transactions, which allocates the computational power that is traditionally supplied by miners to the end device, thus placing the computation burden on a limited IoT device. The various attacks mentioned in the previous paragraph mean that the Tangle IOTA is currently not a suitable solution for IoT networking infrastructure, due to the different threats posed to technology users.

1.4.6 Deep Learning Approaches

The work [20] discussed the disadvantages of the usual mining approach, finding that the confidence trade-off within each transaction in the blockchain is the most important drawback, as it leads to high latency at the confirmation stage among the different nodes. Their solution was based on the use of an AI algorithm to calculate the average transaction for each node. The average transaction generates a threshold value to categorise nodes into super, random, and unknown nodes. The work introduced a modified AlexNet by made it fit a capability assessment system. The network is forced to fit the average transaction based on a matrix constructed by iterating through the nodes and acquiring from them the node tree properties, which are the nature of the network and safety elements and some independent variables. The use of thresholds to obtain these nodes is the subject of debate due to the rigid, detailed network and resource-dependent characteristics, which introduce a monopoly based on the sophistication of the mining environment.

In [6] proposed a proof of useful work based on the training of deep learning models; their suggested solution derived a deep learning architecture from a generated hash value by constructing a map function. However, different hash values can be mapped to the same deep learning structural configuration. The developed model will be subject to training on data, which may be the transactions themselves. This approach starts with the definition of a context-free grammar $G = (V, R, S)$, where V is a nonterminal symbol or is a set of terminal symbols, R is a set of production rules, and S is the starting symbol, and a descriptive example is given in the paper. The developed architecture model was submitted to different nodes for injection within the new appended block within the blockchain. Deep learning has shown impressive results in terms of learning patterns from data. However, its suitability within a consensus mechanism needs to be investigated to find a way to deal with an open context. A search for categories of nodes [20] before taking a delegation approach to solving the leader-based election is another solution from what the Ethereum foundation suggested to switch to PoS from PoW. Baldominos and Saez [6] have shown a lack of coverage of the consensus requirement and suggest a search for a different architecture of deep learning derived from an implementation of a free context grammar, which can lead to recursive and repetitive results. Both solutions suffer from the inability of deep learning to deal with an open context of uncontrolled participation in a leader-based election, as in any consensus mechanism within a distributed ledger technology. Consequently, the adoption of this approach within the IoT sector is not considered.

1.4.7 Soft Computing

The work by Chen [19] claimed that the use of a soft computing approach as a traceability method could lead to a better result in terms of rapidity. This author identified the big data operation to validate transactions to be a derivation of the extensive transaction features coming from different businesses. Raising the fact that a long, linear, and immutable ledger that records each transaction within a chain of blocks, but as well holds partial historical useless information due to the unspent transaction output (UTXO) model set when it creates new Bitcoin. The solution was inspired by the astonishing ability of deep learning to identify patterns within data through its feature representation approach and was adopted to make the mining process more efficient. The solution involved the use of Takagi-Sugeno fuzzy cognitive maps as a traceability chain algorithm within the blockchain network; it present each block metadata. The proposal is a combination of a Takagi-Sugeno fuzzy artificial neural network (T-S FANN) with fuzzy cognitive mapping (FCM). The T-S FANN is a fuzzy system that describes a non-linear representation that is deconstructed into many linear models, while the FCM is a graph constructed from nodes representing concepts and arcs representing causality and links power between them and proposed to serve as a state transition.

This solution still involves a leader and follower approach and focuses on the state transition mechanism by claiming that a rapid conclusion to the validity of the new appended information can eliminate the different attacks and the adoption of the technology within a further domain. It is based on a deep learning concept and uses three hidden layers. Firstly, a feature graph takes eight features as input and multiplies them by an adjacency matrix to measure the effect of those features and make an inference. Secondly, a state transition graph is used to build an account balance, and the last layer is applied only after the validation of the transaction to build a transaction association. The input is fuzzified in a comparable way to the rules database, and the output will be the result that describes the power to the next block appended. This is based on the approach described by Agrawal et al. [1] for generating rules and mining the database by dividing it into three steps (classification, association, and sequence) and building a linked chain.

The solution aims to process the transaction of information in the consensus mechanism. Thus, the adoption of the technique in a particular context such as wearable devices is very appropriate, in which the search algorithm can be enabled with reinforcement learning to help decision-making.

1.5   Data Organisation and Consensus: Criticisms

Consensus is a result of information that is searched for and found within the distributed ledger. The first well-performing proposal was within the Bitcoin platform [59], in which it was based on a search for dispersed objects within the ledger named UTXO. The search starts by investigating all the related unspent UTXO within the historical transactions and linking them to new spent and a change UTXO nested within the newly generated transactions, i.e. the newly appended block. This approach involves an expensive direct search, and several implementations have tried to separate the coin history from the transaction history to enable more rapid referencing. Moreover, a unique linear ledger leads to forking and latency in transaction finality due to the time it takes the community to come to a consensus on it. Sompolinsky and Zohar [72] proposed the use of a tree rather than a linear ledger to optimise the scalability issues. The approach is based on eliminating the thread coming from following the longest chain by adopting a strategy for selecting the heaviest subtree, and consequently allows for controlled forking from negligible miners and is prone to self-gain attacks by miners. However, uncle blocks and forking conflict are much higher. Popov [62] proposed the use of a DAG within the distributed ledger technology with the aim of achieving parallel handling of transactions. This solution dropped the concept of a block for a transaction, and the appending of a new transaction called tip requires validation of two previous ones. Some conflicts can be solved with a voting mechanism that can generate numerous messages for bandwidth within a permissionless blockchain. Other authors have suggested sharding to speed up the treatment of data, such as Chow et al. [22] and Zamani et al. [80]. Although this solution looks appealing, sharding on a vertical level is impossible with transaction data, since the system requires all of the fields for the next step. On a horizontal level, this can be beneficial, but it needs to be implemented internally, or it will be subject to manipulation by concurrent miners.

The sharing of knowledge within the IoT infrastructure raises concerns about privacy, a central point of failure, and massive manipulation and monitoring of data. The use of a zero-knowledge proof in a distributed setting, such as in Zerocash [67], is a promising solution. However, consensus among the different nodes on the shared replica is crucial because the gathered data will be subject to monitoring. Consequently, the use of valid data is vital, and different implementations of the PoW are vulnerable to several selfish mining techniques that lead to the network performance being undermined. This technique is still vulnerable to the majority hash power, the adoption of the technique within the real-world scenario must study the practicality of breaking it, and various solutions have been proposed to make it more efficient by suggesting different forms of useful work. However, most of these suffer from conceptual drawbacks that make them vulnerable to attackers.

PoS preserves randomness in the choice, and this can be a high-performing solution in many cases of implementation of the IoT, especially when coupled with BFT. However, the unique use of BFT as a consensus mechanism is a reinvention of the wheel in some approaches, due to the implementation of the same technique from server replicas, and most cloud-based providers offer this approach to eliminate the possibility of central failure. The implementation of the deep learning model as a proof of concept is impractical, and it makes no sense to derive an architecture from the hash value, as proposed by Baldominos and Saez [6], where different hash values can lead to many previous found architecture. The selection of the supernodes in the study by Chen et al. [20] could be hybridised with BFT after initiating the network with PoW to facilitate the selection of honest miners, based on the assumption that participants who earn rewards from the network are always honest. The Tangle IOTA white paper stays very far from recommending its practical implementation within the IoT infrastructure, due to its vulnerability and philosophical unsuitability, despite claims of its advantages. The work by Chen [19] is promising for transactions of information and may be very suitable within the context of the IoT. As can be seen from the discussion above, none of the available consensus mechanisms can offer a perfect solution within large-scale networked infrastructures such as smart cities and networked cars, due to the first philosophical implementation stated in this specific use case.

Table 1.1 is a summary of the different problems, ledger type suitability, and recommendation within the IoT sector of the consensus approaches introduced in the previous section. Thus, the need for a consensus mechanism dedicated to the IoT is a solution that can bring the blockchain features within the IoT sectors. The consensus mechanism must address the following criteria:

- Zero-fee: The high message exchange between the IoT devices must be handled only with the elimination of any fee in the validation process.
- Dynamic data structure: The huge number of generated data will lead to big data that must be subject to continuous maintenance.
- Search algorithm: The search for relevant information to validate the new one is a very expensive step; consequently, the use of artificial intelligence techniques can be a good solution.

Table 1.1 Consensus comparison

	Disadvantage	Network failure
PoW	Resource consumption [79]	51% attack [10]
BFT	Message complexity [41]	1/3 of the community [41]
PoS	Monopoly [40]	51% of stake [40]
IOTA tangle	Splitting attack [12]	1/3 of the community [68]
DL approaches	Conceptual problem Sect. 1.4.6	1/3 of stakeholder
Soft computing	The search is very expensive Sect. 1.4.7	1/3 of the community [19]
	The ledger type	Suitability for IoT
PoW	Can be any form	High-level component with low communication
BFT	Can be any form	Closed topology
PoS	Can be any form	Topology with high trust
IOTA tangle	DAG	Not suitable
DL approaches	Can be any form	Not suitable
Soft computing	DAG	Suitable with caution to the search

- Introduction of two layers: a layer of validation and a layer of injection to separate between validating the transaction and injecting aside its related information.

1.6 Conclusion

This work has studied the consensus mechanism within blockchain technology and has raised concerns for the gap of research and work explicitly dedicated to the consensus in this use case. It has explained blockchain technology from technical and philosophical points of view focusing on the consensus, and this study can be summarised as follows:

- The introduction of the blockchain technology from a technical/historical point of view, and the analysis the different work done within the IoT sector on integration.
- Explanation of consensus philosophy and functioning.
- Discussion of the different attacks and malicious behaviour that lead to malfunctioning of the platform.
- Discussion of the suitability of available consensus mechanisms within the IoT sector.
- Finally, a discussion of data structures and concerns over the implementation of consensus mechanisms.

References

1. Agrawal, R., Imieliński, T., & Swami, A. (1993). Mining association rules between sets of items in large databases. In *Proceedings of the 1993 ACM SIGMOD international conference on management of data* (pp. 207–216).
2. Ali, A., Latif, S., Qadir, J., Kanhere, S., Singh, J., Crowcroft, J., et al. (2019). Blockchain and the future of the internet: A comprehensive review. *arXiv preprint arXiv:1904.00733*.
3. Amir, Y., Coan, B., Kirsch, J., & Lane, J. (2010). Prime: Byzantine replication under attack. *IEEE Transactions on Dependable and Secure Computing, 8*(4), 564–577.
4. Back, A., et al. (2002). Hashcash-a denial of service counter-measure computer science.
5. Bag, S., Ruj, S., & Sakurai, K. (2016). Bitcoin block withholding attack: Analysis and mitigation. *IEEE Transactions on Information Forensics and Security, 12*(8), 1967–1978.
6. Baldominos, A., & Saez, Y. (2019). Coin. Ai: A proof-of-useful-work scheme for blockchain-based distributed deep learning. *Entropy, 21*(8), 723.
7. Ball, M., Rosen, A., Sabin, M., & Vasudevan, P. N. (2017). Proofs of useful work. *IACR Cryptology ePrint Archive, 2017*, 203.
8. Bayer, D., Haber, S., & Stornetta, W. S. (1993). Improving the efficiency and reliability of digital time-stamping. In *Sequences II* (pp. 329–334). Berlin: Springer.
9. Belotti, M., Kirati, S., & Secci, S. (2018). Bitcoin pool-hopping detection. In *2018 IEEE 4th international forum on research and Technology for Society and Industry (RTSI)* (pp. 1–6). IEEE.
10. Bentov, I., Lee, C., Mizrahi, A., & Rosenfeld, M. (2014). Proof of activity: Extending bitcoin's proof of work via proof of stake [extended abstract] y. *ACM SIGMETRICS Performance Evaluation Review, 42*(3), 34–37.
11. Bonneau, J., Miller, A., Clark, J., Narayanan, A., Kroll, J. A., & Felten, E. W. (2015). Sok: Research perspectives and challenges for bitcoin and cryptocurrencies. In *2015 IEEE symposium on security and privacy* (pp. 104–121). IEEE.
12. Bu, G., Gürcan, Ö., & Potop-Butucaru, M. (2019). G-iota: Fair and confidence aware tangle. In *IEEE INFOCOM 2019-IEEE conference on computer Communications workshops (INFOCOM WKSHPS)* (pp. 644–649). IEEE.
13. Buccafurri, F., Lax, G., Nicolazzo, S., & Nocera, A. (2017). Overcoming limits of blockchain for iot applications. In *Proceedings of the 12th international conference on availability, reliability and security* (pp. 1–6).
14. Buterin, V. (2013). A next generation smart contract & decentralized application platform. *White Paper, 3*(37) Ethereum Foundation.
15. Buterin, V., & Griffith, V. (2017). Casper the friendly finality gadget. *arXiv preprint arXiv:1710.09437*.
16. Castro, M., Liskov, B., et al. (1999). Practical byzantine fault tolerance. *OSDI, 99*, 173–186.
17. Charapko, A., Ailijiang, A., & Demirbas, M. (2018). Bridging paxos and blockchain consensus. In *2018 IEEE international conference on internet of things (iThings) and IEEE Green computing and communications (GreenCom) and IEEE cyber, physical and social computing (CPSCom) and IEEE smart data (SmartData)* (pp. 1545–1552). IEEE.
18. Chatterjee, K., Goharshady, A. K., Ibsen-Jensen, R., & Velner, Y. (2018). Ergodic mean-payoff games for the analysis of attacks in crypto-currencies. *arXiv preprint arXiv:1806.03108*.
19. Chen, R.-Y. (2018). A traceability chain algorithm for artificial neural networks using t–s fuzzy cognitive maps in blockchain. *Future Generation Computer Systems, 80*, 198–210.
20. Chen, J., Duan, K., Zhang, R., Zeng, L., & Wang, W. (2018). An ai based super nodes selection algorithm in blockchain networks. *arXiv preprint arXiv:1808.00216*.
21. Chiang, T. F., Chen, S. Y., & Lai, C. F. (2018). A tangle-based high performance architecture for large scale iot solutions. In *2018 1st international cognitive cities conference (IC3)* (pp. 12–15). IEEE.

22. Chow, S. S., Lai, Z., Liu, C., Lo, E., & Zhao, Y. (2018). Sharding blockchain. In *2018 IEEE international conference on internet of things (iThings) and IEEE Green computing and communications (GreenCom) and IEEE cyber, physical and social computing (CPSCom) and IEEE smart data (SmartData)* (pp. 1665–1665). IEEE.
23. De Roode, G., Ullah, I., & Havinga, P. J. (2018). How to break iota heart by replaying? In *2018 IEEE Globecom workshops (GC Wkshps)* (pp. 1–7). IEEE.
24. Deirmentzoglou, E., Papakyriakopoulos, G., & Patsakis, C. (2019). A survey on long-range attacks for proof of stake protocols. *IEEE Access, 7*, 28712–28725.
25. Dillenberger, D., Novotny, P., Zhang, Q., Jayachandran, P., Gupta, H., Hans, S., Verma, D., Chakraborty, S., Thomas, J., Walli, M., et al. (2019). Blockchain analytics and artificial intelligence. *IBM Journal of Research and Development, 63*(2/3), 5–1.
26. Dubois, S., Masuzawa, T., & Tixeuil, S. (2011). Bounding the impact of unbounded attacks in stabilization. *IEEE Transactions on Parallel and Distributed Systems, 23*(3), 460–466.
27. El Kafhali, S., Chahir, C., Hanini, M., & Salah, K. (2019). Architecture to manage internet of things data using blockchain and fog computing. In *Proceedings of the 4th international conference on big data and internet of things* (pp. 1–8).
28. Eyal, I. (2015). The miner's dilemma. In *2015 IEEE symposium on security and privacy* (pp. 89–103). IEEE.
29. Eyal, I., & Sirer, E. G. (2014). Majority is not enough: Bitcoin mining is vulnerable. In *International conference on financial cryptography and data security* (pp. 436–454). Cham: Springer.
30. Fakhri, D., & Mutijarsa, K. (2018). Secure iot communication using blockchain technology. In *2018 international symposium on electronics and smart devices (ISESD)* (pp. 1–6). IEEE.
31. Florea, B. C. (2018). Blockchain and internet of things data provider for smart applications. In *2018 7th Mediterranean conference on embedded computing (MECO)* (pp. 1–4). IEEE.
32. Frederick, M., & Jaiswal, C. (2018). Bid: Blockchaining for iot devices. In *2018 9th IEEE annual ubiquitous computing, Electronics & Mobile Communication Conference (UEMCON)* (pp. 806–811). IEEE.
33. Gaži, P., Kiayias, A., & Russell, A. (2018). Stake-bleeding attacks on proof-of- stake blockchains. In *2018 Crypto Valley conference on Blockchain technology (CVCBT)* (pp. 85–92). IEEE.
34. Georghiades, Y., Flolid, S., & Vishwanath, S. (2019). Hashcore: Proof-of-work functions for general purpose processors. In *2019 IEEE 39th international conference on distributed computing systems (ICDCS)* (pp. 1951–1959). IEEE.
35. Goodman, L. (2014, August 3). *Tezos: A self-amending crypto-ledger position paper.*
36. Gramoli, V. (2017). From blockchain consensus back to byzantine consensus. *Future Generation Computer Systems, 107*, 760–769.
37. Haber, S., & Stornetta, W. (1991). How to time-stamp a digital document. In *Advances in cryptology-CRYPTO' 90. CRYPTO 1990. Lecture notes in computer science* (Vol. 537). Berlin, Heidelberg: Springer.
38. Hazari, S. S., & Mahmoud, Q. H. (2019). A parallel proof of work to improve transaction speed and scalability in blockchain systems. In *2019 IEEE 9th annual computing and communication workshop and conference (CCWC)* (pp. 0916–0921). IEEE.
39. Heilman, E., Narula, N., Tanzer, G., Lovejoy, J., Colavita, M., Virza, M., & Dryja, T. (2019). Cryptanalysis of curl-p and other attacks on the iota cryptocurrency. *IACR Cryptology ePrint Archive, 2019*, 344.
40. Houy, N. (2014). It will cost you nothing to "kill" a proof-of-stake crypto-currency. *Economics Bulletin, 34*(2), 1038–1044.
41. Jalalzai, M. M., Busch, C., & Richard, G. G. (2019). Proteus: A scalable bft consensus protocol for blockchains. In *2019 IEEE international conference on Blockchain (Blockchain)* (pp. 308–313). IEEE.
42. Jiang, Y., & Lian, Z. (2019). High performance and scalable byzantine fault tolerance. In *2019 IEEE 3rd information technology, networking, electronic and automation control conference (ITNEC)* (pp. 1195–1202). IEEE.

43. Jiang, Y., Wang, C., Huang, Y., Long, S., & Huo, Y. (2018). A cross-chain solution to integration of iot tangle for data access management. In *2018 IEEE International conference on internet of things (iThings) and IEEE Green computing and communications (GreenCom) and IEEE cyber, physical and social computing (CPSCom) and IEEE smart data (SmartData)* (pp. 1035–1041). IEEE.
44. Kang, J., Xiong, Z., Niyato, D., Ye, D., Kim, D. I., & Zhao, J. (2019). Toward secure blockchain-enabled internet of vehicles: Optimizing consensus management using reputation and contract theory. *IEEE Transactions on Vehicular Technology, 68*(3), 2906–2920.
45. King, S., & Nadal, S. (2012, August 19). PPcoin: Peer-to-peer crypto-currency with proof-of-stake. *Self-Published Paper.*
46. Kotla, R., Alvisi, L., Dahlin, M., Clement, A., & Wong, E. (2007). Zyzzyva: Speculative byzantine fault tolerance. *ACM SIGOPS Operating Systems Review, 41*(6), 45–58.
47. Król, M., Sonnino, A., Al-Bassam, M., Tasiopoulos, A., & Psaras, I. (2019). Proof- of-prestige: A useful work reward system for unverifiable tasks. In *2019 IEEE international conference on Blockchain and Cryptocurrency (ICBC)* (pp. 293–301). IEEE.
48. Kroll, J. A., Davey, I. C., & Felten, E. W. (2013). The economics of bitcoin mining, or bitcoin in the presence of adversaries. *Proceedings of WEIS, 2013*, 11.
49. Lamport, L. (1998). The part-time parliament. ACM transactions on computer systems. *ACM Transactions on Computer Systems, 16*(2), 133.
50. Lamport, L. (2011). Byzantizing paxos by refinement. In *International symposium on distributed computing* (pp. 211–224). Cham: Springer.
51. Lamport, L. (2019). Time, clocks, and the ordering of events in a distributed system. In *Concurrency: The works of Leslie Lamport* (pp. 179–196).
52. Lamport, L., Shostak, R., & Pease, M. (1982). The byzantine generals problem acm transactions on progamming languages and systems. *ACM Transactions on Programming Languages and Systems, 4*(3), 382–401.
53. Liao, K., & Katz, J. (2017). Incentivizing blockchain forks via whale transactions. In *International conference on financial cryptography and data security* (pp. 264–279). Springer.
54. Liu, Z., Luong, N. C., Wang, W., Niyato, D., Wang, P., Liang, Y.-C., & Kim, D. I. (2019). A survey on applications of game theory in blockchain. *arXiv preprint arXiv:1902.10865.*
55. Malkhi, D., Nayak, K., & Ren, L. (2019). Flexible byzantine fault tolerance. In *Proceedings of the 2019 ACM SIGSAC conference on computer and communications security* (pp. 1041–1053).
56. Mendki, P. (2019). Blockchain enabled iot edge computing. In *Proceedings of the 2019 international conference on blockchain technology* (pp. 66–69).
57. Merkle, R. C. (1989). A certified digital signature. In *Conference on the theory and application of cryptology* (pp. 218–238). Amsterdam: Springer.
58. Nakahara, R., & Inaba, H. (2018). Proposal of fair proof-of-work system based on rating of user's computing power. In *2018 IEEE 7th global conference on consumer electronics (GCCE)* (pp. 746–748). IEEE.
59. Nakamoto, S., et al. (2008). A peer-to-peer electronic cash system. *Bitcoin.*https://bitcoin.org/bitcoin.pdf.
60. Ongaro, D., & Ousterhout, J. (2014). *In search of an understandable consensus algorithm* (pp. 305–319).
61. Pass, R., & Shi, E. (2017). Hybrid consensus: Efficient consensus in the permission- less model. In *31st international symposium on distributed computing (DISC 2017)*. Schloss Dagstuhl-Leibniz-Zentrum fuer Informatik.
62. Popov, S. (2016). The tangle. *cit. on* p. 131.
63. Puthal, D., & Mohanty, S. P. (2018). Proof of authentication: Iot-friendly blockchains. *IEEE Potentials, 38*(1), 26–29.
64. Rabin, M. O. (1983). Randomized byzantine generals. In *24th annual symposium on foundations of computer science (sfcs 1983)* (pp. 403–409). IEEE.

65. Rong, Y., Zhang, J., Bian, J., & Wu, W. (2019). Erbft: Efficient and robust byzantine fault tolerance. In *2019 IEEE 21st international conference on high performance computing and communications; IEEE 17th international conference on Smart City; IEEE 5th international conference on data science and systems (HPCC/SmartCity/DSS)* (pp. 265–272). IEEE.
66. Rosenfeld, M. (2011). Analysis of bitcoin pooled mining reward systems. *arXiv preprint arXiv:1112.4980*.
67. Sasson, E. B., Chiesa, A., Garman, C., Green, M., Miers, I., Tromer, E., & Virza, M. (2014). Zerocash: Decentralized anonymous payments from bitcoin. In *2014 IEEE symposium on security and privacy* (pp. 459–474). IEEE.
68. Sayeed, S., & Marco-Gisbert, H. (2019). Assessing blockchain consensus and security mechanisms against the 51% attack. *Applied Sciences, 9*(9), 1788.
69. Shabandri, B., & Maheshwari, P. (2019). Enhancing iot security and privacy using distributed ledgers with iota and the tangle. In *2019 6th international conference on signal processing and integrated networks (SPIN)* (pp. 1069–1075). IEEE.
70. Singh, M., Singh, A., & Kim, S. (2018). Blockchain: A game changer for securing iot data. In *2018 IEEE 4th world forum on internet of things (WF-IoT)* (pp. 51–55). IEEE.
71. Sobti, R., & Geetha, G. (2012). Cryptographic hash functions: A review. *International Journal of Computer Science Issues (IJCSI), 9*(2), 461.
72. Sompolinsky, Y., & Zohar, A. (2015). Secure high-rate transaction processing in bitcoin. In *International conference on financial cryptography and data security* (pp. 507–527). Amsterdam: Springer.
73. Szabo, N. (1997). Formalizing and securing relationships on public networks. *First Monday, 2*(9).
74. Tracey, D., & Sreenan, C. (2019). How to see through the fog? Using peer to peer (p2p) for the internet of things. In *2019 IEEE 5th world forum on internet of things (WF-IoT)* (pp. 47–52). IEEE.
75. Vasin, P. (2014). *Blackcoin's proof-of-stake protocol v2* (Vol. 71). https://blackcoin.co/blackcoin-pos-protocol-v2-whitepaper.pdf.
76. Viriyasitavat, W., & Hoonsopon, D. (2019). Blockchain characteristics and consensus in modern business processes. *Journal of Industrial Information Integration, 13*, 32–39.
77. Weking, J., Mandalenakis, M., Hein, A., Hermes, S., Böhm, M., & Krcmar, H. (2020). The impact of blockchain technology on business models–a taxonomy and archetypal patterns. *Electronic Markets, 30*, 285–305.
78. Werner, S. M., Pritz, P. J., Zamyatin, A., & Knottenbelt, W. J. (2019). Uncle traps: Harvesting rewards in a queue-based ethereum mining pool. In *Proceedings of the 12th EAI international conference on performance evaluation methodologies and tools* (pp. 127–134).
79. Yu, Y., & Prasanna, V. K. (2002). Power-aware resource allocation for independent tasks in heterogeneous real-time systems. In *Proceedings of the ninth international conference on parallel and distributed systems, 2002* (pp. 341–348). IEEE.
80. Zamani, M., Movahedi, M., & Raykova, M. (2018). Rapidchain: Scaling blockchain via full sharding. In *Proceedings of the 2018 ACM SIGSAC conference on computer and communications security* (pp. 931–948).
81. Zhou, D. H. (2019). *hhohho/Learning-Blockchain-In-Java-Edition-2 learn blockchain*. https://github.com/hhohho/Learning-Blockchain-In-Java-Edition-2. Blockchain platform.

Chapter 2
Enablers and Inhibitors for IoT Implementation

Cesa-Hugo Muñoz-Flores and Jordi Olivella-Nadal

Abstract IoT implementation depends on a good extend on human and technological resources availability and cultural aspects and priorities of the organizations. According to their state, the different factors can be enablers or inhibitors of IoT implementation. Since IoT implementation is a case of digitalization, main elements of digitalization and most typical enablers and inhibitors are presented. Based on scientific and professional literature, the specific enablers and inhibitors of IoT are presented. They involve technological enablers (ability to provide power to the devices, connectivity, communication capability between elements and data handling capacity), strategic enablers (IoT adoption as a strategic element, formulation of a global architecture of IoT), organizational enablers (digital talent and skills and digital culture), organizational barriers (need for standardization, security risks, privacy restrictions, cost and regulatory issues), and cultural barriers (perception of complexity and lack of trust).

Keywords Digital transformation · Internet of things · Transformation enablers · Transformation barriers

2.1 Introduction

In any technological novelty, concept definition comes first, specific technology developments come later, and implementation is the last step. When the innovation

C.-H. Muñoz-Flores
Transformación TI, Telefónica Perú, Lima, Peru

J. Olivella-Nadal (✉)
Institute of Industrial and Control Engineering, Universitat Politècnica de Catalunya – BarcelonaTech, Barcelona, Spain

Management Department, Universitat Politècnica de Catalunya – BarcelonaTech, Barcelona, Spain
e-mail: jorge.olivella@upc.edu

© Springer Nature Switzerland AG 2021
F. P. García Márquez, B. Lev (eds.), *Internet of Things*, International Series in Operations Research & Management Science 305,
https://doi.org/10.1007/978-3-030-70478-0_2

consists of a single functionality, the three steps can follow each other smoothly. It is not the case of Internet of Things (IoT). While the concept has been widely developed and has a strong support from academia, industry, and administrations, most specific solution developments are still in its first phases, and wide implementation seems a far objective. Although IoT is regarded as disruptive idea of combination of digital technologies and communication solutions with high impact on everyday life and behavior of potential users, its practical development and implementation is complex and demanding and depends on a set of factors and circumstances [1]. Its practical development and implementation are complex and demanding and depend on a set of factors and circumstances.

The development and implementation of IoT is strongly influenced by human and technological resources availability and by cultural aspects and priorities of the organizations. Each of these factors can be an enabler, when its state is clearly favorable to the IoT initiatives and needs, or an inhibitor, in the opposite case. None of these factors are totally indispensable, since a strong determination of the management of a company or the dedication of enough resources can overcome the initial limitations of the organization or its environment. However, it seems clear that this kind of factors is going to have a strong influence on the difficulties to confront and the final success of the initiatives.

IoT implementation is a particular digitalization case, which is why the main generic enablers and barriers of digitalization are introduced first. In this sense, Sect. 2.2 focuses on drawing up, first, the elements of the digitalization processes and, later, the main enablers and barriers of said processes. Section 2.3 below introduces the essential elements of the IoT and details the various technology, strategic and organizational enablers, as well as the organizational and cultural barriers. Finally, Sect. 2.4 sets out the conclusions of this chapter.

2.2 Enablers and Barriers to Digitalization

2.2.1 Digitalization Process Elements

Digital technologies are the result of a record-breaking evolution of the hardware, software, and network technological capabilities. This evolution has had an exponential-type behavior among the main variables such as the processing capability, storage, and the communication speed [2]; while enabling the progress among the technologies, such integration into these processes, products, and business models of companies is pivotal to the growth of companies [3]. The fast evolution of these technologies has driven organizations to search for ways to benefit from its use in the most advantageous way, in order to change or make products, processes, and even their business models better.

Digitalization can be defined as the use of digital technologies changing a business model and creating new opportunities to growth both income and value

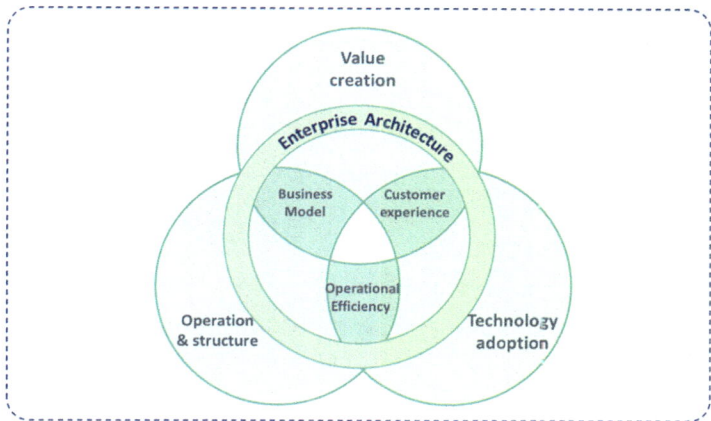

Fig. 2.1 Organizational elements of digitalization

and refers to the process of moving toward a digital business [4]. Other definitions of digitalization give us a broader approach and envisages digitalization as the introduction of digital technologies into the companies and as a transformation engine for organizations [5]. Therefore, the key to digitalization is to exploit new digital technologies and integrate them into the products, processes, and business models, through a process known as digital transformation.

Digitalization has a wide interaction with the different strategic, operational, and business aspects that are linked to activities within the organizations. It is a two-way interaction, while the various elements influence on, and are influenced by, the activity in these different aspects. System architecture is considered as a comprehensive approach that will provide coherence to the business processes, as well as to the systems. This approach is reflected in Fig. 2.1.

As digitalization does not have an endpoint but rather becomes a process of digital maturity; it shall require a continuous alignment of culture, people, structure, and tasks to profit from digital technologies [6, 7]. Therefore, "digitalization" should be understood as an ongoing process of digital maturity progress through the increased use of digital technologies and the promotion of organizational practices that creates a digital culture [8].

Numbers of factors lead organizations to implement a digitalization strategy. These factors are called digitalization drivers that may be both internal and external. Among the internal drivers, we can focus attention on the need for an operational efficiency and productivity of the firms [9], as well as the opportunity to innovate [10] and the search for sustainability [11]. Furthermore, the external drivers include the generalization of digitalization [9], the competitive pressure, customers' expectations [6], and the pressure from the industry disruptors [12].

Furthermore, transformation can be implemented by the enabling factors or hindered by inhibitors. These factors weigh on cultural change and the tendency toward transformation. In Fig. 2.2, the scheme depicts how the digitalization of

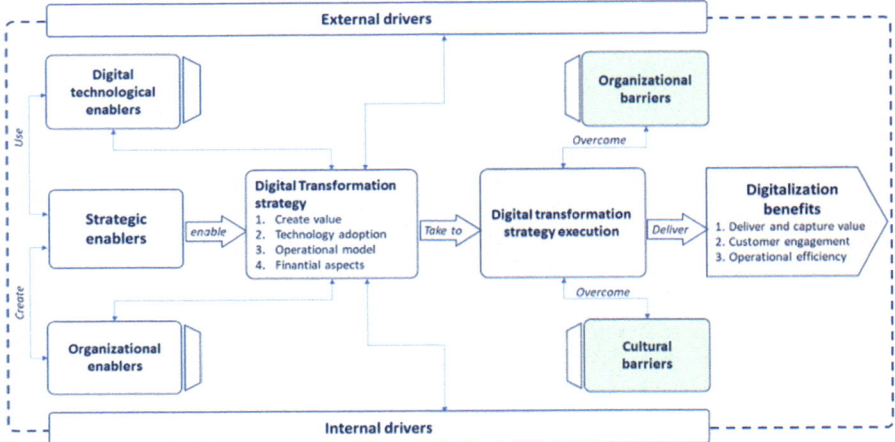

Fig. 2.2 Digitalization process and factors affecting it

a company is driven by both internal and external pressures, and it is facilitated by the technological, strategic, and organizational enablers and narrowed by the organizational and strategic barriers. During the strategy formulation, the concept of how to take advantage of the supportive forces and overcome the barriers is defined, but the latter becomes clearer during the strategy execution.

In order to enable the use of digital technologies and support corporate transformation processes, it is crucial to develop a digital culture within the organizations to shorten the adaptation gap that may exist in the digital scenario, as well as within the regulatory entities and government, to assimilate and define the standards and policies for the digital ecosystem. The development of a digital culture may be facilitated by certain factors driving and accelerating the digitalization; however, it can also be slowed down by other factors that inhibit the development of such culture among organizations. The abovementioned factors will be explained in the following bullets.

A summary of the key concepts and characteristics discussed in this chapter are shown in Annex 1.

2.2.2   Enablers

Digitalization enablers refer to those elements controlled by the organization and enabling the use of primary digital technologies to connect objects and comply with the digital business strategies. The key enablers of digitalization search for harness the technology that connects objects. We can group these enablers as strategic, technology, and organizational enablers.

2.2.2.1   Technology Enablers

Digital technologies refer to the transformation enabler that once adopted by people will allow carrying out the tasks defined and create a culture within organizations and all in alignment with a response to the dynamic environment in a sustainable, digital, and coherent way [13]. The capabilities that enable technologies are summarized below.

Connectivity Regarding connectivity, companies move toward the transformation of their digital channels that are used by their customers, and of the way their employees work when they are connected to their platforms and of the interactions with suppliers.

Localization The possibility of knowing the real-time location of all type of elements is one of the key enablers of digitalization.

Data Management and Analytics Data management technology, empowered with analytical Big Data models, enables to collect, process, analyze, and interpret the data.

Automation Digital technologies allow firms to move from the abstract to concrete digital solutions and from that point on to advance into a digital business through a digitization process.

2.2.2.2   Strategic Enablers

Strategic enablers determine the course of action of digitalization and address the aspects of adopting technology, and the creation of value through a business model and products, as well as the structural changes, processes, and operations within the firm's organization, all this framed in the organization financial capacity. These enablers are essential to make digitalization feasible, and they shall include as follows:

Vision A comprehensive digital vision and a visionary thinking about the organization's digital future is what is expected of the digitalization leadership. A true transformative vision focuses on business rather than on technology, as it is compelling for the lower levels and brings change to customer experience, operational dimension, and business model, as well as it is created at the highest organization level [3, 14]. In addition, it must also be shared and common to the entire organization to achieve a successful digitalization [8].

Digital Transformation Strategy The digital strategy determines *the objectives (the what) of* a company to be achieved, and it is necessary to complete a perspective that will determine *the how*; this concept is defined in the digitalization strategy, which is based on the strategies of the dimensions of the value creation, technology adoption, and operational (structural) model and on the financing of this process [11].

Innovative Capacity Digital innovation introduces solutions combining technologies to produce elements that allow companies to achieve new ways of doing business, based on general-purpose technologies such as ICT, Information and Communications Technology enabling the deployment of innovative solutions in the different scopes of both the organizations and society [2, 15].

2.2.2.3 Organizational Enablers

These enablers are linked to the dynamics of the alignment of people, culture, tasks, and structure, in such a way as to adapted to the digital environment that organizations face in this era [7]. The main organizational enablers are:

Structure When an organization has a structure that suits to its circumstances during the digitalization process, it enables the cultural change of the organization in order to achieve the adoption of technologies and to adapt the firm to the new digital environment and turn it into a digital business.

Dynamic Capabilities These capabilities empower the firm to develop both internal and external organizational competences in a dynamic way and to reconfigure and integrate them with the functional capabilities and achieve new competitive advantages that enable to address the fast-changing environments [16] such as the current digital scenario.

Organizational Agility Implementing agility practices, values, as well as tools in a way of enablers for digitalization and cultural change, facilitate the adoption of digital technologies. Organizational agility encompasses the detection of market opportunities, combining the digital technologies, assets, and relationships to implement them in a fast and innovative way [17]. A data analytics-driven approach enables agility, which is based on build-measure-learn approach. Companies adopt an agile development to incorporate new services through a digital platform, one of the strategic assets for a company which undertakes digitalization through multifunctional teams delivering these type of services [18, 19]

Talent and Digital Skills Talented people empower the organization to achieve, on the one hand, digital capabilities (which includes mastering social media topics, data analytics, virtualization, cloud computing, and digital architecture [20, 21]) and, on the other hand, leadership skills (which require a clear vision of transformation and talent management).

Digital Culture The achievement of a digital culture is essential for the digitalization process. This implies getting people to acquire a change-oriented mindset, a sense of agility and innovation, willingness to take risks, and a delegated decision-making and encourage working with multifunctional teams [13, 14].

2.2.3 Barriers

Likewise, as there are enablers used to incorporate technologies into the business strategies, there are also barriers that represent challenges to overcome, in order to move forward with the digitalization process.

2.2.3.1 Organizational Barriers

Organizational Inertia Organizations evolve and reach a growth rate based on certain capabilities embedded in their existing organizational routines, structures, and processes [22]. It is unlikely that these factors from the past will have the same importance in the novel digital scenarios to create solutions and to take advantage of digital technologies in a suitable way and to digitally transform products, processes, and business models [23].

Resistance to Change On the digital scenario, resistance to an organizational change is evident in people, mainly in mid-level employees and managers, becoming a significant barrier that limits transformation and innovation. The reason of this resistance is the feeling of fear of people facing the unknown, losing their jobs, or not having the necessary skills to adopt solutions based on new technologies and not having the desired performance [24].

Inappropriate Organization Structure A barrier to executing the digitalization strategies is the inappropriate organization structure. Often the firms are not appropriately organized and the new roles and units that must emerge as a result of the transformation progress and in response to the evolution of the technology and the market have not been taken into account [22].

Limited Financial Capability Failure to allocate financial resources to an effort, limiting the investment in talent, or reducing the resources for innovation through experimentation and iteration will represent a barrier that will slow down the digitalization process [23].

Security and Privacy Issues The security and privacy demanded by consumers interacting with digital elements, whether as customers, employees, or members of any community, represent a barrier to the digitalization progress of any organization. The need then arises to change the perception of security and privacy, which had been transformed from being a threat to a source of benefits for people [17].

2.2.3.2 Cultural Barriers

Lack of Sense of Urgency The digital technology evolution is rapidly changing the current scenario and challenges organizations to adapt quickly, so that technologies can be harnessed, and to reduce the adaptation gap. Organizations need to incorporate a sense of urgency into their culture, from which to respond to competitors and disruptors, and adapt to the new digital scenario and implement more effective operations. eliminating the risk of disappearing in the hands of disruptors that arise and develop without restrictions and with unconventional strategies [12].

Silo Work Mindset The organizational structures of many companies respond to functions and are organized into departments each one with objectives to fulfill. As companies grow and become successful firms, operating in organizational silos with their own processes, data definitions, and systems tends to strengthen and, as paradox, limit their ability to share a common vision and goals [21].

Risk Aversion A barrier that often becomes evident in the digital scenario is the reluctance to take risks, especially when it is part of the corporate culture. This makes the firm adopt conservative characteristics, according to which it assumes a role in the following of digital initiatives based on the result obtained by its competitors who have already undertaken their digitalization process, which is a mistake in a digital scenario [25, 26].

Lack of Collaboration This barrier is distinctive of organizations in which an operational efficiency based on functional units has prevailed. The digital scenario demands an implementation of collaboration within the principles and values of the organization, with an inter-functional nature, regardless the hierarchies between internal units, in order to enable the digitalization [27].

2.3   Enablers and Barriers to IoT Implementation

The digitalization of a company with IoT is defined as the process of convergence between elements of the physical and the digital worlds through the adoption, integration, and use of the digital technologies that make up the IoT to transform its products, processes, and business models [19, 28]. Some examples of companies integrating IoT as part of their digitalization are General Electric, which has been venturing into digital services rather than just doing it through products; Siemens, which has digitalized its operational and maintenance processes for underground trains in London; and Caterpillar with its CAT Detect solution combining vehicle tracking systems, CCTV, and RFID to monitor and provide security to construction operations [28]. These digitalization processes formulate strategies aiming to take advantage of enablers and overcome the barriers arising in the IoT implementation solution.

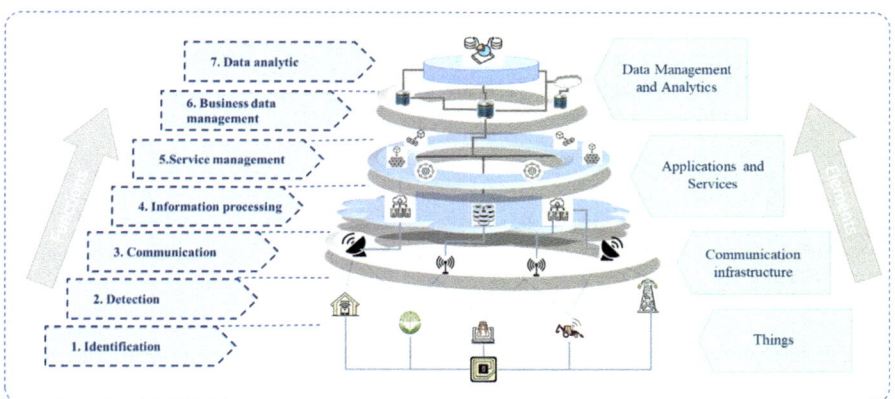

Fig. 2.3 Elements of the IoT solution

2.3.1   IoT Elements

In the context of the digitalization advancement of companies, there is a growing interest in the development and use of the Internet of Things (IoT), a technology that truly transforms the relationship between people and the ecosystem of objects (radio frequency tags, sensors, actuators, mobile phones, among others), with which it interacts in the daily living and in the workplace. IoT is a digital technology that can only exist if there is a combination of digital technologies starting with a breakthrough in communications, information technology, electronics, and social sciences [1] and clearly requires considerable improvements in mobility, cloud computing and data analytics and based on a very strong Internet.

As shown in Fig. 2.3, the elements of an IoT solution contain objects, a communication network, platforms for information processing, applications with services, orchestration platforms, and data management. IoT solution integrates the elements listed below:

Objects, made up of people, physical objects, and equipment fitted with sensors, and actuators, which requires the identification of the object and the data detection of the same, as well as from its environment.

Communication infrastructures, which are connected to a network for transporting the data of the objects to and from the platforms for information processing.

Applications and services, with different functionalities to fulfill the purpose of connection, management and control of objects, are critical elements that allow the processing of information and the management of the services involved.

Data management and analysis, made up of databases and different analytical tools.

The adoption of IoT by an organization requires certain enablers, depending on the strategic vision and leadership with which the solution is boosted and to overcome barriers, in order to adopt and mainly to implement this digital technology. Although the study of IoT solutions is still in its early stage, certain similarities regarding the enablers and barriers are obtained, and based on the review of the available information in the specialized literature and from the case studies, we will review the latter below.

2.3.2   Enablers

2.3.2.1   Technology Enablers

The implementation of IoT requires a set of technological capabilities, which can be grouped into those mentioned below.

Ability to Provide Power to Devices

IoT implementation involves the setting up of a system of objects interconnected with their corresponding devices, which are able to identify each other with the largest possible physical range, delivering their data and those of their environment and exchanging information with the other elements. Many of the objects are passive, so they lack the power sources; they need to be active and fulfill their connecting features, to store and process the data they exchange with other objects and to validate and decode secure accesses. Optimizing devices so they can consume less power and have a supply that ensures their operability will be an important enabler for IoT.

Connectivity

Connectivity is the ability to connect an element to a network to exchange data, applying certain transmission protocols, so that the element delivers and receives information from one or more elements that make up a different network to. Connectivity is an enabler as it holds the ability to connect different objects and exchange data at high speed, low latency (delay between data sending and arrival), and performance, and without it, applications cannot be used by IoT. This enabler entails the need of adoption of communication protocols within the network infrastructure layers, applications, and services.

The need for connectivity impacts different areas, such as network infrastructure, to apply IoT in order to provide affordable, reliable, and scalable communication [29, 30], and applications, ensuring the integration between applications that uses different programming languages [30].

Ability to Communicate Between Elements

It is the ability allowing the connected elements to exchange data at the traffic levels that the system will produce with other devices with different characteristics, whether physical, functional, or technical, ensuring the interoperability, confidence, and security, and fulfilling the functions defined by the business. The elements may include RFID readers, sensors, or sensor networks as well as actuators, communication devices, computing servers and platforms, and data management servers. The sensors detect the data associated with the objects and their environment, and the actuators take defined and ordered actions from the applications [1, 31]. This enabler should allow a fast, interoperable, secure, and reliable communication.

Data Handling Capacity

The handling of data as a result of the adoption of IoT implies adopting capacities that ensures the consistency of data since its creation, transport, storage, and use for different functions, including data analytics, as part of the digitalization of the firm adopting IoT [13]. Interconnection of physical objects, people, animals, plants, smartphones, household appliances, and cars, endowed with different degrees of intelligence, will produce a data exchange and management on a massive scale, crossing interfaces between different networks and making Big Data necessary for data extraction and aggregation, and for information analysis and generation [30]. IoT data is generated when setting up the connected elements and mainly during the operation involving the large number of devices within the solution, which is why this enabler is required to ensure smart and efficient data management in environments other than those conventional, to store, structure, process, and generate responses in acceptable times [29].

This capability is considered an enabler as it will allow the following:

Collect and store the data produced by the different elements; store and transform them into a standard format that can be processed and analyzed to achieve the benefits of IoT [30, 32]. Capturing data when performed on different devices deployed to different networks and in different physical locations shall involve the handling of large amounts of data. Technology supported by cloud computing technologies enables dynamic data collection and storage to be achieved [32].

Manage the data obtained from the IoT elements, determining the truly valuable data, mainly in the scenarios where these are unstructured. For instance, colors, shapes, sizes, and facial recognition features are captured by image sensors [33]; IoT requires devices to be smartly connected and endowed with the ability to communicate, collect, and process large amounts of quality data to effectively get value from IoT and help to overcome the skepticism inherent in business related to security, privacy, and resistance to change [24, 32].

Making analytical capabilities available. After the processing in the different computing instances, the highest value is achieved from the processing and from the data that is collected from different elements and correlated using analytical models. This processing is powerful but sensitive in terms of information processing, since any error could lead to wrong decisions. It requires integrating cutting-edge tools and technologies in order to obtain benefits [29].

2.3.2.2 Strategic Enablers

IoT Adoption as a Strategic Element

The fact that IoT is adopted as a strategic element implies that it is adopted to transform both the products and services delivered to the customer, business processes, or a new business model. This vision when communicated to the entire organization facilitates the application of IoT, in order to improve the customer experience, the work of employees, and/or the interaction with suppliers; they will widely perceive the IoT benefits as better products, a greater operational efficiency of the company, and as better ways of working and interacting between employees and suppliers. It is considered an enabler since its definition and all the way through the final implementation of the IoT adoption strategy, making the transformation feasible and when giving it a business direction and purpose.

Formulation of a Global IoT Architecture

The formulation of a global IoT architecture has been proposed, which will be the definition of how the elements of the IoT solution are represented, structured, and organized. The architecture will consider, on the one hand, the objects, sensors/actuators, communication network, processing systems, services, as well as the data [30]. On the other hand, the standards both at the industry and digital technology level need to be adopted. IoT innovation potential for developing applications is still emerging [29], and architecture is a key strategic enabler to harness such potential, which is defined based on the business model that comprises the value creation architecture [34]. The architecture will consist of lower-level architectures, such as business process architecture, systems architecture, and technological architecture (hardware and network) [31].

Technological and system architecture level allows structuring the information management capabilities generated by the IoT elements for its operation and organizing them into four sublevels (layers): the first one refers to the objects (perception) from where the data is captured, the second one refers to the routing and transport of the data (network), and the third one shows the task decisions on the data (services) and finally the information processing (application). From the business perspective, the architecture adopts a service-oriented approach (SOA) and allows the sublevels to work in a customer-supplier relationship where one element becomes a supplier and the other one is a customer, making it easier to segment the roles of the components which, taken as a whole, allow fulfilling the functions by orchestrating and combining defined, autonomous, and interoperable elements called services [1].

The formulation of the architecture is a critical enabler as it allows the construction of the IoT solution, in a flexible and scalable way, rather than acquiring technologies and implementing them without having any model or reference aligned with the organization's strategy.

2.3.2.3 Organizational Enablers

The organizational enablers allowing an IoT adoption include the organizational structure, dynamic capabilities, organizational agility, digital talent, skills, as well as a digital culture. The first three described as part of organizational digitalization can be applied to IoT, but the last two, are consider to have a particular meaning in relation to this digital technology context.

Talent and Digital Skills

Talent refers to the ability of people to cleverly understand and solve problems to achieve goals, and the skills refer to the abilities, or expertise, that people have to perform tasks. Mainly, it refers to both the digital talent and skills, such as the capabilities and expertise to plan, design, build, and implement solutions using the digital technologies and applying them to IoT adoption. Among them, we can distinguish the following ones:

Digital Talent Defining and implementing IoT adoption as part of the digitalization strategy require an understanding of both the physical and cyber worlds. It is a crucial enabler that allows combining different information, communication, and electronic technologies and summons professionals to work in multifunctional teams, as well as encouraging innovation to build digital vision.

Digital Skills Organizations must have people with expertise in electronics, communications, cloud computing, mobility, data analytics, and application development and integration whether these are merchandising or custom developments in the adoption of IoT. Professionals with expertise in data science, security, and information protection are required as well.

Digital Culture

Culture refers to a set of standards and values guiding human behavior [35]. Digital culture is related to the standards and values enabling us to adopt digital technologies. The values leading the applicable digital culture to the adoption of

IoT are a sense of innovation, agility, autonomy, and shared information. These sets of values are determining factors to make feasible IoT solutions. The following elements of digital culture can be considered:

Sense of innovation, which will enable obtaining proper solutions in the different components of IoT, in the detection and transport of data, and in the processing and actions delivering value to people. It is a change of mindset that extricates the traditional constraints and shows the possibilities that technology provides in the business context and where the strategy defines IoT as a feasible solution, reusing and improving previous solutions [3].

Sense of agility refers to the ability of people to move quickly when planning, executing, reviewing, and iterating to deliver incremental value in shorter periods. Agility is required in decision-making, execution, and correction of improvements. IoT is a combination of many technologies, consequently executing and delivering value with agility which can be important for considering its adoption.

Autonomy, which enables multifunctional working teams to organize, plan, and execute the projects that make up the IoT solution. A more horizontal and less hierarchical relationship between people empowered to make decisions throughout the layout, construction, and implementation of solutions with many edges such as IoT is a key enabler.

Shared information, since in IoT projects it is important to share information due to the high level of integration it requires. Communication is a digital enabler that is leveraged in a culture of transparency and sharing information; otherwise the operational problems will happen during operations.

2.3.3   Barriers

2.3.3.1   Organizational Barriers

Need for Standardization

Standardization refers to the shared acceptance of an established, accepted, and often followed way, method, pattern, or technology to accomplish a given function or type of activity. Across IoT, standard generation has been taking place through protocols, and although many protocols have been developed for different components of the architecture, standardization for this technology is in its early stages. There are many standards at the device level, IoT interconnection network, and information management in the semantics of the elements and standards ensuring the representation, storage, organization, search, and exchange of information among the IoT elements [1].

None of the layers has a universal standard yet. Even for a single industry, consequently adopting the standards is a barrier to achieving an IoT solution that goes beyond the intranet or extranet. The lack of universal standardization affects all layers of architecture, and standards and frameworks providing basic guidelines for adoption at each level of architecture need to be accomplished. In order to measure the lack of standardization, the participation of regulatory organizations and companies sharing a vision is required. The barriers occur at the level of:

(a) Device standards.

Standardization can represent a barrier, since the following features presented in the IoT system for devices must be considered [32]: their heterogeneity, the need for coexistence and collaboration, the constraints, the absence of mobility patterns, a need for self-configuration, a self-organization and autonomy, and a need for multi-hop communication using different protocols, for the devices requiring connection.

This barrier affects the progress of the IoT adoption, and organizations are discouraged by the lack of clarity of both the elements and networks they need to use to connect, the possibility of using different ways of communication with elements of another network, compatibility in communication, and the use of many intermediaries, which complicate the solution architecture and the IoT infrastructure. Overcoming this barrier supposes adopting technologies in an innovative way, with sufficient forward-looking vision in order to develop extended networks with other companies [36] and with devices from other organizations, considering power restrictions [29], detection range, and data rate.

(b) Standards in the IoT network.

In order to interconnect networks, there are different standards, and there is not one that covers all the adoption needs; therefore, the heterogeneity of devices and platforms must be anticipated [1]. Frameworks providing guidance to organizations are required to define an integration architecture enabling applications to connect to heterogeneous networks.

The standards in the IoT network also face the challenge of ensuring their validity over time, their scalability to operate with networks that uses different protocols, and the existence of frameworks that enables the IoT adoption, as they ensure the interconnection between devices and the device and object management platform with the applications managing the functionality of devices and objects, along with security platforms and communication resources and data repositories.

(c) Standards in information management.

Standardization at this level enables the extraction of knowledge from applications on different platforms, and the functional process of service delivery that is expected by the smart objects and end users as standard. A proper integration architecture makes it easier for IoT elements to exchange data between the different levels, from the sensors detecting the data and delivering it to the service and application platforms, until the data from the orders (or commands) reaches the actuators to change the object conditions [29]. The service-oriented architecture

(SOA) defined in IT, including the use of middleware as an intermediate layer, is appropriate to abstract and reduce complexity, since it makes it feasible to use services from different applications or platforms without having to elaborate codes for each type of service [31]. However, the slow and heterogeneous adoption of service-oriented architectures by many organizations becomes a barrier to progress in the digitalization when adopting IoT. The information management at a semantic level includes the middleware as an intermediate layer, data logic, and technologies for the use of services [1].

Security Risks

A risk represents the probability that an event will occur and may impact the project or the operation of a system [37]. Security refers to the set of strategies, tools, and procedures to ensure the availability of the solution components, its operation, and the data protection of the IoT solution. A security risk represents the probability that an event will happen and affects the protection of the system, impacting the availability of the solution components and its operation, or creates an improper access to data. IoT connects a large number of smart devices geographically deployed in different places and have the ability to communicate with elements of its own network and with other communication and information networks and provide access to services, applications, and data. These multiple features make IoT a vulnerable solution unless some mechanisms for a safe start-to-finish operation are included within the diverse elements of the architecture.

Table 2.1 summarizes the attacks to which the IoT system is exposed, such as improper access, unauthorized data use, or attacks on the system that partially or totally disable the operation of the IoT system (sabotage) [1, 38]. These risks will force firms to adopt a security culture to protect their assets and earn the trust of their customers through preventive policies and mechanisms protecting the integrity of the organization's data, as well as their operations.

The IoT security protocols differ from those used for conventional Internet such as a desktop or personal computer, since a broader view of the risks existing in the elements of multiple levels of IoT is required; the elements providing security have limited resources in terms of power and processing capacity, such as the access from remote networks, and geographic dispersion. Despite the mechanisms in place for the secure transport of data using encryption/decryption of information between the terminals communicating in IoT, security remains an open issue due to the following:

- The object network made up of devices such as RFID and sensors is highly vulnerable. Endowing these elements with authentication mechanisms requires the ability to deploy functionalities with low-power and low-speed resources, which cannot withstand greater task loads, to comply with the security requirements.

Table 2.1 Security risks by IoT layer and affected entity

Element	Most common attacks	Challenge
Devices	Capture and control of node or device and access to sensitive information (group, radio, and matching communication keys) Access and/or alter specific functions, and achieve access to the IoT system Inject fake data into IoT applications, with wrong response, incorrect services, and wrong IoT system operation Illegal eavesdropping on network links Attack on encryption Worn out device	Better authentication and data control
Communication equipment	Consume available IoT services by bombarding the network according to protocols Identity theft/multiple identities Diverting information to malicious node Malicious dodo introduction Alter routing and create loops generating delays Access via RFID	Define blocking schemes, better authentication, secure routing
Application	Id and password phishing through illegal emails and websites Virus infection Malicious script execution	Improve authorization and authentication, use of firewalls

Source: Based on [1, 30]

- Each element in the network must be authenticated, as well as the other device with which it communicates, as it represents an access port to the network and to other networks, from which attacks can be carried out.
- As there are elements that remain a significant part of their time inactive, and with no supervision, it is possible that the data they handle can be altered and fails to maintain its integrity.

In an IoT digitalization scenario, it is necessary to adopt the most suitable security protocols and is still insufficient, since the number of nodes deployed significantly limits the vulnerability of the operating system of the devices [29]. Therefore, security is an important barrier to the progress in the adoption of IoT systems by organizations.

Privacy Restrictions

Privacy refers to the right of individuals and organizations to protect their confidential information. Potential constraints to privacy are a barrier to IoT implementation. It is necessary to overcome this barrier to achieve people's trust regarding the protection of information linked to their daily activities, in which IoT will be able to store and manage the data provided by different connected objects and which are part of people's life. A digitalization that integrates IoT into its business model includes the fact that many people's objects, household appliances, cars, smartphones, and even their clothes and shoes provide data to the IoT system, as this is linked with the invasion to the people's privacy and to the feeling of being watched and to the distrust in the data use that belongs only to each individual. The strengths and benefits of having devices that instantly share data with many people and things simultaneously are an asset; however, it also represents a weakness when looking at the aspects of trust, security, and privacy [38]. The type of information that is collected may range from simple environmental climate data to audio and images of places where people move.

The examination of whether or not the information collected is useful for the delivery of the service and whether the data collected as part of the operation of the system is effectively used as part of the service provisioning, and when this occurs, the said information is destroyed, or if on the contrary and taking advantage of a low-cost storage, this information is not properly stored and falls into the wrong hands that may use it in a nonlegal way. Data protection is a key challenge to overcome this barrier; therefore, it is important that organizations that use of IoT technology ensure the customer the access control capabilities at data level, which means that the collected data, who collect them, and when they collect them are effectively authorized [1]. In addition, all the handling of people's data can be effectively audited; this means that there should be the ability to track the data usage since its creation, modification, and queries, as is done, for instance, in a blockchain application [38].

Cost

The solutions that make possible the interconnection of objects within the same or between different networks are complex. Thus, the development and implementation have a high cost [39].

In order to actually bear the costs of implementing IoT, CEOs and executives of organizations need to effectively understand the benefits that IoT solutions will bring to their organizations. These benefits can be achieved in terms that IoT can actually transform the strategic vision of transformation, the operational efficiency, and customer commitment as well as the business model [40]: the benefits are obtained during the operating time. The key is to obtain these benefits and allow to recover the investment in the shortest possible time. As long as this does not happen, the investment will not be made, and its projection will be a barrier to the abovementioned adaptation strategy.

Regulatory Issues

Although public and private organizations are aware of the opportunities that IoT represents, mainly as a data source to achieve the potential benefits above discussed, and to become organizations with greater operational efficiency, customer understanding, and more suitable proposals to customers, still governments need to develop a legal framework for inter-organizational agreements by incorporating contractual relationships with business, information processing, and confidentiality agreements within a digital scenario. The lack of this legal framework becomes a legal and regulatory barrier to IoT implementation [39].

Governments have a role to play in IoT development within both private and public organizations, and in this respect, they need to develop policies and regulations governing the implementation of IoT solutions and fostering innovation to prioritize the well-being of citizens. A digital government that while regulating companies also encourages their own digitalization, by offering tax advantages, has to be implemented.

Legal information systems for the governmental authorities must be developed to enable the massive development of IoT which involves organizations, to ensure security standards and regulate the operation. Regulatory policies on the use of frequency bands, network use, power, and sustainable development of digital solutions are also pending.

2.3.3.2 Cultural Barriers

Perception of Complexity

The management of a transformation with IoT involves many stakeholders, from both the public and private sectors, who need to make commitments, for projects to be successful. If within an organization it is already complex to achieve an alignment under a common objective, achieving this objective when there exist external stakeholders increases the difficulty to do so, which is why the adoption of IoT will be perceived as more complex. As there exist a large number of initiatives, industry consortia and research entities aimed to establishing standards and best practices, leading to the formulation of reference frameworks and architecture models, created by experts from different countries and industries, with the aim to transfer experiences, best practices, available technology opportunities, and potential implications as a road map for various stakeholders. However, while the intent of this wide variety of models and frameworks is to overcome the existing confusion, the large number of models in turn becomes a source of confusion for the different stakeholders, mainly for beginners who venture into this type of solutions [41]. On the digital stage, many jobs become simpler, while others become more complex when it comes to achieving integrated solutions [42]. This perception is a barrier that can be overcome if we:

Break silo mentality and people manage to see not only beyond the departmental area but also beyond their organization.

Promote collaboration, between professionals from different disciplines and areas, reusing solutions achieved in other areas or organizations.

The need for an organization to achieve management skills and achieve strong relationships between IT, communications, and business areas to develop digital skills applicable to IoT and rely on a framework that properly focuses the strategy guides digital projects, supports adoption, and mobilizes the necessary organization to achieve the deployment [3].

Lack of Trust

Trust refers to a cultural component rooted in people that may greatly limit the use of IoT, and it is hard to maintain, as the network of connected objects is broader, since it involves the information of manufacturers, suppliers, and service operators. The lack of trust in IoT exists due to the lack of security and confidentiality regarding information but also due to service quality, the operational failures, and the vulnerability of the solutions. Citizens will trust organizations to the extent that they offer quality service, as well as a robust and reliable infrastructure, confidentiality, and protection of their information [1]. Trust is built on a technical level, especially by establishing relationships of trust among the different elements of the IoT solution but above all by delivering creative solutions to the customer with a:

Sense of urgency, to deliver quality and timely IoT solutions to customers, users, and employees.

Willingness to take risks, to propose solutions to reduce technical problems for customer, users, and employees.

This sense of trust must be translated into a quality of service and data security but also based on the organization's capacity so that a system with so many elements fails to be attacked by internal or external hackers, since any failure of these can destroy people's trust and therefore the adoption process.

2.4 Conclusions

A widespread IoT implementation within an organization implies a whole series of both technical and organizational requirements. The implementation plans that are adopted, both at the general and more specific levels within the organization, will be developed in an environment with elements that enable or hinder their execution, as appropriate. An analysis of these elements, based on the literature, has been submitted.

Based on the conducted analysis, We have identified the technological enablers (the ability to provide power to the devices, the connectivity, the communication capability between the elements and data handling capacity), the strategic enablers (the IoT adoption as a strategic element and the formulation of a global architecture of IoT), the organizational enablers (the digital talent and skills, as well as the digital culture), the organizational barriers (the need for a standardization, security risks, privacy restrictions, cost and regulatory issues), and the cultural barriers (the perception of complexity, as well as the lack of trust).

The identification of these elements may be useful for analyzing potential IoT implementations and for drafting the implementation plans. The study of the importance of the various factors and their possibility to be considered as indispensable relates to subsequent works. Likewise, the way to create enablers and overcome barriers also deserves further studies.

A.1 Annex 1

A.1.1 Summary of Main Concepts and Characteristics

Actuator	Device enabled to perform specific functionalities through orders sent by an application working in a platform or even other device [29]
Connectivity	Ability to set a physical or virtual contact among two or more entities in order to get a peer acknowledge among them, in order to meet the connection needs [43]
Digital strategy	Organizational strategy formulated and executed by leveraging digital resources to create differential value [36]
Digital transformation strategy	How an organization-wide digital strategy might be developed and implemented to get digitalization [44]
Digitalization	It describes the multiple phenomena and socio-technical processes of adoption and use of these technologies in wider individual, organizational, and social contexts [19]
Internet of things	A worldwide network of interconnected objects uniquely addressable, based on standard communication protocols [1]
	"Increasing network of physical objects that feature an IP address for internet connectivity, and the communication that occurs between these objects and other internet-enabled devices and systems" [39]
Interoperability	Capability of two or more objects to work together without any restrictions or additional adjustments, which means it contains integration aspects as endpoint descriptions and communication patterns [39]

IoT application	Software development characterized by enabling data process, make decisions, event transfers, network connectivity, and interoperability [1]
IoT security	Set of feature and mechanisms aimed to secure all layers from applications to infrastructure (including data, devices, platforms, network elements) [1]
IT architecture	Clarity and organizational consensus around technology, data, and business process in terms of well-defined components, which are properly structured to achieve enterprise functions [45]
Protocol	A set of rules and guidelines for communication and interaction between two entities, with physical or virtual exchange. A set of procedures in telecommunications connections that the terminals or nodes use to send signals back and forth [4]
RFID	Radio-frequency identification (RFID) is a label to tag and identify some objects. They have been initially targeted to architect the IoT [29]
Sensors	Instruments used to sense conditions, characteristics or properties from objects, and the environment surrounding the object [29]
Standardization	Effort to adopt standards in order to perform specific functions in the context of IoT, such as communication, data transport, data exchange, network integration, etc. [1]

References

1. Atzori, L., Iera. A., & Morabito, G. (2010). The internet of things: A survey. *Computer Networks, 54*(15), 2787–2805.
2. Brynjolfsson, E., & Mcafee, A. (2014). The second machine age: Work, progress, and prosperity ina time of brilliant technologies. *Journal Citation Report, 16*(2), 112–115.
3. Westerman, G., Bonnet, D., & McAfee, A. (2015). Leading digital: Turning technology into business transformation. *Choice Reviews Online, 52*(06), 52-3197–52–3197.
4. Gartner. Gartner Glossary. *Web Site*. [Online]. Available: https://www.gartner.com/en/glossary. Accessed 29 June 2020.
5. Hess, T. (2016). Digitalisierung — Enzyklopaedie der Wirtschaftsinformatik. In © *2008–2018, Lehrstuhl für Wirtschaftsinformatik (insb. Prozesse und Systeme), Universität Potsdam*. [Online]. Available: https://www.enzyklopaedie-der-wirtschaftsinformatik.de/wi-enzyklopaedie/lexikon/technologien-methoden/Informatik%2D%2DGrundlagen/digitalisierung/index.html/. Accessed 29 Feb 2020.
6. Kane, G. (2019). The technology fallacy: People are the real key to digital transformation. *Research-Technology Management, 62*(6), 44–49.
7. Tushman, M., & Nadler, D. (1986). Organizing for innovation. *California Management Review, 28*(3), 74–92.
8. Ivančić, L., Vukšić, V., & Spremić, M. (2019). Mastering the digital transformation process: Business practices and lessons learned. *Technology Innovation and Management Review, 9*(2), 36–50.
9. Gal, P., Nicoletti, G., von Rüden, C., Sorbe, S., & Renault, T. (2019). Digitalization and productivity: In search of the holy grail - firm-level empirical evidence from European countries. *International Products Monitoring, 37*, 39–71.
10. Cardona, M., Kretschmer, T., & Strobel, T. (2013). ICT and productivity: Conclusions from the empirical literature. *Information Economics and Policy, 25*(3), 109–125.

11. Hess, T., Matt, C., & Benlian, A. (2016). Options for formulating a digital transformation strategy. *MIS Quarterly Executive, 15*(1540–1960), 123–139.
12. Downes, L., & Nunes, P. F. (2013). Big-bang disruption. *Harvard Business Review, 91*(3), 1–12.
13. Kane Gerald, N. B., Palmer, D., Phillips, A. N., & Kiron, D. (2016). Aligning the future for its digital organization. *Sloan Management, 58180*, 7–9.
14. Singh, A., & Hess, T. (2017). How chief digital officers promote the digital transformation of their companies. *MIS Quarterly Executive, 16*, 5.
15. Wiesböck, F., & Hess, T. (2019). Digital innovations: Embedding in organizations. *Electronic Markets, 30*(2), 75–86.
16. Teece, D. J., Pisano, G., & Shuen, A. (2008). Dynamic capabilities and strategic management. In *Technological know-how, organizational capabilities, and strategic management: Business strategy and Enterprise development in competitive environments* (pp. 27–52). Singapore: World Scientific Publishing.
17. Vial, G. (2019). Understanding digital transformation: A review and a research agenda. *Journal of Strategic Information Systems, 28*(2) Elsevier B.V., 118–144.
18. Sebastian, I. M., Ross, J. W., Moloney, K. G., Fonstad, N. O., Beath, C., & Mocker, M. (2017). How big old companies navigate digital transformation. *MIS Quarterly Executive, 16*(3), 197–213.
19. Legner, C., et al. (2017). Digitalization: Opportunity and challenge for the business and information systems engineering community. *Business and Information Systems Engineering, 59*(4), 301–308.
20. Ross, J. W., Sebastian, I. M., & Beath, C. M. (2016). How to create a great digital strategy. *CISR Research Brief, 16*(3), 1–4.
21. Westerman, A., Calméjane, G., Bonnet, C., Ferraris, D., & McAfee, P. (2011). *Digital transformation: A roadmap for billion-dollar organizations: MIT Center for digital business and Capgemini consulting.* [Online]. Available: https://www.capgemini.com/wp-content/uploads/2017/07/Digital_Transformation__A_Road-Map_for_Billion-Dollar_Organizations.pdf. Accessed 9 Mar 2019.
22. O'Reilly, C. A., & Tushman, M. L. (2008). Ambidexterity as a dynamic capability: Resolving the innovator's dilemma. *Research in Organizational Behavior, 28*, 185–206.
23. Kane, G. C., Palmer, D., Philips, A. N., Kiron, D., & Buckley, N. (2018). Coming of Age Digitally: Learning, Leadership, and Legacy. D.gital Business Report: *MIT Sloan Management Review in collaboration with Deloitte.* June 5, 2018. Accessed June 16, 2018. https://sloanreview.mit.edu/projects/com-ing-of-age-digitally/?gclid=EAIaIQobChMImqjnjIjZ2wIV1-EbCh20gwYkE-AEYASAAEgIT6PD_BwE.
24. Horváth, D., & Szabó, R. Z. (2019). Driving forces and barriers of industry 4.0: Do multinational and small and medium-sized companies have equal opportunities? *Technological Forecasting and Social Change, 146*, 119–132.
25. Westerman, G., & Bonnet, D. (2015). Revamping your business through digital transformation. *MIT Sloan Management Review, 56*(3), 10–13.
26. Westerman, G., & Mcafee, A. (2012). *A major research initiative at the MIT Sloan School of Management Research Brief the Digital Advantage: How digital leaders outperform their peers in every industry.*
27. Chanias, S., Myers, M. D., & Hess, T. (2019). Digital transformation strategy making in pre-digital organizations: The case of a financial services provider. *The Journal of Strategic Information Systems, 28*(1), 17–33.
28. Gebauer, H., Fleisch, E., Lamprecht, C., & Wortmann, F. (2020). Growth paths for overcoming the digitalization paradox. *Business Horizons, 63*(3), 313–323.
29. Al-Fuqaha, A., Guizani, M., Mohammadi, M., Aledhari, M., & Ayyash, M. (2015). Internet of things: A survey on enabling technologies, protocols, and applications. *IEEE Communication Surveys and Tutorials, 17*(4), 2347–2376.

30. Lin, J., Yu, W., Zhang, N., Yang, X., Zhang, H., & Zhao, W. (2017). A survey on internet of things: Architecture, enabling technologies, security and privacy, and applications. *IEEE Internet of Things Journal, 4*(5), 1125–1142.
31. Whitmore, A., Agarwal, A., & Da Xu, L. (2015). The internet of things—A survey of topics and trends. *Information Systems Frontiers, 17*(2), 261–274.
32. Bello, O., & Zeadally, S. (2016). Intelligent device-to-device communication in the internet of things. *IEEE Systems Journal, 10*(3), 1172–1182.
33. Mao, Y., You, C., Zhang, J., Huang, K., & Letaief, K. B. (2017). A survey on Mobile edge computing: The communication perspective. *IEEE Communications Surveys and Tutorials, 19*(4) Institute of Electrical and Electronics Engineers Inc., 2322–2358.
34. Teece, D. J. (2010). Business models business strategy and innovation. *Long Range Planning, 43*(2–3), 172–194.
35. Westerman, G., Soule, D. L., & Eswaran, A. (2019). Building digital-ready culture in traditional organizations. *MIT Sloan Management Review, 60*(4), 59–68.
36. Bharadwaj, A., El Sawy, O. A., Pavlou, P. A., & Venkatraman, N. (2013). Digital business strategy: Toward a next generation of insights. *MIS Quarterly, 37*(2), 471–482.
37. Aven, T. (2010). On how to define, understand and describe risk. *Reliability Engineering and System Safety, 95*(6), 623–631.
38. Skarmeta, A. F., et al. (2018). IoTCrawler: Browsing the internet of things. In *2018 global internet of things summit, GIoTS 2018*.
39. Brous, P., & Janssen, M. (2015). A systematic review of impediments blocking internet of things adoption by governments. In *Lecture notes in computer science (including subseries lecture notes in artificial intelligence and lecture notes in bioinformatics)* (Vol. 9373, pp. 81–94).
40. Liu, V. (2017). *Business benefits of the internet of things: A Gartner trend insight report.* Gartner Research. Stamford, Connecticut, USA. https://doi.org/G00333540.
41. Bader, S. R., Maleshkova, M., & Lohmann, S. (2019). Structuring reference architectures for the industrial internet of things. *Future Internet, 11*(7), 151.
42. Padyab, A., Habibipour, A., Rizk, A., & Ståhlbröst, A. (2020). Adoption barriers of IoT in large scale pilots. *Information, 11*(1), 23.
43. TMForum. (2020). TR255A connectivity patterns for virtualization management v4.0. *TM Forum.* [Online]. Available: https://www.tmforum.org/?s=connectivity+need. Accessed 29 June 2020.
44. Matt, C., Hess, T., & Benlian, A. (2015). Digital transformation strategies. *Business and Information Systems Engineering, 57*(5), 339–343.
45. Ross, J. W., & Westerman, G. (2004). Preparing for utility computing: The role of IT architecture and relationship management. *IBM Systems Journal, 43*(1) IBM Corporation, 5–19.

Chapter 3
The Combination of AI, Blockchain, and the Internet of Things for Patient Relationship Management

Mohame Ikbal Nacer, Simant Prakoonwit, and Ismail Alarab

Abstract The use of the Internet of Things (IoT) in the healthcare sector has shown to be a promising solution to reduce the workload of doctors and provide better service to patients. However, shared data may be subject to theft or misuse due to the security issues on various devices. Moreover, transparency among stakeholders, confidentiality, and micropayments need to be addressed. The objective of this work is to use federated learning over blockchain data generated from IoT devices with the usage of zero-knowledge proof or confidential transactions. The proposed architecture ensures the user a level of privacy set by them while making sure of sharing relevant insights with the concerned parties.

Keywords Blockchain · Consensus · Artificial intelligence · Deep learning · Internet of Things · Zero-knowledge proof · Health care

3.1 Introduction

Patients who suffer from illnesses such as cancer and Alzheimer's need ongoing care from personal doctors, keeping in mind the cost of a private hospital is very high and very crowded. There is growing use of wearable IoT devices which are one or a set of devices that share information within a network or with an end-storing framework. The shared information can operate the devices collaboratively or perform the desired functionality. Nevertheless, the centralisation of cloud data storage has raised many questions about confidentiality, security, and tolerance to failure. Moreover, the questions of where the data is located and who is the owner of it are critical. Artificial intelligence and deep learning have shown impressive results in health data and biological research in terms of prediction and analysis.

M. I. Nacer (✉) · S. Prakoonwit · I. Alarab
Bournemouth University, Bournemouth, UK
e-mail: mnacer@bournemouth.ac.uk; sprakoonwit@bournemouth.ac.uk; ialarab@bournemouth.ac.uk

© Springer Nature Switzerland AG 2021   49
F. P. García Márquez, B. Lev (eds.), *Internet of Things*, International Series in Operations Research & Management Science 305,
https://doi.org/10.1007/978-3-030-70478-0_3

On the other hand, blockchain is based on coupling cryptographic techniques with distributed algorithms to give the world's first cryptocurrency that has eliminated the trusted party within the financial transaction. Hence, by applying the technique to the transaction of information is very promising. Therefore, the combination of the three technologies can provide the healthcare industry with a solution that addresses the issues of security and privacy.

The IoT is referred to by several generic terms such as the Internet of Everything (IoE), the Internet of Nano Things (IoNT), the Web of Things (WoT) and Machine to Machine (M2M). However, the background of this different infrastructure is the same, namely, devices communicate via a network. The communication can take many forms; it can be a collaboration or simple data transmission [19, 24]. The adoption of IoT in different industries to increase productivity or improve performance is currently popular in research. Work by Yang et al. [45] proposed the use of the shared information among vehicles to predict a faster path within a network of connected cars. The work in Ref. [20] discussed the implementation of smart houses. Also, several studies have explored the usage of wearable devices, such as Refs. [1, 8, 25]. However, security has always been an issue within this technology because of the lack of standards. Moreover, the central cloud-based architecture can lead to either failure or attacks that exploit many vulnerabilities within the vast network of connected devices. In addition, business or personal data can be exploited by a third party due to the vulnerabilities [44].

Artificial intelligence is the art of making machines learn automatically without hardcoding knowledge. Several approaches have been proposed, such as symbolic programming [22] and probabilistic inference [13], but their usage is more prominent in the control system. However, function-based methods such as analytic machine learning or pattern recognition approaches such as deep learning have shown impressive results on health data. Caroprese et al. [4] presented various achievements from the deep learning pioneers in the healthcare sector. The paper discussed the Deepr system [42], which is a convolutional neural network as it features an extraction algorithm to predict the risk for different patients. Moreover, Deep Patient [23] trains a stake autoencoder by overfitting the data before calculating the different values within the prediction stage to each class of disease; it has shown impressive results on disease tagging. Also, DoctorAI [9] builds a generalising architecture from patient data aiming to predict future events by using the recurrent convolutional neural network.

Blockchain is a technology based on sharing a registry among different peers empowered with a consensus mechanism to validate its integrity. The core of the blockchain architecture is in its consensus. The proof of work (PoW) is by making the miner invest with hardware resources by querying a one-way function described as an NP-complete problem. There are many proposals discussed in the literature to optimise resource consumption of the PoW, such as the proof of stake (PoS) and the proof of concept (POX). The suitability of PoS in the IoT platform is due to the fact that stakeholders are interested in keeping the ledger valid. The PoS such as Autoboros [20] is based on implementing the Follow the Satoshi Algorithm, which works by randomly selecting a coin before surfing the ledger to investigate the owner to be a candidate for leadership. Casper [3] is a proposal that combined the byzantine fault tolerance (BFT) with a PoS to benefit from both the techniques. Moreover, some artificial intelligence proposals were made in the consensus study, such as in Jianwen [7] for node selection. Also, the Takagi Sugeno artificial neural network combined with cognitive mapping for faster transaction traceability (Chen [6]).

The adoption of the BFT has been widely discussed, but the hybrid consensus solution aimed to take advantage of the characteristics of each consensus separately and could be suitable for the IoT industry. The Tangle [31] proposed the use of a novel consensus approach that makes each participant validate two transactions besides running the proof of work in the hashcash approach to eliminate the spamming. However, sometimes there is a need for more privacy to eliminate traceability within the blockchain. Thus, the adoption of zero-knowledge by the implementation of zero-knowledge succinct noninteractive arguments of knowledge (Zk-Snark) was first proposed in Zerocoin [36] and later implemented in Zcash [15] as a forked chain from the Bitcoin.

This work proposes a novel architecture that provides the user with a secure, transparent, and robust communicative platform between the used device and the end-storing platform. Moreover, distribution increases the trustability of the data. Consequently, different doctors can teach their models over each other dataset without any relevant personal information leading to high integrity in the system. The solution aims to combine the three technologies into a single system and to benefit from each technique. There are many works in the literature that have taken advantage of these techniques separately or binomially, but the combination of the three has high potential to make people's lives easier. The next section will introduce the different works in the literature that present the use of those three technologies in the health sector; it will also discuss the drawback of each of them. The third section will present the different components of the architecture separately. The fourth section will present the architecture and discuss its functioning. The fifth section is dedicated to a discussion to compare it with available solutions before a conclusion.

3.2   Related Work

The development of the healthcare system based on the use of wearable devices was discussed in Ref. [35]. Afterwards, it was implemented for the long-term institution for elders in Taiwan [16], in which wearable devices were configured in proactive or passive mode to serve a certain kind of illness with particular services. Nevertheless, the solution suffers from the centralisation of data that leads to low security. Moreover, the implementation is to be dedicated to a local network of a hospital and not generative. Muhtharaman et al. [39] discussed the implementation of IoT use cases in healthcare by setting an ontology of communication. The proposal builds well-structured semantics for a multi-agent system that will manage a collection from different devices for analysis and prediction. Caroprese et al. [4] discussed the use of cloud computing to harness the hardware power for data processing and how to manage it. The work in Ref. [42] discussed the security of communication within the platform and proposed a model for a sophisticated key generation that protects against the Man in the Middle Attack.

The deep learning approach is the focus of interest in the health sector due to the availability of big data and the importance of a pattern recognition approach in such a scenario. Che et al. [5] discussed how to deal with missing data, how to build a model and demonstrated the superiority of their approach compared to previous works in feature discovery. The work in Ref. [29] proposed the usage of deep learning architecture dedicated to facial recognition to predict the elderly person's pain and report it through the network with the use of IoT devices. In Ref. [40], the authors discussed the injection of the recent advancement of deep learning within a decision support system for patient management under the name of the STARR project; it proposed an execution architecture as well. Sheng et al. [37] built a library of short-term activity before training a convolutional neural network over it to track human behaviour through wearable sensors. Deep learning performance is excellent, but the price of performance is over its interpretability.

The lack of theory about how to build deep learning architecture and most of the search techniques for the found ones is based on the experimental approach because all world events are complex and cannot be described with the available mass distribution functions. However, many researchers have proposed giving interpretability to the converged list of functions and mapping matrix, such as the reverse engineering approach in Ref. [30]. Moreover, deep learning needs a lot of data, and sometimes the data owner does not like to share it for privacy reasons, and that led to the rise of federated learning (FL) which was proposed to deal with learning over decentralised data. Nilsson et al. [27] have studied the backdoor attack on the two kinds of learning with FL, which is sequential and average concluding that the approach is vulnerable to this type of attacks. The work in Refs. [18, 21] has proposed the use of blockchain as a recording mechanism for updating among the different nodes. Froelicher et al. [12] have proposed the use of a decentralised system enabled by zero-knowledge proof to learn over geographically distributed data.

Blockchain technology is a data structure built on a hash function; each element of the chain is a block that contains a list of transactions, timestamp, hash digest built recursively from a Merkle tree, and a previous block hash. The different participants within the network are either self-beneficial through its use, such as a light Bitcoin wallet [26] or high-level interesters in maintaining the ledger validity for rewards such as miners. Singh et al. [38] have identified the blockchain as a game changer in the IoT sector. Moreover, the paper presented the architecture of how the blockchain is going to orchestrate the different data acquisitions, eliminate the central failure, and give better transparency to different stakeholders and users. However, blockchain is not a mature technology, and the cryptocurrency field is currently its focus. Also, the adoption of the technique in the IoT sector can provide transparency, privacy, and resilience to failure. The core of the blockchain technology is in the consensus. Different proposals within this technology need revision because of the requirements of a zero-fee transaction. Nevertheless, many implementations of the IoT solution with the proof of stack consensus are proposed such as in Refs. [11, 17, 28, 32] due to its philosophy based on the fact that stakeholders are more interested in keeping the network alive.

AI is a centralised, data-driven technique that provides the user with high predictability and analysis of data based on hard-coded or automatically constructed rules. In addition, it assists in the decision-making process. However, there are many disadvantages to the approaches discussed in the literature. The use of federated learning aims to decentralise the learning process but without any consideration of competitiveness between the different peers. On the other hand, IoT devices offer high trackability but many concerns regarding the security of shared data. The blockchain can respond to competitiveness concerns between different peers by using a consensual mechanism and offer great transparency regarding shared data. Thus, this work aims to inherit from the three technologies the different techniques to manage competitiveness in the distributed system, data analysis, and trackability.

3.3   The Model

This section is decomposed into three parts to discuss the functioning of the different components of the system separately before introducing the architecture. Firstly, the data structure discusses the implemented data and its organisation, the use of encryption over the data, and the data acquisition model. The second part discusses the use of artificial intelligence and federated learning over the different data structures, and the third part is dedicated to the adopted consensus.

3.3.1   The Data Structure

Health mentoring data is a transaction based on types with associated values generated from sensing devices, where some associate a batch of types to another batch of values with the use of two tables. However, sometimes it is just a submission of values in a certain order. Unstructured data is a problem of the blockchain data structure. Also, transaction validity requires validation of the whole chain. In addition, there is a high level of transaction submission in a typical IoT application, and this process of validation is burdensome. Also, sometimes data are a sequence of unrelated transactions. Moreover, the different cryptographic techniques adopted by the blockchain must be parametrised differently to serve the expected high performance within the IoT domain. Consequently, this work proposes that each transaction will yield a statue that stood for the patient's health inferred from the submission and recorded within the block beside the Merkle tree, the hash of the previous block, and timestamp. The following is a block data structure demonstrated in Fig. 3.1.

Fig. 3.1 Block components

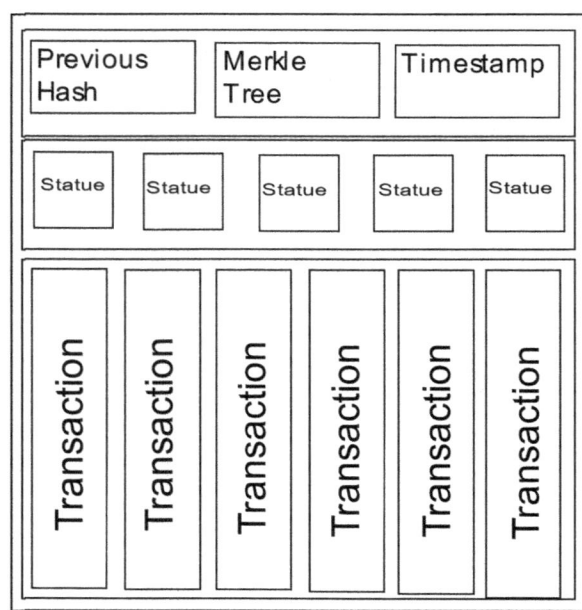

Algorithm 3.1 Trails

```
input : patients, graphRegistry, n
output: trails
convergence ← 1;
static trails ← Array < ant > [n];
procedure RUNANT(patient, graph, ant)
block ← randomStart(graph);
trail ← sur f TheGraph(Graph, patient)
ant.setTrail(trail)
end procedure
n ← size(patient) × random(1, 20)
n_t ← size(patient)
i ← n
j ← 0
whileconvergance ≥ 1 × 10 do
    Create N ant Thread dedicated to patients
    listO f ants ← createThread(n)
    whilei ≥ 0 do
        whilej ≤ n_tdo
            listO f ants[i] ← RunAnt(patient[ j], graph,
                                    listO f ants[i])
            j++
        end
        i-;
        j ← 0
    end
    list ← Optimizedtrail(patients, listO f ants)
    Convergence ← editDistanceNormalized(trails, list)
    trails ← list
end
```

Organising the block into a chain will result in an expensive search algorithm, and finding related information is a crucial step, sometimes due to the particular patients. The Tangle [31] proposed by the IOTA foundation is to serve as a cryptocurrency within IoT platforms. It uses dynamic acyclic graph (DAG) as a data structure leaving it vulnerable to many attacks. This is, firstly, because of the dropping of the concept of the block. Secondly, the dispersed injection of data across the edges of the graph makes the search expensive in the case of massive data growth. Consequently, due to the need for specific customer management at some point, this work proposes the implementation of a graph of block empowered with memory references between identity-related transactions. Consequently, pointing to the first transaction will allow jumping to other references and surf the whole chain of related information. Algorithm 3.1 demonstrates how to optimise trails to the first transactions of each patient.

Algorithm 3.1 starts by calculating an expected number of ants, which is the multiplication of patients' numbers with a random number. Later several variables are initiated, such as the i, j for looping, and n that holds the size of the patient vector. The function *createThread* will create an n of ant where each one is a thread dedicated to a patient as a target. The procedure *runant* will be launched by each ant separately with a target, the first sequential number of the patient. It will keep updating trails until there are no more changes, consequently stopping. Blum et al. [2] have described the ant colony algorithm and its functioning.

Although the blockchain can provide a high level of transparency and keep the identity private due to the use of RSA keys, some patients need to eliminate potential traceability. Thus, the adoption of two security layers is required, firstly, by using the zero-knowledge proof to provide proof of ownership on unlinked transactions or by the usage of the confidential transaction. The security layers' choices are based on making the data visible for further analysis but unlinking it from any identity or limiting it to the predicted algorithm. The level one security is based on the provider exchanges of the encryption keys with the patient under secure schema to record encrypted data. The decision to keep it in the public ledger is to provide transparency between different stakeholders and competitors in the case of sharing insights by running analytics methods. The level two security is by unlinking the transaction from the identity with the use of the zero-knowledge proof but providing the data content for free analyses.

The zero-knowledge snark is composed of four ingredients. Firstly, coding the proof into polynomials: $t (x) h (x) = w (x) v (x)$. Secondly, submitting this last function to a secret evaluation point called conciseness by random sampling, ensuring homomorphic properties. Precisely, the zero-knowledge approach is by obfuscating the s true value [34]. However, the use in blockchain architecture is about dissociating the transaction from identity but providing proof of the ownership. Mathematically, zero-knowledge snark based on the adoption of the generation of the prover and verifier circles to be set between the two parties.

First, the process begins by creating the two proofs by defining a mathematical equation to solve such $x^2 + x^2 + 3 = 35$. Second is to flatten t in several calculation steps; each is a simple mathematical operation:

1. $out1 = x \times x$
2. $out2 = x \times x$
3. $out3 = out2 + out1$
4. $out = out3 + 3$

Third is to convert it to a Rank-1 Constraint System (R1CS), which is three matrices, where each element is a Boolean and describes the presence of the variable or a constant. The resulting matrices will be subject of a shared witness vector that stands for the proof of ownership (Fig. 3.2).

3.3.2   Federated Learning

The federated learning (FL) proposed to train a machine learning model in a decentralised fashion to take advantage of the different data centres with huge stoked data that cannot be made for public use due to confidentiality agreements. The work in Ref. [43] proposed the use of FL over battery-powered devices and described a model with a two-layer trade-off with 20% energy consumption. Nilsson et al. [27]

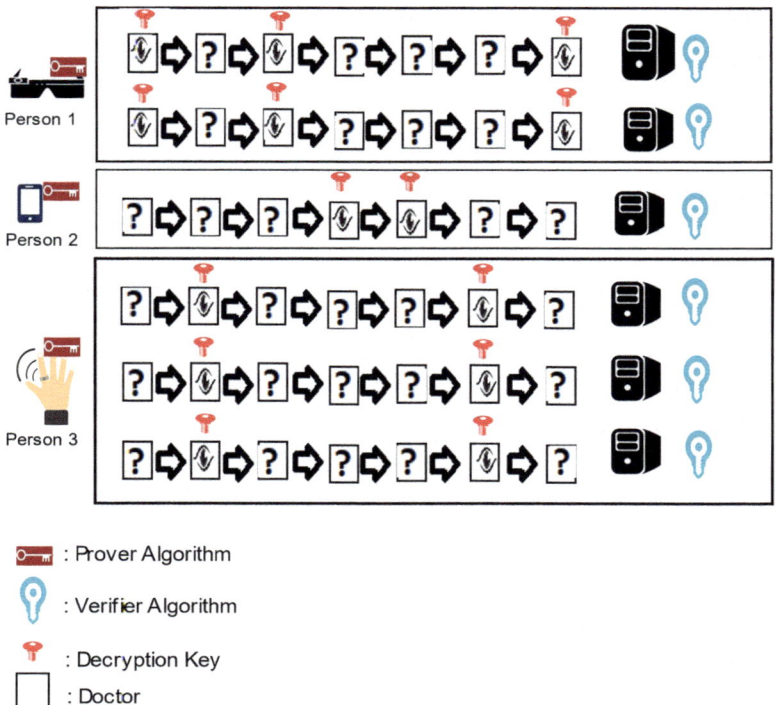

Fig. 3.2 Data acquisition pipeline

have compared the use of federated learning with a centralised one eliminating the different real-world constraints such as the heterogeneity of the data and different server limitations. However, it reported the efficiency of the average model. In Algorithm 3.2, different nodes will submit the updating parameters to the chain of the block to eliminate the high-level packet exchange, in which the branch of transaction related to the machine learning model is saved.

Algorithm 3.2 Federated Learning

```
input: lastsequentialNumber, &graph
output: models
while sleep(lastsequentialNumber, height)do
      data ← getDataFrom(graph, lastsequentialNumber)
      train ← train(supervisedModel, UnsupervisedModel)
      submit(Train, graph)
      enquireModel(graph)
      models ← models.updateAV G(supervisedModel,
      UnsupervisedModel)
end
```

Some artificial intelligence models need supervised learning. Consequently, there may be a need for personal data in the case of customer immigration from the doctor to another database. However, some methods are based on pattern recognition, and the need is limited to the generated values per IoT device. Moreover, analytics methods with business targets must be spotted and eliminated unless with the use of complex deep learning architecture to eliminate any interpretability. Algorithm 3.2 is how to train such models, in which it starts by enquiring data from the blockchain with the last sequential number at which the system stops training for the last time. It will run a partial fit to the data over a list of different models. Each doctor is a training model over his associated data using *train*, and the confidential transaction is decrypted temporally before submitting it with *submit()*. *EnquireModel()* is a blocked synchronised method requires from the blockchain of the updated model to run an average update over it.

3.3.3   Consensus

The use of blockchain technology aims to eliminate the central point of failure and to guarantee transparency in this context. Also, the adoption of the blockchain is to provide a level of confidentiality to the identity by mapping it to the public key, and this work creates a client registry that maps the public key to personal information inside each node separately for a faster search. However, the consensus must be on three levels, which are also the validity, authenticity, and accordance among validators. Moreover, the validity of the IoT data does not only come from the ledger, but it is a validation process that depends on external variables such as the state of the policy and customer offered service.

Algorithm 3.3 Decide

```
input : data
output: validpart, invalidpart
i ← 0;
size ← data.size()
while i ≤ size do
    path ← Trails(data[i]):
    lastTransaction ← jumpToTransaction(path)
    time ← timeDifference(data[i], lastTransaction)
    check ← checkIdentityAndService(data[i])
    statue ← checkPolicy(data[i])
    if decide(time, check, statue) then
        validpart.add(data[i])
    else
        invalidpart.add(data[i])
    end
    i++;
end
```

Algorithm 3.4 Consensus

```
input : LastValidator, Models
while true do
    block ← SleepTillblockMeetCriteria()
    while true do
        if lastValidator = ID then
            e ← randomNumber():
            s ← mod (NodesSize/e)
            send(s, block)
        else
            S ← sleepTillreceiveValidator()
        end
        if s = ID then
            validPart, invalidPart ← block.decide()
            validPart.PredictStatue(models)
            requestPayment(invalidPart)
            Broadcast(validPart)
            block ← validPart
        else
            block ← sleepTillreceiveBlock(s)
        end
        if block = Nul then
            updateReferences(block, Graph) Break;
            LastValidator ← s
        end
    end
end
```

Algorithm 3.3 starts by running Algorithm 3.1 and gets the trail to the first transaction of the submitted identity. Evaluating the patient's electronic behaviour makes the level of throughput under the Ethernet box capacity and eliminates any packet losses using the function *timeDifference(Transaction)*. Secondly, it evaluates the identity of the associated public key to check if the client is registered to send such data to use a particular service with the function *checkIdentityAndService(Transaction)*. Finally, it enquires about the policy statue *checkPolicy(Transaction)* before making a decision that will lead to adding it as a valid transaction to be injected or an invalid transaction.

The consensus in Algorithm 3.4 starts by *SleepTillblockMeetCriteria( )*, which is a synchronised blocking function until the number of transactions meets the minimum within a dependent time. The last validator will initiate a random number to modules it over a number node, and the result is the identity of the next validators. It will be broadcasted among nodes; while the other node will be pending, the validator will run the *decide( )* predict statue of the patient and request payment from invalid transaction senders before broadcasting the new block. All nodes will update their references and link the transaction in the blockchain.

3.4   Architecture

The work proposed an architectural combination of the usage of wearable devices with a system based on blockchain network and take advantage of artificial intelligence models through the use of federated learning. The usage of the ZK proof and confidential transaction provided two levels of security. However, the high level of expected transactions leads to eliminating the overuse of the Zk proof. In addition, patients have the flexibility to choose the type of security level corresponding to the type of service used and, therefore, the use of confidential transactions for patients who need continuous monitoring. There is needed for sequential data. While other types of users can dissociate themselves from the transaction, their data will be the subject of research and analysis. Figure 3.3 is a component architecture of the system.

Figure 3.3 is a combination of three major components, which are the *server*, *client*, and the *IoT device*. The instances of the same *server* will gossip to each other to come to a consensus on data and share the trained AI model. The *IoT device* will communicate with the *client* through Bluetooth, whereas the *client* will submit the data through Wi-Fi. Moreover, Fig. 3.4 illustrates the internal architecture of the server application, which contains a *graph* composed of many *blocks*. Each *block* is composed of many transactions with associated health statues, Merkle tree, previous block hash value, and a timestamp. Each transaction is composed of a public sender key and generated value from the *IoT device*. *UtilityMethods* class contains all the methods to encrypt, process, and search over the graph. *Train* is a general class for both supervised and unsupervised learning that will be trained over blockchain data.

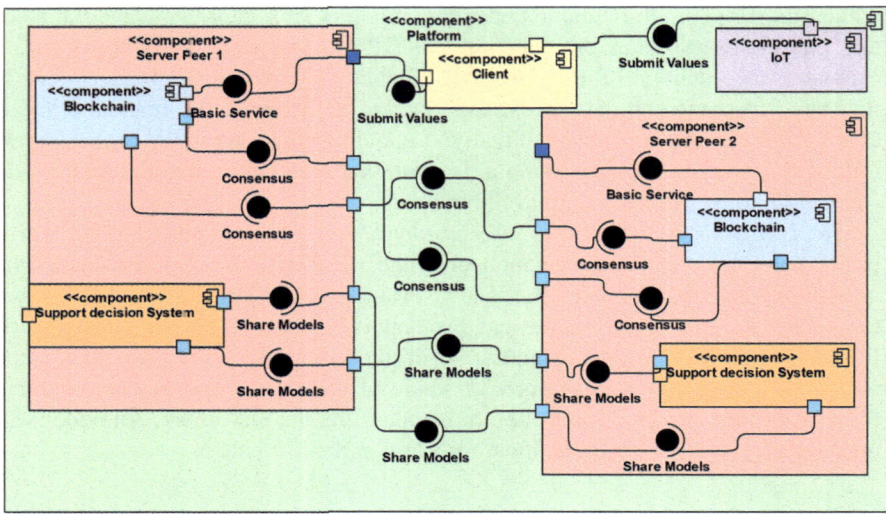

Fig. 3.3 Component architecture

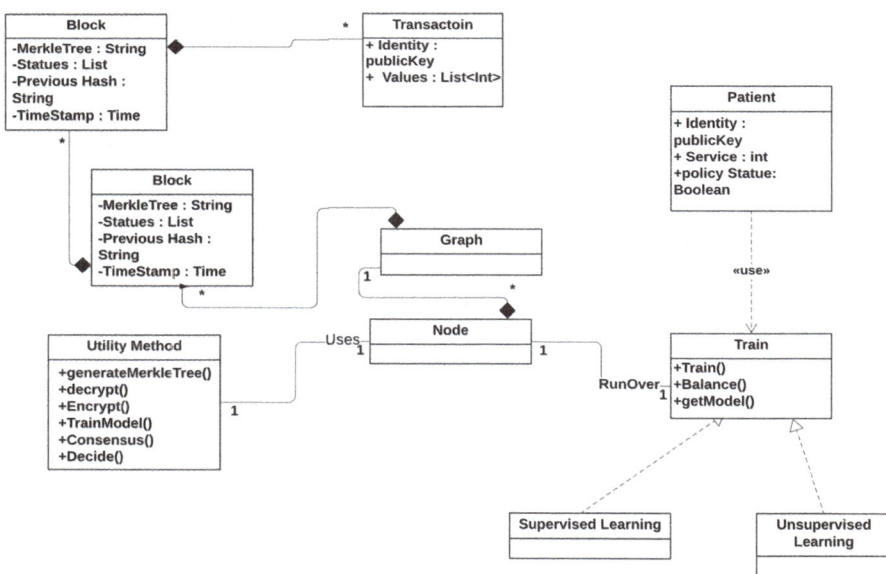

Fig. 3.4 UML server model

3.5 Discussion

The different AI solutions such as Deep Patient, Deepr, and Doctor AI [8, 23, 42] are to make use of health data to predict either future events or support decision-making. However, data trustability issues have been raised in Ref. [41] and solved by proposing the blockchain as a recording data structure. On the other hand, the use of wearable devices in the health sector to monitor the patient continuously is proposed in Ref. [16]. Nevertheless, it was dedicated to a local hospital without any conceptual consideration of openness to gather more data as well as the distribution to increase the integrity of the shared data. Privacy is an issue because of centralisation that leads to a lack of transparency between the stakeholders apart from central failure.

Huang et al. [16] have proposed the usage of blockchain technology in a private consortium to increase many security concerns within the health sector besides the trustability of the data generated from it. Griggs et al. [14] have proposed the use of blockchain to manage data transmission in the healthcare sector with the use of smart contracts running on the Ethereum platform. However, the proof of work is not suitable for a high transmission use case. The work in Ref. [33] proposed a new architecture, which uses blockchain to preserve confidentiality without any consideration of the huge amount of data generated to the blockchain. Also, using the proof of work with Bitcoin ideology is not practical in IoT. Thus, although the system has shown privacy and security features, it costs many other features such as scalability and rapidity. Dwivedi et al. [10] have addressed privacy concerns with the use of blockchain, but the aim was only to take advantage of the encryption keys. However, the solution has eliminated the use of the distribution, which lead to poor integrity.

This work addressed the blockchain use for patient management by preserving all its criteria of distribution and transparency. Moreover, it addressed the problem of unstructured data that leads to expensive searches by proposing the use of an ant algorithm to find the first transaction and link-related transactions, with the use of memory references. Also, it proposed the use of PoS with the external variable to validate the new block of transactions. Moreover, the use of FL to share models between doctors and the patient data has been secured firstly by attaching the identity to a public key before using encryption or ZK proof.

The proposed approach combined the three technologies in one. It makes use of the different features that the blockchain offers to build a platform that is secure, transparent, trustworthy, and resistant to failure. Moreover, it made use of federated learning and took advantage of the non-interpretability of deep learning architectures and some other analytics methods to provide secure, predictable models. Finally, the generated data comes from a wearable IoT device. Table 3.1 is a demonstration of other proposal characteristics and how the proposed architecture inherited all the features.

Table 3.1 Comparison (characteristic inheritance)

	Trackability	Predictability	Security
Decision support system (Deepr, etc.)	Not considered	High	High
Wearable devices	High	Not considered	Medium
Blockchain in healthcare [1–2]	Not considered	Not considered	High
The proposed architecture	High	High	High
	Transparency	Trustability	Resilience to failure
Decision support system (Deepr, etc.)	Not considered	Not considered	Not considered
Wearable devices	Not considered	Not considered	Not considered
Blockchain in healthcare [1–2]	High	High	High
The proposed architecture	High	High	High

The solution can also inherit disadvantages within each separate technique, and it can cause very interesting combinatorial problems. Thus, many research problems can be raised within this system, such as:

1. The right to be forgotten within blockchain technology.
2. Operation of the Simi-synchrony model combined with federated learning.
3. Study of confidentiality issues regarding the public availability of encrypted data.
4. A study discusses the architectural design that ensures the lack of interpretability of deep learning models.
5. Detection and prevention of data loss.
6. The study of each component taking into account the contractual reliability of the other components.

3.6   Conclusion

The use of IoT devices in the health sector has proven to be a potential solution to monitor patients. However, a different solution proposed the usage of blockchain as trackable technology that generates trustable data. Moreover, different systems used artificial intelligence to generate insight from the gathered data. This work proposed the combination of tree technology to offer a solution that can provide the best from each technology. This work can be summarised as follows:

- A data structure with the attached patient statue with use of memory references
- The use of an ant algorithm to optimise trails to find the first transactions
- Federated learning with complex deep learning architecture to secure the privacy of the shared model
- Mixture of proof of stake with external variables as a consensus mechanism
- A demonstration of the architecture before comparison with previous works

References

1. Ahmad, N., George, R. P., & Jahan, R. (2019). Emerging trends in IoT for categorized health care. In *2019 2nd International Conference on Intelligent Computing, Instrumentation and Control Technologies (ICICICT)* (Vol. 1, pp. 1438–1441). Kannur, India.
2. Blum, C. (2005). Ant colony optimisation: Introduction and recent trends. *Physics of Life Reviews, 2*(4), 353–373.
3. Buterin, V., & Griffith, V. (2017). Casper the friendly finality gadget. *arXiv preprint arXiv.* 1710.09437.
4. Caroprese, L., Veltri, P., Vocaturo, E., & Zumpano, E. (2018). Deep learning techniques for electronic health record analysis. In *2018 9th International Conference on Information, Intelligence, Systems and Applications (IISA)* (pp. 1–4). Zakynthos, Greece.
5. Che, Z., & Liu, Y. (2017). Deep learning solutions to computational phenotyping in health care. In *2017 IEEE International Conference on Data Mining Workshops (ICDMW)* (pp. 1100–1109). New Orleans, LA, USA.
6. Chen, R. Y. (2018). A traceability chain algorithm for artificial neural networks using T–S fuzzy cognitive maps in blockchain. *Future Generation Computer Systems, 80*, 198–210.
7. Chen, J., Duan, K., Zhang, R., Zeng, L., & Wang, W. (2018). An AI based super nodes selection algorithm in blockchain networks. *arXiv preprint arXiv.* 1808.00216.
8. Choi, E., Bahadori, M. T., Schuetz, A., Stewart, W. F., & Sun, J. (2016). Doctor AI: Predicting clinical events via recurrent neural networks. In *Machine learning for healthcare conference* (pp. 301–318). LA, Los Angeles, CA, USA.
9. Coelho, C., Coelho, D., & Wolf, M. (2015). An IoT smart home architecture for long-term care of people with special needs. In *2015 IEEE 2nd World Forum on Internet of Things (WF-IoT)* (pp. 626–627).
10. Dwivedi, A. D., Srivastava, G., Dhar, S., & Singh, R. (2019). A decentralised privacy-preserving healthcare blockchain for IoT. *Sensors, 19*(2), 326.
11. Frederick, M., & Jaiswal, C. (2018). BID: Blockchaining for IoT devices. In *2018 9th IEEE Annual Ubiquitous Computing, Electronics & Mobile Communication Conference (UEMCON)* (pp. 806–811).
12. Froelicher, D., Troncoso-Pastoriza, J. R., Sousa, J. S., & Hubaux, J.-P. (2020). Drynx: Decentralised, secure, verifiable system for statistical queries and machine learning on distributed datasets. In *IEEE Transactions on Information Forensics and Security.*
13. Golmard, J.-L. (1993). Probabilistic inference in artificial intelligence: The method of Bayesian networks. In *Philosophy of probability* (pp. 257–291). Dordrecht: Springer.
14. Griggs, K. N., Ossipova, O., Kohlios, C. P., Baccarini, A. N., Howson, E. A., & Hayajneh, T. (2018). Healthcare blockchain system using smart contracts for secure automated remote patient monitoring. *Journal of Medical Systems, 42*(7), 130.
15. Hopwood, D., Bowe, S., Hornby, T., & Wilcox, N. (2016). *Zcash protocol specification.* San Francisco: GitHub.
16. Huang, P.-C., Lin, C.-C., Wang, Y.-H., & Hsieh, H.-J. (2019). Development of health care system based on wearable devices. In *2019 Prognostics and System Health Management Conference (PHM-Paris)* (pp. 249–252).
17. Kang, J., Xiong, Z., Niyato, D., Ye, D., Kim, D. I., & Zhao, J. (2019). Toward secure blockchain-enabled internet of vehicles: Optimising consensus management using reputation and contract theory. *IEEE Transactions on Vehicular Technology, 68*(3), 2906–2920.
18. Kim, Y. J., & Hong, C. S. (2019). Blockchain-based node-aware dynamic weighting methods for improving federated learning performance. In *2019 20th Asia-Pacific Network Operations and Management Symposium (APNOMS)* (pp. 1–4). Matsue, Japan.
19. Lee, S.-H., & Lee, D.-W. (2015). Review on current situations for internet of things. In *2015 7th International Conference on Multimedia, Computer Graphics and Broadcasting (MULGRAB)* (pp. 19–21). Jeju, Korea (South).

20. Lytvyn, V., Vysotska, V., Mykhailyshyn, V., Peleshchak, I., Peleshchak, R., & Kohut, I. (2019). Intelligent system of a smart house. In *2019 3rd International Conference on Advanced Information and Communications Technologies (AICT)* (pp. 282–287). Lviv, Ukraine.
21. Majeed, U., & Hong, C. S. (2019). Flchain: Federated learning via mec-enabled blockchain network. In *2019 20th Asia-Pacific Network Operations and Management Symposium (APNOMS)* (pp. 1–4). Matsue, Japan.
22. McCarthy, J. (1960). Recursive functions of symbolic expressions and their computation by machine, part I. *Communications of the ACM, 3*(4), 184–195.
23. Miotto, R., Li, L., Kidd, B. A., & Dudley, J. T. (2016). Deep patient: An unsupervised representation to predict the future of patients from the electronic health records. *Scientific Reports, 6*(1), 1–10.
24. Miraz, M. H., Ali, M., Excell, P. S., & Picking, R. (2015). A review on Internet of Things (IoT), Internet of Everything (IoE) and Internet of Nano Things (IONT). In *2015 Internet Technologies and Applications (ITA)* (pp. 219–224).
25. Mishra, S. S., & Rasool, A. (2019). IoT health care monitoring and tracking: A survey. In *2019 3rd International Conference on Trends in Electronics and Informatics (ICOEI)* (pp. 1052–1057). Tirunelveli, India.
26. Nakamoto, S. (2019). *Bitcoin: A peer-to-peer electronic cash system.* Technical report, Manubot.
27. Nilsson, A., Smith, S., Ulm, G., Gustavsson, E., & Jirstrand, M. (2018). A performance evaluation of federated learning algorithms. In *Proceedings of the second workshop on distributed infrastructures for deep learning* (pp. 1–8). Rennes, France.
28. Niya, S. R., Schiller, E., Cepilov, I., Maddaloni, F., Aydinli, K., Surbeck, T., et al. (2019). Adaptation of proof-of-stake-based blockchains for IoT data streams. In *2019 IEEE International Conference on Blockchain and Cryptocurrency (ICBC)* (pp. 15–16). Seoul, Korea (South).
29. Nugroho, H., Harmanto, D., & Al-Absi, H. R. H. (2018). On the development of smart home care: Application of deep learning for pain detection. In *2018 IEEE-EMBS Conference on Biomedical Engineering and Sciences (IECBES)* (pp. 612–616). Sarawak, Malaysia.
30. Oh, S. J., Schiele, B., & Fritz, M. (2019). Towards reverse-engineering black-box neural networks. In *Explainable AI: Interpreting, explaining and visualising deep learning* (pp. 121–144). Springer.
31. Popov, S. (2018). The tangle (2016). Verfügbar: http://www.tangleblog.com/wpcontent/uploads/2016/11/IOTA Whitepaper.pdf. Zugriff am 22.05.2019.
32. Puthal, D., & Mohanty, S. P. (2018). Proof of authentication: IoT-friendly blockchains. *IEEE Potentials, 38*(1), 26–29.
33. Rahulamathavan, Y., Phan, R. C.-W., Rajarajan, M., Misra, S., & Kondoz, A. (2017). Privacy-preserving blockchain based IoT ecosystem using attribute-based encryption. In *2017 IEEE International Conference on Advanced Networks and Telecommunications Systems (ANTS)* (pp. 1–6). Bhubaneswar, India.
34. Reitwiessner, C. (2016). zksnarks in a nutshell. *Ethereum Blog, 6*, 1–15.
35. Sankar Bhunia, S. (2015). Adopting internet of things for provisioning health-care. In *Adjunct proceedings of the 2015 ACM international joint conference on pervasive and ubiquitous computing and proceedings of the 2015 ACM international symposium on wearable computers* (pp. 533–538). Osaka, Japan.
36. Sasson, E. B., Chiesa, A., Garman, C., Green, M., Miers, I., Tromer, E., & Virza, M. (2014). Zerocash: Decentralised anonymous payments from Bitcoin. In *2014 IEEE symposium on security and privacy* (pp. 459–474). Berkeley, CA, USA.
37. Sheng, M., Jiang, J., Su, B., Tang, Q., Yahya, A. A., & Wang, G. (2016). Short-time activity recognition with wearable sensors using convolutional neural network. In *Proceedings of the 15th ACM SIGGRAPH conference on virtual-reality continuum and its applications in industry-volume 1* (pp. 413–416). Zhuhai, China.
38. Singh, M., Singh, A., & Kim, S. (2018). Blockchain: A game changer for securing IoT data. In *2018 IEEE 4th World Forum on Internet of Things (WF-IoT)* (pp. 51–55).

39. Thangaraj, M., Ponmalar, P. P., Sujatha, G., & Anuradha, S. (2016). Agent based semantic Internet of Things (IoT) in smart health care. In *Proceedings of the 11th international knowledge management in organisations conference on the changing face of knowledge management impacting society* (pp. 1–9). Hagen, Germany.
40. Vidaković, M., Ć osić, S., Ć osić, O., Kaštelan, I., & Velikić, G. (2019). Adding AI to the decision support system used in patient health assessment. In *Proceedings of the 13th EAI international conference on pervasive computing technologies for healthcare* (pp. 399–402). Trento, Italy.
41. Wang, T., Wu, X., & He, T. (2019). Trustable and automated machine learning running with blockchain and its applications. *arXiv preprint arXiv*. 1908.05725.
42. Nguyen, P., Tran, T., Wickramasinghe, N., & Venkatesh, S. (2017). Deepr: *A Convolutional Net for Medical Records, in IEEE Journal of Biomedical and Health Informatics, 21*(1), 22–30. https://doi.org/10.1109/JBHI.2016.2633963.
43. Xu, Z., Li, L., & Zou, W. (2019). Exploring federated learning on battery-powered devices. In *Proceedings of the ACM Turing Celebration Conference-China* (pp. 1–6). Chengdu, China.
44. Yadav, E. P., Mittal, E. A., & Yadav, H. (2018). IoT: Challenges and issues in Indian perspective. In *2018 3rd International Conference on Internet of Things: Smart Innovation and Usages (IoT-SIU)* (pp. 1–5). Bhimtal, India.
45. Yang, T., Wolff, F., & Papachristou, C. (2018). Connected car networking. In *NAECON 2018-IEEE National Aerospace and Electronics Conference* (pp. 60–64). Dayton, OH, USA.

Chapter 4
Bibliometric Characteristics of Highly Cited Papers on Internet of Things Assessed with Essential Science Indicators

Ming Tang and Huchang Liao

Abstract The Internet of Things (IoT) has been undergoing a rapid development and has obtained increasing visibility. A large number of scientific research achievements have been published. This study aims to provide a bibliometric review for highly cited papers in the field of IoT using the Essential Science Indicators, a widely used database to evaluate scientific outputs. Through the retrieval process, 388 papers were identified as highly cited papers. Based on these 388 papers, we analyze their characteristics from four perspectives: annual and discipline distributions; productive players in terms of journals, countries, institutes, and authors; top 15 most cited papers; and author keyword analysis. Interesting results are given after the analyses. Through author keyword analysis, we also provide research trends of the IoT for future study. It is hoped that our work will be helpful for practitioners and scholars who are interesting in the IoT.

Keywords Internet of Things · Bibliometric · Highly cited papers · Essential Science Indicators

4.1 Introduction

The concept of the Internet of Things (IoT) was first proposed by Kevin Aston in 1999 to characterize the globally increasing Internet-based technologies [1]. It is an information carrier based on Internet and traditional telecommunication network and brings the newest evolution of the Internet by extending communication among all kinds of smart things [2]. Executives believe that the IoT will be the most important emerging technology, ranking higher than robotics and artificial intelligence [3]. A study published by Forbes insights, which examined more than

M. Tang · H. Liao (✉)
Business School, Sichuan University, Chengdu, China

© Springer Nature Switzerland AG 2021
F. P. García Márquez, B. Lev (eds.), *Internet of Things*, International Series in Operations Research & Management Science 305,
https://doi.org/10.1007/978-3-030-70478-0_4

500 executives in Europe, America, and Asia Pacific, representing a range of industries, including companies with at least 500 employees, confirmed the progress of the IoT around the world (Insight team). Ninety percent of all surveyed executives who are in charge with the IoT initiatives believed that the IoT will play a critical role in the future development of business [3]. It was estimated that there will be 29 billion interconnected things by 2022 [4]. The popularity of the IoT has paved the way for countless applications that can improve the quality of our social life. Because of the demand of technical innovations and applications, a huge number of scientific achievements have been obtained in the last two decades since 1999, especially in the past 5 years [3].

A literature review of the IoT has been published from a theoretical framework perspective [3] or in terms of specific aspects such as smart manufacturing [5], supply chain management [6], and energy systems [7]. Several studies used bibliometric methods to quantitatively analyze the literature regarding the IoT [8–10]. However, as far as it knows, there is a lack of bibliometric analysis for highly cited papers (HCPs) in the domain of the IoT based on Essential Science Indicators (ESI) using bibliometric methods. The ESI, which was launched by the Institute for Scientific Information [11], is a database that collects scientific literature according to their performances. It can track the trends of scientific developments for different research fields and provides information on papers that enter the top 1% by the frequency of citations for each year in the last 10 years [12]. It can be used to identify influential players and hot topics in a research field and thus has been widely used to evaluate scientific outputs of countries, institutes, and authors [13]. Bibliometric study based on the HCPs is an emerging topic. Unlike traditional bibliometrics, it is based on the analysis of influential papers in a specific field. Existing studies did not focus on this topic in the field of the IoT.

This study focuses on the HCPs related to the IoT (IoT-HCPs). We analyze the IoT-HCPs in terms of the following aspects: (1) annual and discipline distributions; (2) productive journals, countries, institutes, and authors; (3) the top 15 most cited papers; (4) author keyword analysis covered by the literature detected.

The rest of this study is organized as follows: Section 4.2 describes the data and methods used in this study. Section 4.3 presents results in detail. Section 4.4 ends the study with concluding remarks.

4.2 Data and Methods

In this study, the data were collected from the core database of Web of Science (WoS). The collection strategy is TS="Internet of Things." More than 35,000 records were returned on Dec 9, 2019. Among all these papers, 388 papers were marked as the HCPs. Regarding the document type, 335 are articles, 50 are reviews, and 3 are proceedings papers. These 388 studies were downloaded in a tab delimited file format containing the information including title, abstract, keywords, authors, affiliations, publication year, sources, citations, and cited references.

Some indicators have been adopted to evaluate scientific outputs, including the number of publications, number of citations, average number of citations (AC), impact factor (IF), and H-index [14]. To carry out keyword co-occurrence analysis, the bibliometric software VOSviewer [15] is adopted in this study. In addition, CiteSpace [16] is used to make a timeline visualization map.

When counting the number of countries, we did some data processing work. Papers from England, Scotland, Wales, and Northern Ireland were classified into the UK. Papers from Hong Kong and Taiwan were included in China. If a paper was written in the form of international collaboration, then each country would be counted once. When carrying out author keyword analysis, we merged words with the same meaning but in different representation forms. For instance, "Internet of Things," "Internet of Things (IoT)," and "Internet-of-Things" were merged into "IoT."

4.3 Results

In the following, the 388 IoT-HCPs are analyzed from four perspectives: (1) distribution status; (2) productive journals, countries, institutes, and authors; (3) the top 15 cited papers; and (4) author keyword analysis.

4.3.1 Distributions of the IoT-HCPs

The annual distribution of 388 IoT-HCPs is presented in Fig. 4.1. In the first 4 years, the number of the IoT-HCPs is small. In the following 5 years, the number of the IoT-HCPs increases dramatically. This indicates that the IoT is a burgeoning research direction in recent years. In 2018, the number reaches its highest value. In 2019, it has a decrease since the collection of papers in 2019 has not been completed.

All these 388 IoT-HCPs are distributed in 12 ESI fields. A majority of these studies belong to "Computer Science" and "Engineering," which account for 54.64% (212) and 29.38% (114), respectively. The IoT has a strong dependence on computer science in this information age. Computer science and technology makes use of intelligent perceptions and recognition technology and communication technology, and as a result, the IoT is widely used in the network and real life. There is also a close relationship between the IoT and engineering. Many universities set up a major in "IoT Engineering," which aims to cultivate senior engineers and technical talents with broad and professional knowledge such as communication technology, network technology, and sensor technology. The following five ESI fields include Materials Science (3.87%); Chemistry (2.58%); Social Science, general (2.06%); Economic and Business (1.55%); Physics (1.29%); and others (see Fig. 4.2).

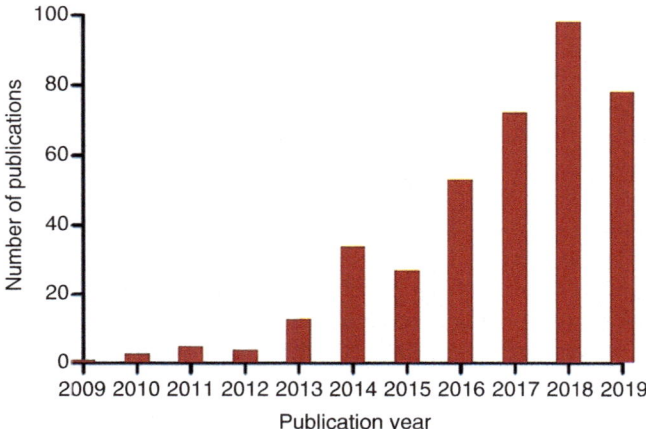

Fig. 4.1 Annual distribution of the IoT-HCPs (2009–2019)

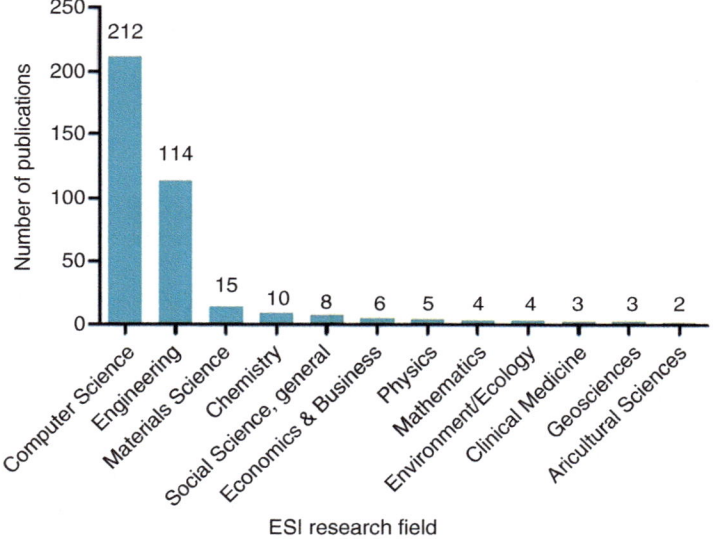

Fig. 4.2 Field distribution of the IoT-HCPs (2009–2019)

4.3.2 Productive Players

This section analyzes productive players with respect to journals, countries, institutes, and authors.

All these 388 studies were distributed in 113 journals. Table 4.1 presents the top 15 productive journals. *IEEE Internet of Things Journal* ranks first with 57

Table 4.1 The top 15 productive journals (2009–2019)

Rank	Journal	TP	TC	AC	IF
1	IEEE Internet of Things Journal	57	7195	126.23	9.515
2	IEEE Access	43	3980	92.56	4.098
3	IEEE Transactions on Industrial Informatics	29	4073	140.45	7.377
4	Future Generation Computer Systems-The International Journal of Escience	21	4820	229.52	5.768
5	IEEE Communications on Magazine	21	4247	202.24	10.356
6	IEEE Communications Surveys and Tutorials	20	4880	244	22.973
7	Journal of the Network and Computer Applications	12	1467	122.25	5.273
8	Computer Networks	10	6934	693.4	3.03
9	IEEE Network	7	671	95.86	7.503
10	IEEE Journal on Selected Areas in Communications	6	841	140.17	9.302
11	Ad Hoc Networks	5	1667	333.4	3.49
12	IEEE Transactions on Wireless Communications	5	423	84.6	6.394
13	IEEE Wireless Communications	5	827	165.4	11.0
14	International Journal of Production Research	4	322	80.5	3.199
15	Proceedings of the IEEE	4	492	123	10.694

Note. TP, total publications; TC, total citations; AC, average number of citations per publication; IF, impact factor

publications. This journal mainly publishes papers on various topics in the IoT, such as system architecture, enabling technologies, communication, and networking protocols (https://ieeexplore.ieee.org/xpl/RecentIssue.jsp?punumber=6488907). *IEEE Access* and *IEEE Transactions on Industrial Informatics* are in the second and third place, with 43 and 29 publications, respectively. *Computer Networks* has the highest value of AC (693.4), although its IF is the lowest (3.03) in 15 journals.

Next, we analyze the distribution status of countries. These 388 papers are from 55 countries, including 26 European countries, 18 Asian countries, 5 American countries, 4 African countries, and 2 Oceania countries. The top 15 productive countries are shown in Table 4.2. Their TP, TC, AC, H-index, international collaboration publications (ICP), first-author publications (FP), and corresponding-author publications (CP) are also provided. A paper's first author usually undertakes the major part of work. A paper's corresponding author is responsible for communication with other people and is usually the director of a research project [17]. The most productive country is China (189), followed by the USA (134), the UK (47), and Canada (34). Sweden has the highest percentage of ICP (100%). However, its percentages of FP and CP are low. There are also some countries like Canada, Saudi Arabia, Germany, Japan, and France which have the similar phenomenon. This can be attributed to their advanced technological, theoretical, and financial supports. Scholars in this field around the world need to cooperate with institutes of these countries. Several countries like China and Italy have low degree of international cooperation but have high percentages of FP and CP. This suggests that China and Italy's authors have primary contributions of their IoT-HCPs. To sum up, scholars

Table 4.2 The top 15 productive countries (2009–2019)

Rank	Country	TP	TC	AC	H-index	ICP (%)	FP (%)	CP (%)
1	China	189	17,852	94.46	73	128(67.72)	157(83.07)	153(80.95)
2	The USA	134	21,671	161.72	76	103(76.87)	55(41.04)	67(50)
3	The UK	47	6397	136.11	34	34 (72.34)	16 (34.04)	19 (40.43)
4	Canada	34	2306	67.82	26	31 (91.18)	11 (32.35)	15 (44.12)
5	Italy	33	12,372	374.91	28	16 (48.48)	23 (69.70)	25 (75.76)
6	South Korea	28	2796	99.86	25	21 (75)	11 (39.26)	20 (71.43)
7	Australia	26	6710	258.08	21	15 (57.69)	12 (46.15)	18 (69.23)
8	India	22	2288	104	20	17 (77.27)	9 (40.91)	8 (36.36)
9	Sweden	19	2350	123.68	18	19 (100)	4 (21.05)	3 (15.79)
10	Saudi Arabia	14	1265	90.36	12	13 (92.86)	4 (28.57)	5 (35.71)
11	Germany	13	1963	151	13	11 (84.62)	5 (38.46)	6 (46.15)
12	Japan	13	847	65.15	11	11 (84.62)	5 (38.46)	4 (30.77)
13	Spain	13	2696	207.38	13	7 (53.85)	6 (46.15)	6 (46.15)
14	Malaysia	12	906	75.5	10	9 (75)	8 (66.67)	7 (58.33)
15	France	11	1243	113	11	10 (90.91)	3 (27.27)	5 (45.45)

TP, total publications; TC, total citations; AC, average number of citations per publication; ICP, international collaboration publications; FA, first-author publications; CP, corresponding-author publications.

from Canada, Saudi Arabia, and France are more likely to cooperate with other countries' scholars. Chinese, Italian, Australian, and Spanish scholars are more likely to do research independently.

Figure 4.3 displays the international collaboration on the IoT using the VOSviewer software package. In Fig. 4.3, the size of a node is determined by the frequency of a country. If a country has more IoT-HCPs, then its corresponding node will be larger. A link between two nodes indicates that two countries have academic collaboration relationship. In VOSviewer, a link has a link strength, which represents the collaboration intensity. The link strength between China and the USA is the highest (80), which denotes that these two countries have extensive communication and cooperation in the IoT field.

Next, we take a sight in the distribution status of institutes. All these 388 IoT-HCPs are distributed in more than 500 institutes. In total, 17.53% (68) of all papers are single-institute publications, and 82.47% (320) are multi-institute publications. The average number of institutes per paper is 3.21. The top 15 productive institutes ordered by the number of papers are listed in Table 4.3. The TP, TC, AC, H-index, as well as two world university rankings are displayed in Table 4.3. There are some research-based institutes that do not participate in the world university ranking, such as the Chinese Academy of Sciences. The last column of Table 4.3 is the country that an institute belongs to. As we can see from Table 4.3, the Chinese Academy of Sciences leads the list with 32 IoT-HCPs. Chinese institutes make up the majority of the list. This indicates that China plays a critical role in the development of the IoT.

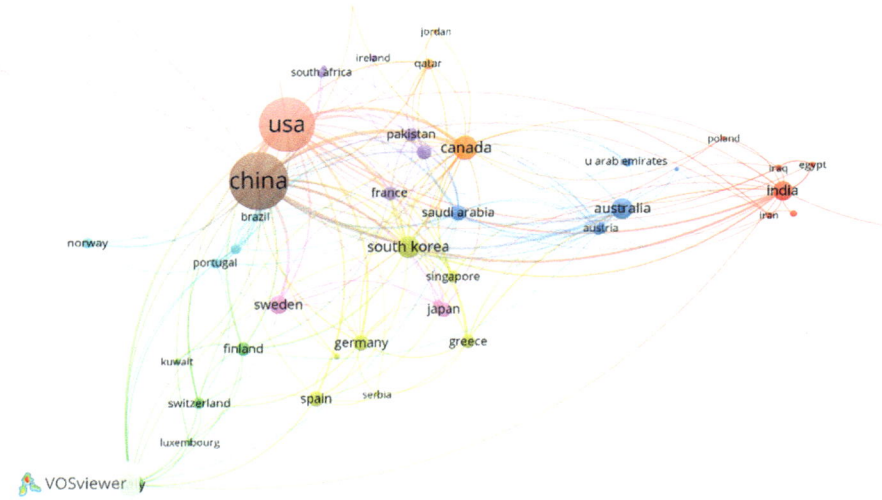

Fig. 4.3 The visualization of international collaboration (2009–2019)

Next, active authors will be presented. Only 18 papers were written by independent authors, which indicates that the IoT is a highly cooperative field. All 388 IoT-HCPs are authored by 1425 authors, among which 1229 (86.25%) authors contributed 1 paper, 124 (8.70%) contributed 2 papers, and 72 (5.05%) authors contributed 3 or more papers. The average number of authors per paper is 4.65. The top 15 active authors and several related indicators including TP, TC, AC, FP, and CP are shown in Table 4.4. Note that an author may belong to multiple organizations. Dr. Xu from the Old Dominion University, the USA, and the Chinese Academy of Sciences, China, has 16 IoT-HCPs and takes the first place. His AC is also the highest. Dr. Liu from the Central South University, China, has 14 papers. Dr. Qiu from the Tianjin University, China, and Dr. Tao from the Beihang University, China, have the largest number of FP papers. Dr. Liu from the Central South University has the largest number of CP papers.

4.3.3 The Top 15 Most Cited Papers

Table 4.5 shows the top 15 most cited papers, including 14 articles and 1 review. Note that the document type of a paper is determined by authors when submitting the manuscript in the online submission system of a journal. Therefore, some reviews will be marked as articles artificially in WoS. In fact, all papers in Table 4.5 can be classified into the review type. According to Liao et al. [11], reviews usually can obtain more citations than regular articles. As shown in Table 4.5, three papers were published in *IEEE Internet of Things Journal*. *Future Generation Computer*

Table 4.3 The top 15 productive institutes (2009–2019)

Rank	Institute	TP	TC	AC	H-index	ARWU	QS	Country
1	Chinese Academy of Sciences	32	5185	162.03	26	–	–	China
2	Dalian University of Technology	22	878	39.91	17	201–300	571–580	China
3	Central South University	19	660	34.74	17	151–200	801–1000	China
4	Old Dominion University	17	4426	260.35	17	601–700	–	USA
5	Shanghai Jiao Tong University	16	3198	199.88	16	82	59	China
6	King Saud University	12	961	80.08	10	151–200	256	Saudi Arabia
7	Beihang University	11	1388	126.18	11	201–300	491	China
8	Georgia Institute of Technology	11	1478	134.36	10	101–150	69	USA
9	University of Science & Technology of China	11	3055	277.73	11	101–150	98	China
10	Huaqiao University	9	286	31.78	9	–	–	China
11	Tsinghua University	9	2413	268.11	9	43	17	China
12	University of Electronic Science and Technology of China	9	343	38.11	9	151–200	751–800	China
13	Huazhong University of Science and Technology	8	1617	202.13	8	101–150	415	China
14	Hunan University of Science & Technology	8	264	33	8	–	–	China
15	Xidian University	8	699	87.38	8	601–700	–	China

TP, total publications; TC, total citations; AC, average number of citations per publication; ARWU, academic ranking of world universities; QS, Quacquarelli Symonds world university rankings

Table 4.4 Top 15 productive authors (2009–2019)

Rank	Author	Institute	TP	TC	AC	FP	CP
1	Xu, LD	Old Dominion University/Chinese Academy of Sciences	16	4372	273.25	2	3
2	Liu, AF	Central South University	14	424	30.29	1	7
3	Vasilakos, AV	Lulea University of Technology	11	1868	169.82	0	0
4	Wang, T	Huaqiao University	10	309	30.9	2	1
5	Li, X	Hunan University of Science & Technology	9	342	38	2	2
6	Qiu, T	Tianjin University	7	386	55.14	5	4
7	Tao, F	Beihang University	7	1121	160.14	5	5
8	Yang, LT	University of Electronic Science and Technology of China	7	510	72.86	0	4
9	Zhang, L	University of Electronic Science and Technology of China	7	1032	147.43	2	1
10	Chen, M	Huazhong University of Science and Technology	6	1313	218.83	4	3
11	Chen, ZK	Dalian University of Technology	6	248	41.33	0	0
12	Choo, KKR	University of Texas at San Antonio	6	227	37.83	0	1
13	Fortino, G	University of Calabria	6	464	77.33	0	0
14	Zhang, Y	University of Oslo	6	524	87.33	0	2
15	Li, P	Ostwestfalen-Lippe University of Applied Sciences	6	259	43.17	1	0

TP, total publications; TC, total citations; AC, average number of citations per publication; ICP, international collaboration publications; FA, first-author publications; CP, corresponding-author publications.

Systems-The International Journal of EScience, *IEEE Communications Surveys and Tutorials*, and *IEEE Communications Magazine* contribute two papers. The paper titled "The Internet of Things: A survey" [18] received more than 4900 citations in the WoS. In Google Scholar, it has more than 12,000 citations. This survey reported different visions of IoT, reviewed enabling technologies, and addressed the major issues faced by the research community. There are also some surveys [19, 20, 22] providing a systematic summarization for vision, applications, and future research directions. Some papers focused on applications of the IoT in a specific field such as smart cities [21] and industries [23]. Two papers reviewed the 5G (fifth-Generation) network [27, 31]. The ultimate goal of the IoT is the interconnection of all things. The mobile communication technology restricts its development. Nowadays, many terminals cannot access the network. The emergence of 5G is an opportunity for the sharp development of the IoT.

Table 4.5 The top 15 productive authors (2009–2019)

Rank	Title	Authors	Journal	TC	ACY
1	The Internet of Things: A survey [18]	Atzori, L; Iera, A; Morabito, G	Computer Networks	4936	493.60
2	Internet of Things (IoT): A vision, architectural elements, and future directions [19]	Gubbi, J; Buyya, R; Marusic, S; Palaniswami, M	Future Generation Computer Systems-The International Journal of Escience	3292	470.29
3	Internet of Things: A survey on enabling technologies, protocols, and applications [20]	Al-Fuqaha, A; Guizani, M; Mohammadi, M; Aledhari, M; Ayyash, M	IEEE Communications Surveys and Tutorials	1577	315.40
4	Internet of Things for smart cities [21]	Zanella, A; Bui, N; Castellani, A; Vangelista, L; Zorzi, M	IEEE Internet of Things Journal	1493	248.83
5	Internet of things: Vision, applications and research challenges [22]	Miorandi, D; Sicari, S; De Pellegrini, F; Chlamtac, I	Ad Hoc Networks	1284	160.50
6	Internet of Things in industries: A survey [23]	Xu, LD; He, W; Li, SC	IEEE Transactions on Industrial Informatics	1189	198.17
7	Recommender systems survey [24]	Bobadilla, J; Ortega, F; Hernando, A; Gutierrez, A	Knowledge-Based Systems	958	136.86
8	Big data: A survey [25]	Chen, M; Mao, SW; Liu, YH	Mobile Networks & Applications	872	145.33
9	Context aware computing for the Internet of Things: A survey [26]	Perera, C; Zaslavsky, A; Christen, P; Georgakopoulos, D	IEEE Communica-tions Surveys and Tutorials	1032	147.43
10	Non-Orthogonal multiple access for 5G: Solutions, challenges, opportunities, and future research trends [27]	Dai, LL; Wang, BC; Yuan, YF; Han, SF; Chih-Lin, I; Wang, ZC	IEEE Communications Magazine	833	166.60
11	Mobile crowdsensing: Current state and future challenges [28]	Ganti, RK; Ye, F; Lei, H	IEEE Communica-tions Magazine	765	85.00

	Title	Authors	Journal	TC	ACY
12	Edge computing: Vision and challenges [29]	Shi, WS; Cao, J; Zhang, Q; Li, YHZ; Xu, LY	IEEE Internet of Things Journal	711	177.75
13	Research directions for the Internet of Things [30]	Stankovic, JA	IEEE Internet of Things Journal	628	104.67
14	A survey of 5G network: Architecture and emerging technologies [31]	Gupta, A; Jha, RK	IEEE Access	603	120.60
15	Integration of Cloud computing and Internet of Things: A survey [32]	Botta, A; de Donato, W; Persico, V; Pescape, A	Future Generation Computer Systems-The International Journal of Escience	537	134.25

TC, total citations; ACY, average number of citations by year.

Table 4.6 The top 30 author keywords (2009–2019)

Author keyword	Frequency	Total link strength	Author keyword	Frequency	Total link strength
IoT	208	946	RFID	7	38
Cloud computing	38	204	Resource allocation	7	30
Big data	28	142	Industrial IoT	7	25
Wireless sensor networks	28	115	Cyber-physical systems	6	37
Fog computing	25	107	Energy efficiency	6	36
Security	23	98	Smart manufacturing	6	26
Edge computing	19	89	Massive MIMO	5	31
Smart city	19	90	Machine learning	5	24
Blockchain	14	59	Deep learning	5	21
Privacy	12	52	Survey	5	20
Authentication	12	51	Security and privacy	5	18
Sensors	9	41	Enterprise systems	4	29
Energy harvesting	8	43	Supply chain management	4	28
5G	7	50	Smart factory	4	27
Industry 4.0	7	42	Big data analytics	4	25

4.3.4 Author Keyword Analysis

Author keywords are the core and refinement of a paper, which can represent authors' overall understanding and generalization [33]. In a specific research field, author keywords with high frequency are often associated with hot topics [34].

Among 388 IoT-HCPs, authors have used more than 1000 keywords. Table 4.6 presents the top 30 frequent author keywords and their total link strength. The total link strength is the sum of co-occurrence frequency between a keyword and all other keywords. Undoubtedly, "IoT" is the most widely used keyword and appears in the author keyword list in 208 papers. Its total link strength is also the highest, which indicates that "IoT" is closely connected with other author keywords.

Figure 4.4 visualizes the co-occurrence network of author keywords. "IoT" is related to many keywords, such as "big data," "fog computing," "cloud computing," "edge computing," "security," "wireless sensor networks," and "smart city." The link strength between "IoT" and "cloud computing" is the largest. They appeared

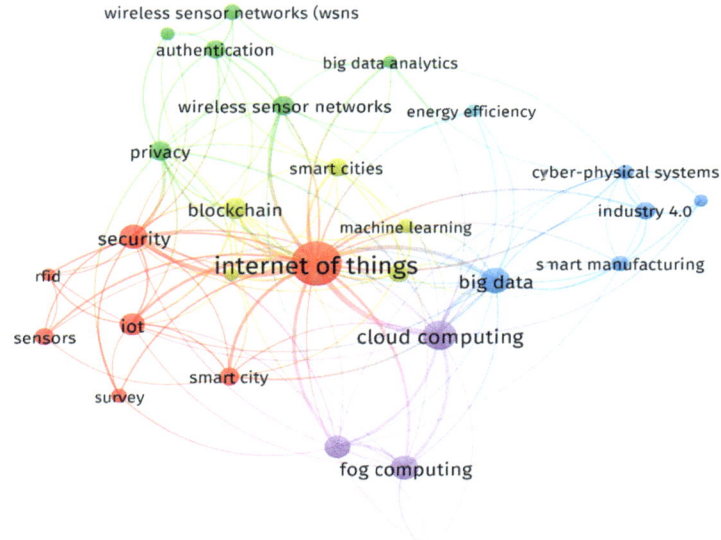

Fig. 4.4 The co-occurrence network of author keywords (2009–2019)

simultaneously in 30 IoT-HCPs. Cloud computing is a set of enabled services in network, providing QoS-guaranteed, inexpensive, and normally personalized computing infrastructures, which can be accessed in a convenient way [35]. Cloud computing is a more mature technology with almost unlimited storage and processing capacity and at least partially solves most of the IoT problems. It provides storage spaces for massive data generated by the IoT and becomes the core to achieve the IoT [36]. Therefore, a novel Internet paradigm that merges these two complementary technologies is expected to change the current and future Internet. This new paradigm is called as CloudIoT by Botta et al. [32]. The second is the link between "IoT" and "big data." The sensors of the IoT generate a large amount of data, which constitutes an important source of big data. Cloud computing, big data, and the IoT have penetrated and integrated with each other. In many applications, they can be seen at the same time. In the future, they will continue to promote and influence each other and better serve all fields of social production and life. Fog computing is an extended concept of cloud computing and has been introduced as a technique to bridge the gap between the IoT devices and remote data centers. Fog has a wide range of advantages, including enhanced security, reduced bandwidth, and reduced latency. It is a suitable paradigm for many IoT services [37].

To analyze the research topics from a dynamic perspective, we make the timeline visualization map based on author keywords using the CiteSpace software package, shown in Fig. 4.5. In Fig. 4.5, a cross-shaped node represents a keyword and its size reflects the frequency. Eight horizontal lines correspond to eight clusters. The right of the horizontal line is the label of the cluster. There are four red figures in the

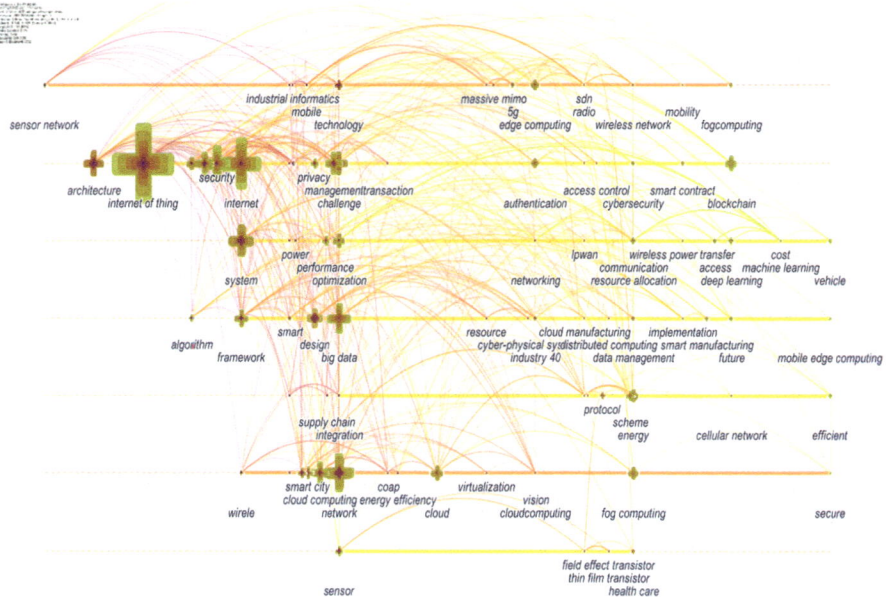

Fig. 4.5 Timeline visualization of author keywords (2009–2019)

top of the map, which represent 4 particular years. The line connecting two nodes indicates that two author keywords appear in some documents simultaneously. Through timeline visualization map, we can identify the evolution of research topics and find out emerging directions. As illustrated in Fig. 4.5, "IoT" is the biggest node without peradventure. Note that this node had an explosion in the year of 2012. Corresponding to Fig. 4.1, the number of IoT-HCPs in the first 4 years (2009–2012) is small. Important author keywords such as "cloud computing" and "big data" appeared in 2014. The concept of big data emerged around the year of 2012. The Obama administration announced the "Big Data Research and Development Initiative" [38], which proposed to use big data to break through technologies in national security, scientific research, and environmental protection. As time goes on, the size of nodes becomes smaller although the number of publications is growing. There are familiar keywords in 2018 and 2019 such as fog computing, blockchain, and deep learning, which indicates that scholars still have interests on these fields. In the near future, it is necessary to pay attention to these topics to further explore the applicability of the IoT.

4.4   Conclusion

This study conducted a bibliometric analysis for IoT-HCPs based on the ESI database. Four aspects including distribution characteristics, productive players, top 15 cited papers, and author keyword analysis were analyzed in detail. Some bibliometric indicators such as the TP, TC, AC, IF, and H-index were adopted. The VOSviewer and CiteSpace software packages were used in international collaboration network, co-occurrence network of author keywords, and timeline visualization of author keywords. Results revealed that the IoT has developed sharply since 2013. *IEEE Internet of Things Journal* is the most influential journal in this field. Chinese institutes and scholars played a critical role. The most cited papers were all reviews. Through keyword analysis, we found that IoT, big data, and cloud computing had close relationships. The combination of IoT with fog computing, block chain, and deep learning is new challenging research direction.

References

1. Ashton, K. (2009). That 'internet of things' thing. *RFID Journal, 22*(7), 97–114.
2. Macedo, E. L. C., de Oliveira, E. A. R., Silva, F. H., et al. (2019). On the security aspects of Internet of Things: A systematic literature review. *Journal of Communications and Networks, 21*(5), 445–457.
3. Nord, J. H., Koohang, A., & Paliszkiewicz, J. (2019). The Internet of Things: Review and theoretical framework. *Expert Systems with Applications, 133*, 97–108.
4. Macedo, E. L. C., et al. (2019). On the security aspects of Internet of Things: A systematic literature review. *Journal of Communications and Networks, 21*(5), 444–457.
5. Yang, H., Kumara, S., Bukkapatnam, S. T. S., & Tsung, F. (2019). The internet of things for smart manufacturing: A review. *IISE Transactions, 51*(11), 1190–1216.
6. Ben-Daya, M., Hassini, E., & Bahroun, Z. (2019). Internet of things and supply chain management: A literature review. *International Journal of Production Research, 57*(15–16), 4719–4742.
7. Bedi, G., Venayagamoorthy, G. K., Singh, R., Brooks, R. R., & Wang, K. C. (2018). Review of Internet of Things (IoT) in electric power and energy systems. *IEEE Internet of Things Journal, 5*(2), 847–870.
8. Mishra, D., Gunasekaran, A., Childe, S. J., Papadopoulos, T., Dubey, R., & Wamba, S. (2016). Vision, applications and future challenges of Internet of Things: A bibliometric study of the recent literature. *Industrial Management & Data Systems, 116*(7), 1331–1355.
9. Nobre, G. C., & Tavares, E. (2017). Scientific literature analysis on big data and internet of things applications on circular economy: A bibliometric study. *Scientometrics, 111*(1), 463–492.
10. Kaba, A., & Ramaiah, C. K. (2019). Bibliometric analysis of research output on the Internet of Things in the Arab world. *DESIDOC Journal of Library & Information Technology, 39*(5), 222–229.

11. Liao, H. C., Tang, M., Li, Z. M., & Lev, B. (2019). Bibliometric analysis for highly cited papers in operations research and management science from 2008 to 2017 based on Essential Science Indicators. *Omega, 88*, 223–236.
12. Zhang, N., Wan, S. S., Wang, P. L., Zhang, P., & Wu, Q. (2018). A bibliometric analysis of highly cited papers in the field of Economics and Business based on the Essential Science Indicators database. *Scientometrics, 116*(2), 1039–1053.
13. Chuang, K. Y., Wang, M. H., & Ho, Y. S. (2011). High-impact papers presented in the subject category of water resources in the essential science indicators database of the institute for scientific information. *Scientometrics, 87*, 551–562.
14. Furnham, A. (2020). What I have learned from my Google Scholar and H index. *Scientometrics, 122*(2), 1249–1254.
15. van Eck, N. J., & Waltman, L. (2010). Software survey: VOSviewer, a computer program for bibliometric mapping. *Scientometrics, 84*(2), 523–538.
16. Chen, C. M. (2006). CiteSpace II: Detecting and visualizing emerging trends and transient patterns in scientific literature. *Journal of the Association for Information Science and Technology, 57*, 359–377.
17. Zhai, T., & Di, L. Z. (2019). Information mining and visualization of highly cited papers on type-2 diabetes mellitus from ESI. *Current Science, 116*(12), 1965.
18. Atzori, L., Iera, A., & Morabito, G. (2010). The Internet of Things: A survey. *Computer Networks, 54*(15), 2787–2805.
19. Gubbi, J., Buyya, R., Marusic, S., & Palaniswami, M. (2013). Internet of Things (IoT): A vision, architectural elements, and future directions. *Future Generation Computer Systems, 29*(7), 1645–1660.
20. Al-Fuqaha, A., Guizani, M., Mohammadi, M., Aledhari, M., & Ayyash, M. (2015). Internet of Things: A survey on enabling technologies, protocols, and applications. *IEEE Communication Surveys and Tutorials, 17*(4), 2347–2376.
21. Zanella, A., Bui, N., Castellani, A., Vangelista, L., & Zorzi, M. (2014). Internet of Things for smart cities. *IEEE Internet of Things Journal, 1*(1), 22–32.
22. Miorandi, D., Sicari, S., De Pellegrini, F., & Chlamtac, I. (2012). Internet of things: Vision, applications and research challenges. *Ad Hoc Networks, 10*(7), 1497–1516.
23. Xu, L. D., He, W., & Li, S. C. (2014). Internet of Things in industries: A survey. *IEEE Transactions on Industrial Informatics, 10*(4), 2233–2243.
24. Bobadilla, J., Ortega, F., Hernando, A., & Gutierrez, A. (2013). Recommender systems survey. *Knowledge-Based Systems, 46*, 109–132.
25. Chen, M., Mao, S. W., & Liu, Y. H. (2014). Big data: A survey. *Mobile Networks and Applications, 19*(2), 171–209.
26. Perera, C., Zaslavsky, A., Christen, P., & Georgakopoulos, D. (2014). Context aware computing for the Internet of Things: A survey. *IEEE Communication Surveys and Tutorials, 16*(1), 414–454.
27. Dai, L. L., Wang, B. C., Yuan, Y. F., Han, S. F., Chih-Lin, I., & Wang, Z. C. (2015). Non-orthogonal multiple access for 5G: Solutions, challenges, opportunities, and future research trends. *IEEE Communications Magazine, 53*(9), 74–81.
28. Ganti, R. K., Ye, F., & Lei, H. (2011). Mobile crowdsensing: Current state and future challenges. *IEEE Communications Magazine, 49*(11), 32–39.
29. Shi, W. S., Cao, J., Zhang, Q., Li, Y. H. Z., & Xu, L. Y. (2016). Edge computing: Vision and challenges. *IEEE Internet of Things Journal, 3*(5), 637–646.
30. Stankovic, J. A. (2014). Research directions for the Internet of Things. *IEEE Internet of Things Journal, 1*(1), 3–9.
31. Gupta, A., & Jha, R. K. (2015). A survey of 5G network: Architecture and emerging technologies. *IEEE Access, 3*, 1206–1232.
32. Botta, A., de Donato, W., Persico, V., & Pescape, A. (2016). Integration of cloud computing and Internet of Things: A survey. *Future Generation Computer Systems, 56*, 684–700.
33. Uddin, S., Khan, A., & Baur, L. A. (2015). A framework to explore the knowledge structure of multidisciplinary research fields. *Public Library of Science, 10*(4), e0123537.

34. Uddin, S., & Khan, A. (2016). The impact of author-selected keywords on citation counts. *Journal of Informetrics, 10,* 1166–1177.
35. Wang, L., Von Laszewski, G., Younge, A., He, X., Kunze, M., Tao, J., & Fu, C. (2010). Cloud computing: A perspective study. *New Generation Computing, 28*(2), 137–146.
36. Botta, A., de Donato, W., Persico, V., & Pescapé, A. (2014). On the integration of cloud computing and Internet of Things. *2014 International Conference on Future Internet of Things and Cloud,* 23–30. Barcelona, Spain.
37. Alrawais, A., Alhothaily, A., Hu, C. Q., & Cheng, X. Z. (2017). Fog computing for the Internet of Things: Security and privacy issues. *IEEE Internet Computing, 21*(2), 34–42.
38. Li, G. J., & Cheng, X. Q. (2012). Research status and scientific thinking of big data. *Bulletin of the Chinese Academy of Sciences, 6,* 647–657.

Chapter 5
A Macroeconomic Aspect of IoT Services: Their Marginal Costs

Takafumi Mizuno

Abstract In macroeconomics, "information" is a copiable product with no additional cost. Despite services on IoT (Internet of Things) treat information, their scalabilities are smaller than other information products. In this chapter, I model IoT services as a composition of information, devices, and electricity and point out that the existence of devices and electricity prevents reducing marginal costs of the services. I mention that the informatization of the computer industry in the past was the replacement of accounting subjects. And I describe that design to scale IoT services is to develop incentives letting others shoulder the costs of devices and electricity.

Keywords Informatization · Marginal cost · Blockchain · Service science

5.1 Introduction

Due to technological improvements in communications and sensors, more and more things have been connected to the Internet. Fifty billion devices will be connected to the Internet in 2020 [1]. In the background, many services on IoT (Internet of Things) have been developed: smart cars, smart homes, smart cities, drones, robots, healthcare applications, and so on. The scale is beyond the number of humans, and they will give us unprecedented changes in our lives and industrial structures.

We want to describe and analyze the services and the changes in the viewpoint of macroeconomics. Many studies argue IoT services' mechanisms and their effects from technological aspects, while few studies mention what the whole IoT services in the world impact us.

T. Mizuno (✉)
Meijo University, Nagoya, Japan
e-mail: tmizuno@meijo-u.ac.jp

© Springer Nature Switzerland AG 2021
F. P. García Márquez, B. Lev (eds.), *Internet of Things*, International Series in
Operations Research & Management Science 305,
https://doi.org/10.1007/978-3-030-70478-0_5

Considering the whole IoT services in macroeconomics is abstracting a common feature from all of them. The feature of IoT services is information; IoT services are information products.

In this chapter, I describe that information is a copiable product with no additional cost. Informatization of a product is reducing its marginal cost. To consider the informatization of IoT services, I review brief histories of the computer industry. And I mention that informatization was the attempt to move accounting subjects.

I provide a model of IoT services for macroeconomics; IoT services consist of information, devices, and electricity. Then I mention that devices and electricity give limitations of scalabilities of IoT services, and describe that design to scale IoT services is to develop incentives letting others shoulder them.

5.2   Information and Business Models

In economics areas, we learn that information is news that reduces the risks and the uncertainty of something. Profit-making prospects and weather forecasts are such information. Receiving them reduces uncertainties, and their worths go away once we get them. This definition, however, is no more than one function of information. Music, movie, and other digital contents are also information used in business areas, and we use them repeatedly. The purpose is not to reduce anything's uncertainty but is sending something to others and receiving it repeatedly in the above examples; information has transferability. Also, there are examples of information whose purpose is not to send to others. Those are programs on devices, database systems, and useful ideas on business. Other than those, noises and vague memories are also information.

All of them have a property that is copiability. In the macroeconomic aspect that gives us a high abstract level viewpoint, information is a product whose marginal cost is zero.

McDonough used information as evaluated data in particular situations, or as data needed to solve specific problems [2]. In the information theory developed by Shannon, information is an amount of uncertainty constructed with the probability [3]. This definition cannot treat contents that lost uncertainty by using repeatedly. More generally, in the cybernetics developed by Wiener, information is everything exchanged between humans and their environments [4]. This definition covers neither ideas nor data that were not sent to others. Noguchi pointed out that copiability is the essence of information, and he defined information as copiable products [5]. This chapter adopts Noguchi's definition for describing what information is.

The essence of information is vital for designing business models. Corporations have to decrease the marginal costs of their products and services. That is why they orient informatization. The ratio that a product contains information represents the scalability of businesses using the products. Decreasing the marginal cost of a product, however, is difficult. Even enterprises of the computer industry have taken a long time to build business models generating profits measuring up to their investments.

Enterprises of the computer industry had sold computers by gluing information products and physical products. The software did not have their evaluated costs, and they bundled in hardware. Only hardware had had a price that included prices of software and services. Selling one unit of software had meant selling a large mainframe computer. Then, in the late 1960s, manufacturers had started to produce compatible hardware, and selling only software had begun. In the middle of the 1980s, the operating system has sold in the market of personal consumers. The selling software looked like selling only information, but it contained physical products: packages and conveyances. Until the early 2000s, many software products are recorded in CD-ROM and packed in plastic cases and transported by truck drivers. But since the middle of the 2000s, download selling and providing online services have seemed to eliminate the marginal costs. Some corporations have dealt with platforms that are solutions for more reducing the interface between the systems and the physical world, and they have become gigantic corporations, also known as GAFA.

Of course, technological improvements have contributed to reducing marginal costs in the history of the computer industry. But, by regarding the transitions of their business models, we can find what informatization is. In macroeconomics, that is the replacement of accounting subjects. Vendors separated software and hardware, and the costs of computers kept by customers went away from vendors' accounts. Download selling removed the costs of packages and conveyances. Platform strategies of enterprises moved physical efforts, which are making their contents, to their customers' accounts.x

5.3   A Model of IoT

Let us consider models of IoT services from the viewpoint of economics.

IoT World Forum provides a reference model of IoT that consists of a seven-layered structure (Table 5.1) [6]. The model represents how IoT systems process data. Physical sensors obtain and transmit environmental data. Computers near the sensors add preliminary treatment to the data, database or storages accumulate the data, and statistical operators and abstraction are applied to them. Computer applications analyze and visualize the data, and people use the data to improve their lives and business processes.

Each layer of the reference model corresponds to procedures and simplifies data flow as interactions between layers; an upper layer sends requests, and a lower layer serves services to the upper. Technicians use the model when they design IoT systems. They can build procedures of a layer without considering detailed implementations of other layers.

Table 5.1 IoT World Forum reference model [6]

Level	Abstract layer
7	Collaboration and processes (involving people and business process)
6	Application (reporting, analytics, and control)
5	Data abstraction (aggregation and access)
4	Data accumulation (storage)
3	Edge computing (data element analysis and transformation)
2	Connectivity (communication and processing units)
1	Physical devices and controllers (the "things" in IoT)

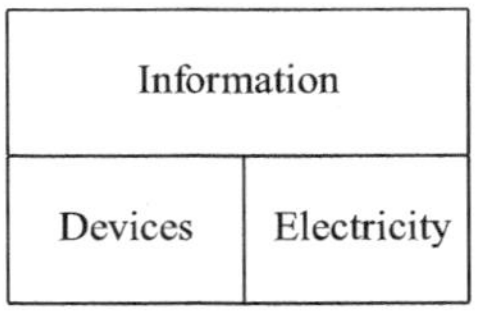

Fig. 5.1 An abstract IoT model. "Information" represents something copiable. "Devices" are physical devices, and "Electricity" runs "Information" and "Devices." "Devices" and "Electricity" are marginal costs of the model

But, when we design business models of IoT services, the reference model is quite too detailed. More abstraction is needed to provide a model to analyze IoT services in macroeconomics.

By considering what is needed when we copy an IoT service, we can provide a model; an IoT service consists of three elements: devices, information, and electricity (Fig. 5.1).

"Devices" are sensors, computers, storages, communication channels, and something that has physical entities. "Information" represents software products, applications, database systems, data, and something copiable. And devices and information need "electricity." "Devices" correspond to levels 1 and 2 in the IoT reference model, and "information" corresponds to level 3–7. "Electricity" does not appear in the IoT reference model. Since the reference model is interested in technological challenges, it ignores the cost side that IoT engineers cannot improve.

The existence of devices is a different feature of IoT services from other information products. Generally, increasing devices connected to the Internet has reduced their costs. The sales number of smartphones containing three or more sensors has increased from 0.5 billion to 1 billion for 5 years since 2010, and the unit price of semiconductor sensors has fallen from 0.7 to 0.4 dollars [7]. IoT services, however, increase their users only in proportion to the number of devices; scaling the services increases their costs linearly. In contrast, high-level information products riding on IoT services can increase the number of their users exponentially by using suitable algorithms.

IoT services are not useful without using general information products such as databases, data analyzing, visualization, reporting, and business judgments. The

Table 5.2 The IoT industrial structure without suitable business designs

Corporation type	Products	Scalability
IoT corporation	Sensor, device, software on device	Linearly, depending on the number of devices
Gigantic corporation	Infrastructure, platform	Exponentially, depending on algorithms

information products, especially processing Big Data from sensors, will deploy on cloud services of gigantic corporations such as GAFA. Since preparing the newest computer systems and maintaining secure software are difficult, using infrastructures of gigantic corporations is inexpensive than constructing infrastructures by each IoT corporation. In the future, more and more information processing will depend on the infrastructures of gigantic corporations.

Deep learning, a breakthrough in the machine learning area since 2010, can learn feature values from sensor data automatically [8]. Feature values are essential for analyzing environments using computers, and human experts designed the values until then. More data and high spec computer systems can learn the feature values for more high accuracy analysis. So gigantic corporations providing infrastructures obtain extensive data, produce high-value services, and grow larger than corporations providing IoT services.

Without suitable business designs, the IoT industry will consist of two types of corporations: corporations providing IoT services and gigantic corporations giving infrastructure (Table 5.2). The profitability of the latter is hugely higher than the former.

On the model, we can measure the scalability of IoT services by their informatization. And how to build new business models using IoT services is how to proceed with their informatization.

5.4 Designing Incentives

We, however, may be able to improve IoT services' profitabilities by designing suitable incentives. A technology overcoming a weak point of gigantic corporations is a hint for that.

Information products of gigantic corporations have a hidden cost. That is electricity. They have paid enormous running costs of data centers and cooling towers. The total of them, denoted as electricity, is comparable to countries or large cities. Google consumed electricity 10.10 TWh in 2018 [9]. For all corporations treating with information services, even gigantic corporations, the electricity prevents reducing marginal costs of their services to zero.

But technological inventions may destroy the structure; blockchain is the example. Blockchains are distributed systems that consist of hundreds of thousands of computers in the world [10]. Some classes of programs and databases can deploy on

Table 5.3 There are what vendors and users have to prepare when a service is copied

Product	What vendors prepare	What users prepare
Software before 1970s	Information, mainframe computer	
Software before 2000s	Information, package, conveyances	
Download selling	Information, electricity	
Software on blockchain	Information	Electricity
IoT service	Information, devices, electricity	
IoT service (suitable design)	? information, devices electricity ?	

blockchains, and distributed ledger systems are running actually on them. At Bitcoin [10], a ledger service on blockchains, owners of computers attending blockchains obtain the chance of getting money in exchange for calculation costs, which is the electricity. The costs are used to maintain the monotonicity of the ledger data.

From the viewpoint of the provider of the service, the marginal cost is zero. The owners of the computers attending the blockchain defray the cost that is electricity. Computers supporting the Bitcoin used 61.76 TWh per year in total [11]. Bitcoin is the service that has accomplished informatization completely.

That is the hint for designing IoT services (Table 5.3). Producing sensors by a corporation and scaling IoT services increase costs for the corporation, while letting others prepare sensors and provide computer resources for the service decreases the marginal costs to zero. Despite its simpleness, systems with no marginal cost had not been realized. But now, such a system exists and runs actually. Designing an IoT service is not only a technological issue but also an economic issue on how to construct incentives making people provide their resources for the service.

So all elements of IoT services, information and devices and electricity, are targets of informatization. The element of information can be improved by developing algorithms, and the elements of devices and electricity can be improved by designing business models and incentives. Theoretically, in macroeconomics, they are products whose marginal costs may be zero.

5.5 Conclusions

In this chapter, information was defined as a product whose marginal cost is zero. That is the most abstract aspect of information. Macroeconomics, which analyzes the whole products of markets, needs the abstraction. IoT services are products that contain the information.

There are studies analyzing information products. The information economics is the most successful study that treats mainly pricings by regarding information asymmetry [12]. To discuss the scalability of information products, I omitted its microeconomic aspects of information in this chapter.

I mentioned Bitcoin as an example of services with no marginal cost. Many studies value its decentralization mechanism. But Bitcoin's impact on the macroeconomics is its scalability. That is supported by informatization designing incentives that remove its marginal cost. In the context, an issue of IoT services is how to design incentives removing the costs of physical devices and electricity.

In the late 1990s to the early 2000s, corporations in the computer industry faced a crisis that gigantic corporations, GAFA, have risen. Products of gigantic corporations are platforms and portals that have large scalabilities. They do not need to sell physical hardware when they increase their customers. IBM, which was the biggest corporation in the computer industry until the 1990s, shifted its business from computer manufacturing to system integration and developed service science in the early 2000s [13]. IBM did not describe clearly the crisis, but we can consider that the purpose of service science is to achieve informatization by designing incentives.

When we design IoT services, we must design who pays the costs of physical devices and electricity of the services. Services without the design enlarge only linearly commensurate with investments in devices. If we design incentives that make others pay the costs of electricity, we can enlarge services more than gigantic corporations.

We expect that artificial intelligence (AI) improves IoT services. Though, until the marginal costs are smaller than human workers or other autonomous low-tech software, we cannot distinguish AI and other information systems in macroeconomics. A service whose marginal costs are removed can destroy industrial structures, even if it provides low-tech functions.

The marginal costs of IoT service might be going to be zero. It raises some issues in macroeconomics. By proceeding Ricard's analysis on comparative advantage, we can say that a product with no marginal cost takes absolute advantage for all others' products, and the product can be exchanged for any amount of others' products. That seems to be impossible. We have to improve studies of comparative advantage to analyze industries treating with information products, such as IoT services.

In macroeconomics, economic agents are limited by scopes of countries or currencies. When a corporation designs incentives removing their hidden costs, the corporation scales more and more. In some cases, they will operate their currency systems with no running costs. The number of sensors of IoT, connected to the Internet, will be 50 billion. Those are beyond the magnitude of the countries. We have to consider how to define economic agents in macroeconomics when such corporations exist.

References

1. Kerravala, Z. (2014). It's Time for Businesses to Embrace the Internet of Things, ZK Research. https://iotbusinessnews.com/download/white-papers/ZK-RESEARCH-time-to-embrace-the-Internet-Of-Things.pdf. Cited 22 April 2020.

2. McDonough, A. M. (1963). *Information Economics and Management Systems*. New York: McGraw-Hill.
3. Abramson, N. (1963). *Information Theory and Coding*. New York: McGraw-Hill.
4. Wiener, N. (1949). *The Human Use of Human Beings, Cybernetics and Society*. Boston: Houghton Mifflin & Co.
5. Noguchi, Y. (1974). *Economic Theory of Information (in Japanese)*. Japan: Toyo-Keizai-Shinpo-sha.
6. Green, J. (2014). A Proposed Internet of Things Reference Model, Internet of Things World Forum. http://cdn.iotwf.com/resources/72/IoT_Reference_Model_04_June_2014.pdf. Cited 17 April 2020.
7. Lineback, R. (2016). Sensor sales keep hitting new records but price erosion curbs growth. In *Research Bulletin*, IC Insights. https://www.icinsights.com/data/articles/documents/895.pdf. Cited 17 April 2020.
8. Krizhevsky, A., Sutskever, I., & Geoffrey, E. H. (2012). ImageNet classification with deep convolutional neural networks. *Advances in Neural Information Processing Systems 25*(Curran Associates), 1097–1105.
9. Google (2019). Environmental Report 2019, Google. https://services.google.com/fh/files/misc/google_2019-environmental-report.pdf. Cited 19 April 2020.
10. Nakamoto, S. (2009). Bitcoin: A Peer-to-Peer electronic cash system. https://bitcoin.org/bitcoin.pdf. Cited 29 April 2020.
11. McCarthy, N. (2019). Bitcoin devours more electricity than Switzerland, Forbs. https://www.forbes.com/sites/niallmccarthy/2019/07/08/bitcoin-devours-more-electricity-than-switzerland-infographic. Cited 19 April 2020.
12. Stiglitz, J. E. (2000). The contributions of the economic of information to twentieth century economics. *Quarterly Journal of Economics, 115*(4), 1441–1478.
13. Spohrer, J., Morris, R., & Maglio, P. (2011). The Invention of Service Science. New York: IBM. https://www.ibm.com/ibm/history/ibm100/us/en/icons/servicescience/. Cited 20 April 2020.

Chapter 6
Biclustering Analysis of Countries Using COVID-19 Epidemiological Data

S. Dhamodharavadhani and R. Rathipriya

Abstract In this work, COVID-19 data were analyzed using the biclustering approach to gain insights such as which group of countries have similar epidemic trajectory patterns over the subset of COVID-19 pandemic outburst days (called bicluster). Countries within these groups (biclusters) are all in the same phase but with a slightly different trajectory. An approach based on the Greedy Two-Way KMeans biclustering algorithm is proposed to analyze COVID-19 epidemiological data, which identifies subgroups of countries that show a similar epidemic trajectory patterns over a specific period of time. To the best of authors' knowledge, this is the first time that the biclustering approach has been applied to analyze COVID-19 data. In fact, these COVID-19 epidemiological data is not a real count because not all data can be tracked properly and other practical difficulties in collecting the data. Even in developed countries, it has huge practical problems. Therefore, if we can use the IoT-based COVID-19 monitoring system to detect the origin of the COVID-19 outbreak, we can identify the real situation in each country. Results confirm that the proposed approach can alert and helps the government authorities and healthcare professionals to know what to anticipate and which measures to implement to decelerate the COVID-19 spread.

Keywords COVID-19 data · Biclustering · Greedy Two-Way KMeans biclustering · nCov · COVID-19 pattern

6.1 Introduction

Due to technological advances, COVID-19 epidemiological data is updated every hour and becomes publicly available. Furthermore, there are several COVID-19 monitoring tools available to provide data on the global spread of COVID-19. These

S. Dhamodharavadhani (✉) · R. Rathipriya
Department of Computer Science, Periyar University, Salem, Tamil Nadu, India
e-mail: vadhaniphd@periyaruniversity.ac.in; rathi_priyar@periyaruniversity.ac.in

© Springer Nature Switzerland AG 2021   93
F. P. García Márquez, B. Lev (eds.), *Internet of Things*, International Series in
Operations Research & Management Science 305,
https://doi.org/10.1007/978-3-030-70478-0_6

data can be analyzed to gain understandings or to identify hidden or predict patterns. Generally, numerous clustering models are used to identify patterns or trends among epidemiological data, but they are based on a global pattern (called cluster centroid) and cannot detect local patterns hidden in these data.

Generally, "a biclustering algorithm groups the rows and columns of a two-dimensional data (called data matrix) simultaneously" [1, 2]. While a clustering is applied to group COVID-19 cases, it has the following limitations:

- It groups either countries or period (pandemic outburst days) of COVID epidemiological data that is only one at a time.
- It fails to identify the countries that have similar trends over a subset of pandemic outbursts day or vice versa.

Therefore, the biclustering concept is used in this paper as a pattern extraction technique that allows identifying groups of countries that cannot be found by a traditional clustering approach. Generally, the clustering approach always identifies a group of countries that exhibits the same epidemic trajectory pattern over entire days of pandemic outbursts. Biclustering overcomes this limitation and groups the countries and the period simultaneously into a submatrix called bicluster. This improves the efficiency of the COVID-19 pattern analysis system.

In the literature, a different variation of biclustering algorithms has been proposed due to their ability to find collections of rows (instances) with a similar pattern under a subset of columns (features) [1, 2]. In Padilha and Campello [3], "Padilha V. A. et. al. presented a comparative study involving seventeen biclustering algorithms and concluded that the choice of the best biclustering algorithm purely depends on the types of patterns that to be discovered and applications." In this review paper [4, 5], "the authors described biclustering algorithms, their quality evaluation measures, and different types of validations used for the biclustering of gene expression data in detail."

As in Fig. 6.1, let us consider the number of COVID-19 confirmed cases of seven countries for nine consecutive days (i.e., time points). A biclustering algorithm extracts the trajectory pattern by considering a subset of countries and days of the given two-dimensional COVID-19 data into a submatrix called bicluster. Here, identified bicluster indicates that countries 3, 4, and 5 have the same COVID-19 epidemic trajectory pattern for the days D3 to D6 which is highlighted in light grey color. However, a traditional clustering method would consider all the days (from D1 to D9) for grouping the similar countries. While countries 3, 4, and 5 may not have similar trajectory pattern for the entire period from D1 to D9, one can easily observe strong similarities for the period D3 to D6. Therefore, countries 3, 4, and 5 can be viewed as a bicluster for the days D3 to D6 rather than as being clustered over the entire days with low similarity.

Biclustering was first proposed by Hartigan [1] to investigate voting data of US states. Harigan used variance as a quality measure to identify the bicluster. Cheng and Church introduced a measure called Mean Square Residue (MSR) to assess the quality of the bicluster [4]. Teng and Chan [4] "defined a statistical score namely Average Correlation Value (ACV) for evaluating a bicluster based on the weighted

Countries	D1	D2	D3	D4	D5	D6	D7	D8	D9
1	V11	V12	V13	V14	V15	V16	V17	V18	V19
2	V21	V22	V23	V24	V25	V26	V27	V28	V29
3	V31	V32	V33	V34	V35	V36	V37	V38	V39
4	V41	V42	V43	V44	V45	V46	V47	V48	V49
5	V51	V52	V53	V54	V55	V56	V57	V58	V59
6	V61	V62	V63	V64	V65	V66	V67	V68	V69
7	V71	V72	V73	V74	V75	V76	V77	V78	V79

Fig. 6.1 Sample dataset

correlation coefficient." In Pontes et al. [6], the authors reviewed the development of various biclustering algorithms in a comprehensive way.

6.2   Problem Description

In the literature, it has been found that most of the biclustering algorithms have used some similarity measure to evaluate the quality of the bicluster as well as for extracting the bicluster [7]. MSR measure is used frequently in many biclustering algorithms. When all the elements in a submatrix have less magnitude value, the mean squared residue is low. According to Aguilar-Ruiz [5] Aguilar Ruiz J.S et al., "biclusters ought to contain a set of rows showing similar behavior, not similar values. A correlated subset of rows will demonstrate pure scaling or shifting patterns across a subset of columns. Such correlation is pattern-based, that is neither linear nor nonlinear."

Consider two biclusters in Fig. 6.2 whose pandemic outburst days vary in harmony under the countries in the bicluster. Despite the fact the countries exhibit the same epidemiological trajectory under the subset of outburst days, the MSR value for these two biclusters is different; there is a huge difference in their value which indicates they are not equally good biclusters.

As can be seen in Fig. 6.2, there is a significant difference in their value, which indicates that they are not equally good biclusters. Comparing these two biclusters graphically, it cannot be concluded that the left-side bicluster is better than the right-side bicluster, as it would be unfair to claim that only countries having less COVID-19 cases for certain days are preferable.

Average correlation value (ACV), a bicluster quality measure, evaluates well all types of biclusters and also tolerates transformations like scaling and translation [7–10]. The ACV of these two biclusters is 0.99. Therefore, MSR is not the best-quality measure to discover bicluster when the variance of COVID-19 cases values is high.

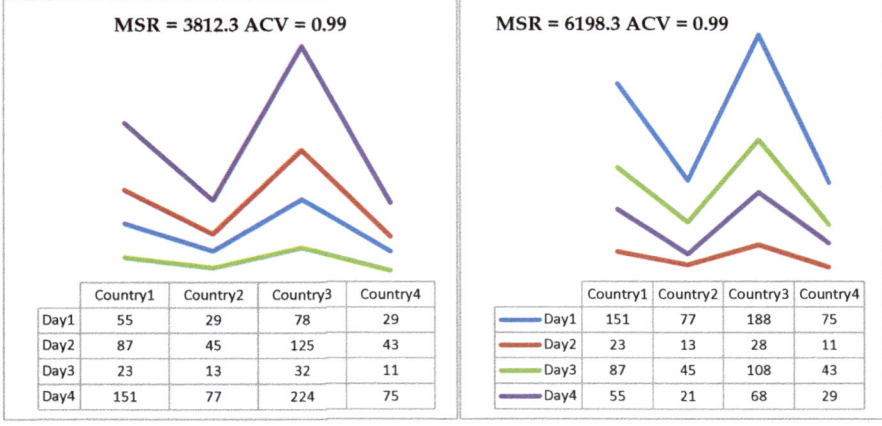

Fig. 6.2 Similar bicluster pattern with different value

Hence, in this research work, correlation-based merit function (ACV) has been used to identify the biclusters.

6.2.1 Greedy Approach: Single Objective Size Maximization-Based Fitness Function

The Greedy approach aims to find maximum size highly correlated biclusters with shifting and scaling patterns. "Therefore, a correlation-based measure can be a good choice of fitness function to find biclusters with these patterns" [7–9]. The shifting and scaling pattern can be represented as in Eq. (6.1):

$$D_y = \alpha * D_x + \beta, \text{ where } \alpha, \beta \in R \qquad (6.1)$$

Let us bicluster B composed by N days, $B = \{d_1, \ldots, d_N\}$, the average correlation value of B, $\rho(B)$, is defined in Eq. (6.2) as follows:

$$\rho(B) = \frac{\sum_{i=1}^{N-1} \sum_{j=i+1}^{N} \rho(d_i, d_j)}{n^2 - n} \qquad (6.2)$$

where $\rho(d_i, d_j)$ is the correlation coefficient between the day d_i and the user d_j.

The correlation coefficient between any two variables X and Y measures the grade of linear dependency between them. It is defined using Eq. (6.3):

$$\rho(X, Y) = \frac{\sum_{i=1}^{n} (x_i - mean(X)) - (y_i - mean(Y))}{\sigma_X * \sigma_Y} \qquad (6.3)$$

where *mean(X) and mean(Y)* are the mean of X and Y and σ_X and σ_Y are the standard deviations of X and Y, respectively. The fitness function used to evaluate the quality of biclusters B (D', C') using Eq. (6.4):

$$\max \; f\left(D', C'\right) = \left|D'\right| * \left|C'\right| \tag{6.4}$$

$$\text{subjected to } g\left(D', C'\right) \; increases \; the \; ACV(B)$$

where $g(D', C') = (1 - \rho(B))$, $|D'|$ and $|C'|$ are the number of pandemic outburst days and countries in the bicluster, respectively; and μ is the correlation threshold.

6.2.2   Data Description

COVID-19 data is used, which have downloaded from the Kaggle website [11–13]. Since 21 Jan 2020, the data is updated daily basis, of the increment of the number of infected people in COVID-19-infected countries across the world. It contains epidemiological data such as time series [14–16] COVID-19 confirmed cases, time series COVID-19 recovered cases, and time series COVID-19 death case but time series COVID-19 new cases derived from the above data [17–22]. For this study, time series data for the abovementioned cases have been taken for the period 11 March 2020 to 10 April 2020. In this period, worldwide millions of peoples are suffering from COVID-19 severely. Also, the epidemiological trajectory moved toward their new peak value in many countries. Figure 6.3 depicts the preprocessed COVID-19 data.

COVID-19 confirmed cases are growing exponentially in most parts of the world. Especially, in the USA, Spain, and Italy, the pandemic is already severe and collapsing their healthcare system [23, 24]. If the current trends continue, it will not take a long time to affect other European countries too. Therefore, a reliable and accurate analysis and forecasting system for COVID-19 spread are required to contain the novel coronavirus spread [25–29].

In this paper [29], the authors presented a simple iterative method to forecast the number of COVID-19 cases, and the insights and strategies on basic principles for COVID-19 are mentioned. According to our knowledge, there is no work yet to pattern analysis e of COVID-19. Therefore, local patterns (i.e., biclusters) are extracted for top 50 COVID-19-infected countries using Greedy Two-Way KMeans Biclustering Algorithms in this work.

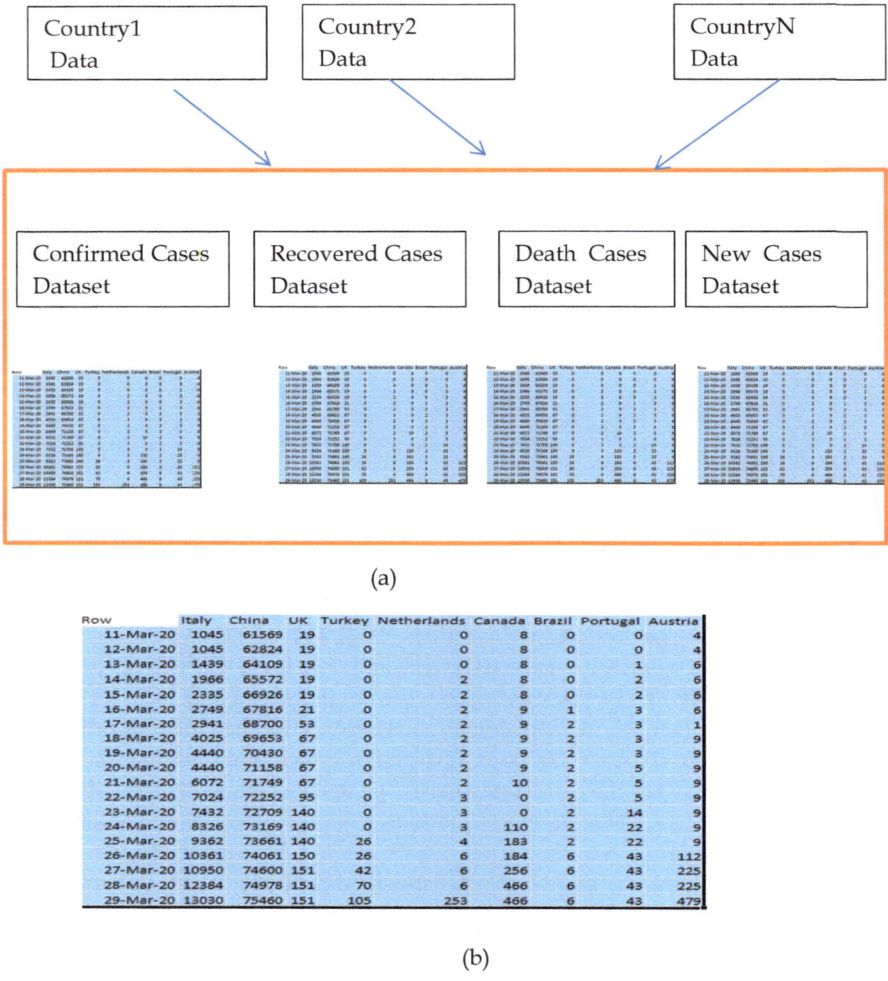

(a)

Row	Italy	China	UK	Turkey	Netherlands	Canada	Brazil	Portugal	Austria
11-Mar-20	1045	61569	19	0	0	8	0	0	4
12-Mar-20	1045	62824	19	0	0	8	0	0	4
13-Mar-20	1439	64109	19	0	0	8	0	1	6
14-Mar-20	1966	65572	19	0	2	8	0	2	6
15-Mar-20	2335	66926	19	0	2	8	0	2	6
16-Mar-20	2749	67816	21	0	2	9	1	3	6
17-Mar-20	2941	68700	53	0	2	9	2	3	1
18-Mar-20	4025	69653	67	0	2	9	2	3	9
19-Mar-20	4440	70430	67	0	2	9	2	3	9
20-Mar-20	4440	71158	67	0	2	9	2	5	9
21-Mar-20	6072	71749	67	0	2	10	2	5	9
22-Mar-20	7024	72252	95	0	3	0	2	5	9
23-Mar-20	7432	72709	140	0	3	0	2	14	9
24-Mar-20	8326	73169	140	0	3	110	2	22	9
25-Mar-20	9362	73661	140	26	4	183	2	22	9
26-Mar-20	10361	74061	150	26	6	184	6	43	112
27-Mar-20	10950	74600	151	42	6	256	6	43	225
28-Mar-20	12384	74978	151	70	6	466	6	43	225
29-Mar-20	13030	75460	151	105	253	466	6	43	479

(b)

Fig. 6.3 Data preprocessing of time series COVID-19 dataset

6.3 Proposed Work: COVID-19 Pattern Identification Using Greedy Two-Way KMeans Algorithms

Given a COVID-19 data matrix D, let n_r be the number of clusters on row (day) dimension and n_c be the number of clusters on the column(country) dimension. After K-means clustering is applied on both dimensions, CC^r is the set of row (day) clusters, and CC^c is the set of column (country) clusters. Let $cc_i{}^r$ be a subset of outburst days and $cc_i{}^r \in C^r$ ($1 \leq i \leq k_r$). Let $cc_j{}^c$ be a subset of countries and $cc_j{}^c \in C^c$ ($1 \leq j \leq k_c$). The pair ($cc_i{}^r$, $cc_j{}^c$) represents a bicluster of D. The results of row dimensional clustering and column dimensional clustering are merged to obtain $n_r \times n_c$ biclusters. These biclusters are called seeds [9].

6.3.1 Optimize Biclusters Using Greedy Approach

In this step, seeds are extended and refined using the Greedy approach. This process adds/removes the rows (outburst days) and columns (countries) into/from the existing bicluster for increasing their volume/improving their ACV, respectively [8, 9, 30].

The purpose of using Greedy heuristic is to increase the volume of the bicluster (seed) without degrading its quality. The volume of a bicluster is defined as the product of several countries and the number of periods (days) in that bicluster. Here, ACV is used as quality criteria to grow the seeds. Insert/remove the days/countries to/from the bicluster if it increases ACV of the bicluster. Enlarging and refining the seed starts from the country list followed by the day list until ACV is increased using a Greedy search procedure.

Pseudo Code: Greedy Two-Way KMeans Biclustering Algorithm

```
Initialize  input data, R -set of rows in the data, C- set of
columns in data
Step 1: Data Preprocessing:  Convert COVID-19 epidemiological
data into the data matrix for Top 50 countries. It is shown
in Fig. 6.2.
Step 2: Pattern Identification:
    Rowcluster(Data,rK)//Apply KMeans clustering algorithms on
    rows of the 'Data'
    Columncluster(Data,cK) //Apply KMeans clustering algorithms
    on columns of the 'Data'
    Combine(Rowcluster, Columncluster)// to form bicluster
Step 3: Optimize the Biclusters
    For each 'B'
          Enlarge (B)
          Refine(B)
    For end
Step 3.1: sub Enlarge()
          br=set of rows in B
          br=set of columns in B
          r= setdifference(R,br)
          c=setdifference(C,bc)
    For each node (row/column)
            If ACV( union(Seed, r/c)) >   ACV(Seed(R, C)) then
                   Add r/c to Seed(R,C)
                   End(if)
      End(for)
            End sub
Step 3.2: sub Refine()
    For each  node r/c in Enlarged Seed
          Remove node r/c from Enlarged Seed
```

R''/C'' be set of rows/columns in R'/C' but not contained r/c
    If ACV (Enlarged Seed(R'',C'')) >
       ACV(Enlarged Seed(R', C')
       Update R'/C'
    End(if)
  End(for)
    End sub
Step 4: **Pattern analysis:** Post process the result

6.4 Results

In this section, the results of the most representative bicluster obtained on the
COVID-19 data are presented and summarized. Tables 6.1, 6.2, 6.3, and 6.4 show
the characteristics of extracted biclusters for Top 50 COVID-19-infected countries'
confirmed cases, death cases, new cases, and recovered cases data, respectively.
These tables contain the following details:

- The number of countries in the biclusters
- Records the number of the time period (days) that the identified correlated pattern
  between the countries in the bicluster is similar
- ACV of the biclusters and
     The volume of the biclusters

Table 6.1 Characteristics of biclusters for COVID-19 confirmed cases

Bicluster index	No. of country	No. of days	ACV	Volume
1	44	21	0.98	924
2	29	17	0.99	493
3	33	8	0.99	264
4	33	7	0.99	231
5	12	16	0.99	192
6	21	7	0.99	147
7	14	8	0.99	112
8	11	8	0.99	88
9	12	7	0.99	84
10	2	31	1	62

Table 6.2 Characteristics of biclusters for COVID-19 death cases

Bicluster index	No. of country	No. of days	ACV	Volume
1	37	16	0.99	592
2	37	9	0.99	333
3	37	6	0.99	222
4	8	16	0.99	128
5	13	9	0.99	117
6	15	6	0.99	90
7	4	16	0.99	64
8	4	31	1	124

Table 6.3 Characteristics of biclusters for COVID-19 new cases

Bicluster index	No. of country	No. of days	ACV	Volume
1	35	12	1	420
2	38	11	0.99	418
3	35	8	0.99	280
4	28	8	0.99	224
5	16	11	0.99	176
6	9	12	0.99	108
7	5	31	1	155

Table 6.4 Characteristics of biclusters for COVID-19 recovered cases

Bicluster index	No. of country	No. of days	ACV	Volume
1	42	19	0.99	798
2	41	8	0.99	328
3	42	4	0.99	168
4	7	19	0.99	133
5	5	19	0.99	95
6	18	4	0.99	72
7	5	31	1	155

This information provides us an idea of how does epidemiological trajectory behaved similarly among the subset of countries taken for the study. From the presented tables, it can be easily noted that all identified biclusters are highly correlated since their ACV almost equals to value 1. It signifies that the Greedy Two-Way KMeans Biclustering approach captured the highly correlated bicluster (i.e., biclusters with scaling and shifting pattern) very well.

It has been observed from Fig. 6.4a–f that:

- From the end of March 2020, the daily increase in COVID-19 confirmed cases has increased at an exponential rate for countries like the USA, Italy, Spain, France, and Germany.
- China has shown a steady trend in the course of COVID-19 confirmed cases for April.

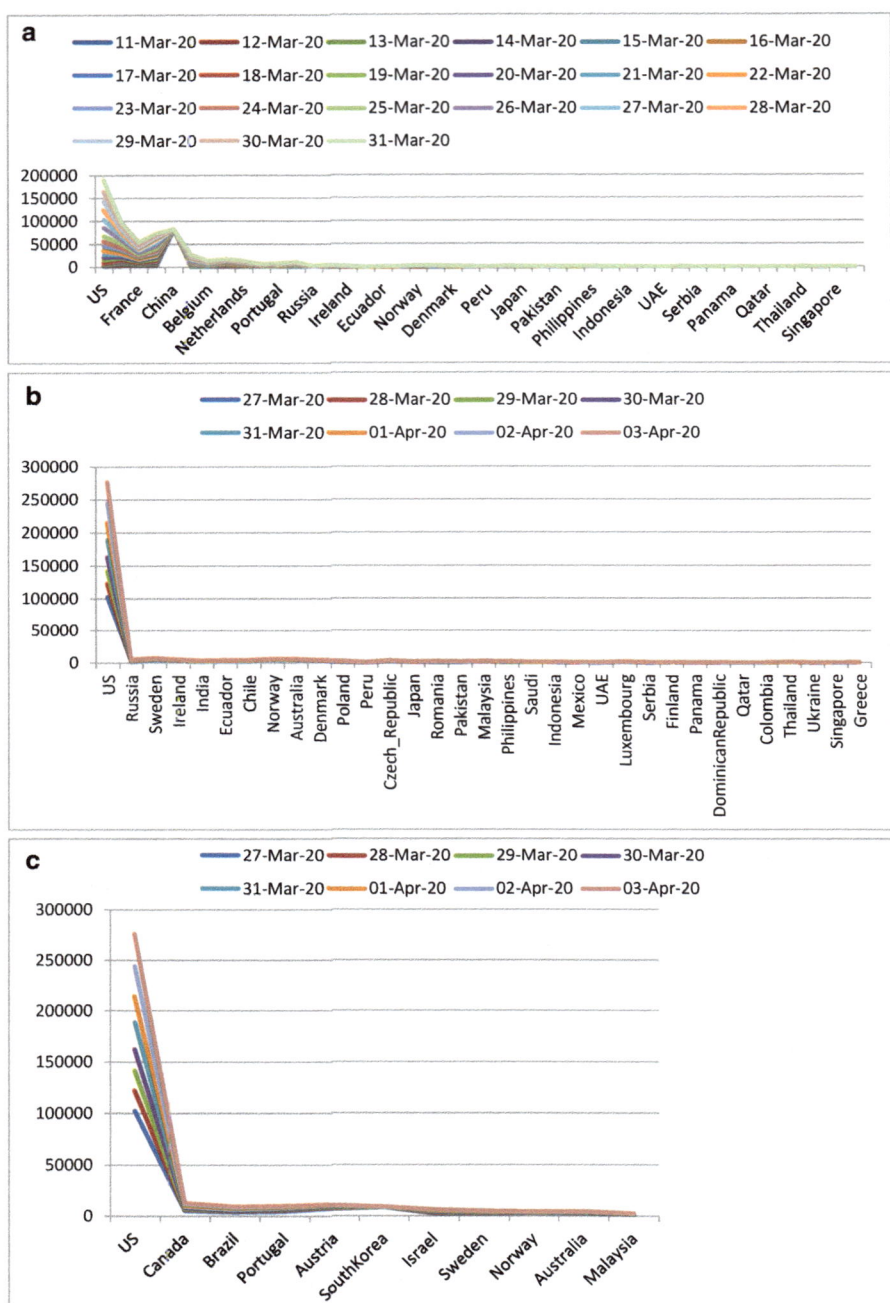

Fig. 6.4 (a)–(f) Incremental pattern for COVID-19 confirmed cases (Table 6.5)

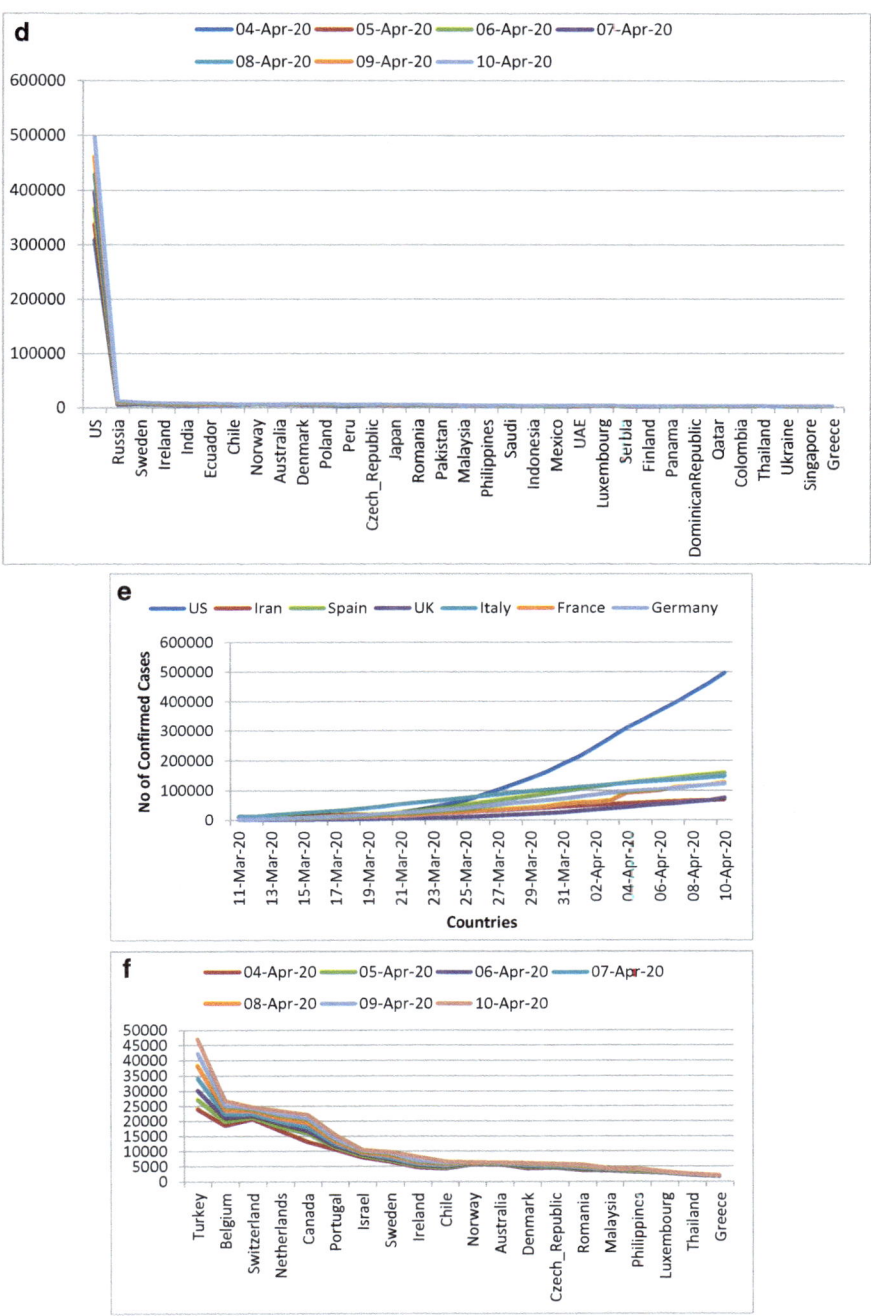

Fig. 6.4 (continued)

Table 6.5 Description of Fig. 6.4

	Countries in the bicluster	Description
4(a)	The USA, Spain, France, Germany, China, the UK, Belgium, Switzerland, Netherlands, Brazil, Portugal, Austria, Russia, Sweden, Ireland, India, Ecuador, Chile, Norway, Australia, Denmark, Poland, Peru, Czech Republic, Japan, Romania, Pakistan, Malaysia, Philippines, Saudi, Indonesia, Mexico, UAE, Luxembourg, Serbia, Finland, Panama, Dominican Republic, Qatar, Colombia, Thailand, Ukraine, Singapore, Greece	COVID-19 confirmed cases for these countries showed increased patterns from 11 March to 20 March. Specifically, for countries the USA, Spain, France, and Germany, cases have risen by more than 1 lakh, but China's cases have steadily increased. Other countries in this bicluster ranged from a few hundred to a few thousand
4(b)	The USA, Russia, Sweden, Ireland, India, Ecuador, Chile, Norway, Australia, Denmark, Poland, Peru, Czech Republic, Japan, Romania, Pakistan, Malaysia, the Philippines, Saudi, Indonesia, Mexico, the UAE, Luxembourg, Serbia, Finland, Panama, Dominican Republic, Qatar, Colombia, Thailand, Ukraine, Singapore, Greece	Except for the USA, for the period from the 27 March to the 3 of April 2020, the confirmed cases of the remaining countries have increased at a lower rate, and their values are less than 2000
4(c)	The USA, Canada, Brazil, Portugal, Austria, South Korea, Israel, Sweden, Norway, Australia, Malaysia	Time period: 27 March to 3 April 2020 In the USA, the number of confirmed cases has increased by 20,000 daily For the rest of the countries in this bicluster, confirmed cases have increased by 1000 daily
4(d)	The USA, Russia, Sweden, Ireland, India, Ecuador, Chile, Norway, Australia, Denmark, Poland, Peru, Czech Republic, Japan, Romania, Pakistan, Malaysia, the Philippines, Saudi, Indonesia, Mexico, the UAE, Luxembourg, Serbia, Finland, Panama, Dominican Republic, Qatar, Colombia, Thailand, Ukraine, Singapore, Greece	Time period: 4 April to 10 April 2020 A daily increase in confirmed cases has risen to 30,000 approximately for the USA and less than 1000 for remaining countries
4(e)	The USA, Spain, Iran, Italy, the UK, France, and Germany	These countries have shown an incremental trajectory for confirmed cases in the time period of 31 days (i.e., 11 March to 10 April 2020). The daily increase in confirmed cases is less than 200 in the early days, gradually increasing to a few thousand But the USA has shown an exponential rate of growth in confirmed cases in April
4(f)	Turkey, Belgium, Switzerland, Netherlands, Canada, Portugal, Israel, Sweden, Ireland, Chile, Norway, Australia, Denmark, Czech Republic, Romania, Malaysia, the Philippines, Luxembourg, Thailand, Greece	For the time period 4 April to 10 April 2020, a daily increase in confirmed cases has risen in a few thousand approximately for the Turkey and Belgium and less than a thousand for remaining countries in this bicluster

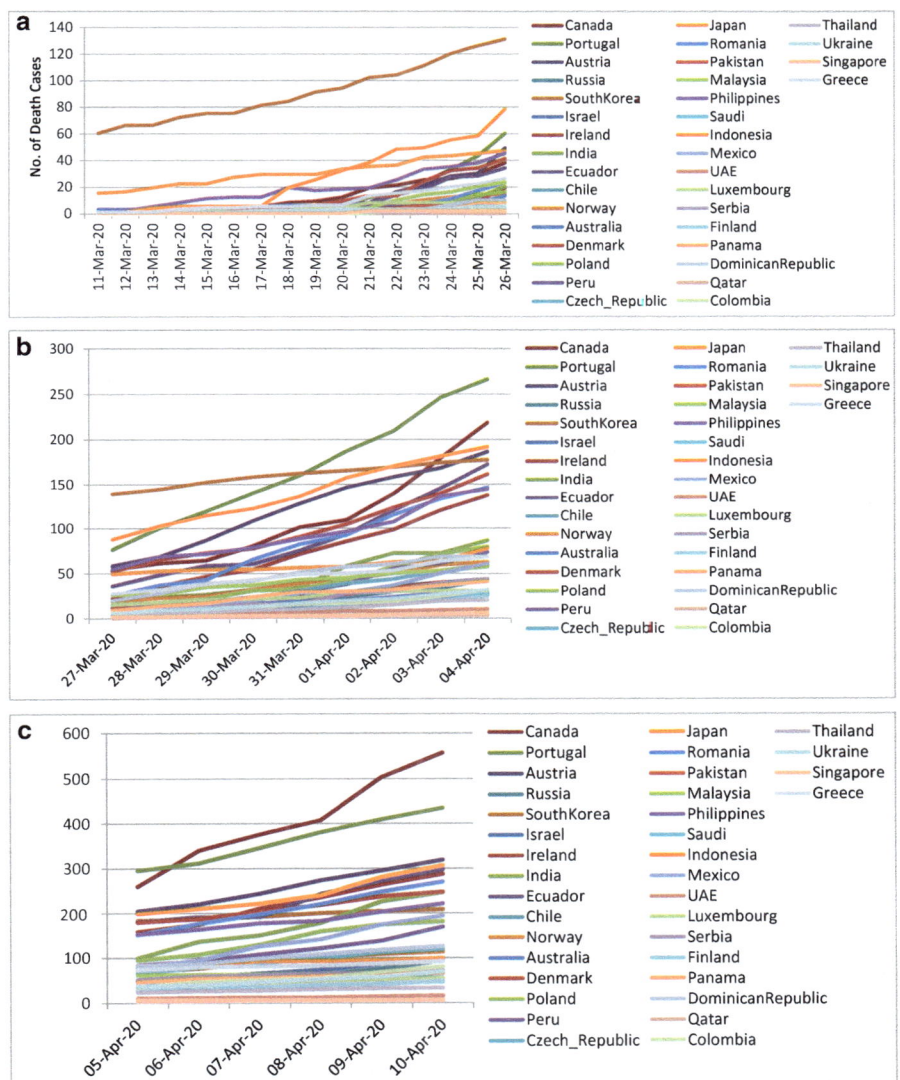

Fig. 6.5 (a)–(g) Incremental pattern for COVID-19 death cases (Table 6.6)

Remaining countries like South Korea, the UK, Turkey, etc. have shown an incremental growth pattern for COVID-19 confirmed cases. Their daily increase of confirmed cases has ranged from a few hundred to a few thousand.

It has been observed from Fig. 6.5a–g that:

- As of 10 April 2020, the USA topped the COVID-19 mortality rate and Italy was second. The USA, Italy, Spain, and Iran have higher mortality rates compared to other countries.

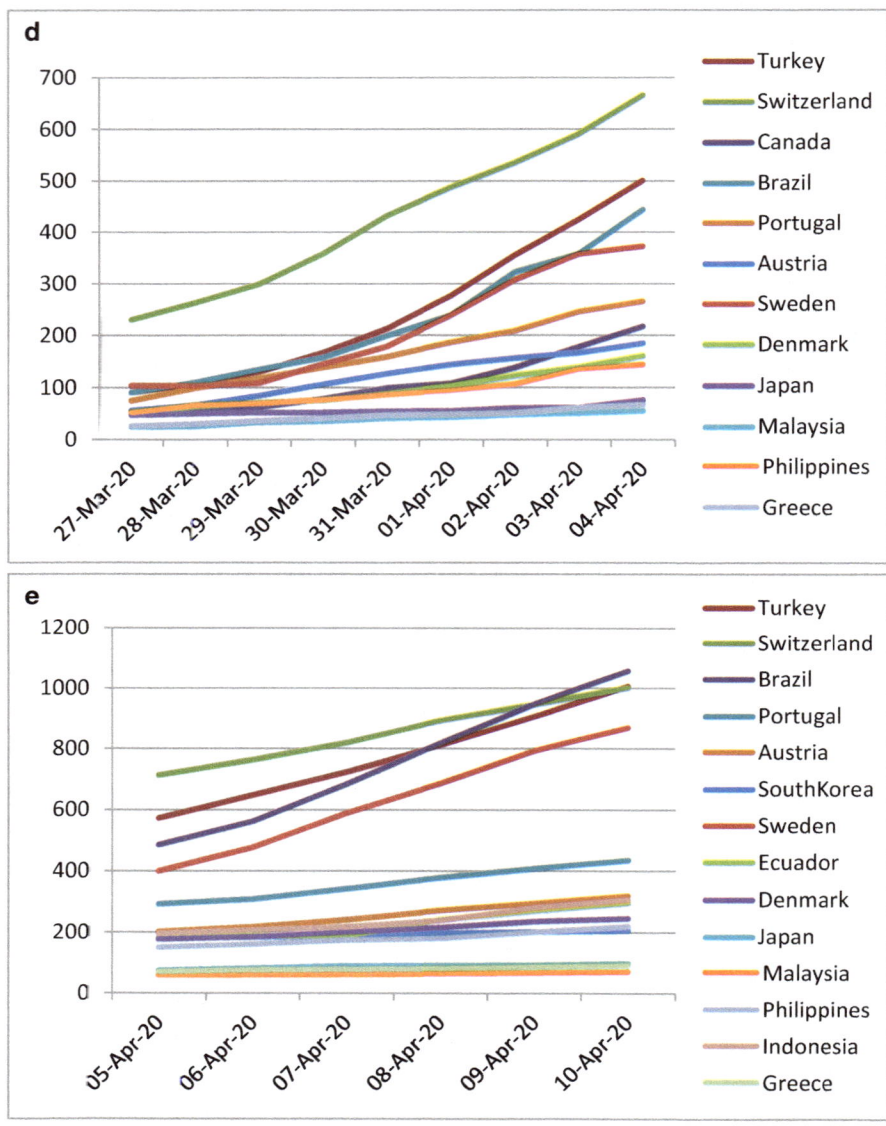

Fig. 6.5 (continued)

- China did not have significant death cases in April month.
- Remaining countries in this bicluster like South Korea, the UK, Turkey, France, Germany, Japan, India, etc. have shown an increased pattern of death cases, but their number is only a few hundred.

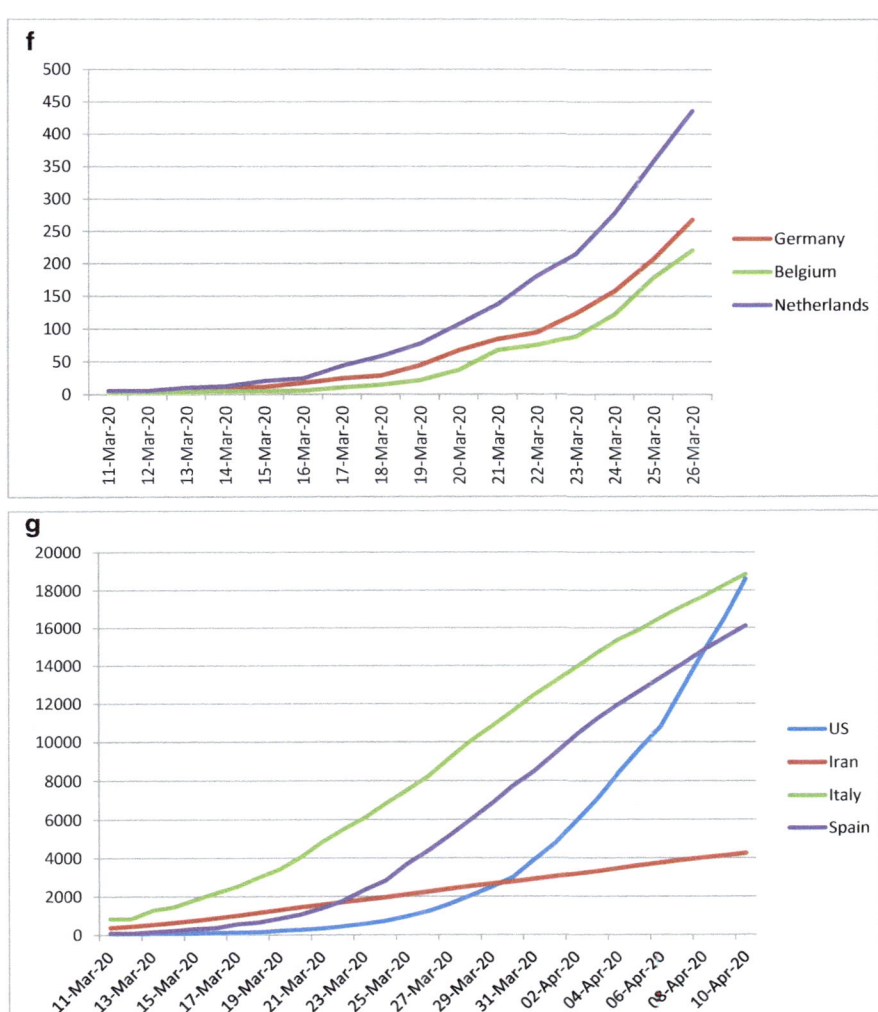

Fig. 6.5 (continued)

It has been observed from Fig. 6.6a–g that:

- All almost countries have an incremental pattern for COVID-19 recovery cases.
- As of April 10, 2020, Germany topped the COVID-19 rescue. The USA, Italy, China, Spain, and Iran have the next five positions in the queue, respectively.
- Compared to the COVID-19 death rate, the COVID-19 recovery rate is low in all countries.

Table 6.6 Description of Fig. 6.5

	Countries in the bicluster	Description
5(a)	Canada, Portugal, Austria, Russia, South Korea, Israel, Ireland, India, Ecuador, Chile, Norway, Australia, Denmark, Poland, Peru, Czech Republic, Japan, Romania, Pakistan, Malaysia, the Philippines, Saudi, Indonesia, Mexico, the UAE, Luxembourg, Serbia, Finland, Panama, Dominican Republic, Qatar, Colombia, Thailand, Ukraine, Singapore, Greece	COVID-19 death cases for these countries have shown increased patterns from 11 March to 20 March. In particular, there are 60 plus daily COVID-19 death cases in Canada during this period. The maximum value for other countries is below 60
5(b)	The USA, Canada, Portugal, Austria, Russia, South Korea, Israel, Ireland, India, Ecuador, Chile, Norway, Australia, Denmark, Poland, Peru, Czech Republic, Japan, Romania, Pakistan, Malaysia, the Philippines, Saudi, Indonesia, Mexico, the UAE, Luxembourg, Serbia, Finland, Panama, Dominican Republic, Qatar, Colombia, Thailand, Ukraine, Singapore, Greece	Time Period: 7 March to 4 April 2020 The number of death cases for the USA has increased by 400 plus daily, with a value of approximately 1500–8000; countries like Canada, Portugal, Austria, South Korea have a daily increase of death cases by 20 plus cases; and remaining countries have a daily increase of 10 cases
5(c)	The USA, Canada, Portugal, Austria, Russia, South Korea, Israel, Ireland, India, Ecuador, Chile, Norway, Australia, Denmark, Poland, Peru, Czech Republic, Japan, Romania Pakistan, Malaysia, the Philippines, Saudi, Indonesia, Mexico, the UAE, Luxembourg, Serbia, Finland, Panama, Dominican Republic, Qatar, Colombia, Thailand, Ukraine, Singapore, Greece	Time period: 5 April to 10 April 2020 In the USA, there were about 2000 cases of daily deaths In the rest of the country, there were about 100 cases of daily deaths
5(d)	Turkey, Switzerland, Canada, Brazil, Portugal, Austria, Sweden, Denmark, Japan, Malaysia, the Philippines, Greece	Time period: 27 March to 4 April 2020 Daily death cases for these countries have increased by approximately 40–50 cases
5(e)	Turkey, Switzerland, Brazil, Portugal, Austria, South Korea, Sweden, Ecuador, Denmark, Japan, Malaysia, the Philippines, Indonesia, Greece	Time period: 5 April to 10 April 2020 daily death cases for countries Turkey, Belgium, Switzerland, Netherlands, Canada, and Portugal have increased by 30–50 cases approximately, whereas remaining countries have increased by 10–20 cases daily
5(f)	Germany, Belgium, the Netherlands	Time period: 11 March to 26 March 2020 In the early days, the number of cases of daily death was very low, but it has gradually increased by 30–50 daily cases
5(g)	The USA, Iran, Italy, Spain	Time period: 11 March to 10 April 2020 In the early days, the number of cases of daily death was very low, but it has gradually increased by a few hundred to a few thousand daily. As of 10 April 2020, the USA topped the COVID-19 mortality rate which is followed by Italy and Spain

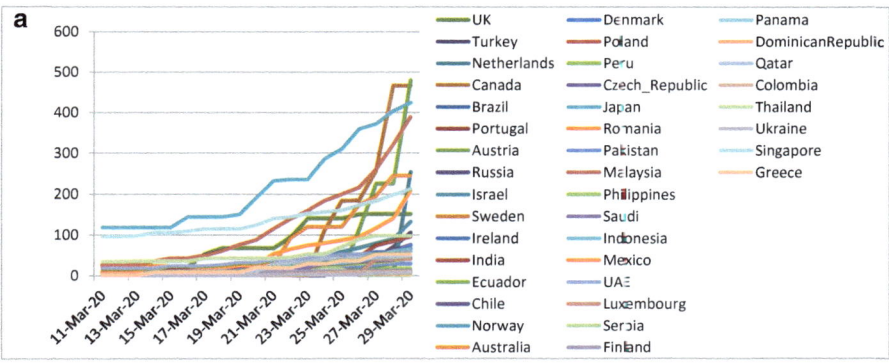

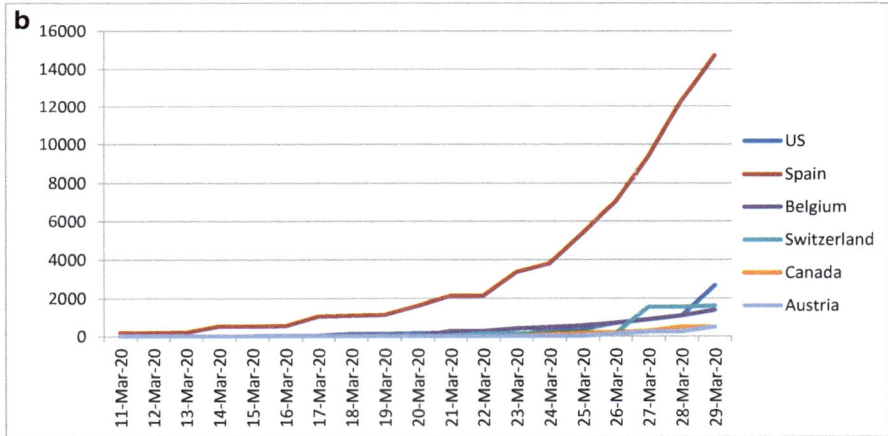

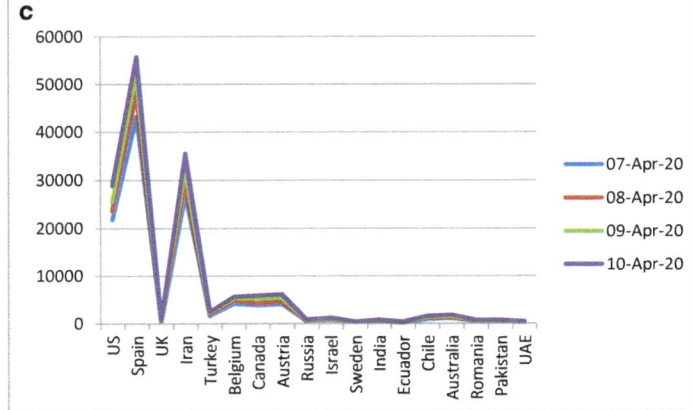

Fig. 6.6 (a)–(e) Incremental pattern for COVID-19 recovered cases (Table 6.7)

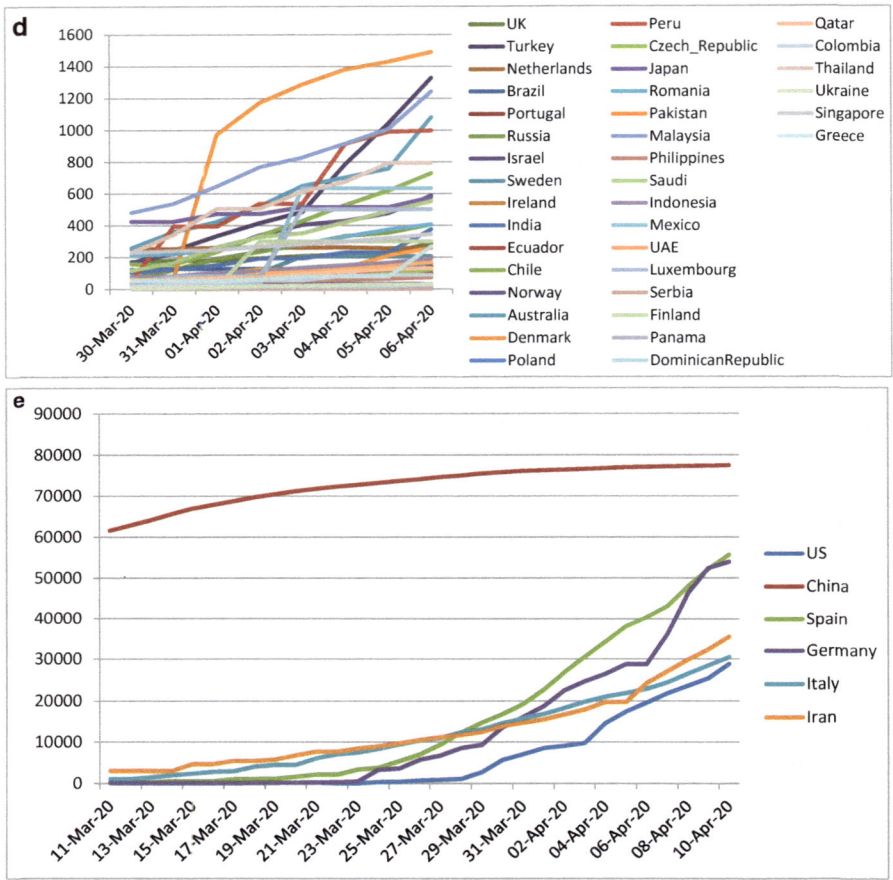

Fig. 6.6 (continued)

6.4.1 Suggestions

There are various official and unofficial websites that provide COVID-19 epidemiological datasets such as the number of confirmed cases, recovered cases, and death cases. In fact, this data is not a real number because not all data can be tracked properly. Even in developed countries, it has huge practical problems. Therefore, if we can use the IoT to detect the origin of the COVID-19 outbreak, we can identify the real situation in each country. Nowadays, people have smartphones with a Wi-Fi connection. With this, it is possible to collect valid COVID-19 epidemiological data using artificial intelligence integrated IoT devices during these infections. In that case, the proposed biclustering method identifies the most effective and correct local patterns from COVID-19 epidemiological data of countries. These patterns are very useful for understanding the prevalence and severity of COVID-19 among countries.

Table 6.7 Description of Fig. 6.6

	Countries in the bicluster	Description
6(a)	The UK, Turkey, the Netherlands, Canada, Brazil, Portugal, Austria, Russia, Israel, Sweden, Ireland, India, Ecuador, Chile, Norway, Australia, Denmark, Poland, Peru, Czech Republic, Japan, Romania, Pakistan, Malaysia, the Philippines, Saudi, Indonesia, Mexico, the UAE, Luxembourg, Serbia, Finland, Panama, Dominican Republic, Qatar, Colombia, Thailand, Ukraine, Singapore, Greece	COVID-19 recovered cases for these countries have shown increased pattern from 11 March to 29 March 2020 In particular, countries like Turkey, Brazil, Netherland, Ireland, Chile, Peru, etc., there was no COVID-19 recovery cases in the second week of March 2020. But gradually it has risen to 100 in all countries
6(b)	The USA Spain, China, Belgium, Switzerland, Canada, Austria	COVID-19 recovered cases for these countries have shown increased pattern from 11 March to 29 March 2020 In the early days, one or two cases have recovered from COVID-19, but by the end of March 2020, it has risen to 1000 plus in these countries
6(c)	The USA, Spain, the UK, Iran, Turkey, Belgium, Canada, Austria, Russia, Israel, Sweden, India, Ecuador, Chile, Australia, Romania, Pakistan, the UAE	Time period: 7 April to 10 April 2020 For the USA, Spain, and Iran, daily recovered cases have increased to 2000 plus approximately, whereas, in remaining countries, daily recovered cases have increased to 100 plus approximately
6(d)	The UK, Turkey, Belgium, the Netherlands, Brazil, Portugal, Russia, Israel, Sweden, Ireland, India, Ecuador, Chile, Norway, Australia, Denmark, Poland, Peru, Czech Republic, Japan, Romania, Pakistan, Malaysia, the Philippines, Saudi, Indonesia, Mexico, the UAF, Luxembourg, Serbia, Finland, Panama, Dominican Republic, Qatar, Colombia, Thailand, Ukraine, Singapore, Greece	Time period: 30 March to 6 April 2020 Daily recovered cases for these countries have increased from 30 to 100 cases approximately
6(e)	The USA, China, Spain, Germany, Italy, Iran	Time period: 11 March to 10 April 2020 In the early days, the number of daily recovered cases was very low, but it has gradually increased from a few hundred to a few thousand daily

On the whole, all countries' epidemiological trajectories have a high correlation with the USA. Therefore, rapid and reliable measures, such as social distance, health practices, and national lockdown, are needed to control the spread of the coronavirus. Otherwise, this virus is likely to spread so badly in all countries, like the USA.

6.5   Conclusion

In this work, an analysis based on the biclustering of COVID-19 epidemiological data has been presented for top 50 COVID-19-infected countries. To the best of our knowledge, the biclustering approach has not been applied for COVID-19 data analysis so far. The main objective of this study was to detect meaningful and reliable patterns in a more optimized way. Instead of clustering, biclustering techniques allow discovering a subset of countries showing similar epidemic trajectory over a specific period (i.e., pandemic outburst days). This work has shown how biclustering methods could fit to study COVID-19 epidemiological time series data. The results obtained by the proposed approach will help public health officials to understand country-wise how COVID-19 is transmitted in humans, recovery rates, and death rates. These patterns are very useful for understanding the prevalence and severity of COVID-19 among countries. In the future, COVID-19 epidemiological data will be collected and stored in the cloud for each country using the IoT-based COVID-19 patient tracking system, and then these data will be more accurate in their numbers. Therefore, these IoT-based epidemiological data play an important role in identifying the precise and accurate epidemiological pathway.

Acknowledgments The first author acknowledges the UGC-Special Assistance Programme (SAP) for the financial support to her research under the UGC-SAP at the level of DRS-II (Ref.No.F.5-6/2018/DRS-II (SAP-II)), 26 July 2018 in the Department of Computer Science.

References

1. Hartigan, J. A. (1972). Direct clustering of a data matrix. *Journal of the American Statistical Association (JASA), 67*, 123–129.
2. Cheng, Y., & Church, G. M. (2000). Biclustering of expression data. In *Proceedings of eighth international conference on intelligent systems for molecular biology* (pp. 93–103). AAAI Press.
3. Padilha, V. A., & Campello, R. J. G. B. (2017). A systematic comparative evaluation of biclustering techniques. *BMC Bioinformatics, 18*(55). https://doi.org/10.1186/s12859-017-1487-1.
4. Teng, L., & Chan, L. W. (2008). Discovering biclusters by iteratively sorting with weighted correlation coefficient in gene expression data. *Journal of Signal Processing Systems, 50*, 267–280.

5. Aguilar-Ruiz, J. S. (2005). Shifting and scaling patterns from gene expression data. *Bioinformatics, 21*(20), 3840–3845.
6. Pontes, B., Giráldez, R., & Aguilar-Ruiz, J. S. (2015). Biclustering on expression data: A review. *Journal of Biomedical Informatics, 57*, 163–180.
7. Anitha, S., & Chandran, C. (2016). Review on analysis of gene expression data using biclustering approaches. *Bonfring International Journal of Data Mining, 6*, 16.
8. Dharan, S., & Nair, A. S. (2009). Biclustering of gene expression data using reactive greedy randomized adaptive search procedure. *BMC Bioinformatics, 10*(Suppl 1), S27, 1–10.
9. Rathipriya, R., Thangavel, K., & Bagyamani, J. (2011). Binary Particle Swarm Optimization based Biclustering of Web Usage Data. *International Journal of Computer Applications, 25*(2), 43.
10. Biswal, B. S., Mohapatra, A., & Vipsita, S. (2018). A review on biclustering of gene expression microarray data: Algorithms, effective measures and validations. *International Journal of Data Mining and Bioinformatics, 21*(3), 230–268. https://doi.org/10.1504/IJDMB.2018.097683.
11. https://www.kaggle.com/vadhani/india-covid-19-time-series-analysis
12. https://www.kaggle.com/vadhani/linear-regression-model-for-india-covid-19
13. https://www.kaggle.com/vadhani/covid19-dataset
14. Dhamodharavadhani, S., & Rathipriya, R. (2019). Region-wise rainfall prediction using MapReduce-based exponential smoothing techniques. In J. Peter, A. Alavi, & B. Javadi (Eds.), *Advances in big data and cloud computing* (Advances in intelligent systems and computing) (Vol. 750). Singapore: Springer.
15. Dhamodharavadhani, S., & Rathipriya, R. (2020). Variable selection method for regression models using computational intelligence techniques. In *Handbook of research on machine and deep learning applications for cyber security* (pp. 416–436). Web. 7 Apr. 2020. IGI Global. https://doi.org/10.4018/978-1-5225-9611-0.ch019.
16. Dhamodharavadhani, S., & Rathipriya, R. (2020). Enhanced logistic regression (ELR) model for big data. In *Handbook of research on big data clustering and machine learning* (pp. 152–176). Web. 7 Apr. 2020. IGI Global. https://doi.org/10.4018/978-1-7998-0106-1.ch008.
17. Fong, S. J., Li, G., Dey, N., Gonzalez-Crespo, R., & Herrera-Viedma, E. (2020). Finding an accurate early forecasting model from small dataset: A case of 2019-nCoV novel coronavirus outbreak. *International Journal of Interactive Multimedia and Artificial Intelligence, 6*(1), 132–140.
18. Benvenuto, D., Giovanetti, M., Vassallo, L., Angeletti, S., & Ciccozzi, M. Application of the ARIMA model on the COVID-2019 epidemic dataset. *Data in Brief, 29*, 105340. Received 14 Feb 2020, Revised 21 Feb 2020, Accepted 21 Feb 2020, Available online 26 Feb 2020.https://doi.org/10.1016/j.dib.2020.105340.
19. WHO|Novel Coronavirus – China. WHO. Archived from the original on 23 Jan 2020.
20. Dehesh, T., Mardani-Fard, H. A., & Dehesh, P. Forecasting of COVID-19 confirmed cases in different countries with ARIMA models. *medRxiv preprint.* https://doi.org/10.1101/2020.03.13.20035345.
21. World Health Organization. (2005). *Emergency Committee regarding the outbreak of novel coronavirus (2019-nCoV).* Statement on the meeting of the International Health Regulations.
22. Sparrow, A. How China's coronavirus is spreading – And how to stop it. *Foreign Policy.* Archived from the original on 31 Jan 2020. Retrieved 2 Feb 2020.
23. Remuzzi, A., & Remuzzi, G. (2020). COVID-19, and Italy: What next? *Lancet.* https://doi.org/10.1016/S0140-6736(20)30627-9.
24. Li, Q., Guan, X., Wu, P., Wang, X., Zhou, L., Tong, Y., et al. (2020). Early transmission dynamics in Wuhan, China, of novel coronavirus–infected pneumonia. *The New England Journal of Medicine, 382*, 1199–1207. https://doi.org/10.1056/NEJMoa2001316.
25. Zhou, T., Liu, Q., Yang, Z., Liao, J., Yang, K., Bai, W., et al. (2020). Preliminary prediction of the basic reproduction number of the Wuhan novel coronavirus 2019-nCoV. *Journal of Evidence-Based Medicine, 13*, 3–7. https://doi.org/10.1111/jebm.12376.

26. Zhao, S., Lin, Q., Ran, J., Musa, S. S., Yang, G., Wang, W., et al. (2020). Preliminary estimation of the basic reproduction number of novel coronavirus (2019-nCoV) in China, from 2019 to 2020: A data-driven analysis in the early phase of the outbreak. *International Journal of Infectious Diseases, 92*, 214–217. https://doi.org/10.1016/j.ijid.2020.01.050.
27. Liu, Y., Gayle, A. A., Wilder-Smith, A., & Rocklöv, J. (2020). The reproductive number of COVID-19 is higher compared to SARS coronavirus. *Journal of Travel Medicine, 27*, taaa021. https://doi.org/10.1093/jtm/taaa021.
28. Lai, A., Bergan, A., Acciarri, C., Galli, M., & Zehender, G. (2020). Early phylogenetic estimate of the effective reproduction number of SARS-CoV-2. *Journal of Medical Virology.* https://doi.org/10.1002/jmv.25723.
29. Perc, M., Gorišek Miksić, N., Slavinec, M., & Stožer, A. (2020). Forecasting COVID-19. *Frontiers of Physics, 8*, 127. https://doi.org/10.3389/fphy.2020.00127.
30. Das, S., & Idicula, S. M. (2010). Greedy search-binary PSO hybrid for biclustering gene expression data. *International Journal of Computer Applications, 2*(3), 1–5.

Chapter 7
IoT Applications in Healthcare

Qi Lin and Qiuhong Zhao

Abstract This chapter aims to review IoT applications in the healthcare domain that are representative and active in practice and research. The chapter introduces the existing IoT products in the healthcare market; reviews the studies on developing, using, and improving IoT healthcare applications; and presents and discusses the recent trend and focus of IoT healthcare applications. First, the chapter describes a general picture of IoT healthcare applications. And then, the chapter studies IoT healthcare applications in three scenarios:

1. Acute disease care. Three applications are introduced to show how IoT benefits acute care: vital sign monitoring, acute care telemedicine, and IoT-based detection and control of infectious diseases.
2. Chronic disease care. The chapter focuses on remote health monitoring used for patients with chronic diseases, especially patients with Alzheimer's disease, diabetes, and heart failure.
3. Self-health management. The chapter pays attention to the most common representative device for self-health management, smartwatches and analyzes the two main functions of smartwatches on self-health management, sleep monitoring and exercise monitoring.

Keywords IoT applications · Healthcare · Acute disease care · Chronic disease care · Self-health management

Q. Lin · Q. Zhao (✉)
School of Economics and Management, Beihang University, Beijing, China
e-mail: qhzhao@buaa.edu.cn

© Springer Nature Switzerland AG 2021   115
F. P. García Márquez, B. Lev (eds.), *Internet of Things*, International Series in
Operations Research & Management Science 305,
https://doi.org/10.1007/978-3-030-70478-0_7

7.1 Introduction

The Internet of Things (IoT) is a concept reflecting a connected world of physical objects, such as vehicles, home appliances, medical devices, and Radio-Frequency Identification (RFID) tags. IoT enables communication among these objects to take place without human intervention requirement in a loop [1]. "The strategic significance of IoT is born of the ever-advancing ability to break that constraint, and to create information, without human observation, in all manner of circumstances that were previously invisible" [2]. In addition to collect and share data, IoT combining these objects with automated systems makes "gather information, analyze it, and create an action" possible to help some with a particular task or learn form a process [3]. IoT is now being applied in different fields. As a typical quick adopter of new technology, the healthcare industry has had some promising applications of IoT. Ultrasounds, thermometers, glucose monitors, electrocardiograms, and more are all starting to become connected, letting doctors and patients themselves learn more about patient health. According to a report by Grand View Research, the global IoT in healthcare market size is projected to reach USD 534.3 billion by 2025 expanding at an annual growth rate 19.9% over the forecast period [4].

With the increasing and aging population, healthcare providers are facing two main challenges: (1) provide safe, accessible, high quality, and integrated health services for patients, persons, families, communities, and populations in general [5], especially for the elderly and the populations that live in rural or remote areas, and (2) reduce healthcare costs to make health coverage more affordable. IoT healthcare applications can help empower doctors to deliver superlative care, make telemedicine and remote health monitoring possible, increase patient engagement and satisfaction, and keep patients safe and healthy. Moreover, IoT has a major impact on reducing healthcare costs and meanwhile improving treatment outcomes significantly [6]. IoT is transforming the future of the healthcare industry. IoT healthcare applications have potentials for not only backing accurate detection and treatment of illness but also providing quality health services at reduced costs or in remote areas [7, 8]. Further, research institutes and related companies like insurance companies can leverage health data collected by IoT devices for research work or decision-making.

Islam et al. [9] review the state-of-the-art IoT healthcare applications in their paper, based on whose work; Balakrishna and Thirumaran [10] divide IoT healthcare applications into two categories: single-condition and clustered-condition applications. This chapter refers to IoT healthcare applications as any application related to healthcare delivery across the healthcare continuum based on IoT devices, systems, and technology [1, 12]. This chapter divides IoT healthcare applications into three categories according to health status of target groups whom IoT healthcare applications work for: (1) applications for people with acute diseases, which work in real-time environments; (2) applications for people with chronic diseases, which emphasize data utilization to produce long-term, personalized, customized treatment plans; and (3) applications for healthy or sub-healthy people, which

Table 7.1 IoT applications in the healthcare domain

Literature	IoT healthcare applications	ADC	CDC	SHM
Baker et al. [13]	Remote health monitoring		✓	
Darshan and Anandakumar [14]	Remote health monitoring		✓	
Dias and Paulo Silva Cunha [15]	Vital sign monitoring	✓	✓	
Gill et al. [16]	Disease detection, especially at earlier stages	✓	✓	
	Customized patient treatment	✓	✓	
	Hospital inventory management			
Laplante and Laplante [11]	Bulimia diagnosis and management		✓	
	Alzheimer's disease and its comorbidities monitoring		✓	
	Safety and violence			
	Scarce shared equipment tracking and management			
Lee et al. [17]	Sleep monitoring			✓
Manikandan et al. [18]	Smart healthcare (SHC) systems	✓		
Mozaffari et al. [19]	Fall detection			✓
Ukil et al. [20]	Anomaly detection	✓	✓	
Yacchirema et al. [21]	Sleep monitoring			✓

Note: In the table, ADC is the acronym for acute disease care, CDC is that for chronic disease care, and SHM is that for self-health management; and the tick means that this application is used in the corresponding scenarios

highlights the awareness of self-health management. The chapter will review both current research works and representative products in practice to show the recent focus and trend of IoT healthcare applications. This chapter begins with drawing a rough picture of IoT healthcare applications (shown in Table 7.1 and Fig. 7.1).

7.2 IoT Applications for Acute Disease Care

Acute diseases refer to diseases that come on rapidly, are accompanied by distinct symptoms, and get better once they are treated, such as a broken bone, a heart attack, a common cold, and a respiratory infection. Acute care is the early and specialist management of patients suffering from a wide range of medical conditions requiring urgent or short-term care. The success of acute care depends on the time, availability, quality, and accuracy of a patient's health data and information. The traditional process of data collection, storage, processing, and retrieval is manual and time-consuming and thus often results in errors and inaccuracy. IoT shows positive effects on lessening monitoring and analysis burden in very fast-paced environments, helping make real changes in acute conditions that require immediate actions. This section will introduce three applications to show how IoT benefits acute care.

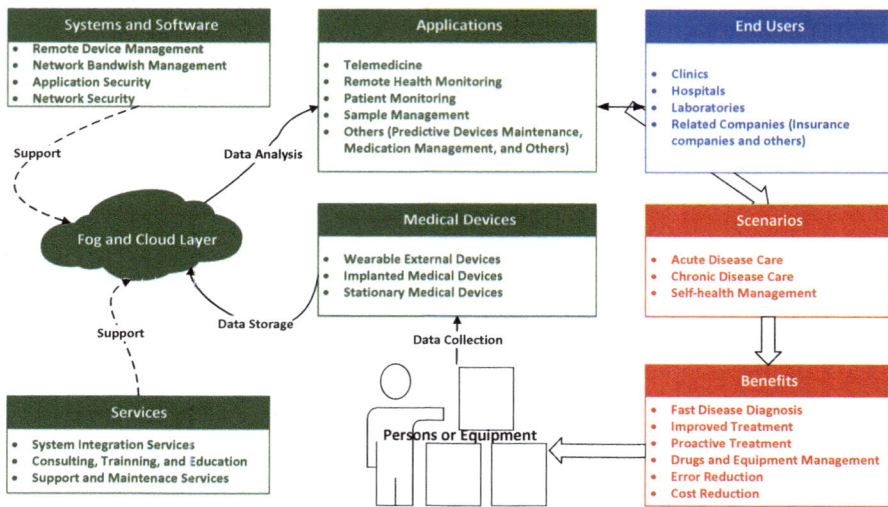

Fig. 7.1 A framework of IoT healthcare applications. (Grand View Research [4])

7.2.1 Vital Sign Monitoring for the Emergency Department

There are four primary vital signs: body temperature, blood pressure, heart rate, and respiratory rate. Depending on the clinical settings, vital signs may include other measurements, such as pain assessment, oxygen saturation, and pulse oximetry. Vital sign monitoring is an essential component of patient care. First, vital signs can provide information for prompt diagnosis and proper treatment; second, by analyzing vital signs, clinicians can identify early signs of patient deterioration; and third, vital signs can be used to predict outcomes after discharge and then readmissions. Traditional intermittent manual vital sign monitoring, such as early warning score systems, runs the risk of undetected patient deterioration due to inadequate frequency of monitoring [22]. Vital sign monitoring systems, driven by IoT and big data analytics technology, allow for automatic, continuous monitoring patients' vital signs and can alert patient deterioration in an earlier stage, which, therefore, can prevent serious adverse events, reduce mortality and hospital costs, and improve patient wellbeing [23]. There are two systems widely used in hospitals (Fig. 7.2). Visensia, a data-driven system, can provide real-time intelligent analysis and alerting of patient deterioration by comparing a correlated set of several vital signs of a patient to the unique Visensia database; and VitalPatch, one of the most discrete and advanced biosensors, can monitor eight physiological measurements continuously, in real time, with clinical-grade accuracy.

Vital signs are critical markers of illness triage and severity in the emergency department (ED) [24]. For example, one with a temperature of 104, heart rate of 120, and blood pressure of 80/40 may with a heart be in sepsis; one rate of 160 may have a supraventricular tachycardia or atrial fibrillation. Hence, recording a full set

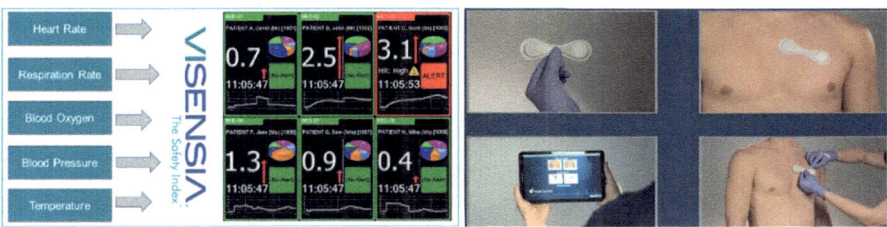

Fig. 7.2 Visensia (left) and VitalPatch (right). (Source: The left and the right panels are provided by OBS Medical at http://www.obsmedical.com/visensia-the-safety-index/ and VitalConnect at https://vimeo.com/289562665, respectively)

of the four primary vital signs at least daily is considered as a standard for patient care on acute hospital wards [25], which can be perfectly implemented by vital sign monitoring systems. In terms of practice, opioid analgesic use is a major cause of morbidity and mortality in the USA. It has been proved that wearable sensors can improve relapse detection in the ED by providing objective, real-time physiologic data on opioid analgesic use [26]. In terms of research, Gao et al. [27] develop a system to facilitate collaborative and time-critical care in the emergency response community using wearable sensors, vital sign monitoring algorithm, prehospital patient care software, and web portals; and Pimentel et al. [28] propose a technique to estimate respiratory rate, a vital sign routinely measured in the ED, using waveform data acquired from wearable sensors. Although practice and research studies have shown positive results of the adoption of vital sign monitoring systems in the ED, further understanding of patient and clinician preferences are requisite for future development.

7.2.2 Acute Care Telemedicine

Telemedicine refers to the practice of caring for patients remotely when providers and patients are not physically present with each other [29], leveraging information technology, video imaging, and telecommunication linkages. As a time-efficient and cost-effective alternative to a drive to a doctor's office, more and more people turn to find medical solutions by telemedicine. Advances of telemedicine are shown in many aspects, including gap service coverage (e.g., nighttime radiology coverage), urgent services (e.g., tele-stroke services and tele-burn services), mandated services (e.g., the delivery of healthcare services to prison inmates), and the proliferation of video-enabled multisite group chart rounds (e.g., Extension for Community Healthcare Outcomes programs) [30].

In this subsection, the chapter pays attention to acute care telemedicine. Acute care telemedicine is simply defined as "the practice of medicine at a distance, enabled by technology, for patients requiring urgent or emergent care." Note

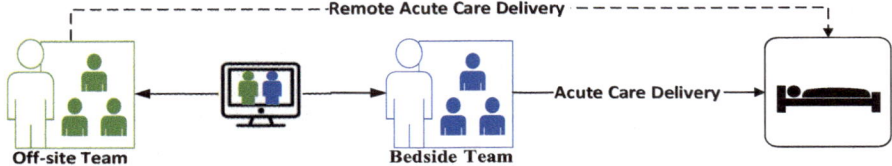

Fig. 7.3 Tele-ICU

that the interactions of acute care telemedicine, unlike in many other clinical applications, are between providers rather than between a provider and a patient [31]. Telemedicine plays its role in many acute conditions, such as acute stroke [32], acute plastic surgical trauma and burns [33], and prompt electrocardiograph diagnosis [34]. For example, SOC Telemed, founded in 2004, is the largest US provider of acute care telemedicine services, including tele-neurology, tele-psychiatry, and tele-intensivist services, and AcuteCare Telemedicine, founded in 2009, is a representative leading practice-based provider of telemedicine services for hospitals seeking around-the-clock stroke and other urgent neurological care. Below a primary use of acute care telemedicine, tele-Intensive Care Unit (tele-ICU), is presented.

Tele-ICU is a care that is provided to critically ill patients by off-site clinicians using audio, video, and electronic links (Fig. 7.3). The care that can be provided by tele-ICU includes the ability to detect patient's instability or laboratory abnormalities in real time, collect additional clinical information from or about the patient, order diagnostic testing, make diagnoses, implement treatment, and render other forms of intensive care such as managing life-support devices and communicate with patients and bedside providers [35]. Tele-ICU enables an off-site team to work together with a bedside team for patient care. By tele-ICU, one centralized care team can manage and provide continuous, professional acute care services to a large number of geographically dispersed ICU locations in real time. What needs to be emphasized is that tele-ICU serves as a supplement, but not a replacement, to the bedside team, delivering proven, enhanced clinical outcomes and respecting hospital's need for delivering care in a financially responsible manner [36, 37]. Khunlertkit and Carayon [38] prove that tele-ICU can reduce on mortality and length of stay, support medication management and improve medication safety, and reduce the risk of patient falls and extubations. Lilly et al. [39] suggest that there are benefits of a tele-ICU intervention beyond what is provided by the daytime bedside team and traditional approaches to quality improvement. Tele-ICU has been proven to be cost-effective in most cases and cost-saving in some cases [40]. Indeed, there is a U-shaped relationship between the economic efficiency and tele-ICU use selected based on severity of illness [41].

7.2.3   *IoT-Based Detection and Control of Infectious Diseases*

Using IoT for infectious disease detection and control is an emerging field and has a substantial positive impact on humanity. For example, "at the Virginia Tech Network Dynamics and Simulation Laboratory, disease monitoring tools such as HealthMap and EpiCaster are merging IoT data with population data, GIS data, land-use information, social media streams, and other sources to detect emerging public health threats" [42].

Detection is the first and most critical step in infectious disease control. Mobile Health (mHealth) devices combined with connected diagnostic devices offers new possibilities to diagnose, track, and control infectious diseases, while the challenge is how to deploy these devices to a clinical care pathway and/or a surveillance system for an infectious disease [43]. Taking dengue fever as an example, Zhu et al. [44] develop an IoT system based on a miniaturized polymerase chain reaction device. The system is connected with an Android-based smartphone via Bluetooth and with the whole world via Long Term Evolution, helping to tackle outbreaks of dengue fever and other diseases such as any type of influenza, malaria, and human immunodeficiency virus. Similar studies have been conducted to develop methods, frameworks, or systems to detect and control different infectious diseases, such as Zika fever [45], Chikungunya fever [46], and Ebola virus disease (2018). Considering the COVID-19, IoT can be used to monitor the air quality continuously. Once the virus is detected, the IoT system should send an alert and analyze the pollution timeline. Additionally, as Bai et al. [47] present in their paper, specialists (clinicians with rich clinical experience, clinicians supporting front-line work in Wuhan, and biomedical, statistical, and information technology engineers) have formulated a consensus, the "COVID-19 Intelligent Diagnosis and Treatment Assistant Program" based on IoT, to diagnose the COVID-19 earlier and to improve its treatment.

The chapter refers readers to Kaushalya et al. [48] who critically review the research work on IoT-based epidemic detection systems and present a summary of their strengths and weaknesses. In a word, IoT has the potential to assist to achieve early identification, isolation, and treatment of infected patients, while to achieve this, a global-scale connectivity of IoT monitoring systems deployed by different countries and regions is needed, which is quite challengeable.

7.3   IoT Applications for Chronic Disease Care

Chronic diseases are defined broadly as conditions that last 1 year or more and require ongoing medical attention or limit activities of daily living or both, such as arthritis, Alzheimer's disease, diabetes, heart disease, high blood pressure, and

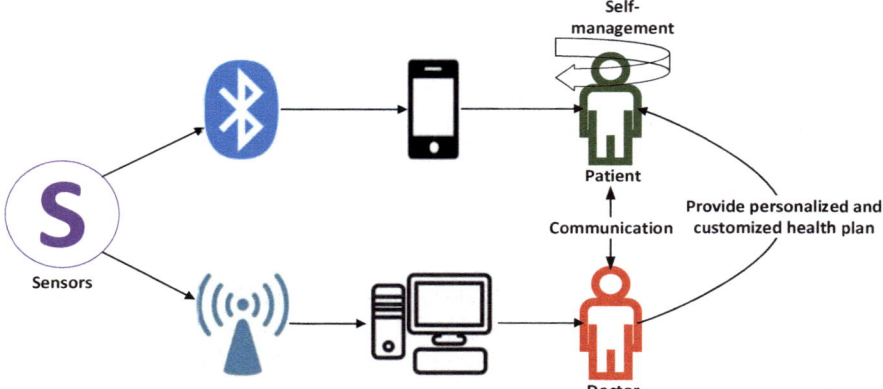

Fig. 7.4 Remote health monitoring for patients with chronic diseases

chronic kidney disease. Compared to acute diseases, chronic diseases are slower to develop, may progress over time, may have any number of warning signs or no signs at all, and yet cannot be cured – only controlled through health plans. IoT healthcare applications for chronic diseases mainly focus on using wearables and other home equipment to keep track of patient health continuously. Such applications enable physicians to identify the best treatment process for patients in the light of analysis of collected data. In this section, the chapter will discuss how IoT healthcare applications benefit patients with chronic diseases.

Remote health monitoring is a healthcare delivery system and method that uses information technology to monitor patient health outside of a traditional clinical setting (Fig. 7.4). By remote health monitoring, health information can be transmitted electronically between patients and physicians, letting patients become a part of addressing their own health problems. Unlike other telehealth delivery methods, remote health monitoring does not require interactive audio-video. It only monitors and collects a patient's health data, and then their physician can grasp their health status remotely and provide them with an appropriate preventive intervention or health plan, helping to avoid emergency care and hospital admissions and improve the patient's quality of care and life. According to the Centers for Disease Control and Prevention (CDC), chronic diseases are leading drivers of the US annual healthcare costs. Remote health monitoring is expected to save up to $36 billion globally over the next 5 years [49].

Most remote health monitoring systems have similar key components. First, sensors and remote transmission technology are required to measure and transmit specific physiological data. Shared data storage is also crucial, as well as software that can assist to analyze health data, offer treatment recommendations, and send an alert when any anomaly is detected. Blount et al. [50] design a platform, called Personal Care Connect (PCC), to facilitate remote monitoring of patients. PCC has features in common with other remote health monitoring systems, while it is a standards-based, open platform that allows for integrating with devices and applications from independent vendors. Baker et al. [13] introduce remote health monitoring for rehabilitation after physical injury, Parkinson's disease, diabetes, heart attacks, and assisted ambient living for the elderly and chronically ill patients, through wearable healthcare systems supported by sensors. Remote health monitoring can aid patients with various chronic diseases but is most widely used for monitoring Alzheimer's disease, diabetes, and heart failure.

7.3.1 IoT Healthcare Applications for Alzheimer's Disease

Alzheimer's disease is a chronic neurodegenerative disease that usually starts slowly and gradually worsens over time until it becomes severe enough to interfere with daily tasks. It is the cause of 60–70% of dementia cases. For the detection of Alzheimer's disease, especially in the early stage, remote health monitoring can be a great solution. Cheng and Zhuang [51] propose a Bluetooth-enabled in-home patient monitoring system, facilitating early detection of Alzheimer's disease. Taking advantage of short-term Bluetooth communication to track an in-home patient's location and record their location information in a local database, their doctor can learn more about the movement pattern of the patient and determine whether a target patient is developing Alzheimer's disease. Varatharajan et al. [52] use dynamic time warping (DTW) algorithm to compare various shapes of foot movements collected from wearable IoT devices and then classify the gait signal for Alzheimer disease diagnosis.

Researchers also work on developing advanced systems based on IoT to monitor patients with Alzheimer's disease. Al-khafajiy et al. [53] propose a smart healthcare monitoring system that has three main layers: wearable devices (patient layer), the cloud (data layer), and the monitoring platform (hospital layer). The system accumulates patients' physiological data via wearable sensors, transmits it to cloud for data processing and analyzing, and finally reports any detection of disorder in the patient's data to their doctor via the monitoring platform. Faria et al. [54] propose a mobile system that is capable of providing the geographic position of the patient carrying the mobile equipment to themselves or an external authorized person such as their family or doctor. It also incorporates hands-free voice communication and fall detection capability, which allows for communication with a distant person, in case of an unexpected incident such as a fall. Elfaki and Alotaibi [55] explore, analyze, and investigate academic and nonacademic mobile applications for Alzheimer's disease over the last 10 years in order to highlight current and future directions from four service perspectives: enhancing human memory, ensuring safety, improving awareness, and facilitating patients' daily activities.

7.3.2   IoT Healthcare Applications for Diabetes

Diabetes is a chronic, metabolic disease characterized by elevated levels of blood glucose, which leads over time to serious damage to the heart, blood vessels, eyes, kidneys, and nerves. According to the WHO, about 422 million people worldwide have diabetes, and 1.6 million deaths are directly attributed to diabetes each year. Indeed, diabetes is one of the leading causes of death in the world. There is not a cure for diabetes yet, but living healthy lifestyles, taking medicine as needed, carrying out diabetes self-management, and keeping healthcare appointments can really help patients reduce the impact of diabetes on their life.

Gia et al. [56] design an IoT-based system architecture from a sensor device to a back-end system for presenting real-time glucose, body temperature, and environmental temperature to end users such as patients and doctors. Ericsson (a Swedish multinational networking and telecommunications company) and its partner, Brighter (a Swedish health-tech company), commercially introduce Actiste in 2019, the world's first complete IoT health solution for monitoring and treating insulin-dependent diabetes. Blood sample, blood glucose measurement, and insulin injection can be completed using a single connected device, Actiste. As Henrik Norström, CEO of Brighter, said, with Actiste, "no matter where in the world patients decide to go, their generated health and treatment data will always be securely stored and available to improve their treatments."

So far, remote healthcare monitoring for diabetes is mainly used to obtain health data and information from patients, while feedback and advice are then given usually by telephones or emails. Such use still requires plenty of human resources, and responses to patients are often delayed. Hence, to achieve cost-effective diabetes management on a large scale, an automated response system that will respond immediately to patients' input and provide advice is needed [57]. AI-Taee et al. [58] present a smartphone platform that understands to what extent the patient's activities comply with their individual treatment plan, derives rule-based health indicators, generates appropriate warnings, and support in terms of feedback advice.

7.3.3   IoT Healthcare Applications for Heart Failure

Heart failure is a chronic, progressive condition where the heart muscle is unable to pump enough blood to meet the body's needs for blood and oxygen. Heart failure is a major public health issue with a prevalence over 23 million worldwide and rising [59]. Despite advanced medical, pharmacological, and surgical treatment, patient outcomes of heart failure are poor, and hospital readmissions are high [60]. Remote health monitoring shows its advantage on heart failure, by allowing earlier identification of decompensation, better adherence to lifestyle changes, medication, and interventions, to reduce the need for hospitalization [61].

The basic function of remote health monitoring is to collect, transmit, and store patients' health data for further analysis remotely, which is not difficult with current technology, while the challenge is how to convert data into better decision-makings [61]. Pecchia et al. [62] combine data mining technology with the remote health monitoring platform for early detection of any worsening in patients' conditions. Yang et al. [63] put forward a non-line-of-sight monitoring system for heart diseases to collect physiological data in real time and support the short-delay and high-reliability response to urgent disease condition. The UCLA Nursing School and the UCLA Wireless Health Institute together develop WANDA, a weight and activity with blood pressure monitoring system, leveraging sensors to monitor patient's activities and wireless communication technology to provide tailored guidance [64]. Researches prove that WANDA has a positive impact on heart failure patients [65, 66].

Future research should focus on issues such as miniaturization of the devices, development of implantable chips, low-cost disposable and/or waterproof sensors, and interoperability with other tracking services [67].

7.4 IoT Applications for Self-Health Management

Recently health perceptions are changing. More and more people pay attention to their lifestyles and health status and show great interest in self-health management. Advances in interactive computing technology, data processing, sensing, and displays have enabled devices to fit into our palm and pockets, which are wrist-worn, head-mounted, or clothing-embedded [68]. The most common representative device is smartwatches (or fitness trackers) that capture health signals and interact with associated smartphones via wireless technologies such as Bluetooth, Wi-Fi, and GPS for the telemetry, management, and analysis of health data (Fig. 7.5).

The health-related functions of smartwatches include workout reminder, step tracker, sleep monitoring, and calorie consumption measurement. Reeder and David [69] summarize the ways in which smartwatches support health in our daily life: enabling self-monitoring of personal activities, obtaining feedback based on activity measures, allowing for in situ surveys to identify patterns of behavior, and supporting bidirectional communication with healthcare providers and family members. So far, smartwatches have penetrated and become one of the focuses of the health market and research. For example, Apple Watch, the most popular smartwatch worldwide, accounts for half of the total 45 million smartwatches shipped in 2018. In this section, the chapter will present how smartwatches change our lifestyles and health status.

There are two main research topics on smartwatches for self-health management. First is activity recognition. Lutze and Waldhor [70] propose a software architecture building on the automatic detection of the events and activities of the elderly's daily life sensors of smartwatches. Then, they (2017) introduce an artificial neuronal net to analyze motion patterns, recognize events and activities, and calculate the

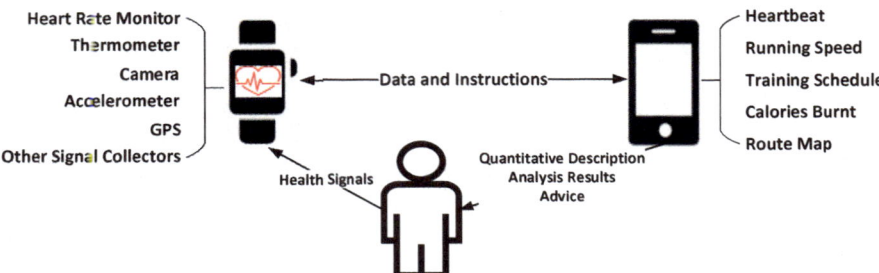

Fig. 7.5 Smartwatches for self-health management

wellbeing of smartwatch users. Bhattacharya and Lane [71] perform a smartwatch-centric investigation of activity recognition using one of the most popular deep learning methods – Restricted Boltzmann Machines (RBMs). The results indicate that RBMs are effective in activity recognition and have acceptable levels of resource use for smartwatches. Second is app design. Dibia [72] designs Foqus, an app running on smartwatches to aid adults with mental health and stress-related conditions, which has three functions: Pomodoro time management, mindful meditation, and message-based priming. Apple Watch launches functions and apps to detect depression levels, which are expected to help cure the mental health of working-class people.

7.4.1 Sleep and Exercise Monitoring Using Smartwatches

Traditional sleep monitoring systems, such as polysomnography, involves a myriad of sensors attached around one's body and therefore is limited to clinical usage [73], while smartwatches enable sleep monitoring to become a habit in our daily life. To some extent, sleep monitoring changes people's perceptions of sleep. On one hand, one can look into smartwatches and apps to track sleep, quantify sleep, and change sleep patterns according to advice from apps by analyzing their sleep data. On the other hand, "while digital apps and devices can't replace formal testing, they can give your doctor a general idea of your total sleep time, your sleep/wake cycle, and how disruptive your sleep may be," as Collen Lance, a sleep medicine expert, said.

Research on sleep monitoring systems on smartwatches has been conducted from the perspectives of frameworks, functions, and algorithms. Based on the portability and interoperability concepts, Pombo and Garcia [73] present a ubiquitous architecture where a smartwatch is combined with a smartphone to implement a sleep monitoring system. The system joins heart rate, accelerometer, and sound signals collected into a smartwatch and includes an application programming interface for data exchange between smart devices. Sun et al. [74] propose SleepMonitor, a smartwatch-based system that leverages the built-in accelerometer to monitor respiratory rate and body positions, the two major physiological parameters in sleep study. To calculate respiratory rate, they design a filter to extract respiratory signals and use frequency analysis to estimate respiratory rate; and to detect body positions, they use machine learning techniques. Chang et al. [75] propose SleepGuard, a novel approach that relies solely on sensors available in an off-the-shelf smartwatch, to capture a rich amount of information about sleep events and contexts, including body posture and movements, acoustic events, and illumination conditions, and to estimate sleep quality and identify factors affecting it most. Although many studies have worked on this area, there still exist challenges waiting to be addressed, such as a lack of standard evaluation methods for consumer-grade devices (e.g., reliability and validity assessment), limitations in the populations studied, consumer expectations, and constraints on resources of consumer-grad devices (e.g., power consumption) [76].

"Getting enough sleep, exercising, and limiting sedentary activities can greatly contribute to disease prevention and overall health and longevity" [77]. Except for sleep monitoring, smartwatches are able to recognize and monitor exercise. "Workout data generated by mobile tracking apps can assist both users and physicians in achieving better health care, rehabilitation, and self-motivation" [78].

Techniques and approaches are developed for activity recognition. Shahmohammadi et al. [79] describe a smartwatch-based active learning method for activity recognition to identify five common daily activities: walking, standing, lying down, sitting, and running. For activity recognition, classification methods are explored, such as convolution neural network [80, 81] and artificial neural network [82]. Topics on exercise monitoring and analysis are also studied. Smartwatches enable users to explicitly log exercise. Hoilett et al. [83] describe a measurement by smartwatches of respiratory rate and heart rate simultaneously, using photoplethysmography, a photosensor, and frequency content analysis.

Although smartwatches are intelligent enough to log users' daily health activities such sleeping and exercise and provide simple analysis to help users understand their health status roughly, more efforts should be exerted to study how to utilize these data to predict underlying diseases.

7.5 Conclusion

IoT ideas have been applying to the healthcare domain and play a critical role in creating smart healthcare. IoT enables healthcare occurring not only in hospital but also at home. Through IoT healthcare applications such as telemedicine, vital sign monitoring, remote health monitoring, and others, patients can be engaged into decision-makings, and big data and accurate information can be obtained, which supports timely diagnosis, appropriate treatment, and customized and personalized healthcare plans. IoT combined with big data analytics technology, the cloud, and other related technologies makes decision-makings faster, more efficient, more proactive, and more accurate. With the concept of self-health management emerges, wearable devices, especially smartwatches, have been changing people's perceptions of health and their lifestyles.

Based on IoT, an interconnected healthcare network can be established, which allows for communication among doctors, patients, equipment, and resources. The network collects and provides a large amount of valuable real-time data, analysis of which can provide support to decision systems and assist to predict future trend of healthcare. Instruction can also be accomplished through the network. Indeed, based on IoT, healthcare systems become digital, structured, networked, and efficient. Despite such benefits, IoT faces some barriers of being adopted in the healthcare industry. First, privacy is of paramount importance because patients expect that certain private information will remain confidential [12]. Blockchain may provide an answer to this difficult problem as blockchain-based approaches can provide decentralized security and privacy, while accompanied by significant energy, delay, and computational overhead, which is not suitable for most resource-constrained IoT devices but is being explored and addressed by researchers [84]. Second, IoT is suffering from the fragmentation and the missing interoperability that resulting in "high entry barriers for developers and currently prevent the emergence of broadly accepted IoT ecosystems" [85]. The interoperability puts forward a high request on data standards. It is almost impossible to force providers and users of IoT systems or devices to execute uniform data standards. A relatively ideal way is to provide conversion among data standards and then provide connectivity between those isolated IoT products based on established communication and data standards. For example, the Semantic Web technologies can be used to support the semantic integration and functional collaborations between IoT healthcare information systems and EHR systems by defining and normalizing health data [86]. Moreover, high costs and the preferences of users mainly referring to doctors, nurses, and patients should be also considered an important risk of the adoption of IoT [87]. Although there are many technological, financial, cultural, social issues that need to be addressed for the success of IoT healthcare applications, the future of IoT in the healthcare domain is bright. We can expect more benefits obtained from IoT healthcare applications as researches and practices are working on overcoming these barriers and are exploring more and better uses of IoT.

References

1. Thibaud, M., Chi, H., Zhou, W., & Piramuthu, S. (2018). Internet of Things (IoT) in high-risk environment, health and safety (EHS) industries: A comprehensive review. *Decision Support Systems, 108*, 79–95.
2. Holdowsky, J., Mahto, M., Raynor, M. E., & Cotteleer, M. (2015). *Inside the internet of things (IoT): A primer on the technologies building the IoT*. New York, Deloitte University Press.
3. Burgess, M. (2018). What is the Internet of Things? WIRED explains. www.wired.co.uk/article/internet-of-things-what-is-explained-iot
4. Grand View Research. (2019). IoT in healthcare market worth $534.3 billion by 2025|CAGR: 19.9%. https://www.grandviewresearch.com/press-release/global-iot-in-healthcare-market. Visit on 30 Aug 2020.

5. The World Health Organization (WHO). (2020). Health service. https://www.who.int/topics/health_services/en/. Visit on 30 Aug 2020.
6. Ramachandran, G., Kannan, S., Sheela, T., Malarvizhi, A., Murali, P. M., & Sureshkumar, G. (2019). Internet of things in healthcare. *Research & Reviews: Journal of Medical Science and Technology, 8*(1), 10–12.
7. Muhammad, G., Rahman, S. M. M., Alelaiwi, A., & Alamri, A. (2017). Smart health solution integrating IoT and cloud: A case study of voice pathology monitoring. *IEEE Communications Magazine, 55*(1), 69–73.
8. Varshney, U., & Chang, C. K. (2016). Smart health and well-being. *Computer, 49*(11), 11–13.
9. Islam, S. R., Kwak, D., Kabir, M. H., Hossain, M., & Kwak, K S. (2015). The internet of things for health care: A comprehensive survey. *IEEE Access, 3*, 678–708.
10. Balakrishna, S., & Thirumaran, M. (2020). Semantic interoperability in IoT and big data for health care: A collaborative approach. In *Handbook of data science approaches for biomedical engineering* (pp. 185–220). Cambridge, MA: Academic Press.
11. Laplante, P. A., & Laplante, N. L. (2015). A structured approach for describing healthcare applications for the Internet of Things. In *2015 IEEE 2nd World Forum on Internet of Things (WF-IoT)* (pp. 621–625). Milan, Italy.
12. Laplante, P. A., & Laplante, N. L. (2016). The internet of things in healthcare: Potential applications and challenges. *It Professional, 18*(3), 2–4.
13. Baker, S. B., Xiang, W., & Atkinson, I. (2017). Internet of things for smart healthcare: Technologies, challenges, and opportunities. *IEEE Access, 5*, 26521–26544.
14. Darshan, K. R., & Anandakumar, K. R. (2015). A comprehensive review on usage of Internet of Things (IoT) in healthcare system. In *2015 international conference on emerging research in electronics, computer science and technology* (pp. 132–136). Mandya, India.
15. Dias, D., & Paulo Silva Cunha, J. (2018). Wearable health devices – Vital sign monitoring, systems and technologies. *Sensors, 18*(8), 2414.
16. Gill, S. S., Tuli, S., Xu, M., Singh, I., Singh, K. V., Lindsay, D., et al. (2019). Transformative effects of IoT, Blockchain and Artificial Intelligence on cloud computing: Evolution, vision, trends and open challenges. *Internet of Things, 100118*, 1–26.
17. Lee, J., Hong, M., & Ryu, S. (2015). Sleep monitoring system using kinect sensor. *International Journal of Distributed Sensor Networks, 11*(10), 875371.
18. Manikandan, R., Patan, R., Gandomi, A. H., Sivanesan, P., & Kalyanaraman, H. (2020). Hash polynomial two factor decision tree using IoT for smart health care scheduling. *Expert Systems with Applications, 141*, 112924.
19. Mozaffari, N., Rezazadeh, J., Farahbakhsh, R., Yazdani, S., & Sandrasegaran, K. (2019). Practical fall detection based on IoT technologies: A survey. *Internet of Things, 100124*, 1–16.
20. Ukil, A., Bandyoapdhyay, S., Puri, C., & Pal, A. (2016). IoT healthcare analytics: The importance of anomaly detection. In *2016 IEEE 30th international conference on advanced information networking and applications* (pp. 994–997). Crans-Mortana, Switzerland.
21. Yacchirema, D., Sarabia-Jácome, D., Palau, C. E., & Esteve, M. (2018). System for monitoring and supporting the treatment of sleep apnea using IoT and big data. *Pervasive and Mobile Computing, 50*, 25–40.
22. Odell, M. (2010). Are early warning scores the only way to rapidly detect and manage deterioration? *Nursing Times, 106*(8), 24–26.
23. Weenk, M., Koeneman, M., van de Belt, T. H., Engelen, L. J., van Goor, H., & Bredie, S. J. (2019). Wireless and continuous monitoring of vital signs in patients at the general ward. *Resuscitation, 136*, 47–53.
24. Gabayan, G. Z., Gould, M. K., Weiss, R. E., Derose, S. F., Chiu, V. Y., & Sarkisian, C. A. (2017). Emergency department vital signs and outcomes after discharge. *Academic Emergency Medicine, 24*(7), 846–854.
25. Cretikos, M. A., Bellomo, R., Hillman, K., Chen, J., Finfer, S., & Flabouris, A. (2008). Respiratory rate: The neglected vital sign. *Medical Journal of Australia, 188*(11), 657–659.

26. Carreiro, S., Wittbold, K., Indic, P., Fang, H., Zhang, J., & Boyer, E. W. (2016). Wearable biosensors to detect physiologic change during opioid use. *Journal of Medical Toxicology, 12*(3), 255–262.
27. Gao, T., Greenspan, D., Welsh, M., Juang, R. R., & Alm, A. (2005). Vital signs monitoring and patient tracking over a wireless network. In *2005 IEEE engineering in medicine and biology 27th annual conference, Shanghai, China, 2005* (pp. 102–105).
28. Pimentel, M. A., Charlton, P. H., & Clifton, D. A. (2015). Probabilistic estimation of respiratory rate from wearable sensors. In *Wearable electronics sensors* (pp. 241–262). Cham: Springer.
29. Vsee. (2020). What is telemedicine?. https://vsee.com/what-is-telemedicine/#1. Visit on 30 Aug 2020.
30. Weinstein, R. S., Lopez, A. M., Joseph, B. A., Erps, K. A., Holcomb, M., Barker, G. P., & Krupinski, E. A. (2014). Telemedicine, telehealth, and mobile health applications that work: Opportunities and barriers. *The American Journal of Medicine, 127*(3), 183–187.
31. Armfield, N. R., & Donovan, T. (2016). Acute care telemedicine. In *The E-medicine, E-health, M-health, telemedicine, and telehealth handbook* (pp. 597–618). Boca Raton.
32. Johansson, T., & Wild, C. (2010). Telemedicine in acute stroke management: Systematic review. *International Journal of Technology Assessment in Health Care, 26*(2), 149–155.
33. Wallace, D. L., Jones, S. M., Milroy, C., & Pickford, M. A. (2008). Telemedicine for acute plastic surgical trauma and burns. *Journal of Plastic, Reconstructive & Aesthetic Surgery, 61*(1), 31–36.
34. Lieberman, J. (2008). How telemedicine is aiding prompt ECG diagnosis in primary care. *British Journal of Community Nursing, 13*(3), 123–126.
35. Lilly, C. M., & Thomas, E. J. (2010). Tele-ICU: Experience to date. *Journal of Intensive Care Medicine, 25*(1), 16–22.
36. Philips Healthcare. (2017). Philips healthcare whitepaper: Calculating the value of a Tele-ICU investment. https://www.usa.philips.com/healthcare/resources/landing/whatisteleicu. Visit on 30 Aug 2020.
37. Silverman, L. (2018). Interview with Lou Silverman, Chairman and CEO of Advanced ICU Care: The role of acute care telemedicine in hospitals. https://thejournalofmhealth.com/the-role-of-acute-care-telemedicine-in-hospitals/. Visit on 30 Aug 2020.
38. Khunlertkit, A., & Carayon, P. (2013). Contributions of tele-intensive care unit (Tele-ICU) technology to quality of care and patient safety. *Journal of Critical Care, 28*(3), 315–3e1.
39. Lilly, C. M., Cody, S., Zhao, H., Landry, K., Baker, S. P., McIlwaine, J., et al. (2011). Hospital mortality, length of stay, and preventable complications among critically ill patients before and after tele-ICU reengineering of critical care processes. *JAMA, 305*(21), 2175–2183.
40. Yoo, B. K., Kim, M., Sasaki, T., Melnikow, J., & Marcin, J. P. (2016). Economic evaluation of telemedicine for patients in ICUs. *Critical Care Medicine, 44*(2), 265–274.
41. Yoo, B. K., Kim, M., Sasaki, T., Hoch, J. S., & Marcin, J. P. (2018). Selected use of telemedicine in intensive care units based on severity of illness improves cost-effectiveness. *Telemedicine and e-Health, 24*(1), 21–36.
42. Shah, H. (2017). How IoT can help detect and control infectious disease outbreaks in real-time. https://www.idigitalhealth.com/news/how-internet-of-things-helps-detect-and-control-infectious-disease-outbreaks-in-realtime. Visit on 30 Aug 2020.
43. Wood, C. S., Thomas, M. R., Budd, J., Mashamba-Thompson, T. P., Herbst, K., Pillay, D., et al. (2019). Taking connected mobile-health diagnostics of infectious diseases to the field. *Nature, 566*(7745), 467–474.
44. Zhu, H., Podesva, P., Liu, X., Zhang, H., Teply, T., Xu, Y., et al. (2020). IoT PCR for pandemic disease detection and its spread monitoring. *Sensors and Actuators B: Chemical, 303*, 127098.
45. Sareen, S., Sood, S. K., & Gupta, S. K. (2017). Secure internet of things-based cloud framework to control zika virus outbreak. *International Journal of Technology Assessment in Health Care, 33*(1), 11–18.
46. Sood, S. K., & Mahajan, I. (2017). Wearable IoT sensor based healthcare system for identifying and controlling chikungunya virus. *Computers in Industry, 91*, 33–44.

47. Bai, L., Yang, D., Wang, X., Tong, L., Zhu, X., Bai, C., & Powell, C. A. (2020). Chinese experts' consensus on the Internet of Things-aided diagnosis and treatment of coronavirus disease 2019. *Clinical eHealth, 3*, 7–15.
48. Kaushalya, S. A. D. S., Kulawansa, K. A. D. T., & Firdhous, M. F. M. (2019). Internet of things for epidemic detection: A critical review. In *Advances in computer communication and computational sciences* (pp. 485–495). Springer, Berlin.
49. Deloitte. (2015). No appointment necessary: How the IoT and patient-generated data can unlock health care value. https://www2.deloitte.com/us/en/insights/focus/internet-of-things/iot-in-health-care-industry.html. Visit on 30 Aug 2020.
50. Blount, M., Batra, V. M., Capella, A. N., Ebling, M. R., Jerome, W. F., Martin, S. M., et al. (2007). Remote health-care monitoring using Personal Care Connect. *IBM Systems Journal, 46*(1), 95–113.
51. Cheng, H. T., & Zhuang, W. (2010). Bluetooth-enabled in-home patient monitoring system: Early detection of Alzheimer's disease. *IEEE Wireless Communications, 17*(1), 74–79.
52. Varatharajan, R., Manogaran, G., Priyan, M. K., & Sundarasekar, R. (2018). Wearable sensor devices for early detection of Alzheimer disease using dynamic time warping algorithm. *Cluster Computing, 21*(1), 681–690.
53. Al-khafajiy, M., Baker, T., Chalmers, C., Asim, M., Kolivand, H., Fahim, M., & Waraich, A. (2019). Remote health monitoring of elderly through wearable sensors. *Multimedia Tools and Applications, 78*(17), 24681–24706.
54. Faria, S. M., Fernandes, T. R., & Perdigoto, F. S. (2008). Mobile web server for elderly people monitoring. In *2008 IEEE international symposium on consumer electronics* (pp. 1–4). Las Vegas, USA.
55. Elfaki, A. O., & Alotaibi, M. (2018). The role of M-health applications in the fight against Alzheimer's: Current and future directions. *Mhealth, 4*(32), 1–13.
56. Gia, T. N., Ali, M., Dhaou, I. B., Rahmani, A. M., Westerlund, T., Liljeberg, P., & Tenhunen, H. (2017). IoT-based continuous glucose monitoring system: A feasibility study. *Procedia Computer Science, 109*, 327–334.
57. Katalenich, B., Shi, L., Liu, S., Shao, H., McDuffie, R., Carpio, G., et al. (2015). Evaluation of a remote monitoring system for diabetes control. *Clinical Therapeutics, 37*(6), 1216–1225.
58. Al-Taee, M. A., Al-Nuaimy, W., Al-Ataby, A., Muhsin, Z. J., & Abood, S. N. (2015, November). Mobile health platform for diabetes management based on the Internet-of-Things. In *2015 IEEE Jordan conference on applied electrical engineering and computing technologies (AEECT-2015)* (pp. 1–5). The Dead Sea, Jordan.
59. Bui, A. L., Horwich, T. B., & Fonarow, G. C. (2011). Epidemiology and risk profile of heart failure. *Nature Reviews Cardiology, 8*(1), 30.
60. Bashi, N., Karunanithi, M., Fatehi, F., Ding, H., & Walters, D. (2017). Remote monitoring of patients with heart failure: An overview of systematic reviews. *Journal of Medical Internet Research, 19*(1), e18.
61. Brahmbhatt, H. D., & Cowie, R. M. (2019). Remote management of heart failure: An overview of telemonitoring technologies. *Cardiac Failure Review, 5*(2), 86–92.
62. Pecchia, L., Melillo, P., & Bracale, M. (2010). Remote health monitoring of heart failure with data mining via CART method on HRV features. *IEEE Transactions on Biomedical Engineering, 58*(3), 800–804.
63. Yang, J., Xiao, W., Lu, H., & Barnawi, A. (2020). Wireless high-frequency NLOS monitoring system for heart disease combined with hospital and home. *Future Generation Computer Systems, 110*, 772–780.
64. Suh, M. K., Evangelista, L. S., Chen, V., Hong, W. S., Macbeth, J., Nahapetian, A., et al. (2010). WANDA B.: Weight and activity with blood pressure monitoring system for heart failure patients. In *2010 IEEE international symposium on "a world of wireless, mobile and multimedia networks"* (pp. 1–6). Montreal, QC, Canada.
65. Lan, M., Samy, L., Alshurafa, N., Suh, M. K., Ghasemzadeh, H., Macabasco-O'Connell, A., & Sarrafzadeh, M. (2012). Wanda: An end-to-end remote health monitoring and analytics system for heart failure patients. In *The conference on wireless health* (pp. 1–8). Bethesda, Maryland, USA.

66. Suh, M. K., Chen, C. A., Woodbridge, J., Tu, M. K., Kim, J. I., Nahapetian, A., et al. (2011). A remote patient monitoring system for congestive heart failure. *Journal of Medical Systems, 35*(5), 1165–1179.
67. Mahoney, E. L., & Mahoney, D. F. (2010). Acceptance of wearable technology by people with Alzheimer's disease: Issues and accommodations. *American Journal of Alzheimer's Disease & Other Dementias, 25*(6), 527–531.
68. Chen, X. A., Grossman, T., Wigdor, D. J., & Fitzmaurice, G. (2014). Duet: Exploring joint interactions on a smart phone and a smart watch. In *The SIGCHI conference on human factors in computing systems* (pp. 159–168). Toronto, Canada.
69. Reeder, B., & David, A. (2016). Health at hand: A systematic review of smart watch uses for health and wellness. *Journal of Biomedical Informatics, 63*, 269–276.
70. Lutze, R., & Waldhor, K. (2015). A smartwatch software architecture for health hazard handling for elderly people. In *2015 international conference on healthcare informatics* (pp. 356–361). Dallas, Texas, USA.
71. Bhattacharya, S., & Lane, N. D. (2016). From smart to deep: Robust activity recognition on smartwatches using deep learning. In *2016 IEEE international conference on pervasive computing and communication workshops* (pp. 1–6). Sydney, Australia.
72. Dibia, V. (2016). Foqus: A smartwatch application for individuals with adhd and mental health challenges. In *The 18th international ACM SIGACCESS conference on computers and accessibility* (pp. 311–312). Reno, Nevada, United States.
73. Pombo, N., & Garcia, N. M. (2016). ubiSleep: An ubiquitous sensor system for sleep monitoring. In *2016 IEEE 12th international conference on wireless and mobile computing, networking and communications* (pp. 1–4). New York, USA.
74. Sun, X., Qiu, L., Wu, Y., Tang, Y., & Cao, G. (2017). Sleepmonitor: Monitoring respiratory rate and body position during sleep using smartwatch. In: The ACM on interactive, mobile, wearable and ubiquitous technologies, 1(3): 1–22.
75. Chang, L., Lu, J., Wang, J., Chen, X., Fang, D., Tang, Z., et al. (2018). SleepGuard: Capturing rich sleep information using smartwatch sensing data. *The ACM on Interactive, Mobile, Wearable and Ubiquitous Technologies, 2*(3), 1–34.
76. Roomkham, S., Lovell, D., Cheung, J., & Perrin, D. (2018). Promises and challenges in the use of consumer-grade devices for sleep monitoring. *IEEE Reviews in Biomedical Engineering, 11*, 53–67.
77. Rosenberger, M. E., Buman, M. P., Haskell, W. L., McConnell, M. V., & Carstensen, L. L. (2016). 24 hours of sleep, sedentary behavior, and physical activity with nine wearable devices. *Medicine and Science in Sports and Exercise, 48*(3), 457.
78. Shen, C., Ho, B. J., & Srivastava, M. (2017). Milift: Efficient smartwatch-based workout tracking using automatic segmentation. *IEEE Transactions on Mobile Computing, 17*(7), 1609–1622.
79. Shahmohammadi, F., Hosseini, A., King, C. E., & Sarrafzadeh, M. (2017). Smartwatch based activity recognition using active learning. In *2017 IEEE/ACM international conference on connected health: Applications, systems and engineering technologies* (pp. 321–329). Philadelphia, Pennsylvania, USA.
80. Jiang, W., & Yin, Z. (2015). Human activity recognition using wearable sensors by deep convolutional neural networks. In *The 23rd ACM international conference on multimedia* (pp. 1307–1310). Brisbane, Australia.
81. Um, T. T., Babakeshizadeh, V., & Kulić, D. (2017). Exercise motion classification from large-scale wearable sensor data using convolutional neural networks. In *2017 IEEE/RSJ international conference on intelligent robots and systems* (pp. 2385–2390). Vancouver, Canada.
82. Kwon, M. C., & Choi, S. (2018). Recognition of daily human activity using an artificial neural network and smartwatch. *Wireless Communications and Mobile Computing, 2018*.

83. Hoilett, O. S., Twibell, A. M., Srivastava, R., & Linnes, J. C. (2018). Kick LL: A smartwatch for monitoring respiration and heart rate using photoplethysmography. In *2018 40th annual international conference of the IEEE engineering in medicine and biology society* (pp. 3821–3824). Honolulu, Hawaii, USA.
84. Dorri, A., Kanhere, S. S., Jurdak, R., & Gauravaram, P. (2017). Blockchain for IoT security and privacy: The case study of a smart home. In *2017 IEEE international conference on pervasive computing and communications workshops* (pp. 618–623). Kona, Big Island, HI, USA.
85. Bröring, A., Schmid, S., Schindhelm, C. K., Khelil, A., Käbisch, S., Kramer, D., et al. (2017). Enabling IoT ecosystems through platform interoperability. *IEEE Software, 34*(1), 54–61.
86. Alamri, A. (2018). Ontology middleware for integration of IoT healthcare information systems in EHR systems. *Computers, 7*(51), 1–15.
87. Brous, P., Janssen, M., & Herder, P. (2020). The dual effects of the Internet of Things (IoT): A systematic review of the benefits and risks of IoT adoption by organizations. *International Journal of Information Management, 51*, 101952.

Chapter 8
An Interactive Visiting System Using BLE Devices

Nuno Garrido, Carlos Serrão, and Bruno Coitos

Abstract This chapter presents a use case based on the development of an interactive, integrated and adaptable visiting system for complex buildings and surrounding grounds (smart places). The system features a mobile application that allows the user to access information from several smart places in a single application and an indoor location and tracking system that infers the user location during the smart place visit. The system calculates the tracking and location of the user based on the positioning of neighbouring BLE devices sensed via Bluetooth on the user's mobile device. The approximate location, behaviour and interests and hence the visiting profile of each user can be inferred by the signals from multiple beacons installed on the building at specific predefined positions. The system also integrates a back-end content management system to allow the creation and management of smart places information and supports information import from BIM tools.

Keywords Indoor Location System · Smart places · BLE · Beacon · BIM

8.1 Introduction

To satisfy the needs of an increasing number of people living or working in most cities, there is a growing urge for sizeable and more complex buildings, such as

N. Garrido (✉)
Instituto de Telecomunicações (IT-IUL), Lisbon, Portugal
e-mail: nuno.garrido@iscte-iul.pt

C. Serrão
Information Sciences, Technologies and Architecture Research Center (ISTAR-IUL), Lisbon, Portugal
e-mail: carlos.serrao@iscte-iul.pt

B. Coitos
Instituto Universitário de Lisboa (ISCTE-IUL), Lisbon, Portugal
e-mail: bmfcc@iscte-iul.pt

© Springer Nature Switzerland AG 2021
F. P. García Márquez, B. Lev (eds.), *Internet of Things*, International Series in Operations Research & Management Science 305,
https://doi.org/10.1007/978-3-030-70478-0_8

hospitals, shopping malls, museums and sports facilities, amongst others [1]. This need creates a challenge for the managers of these buildings or sites since it is necessary to provide relevant information to the users/visitors. Frequently this is done by putting guiding plates, which are a minimal way to realise this task. When considering larger and complex buildings such as hospitals or museums, it is common for users to get lost or have trouble finding their way around and requiring additional information in multiple formats and languages.

Mobile devices have become ubiquitous to everyone transforming themselves into interaction gateways between the digital and the real world [2]. Therefore, mobile devices can be the right approach for this quest and an excellent way to display information about multiple buildings or sites. Furthermore, this can be achieved in a single application, removing the need for multiple applications with different layouts and behaviours to be installed on the end-user's mobile device reducing discomfort and usability problems to the user.

Recently, there has been an increase on the number of available low-cost devices (both sensors and actuators) that have the capability to communicate through several networks and with each other. These devices, commonly known as IoT, are taking advantages of multiple protocols such as Wi-Fi, LoRA, Bluetooth and others to increase their communication and integration. Therefore, IoT has found multiple application domains that range from industrial automation, smart home development, health management, smart city control and management and many more. The potential for the application of IoT keeps growing.

Taking this into consideration, it was decided to propose and develop an integrated system consisting of two different components: (a) a smart and interactive mobile guiding application (named MOG (My Own Guide)), that uses an Indoor Location System (ILS) based on information provided by Bluetooth Low Energy (BLE) beacons and (b) a content management system (CMS) module, which gives the building managers a tool to manage the information displayed to the users efficiently. Users using a specific mobile application on their devices help gather valuable information about its interaction with the building or site.

Considering that the referred buildings or spaces can each have several zones and points of interest, loading all this data into the prototype using only a CMS is not feasible since it is hugely time-consuming. Therefore, it was an opportunity to coordinate our prototype with a tool that could have this information or parts of it, already configured. Currently, most modern buildings go through a Building Information Modelling (BIM) process, where a 3D model of the building or site is created with valuable information about the building, spaces of the building, such as rooms, and other information. Therefore, it was decided to provide an efficient and fast way for the smart place staff to upload files extracted from the BIM tools. This mechanism can speed up the data creation process since by using the BIM model, the building model can include and define the information needed by our prototype, such as the interest zones, groups of interest points and interest points, as well as the location of the beacons in the building, and then upload the files to the CMS which in turn can map this information to the objects defined in the data model.

8.2 Related Work

In the course of our research, the focus was on approaches that aimed at the guidance of users inside complex buildings, especially shopping malls and museums and preferably those featuring BIM. One approach where BIM models are used is [3]; here a BIM tool is used to define emergency paths of buildings that can be extracted and then imported into a firefighter's guidance system. This system includes a mobile application in coordination with an ILS that combines the use of RFID, UWB and WLAN technologies, which allows support to guiding them during emergencies, whenever the intervention of firefighters is required, through the emergency paths defined in the BIM tool. The system also contains a back-office tool, where firefighters outside the building can also see their location in real time inside the building.

In [4], the authors developed a guiding system for museum visitors. In this system, the visitors install a mobile application and answer a couple of questions for profiling purposes that generate a QR code. When the visitor arrives at the museum, museum workers scan the QR code generated by the application and assign visitors a wearable device that must remain with the visitor throughout the visit. This wearable device captures what the visitor is seeing and combines this information with the location of the visitor that is inferred through the sensing of BLE devices signals, allowing the system to identify the piece of art being observed, so that the mobile application can provide additional relevant information for that art piece. This approach is expensive since the museums must guarantee the maintenance and availability of the wearable devices for each visitor, which is hardly practical and affordable.

Another approach focused on enhancing museum visits is [5], where the authors propose the combined use of BLE devices and Wi-Fi areas. In this solution, the museum workers have a web-based tool to manage the information about each piece of art. When the visitor is at the museum, his position is inferred using BLE's signals and then processed taking advantage of Wi-Fi areas data. The disadvantage of this system is that it only supports the Italian language.

As mentioned in the previous section, it is more comfortable and preferable for the users to have information about several buildings or sites in a single mobile application. In this work [6], the authors have not developed the proposed system, but the concept is to combine information from a group of museums that belongs to the same district, namely, Jongno district in South Korea since the authors believe this approach could contribute to the attraction of more visitors to the museums.

Another approach found is [7] where the authors developed a system used to track and guide users on a university campus. BIM was used to define the position of each BLE device and set other additional information about the building (e.g. closest stairs). This information is loaded into the system and read by an algorithm used in the mobile application to calculate the shortest path between two points. Initially, the user selects the desired destination. The mobile application calculates the nearest path inside the building and updates it as long as the user is moving; this is done taking into consideration the BLE signals intercepted to infer his current location in the building.

Several other studies [8–10] were addressed in the context of smart places for large buildings and sites, e.g. offices, zoos and museums, where similar solutions were studied some including the use of BLE devices or a content management system.

From related works [3–6], it was considered the advantages and disadvantages of each approach during the design and evaluation of the proposed prototype. The main focuses of our design were BLE sensing and a simple and intelligent information management system for building managers.

8.3 Prototype Architecture

Considering the different requirements identified for indoor intelligent guidance systems and the review on the state-of-the-art systems, it was possible to detect the need for a more open and generic system that could be easily adapted to multiple different indoor guidance scenarios, at a lower cost. The proposed solution offers an end-to-end framework, for smart building managers, to create and distribute specific content to visitors, tailor visiting experiences, customise the "in-building" navigation and parametrise the end-user's smartphone application.

The prototype architecture depicted in Fig. 8.1 was designed and developed to give smart building managers a fast and effective way to provide information to the building users without the need to install a specific application for each building and bring a more practical and comfortable solution that allows access to information about several buildings in a single mobile application. The system is composed of several distributed components that are described individually: two databases that interact with a content management system, a mobile application and a set of BLE physical devices.

The implementation of the described prototype required the usage of a server to host the content management system. This server was deployed on a Linux machine (Intel Core i3 processor, 16 GB RAM, 1 TB HDD), running the latest version of Ubuntu Server 18.04, with an installation of the Apache HTTP Server 2.4, the MariaDB 10.4.x database management server and the PHP 7.x development stack. All of these components are open-source software.

The mobile application was developed as an Android native Java-based application, running on all Android devices that support at least API level 23 (Android 6.0 Marshmallow). For the development of the application, it was used the Android Studio IDE. The back end of the prototype was implemented on Firebase using free accounts.

The following sections of the chapter present the different components of the developed system prototype. We start by describing the databases that are used by the system followed by an overview of the BIM component that might be used to import building indoor location information to the system. After this, the content

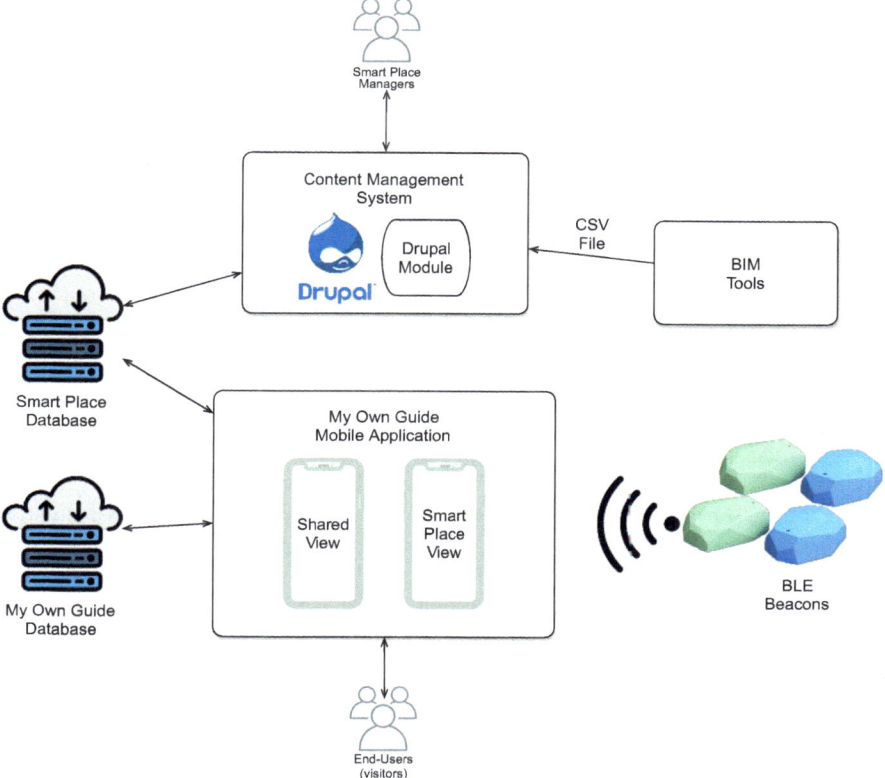

Fig. 8.1 Prototype architecture

management system used to manage the smart place content is presented. Finally, the end-users' mobile application is presented.

8.3.1 Databases

To support all the information on the system prototype, it was defined in one central database that is the MOG database (MD) and also a database for each smart place that was named smart place database (SPD). This design choice was made to provide smart place managers with total control over their database and of the contents that will be presented to the visiting users. The MD contains general information about a new smart place existence on the global system (pointing the system to the specific SPD whenever a smart place is selected), while the SPD contains information about one specific smart place. The smart place managers entirely manage the SPD, while the MOG system administrators manage the MD.

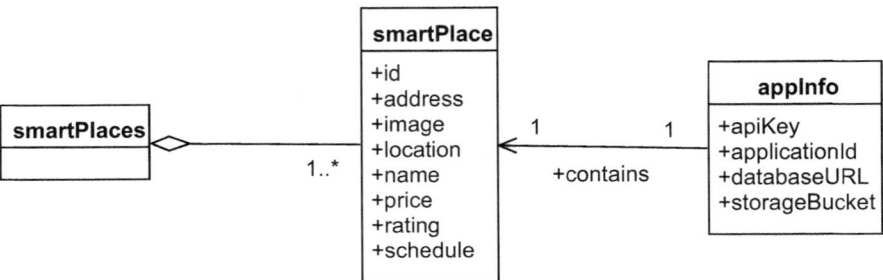

Fig. 8.2 MOG database model (MD)

Taking into consideration the agility of the prototype development, Firebase [11] was the platform selected to hold the online databases. Firebase allows fast development since it provides all the needed services and a simple way to connect to different databases. Moreover, Firebase allows easy system scalability and adaptability, through the usage of non-relational databases where JSON-formatted documents and collections are used to represent and manage the data. Although the selection is made for the prototype development, the system can quickly adapt to support other types of databases or external data-related special-purpose APIs.

MD is used to store general-purpose, high-level information about the featured smart places but, most importantly, to store information about each smart place database in order to establish an interactive connection to them as depicted in Fig. 8.2.

For SPD it was implemented an internationalisation mechanism in the database. In order to achieve that, it was created a specific "language" object that allows each smart place manager to define the different content languages that are available to the mobile application end-users. For each of the supported languages, the smart place managers will need to provide the appropriate content in the different identified languages. The process is specific of the smart place managers because some smart places may have content in multiple languages, while others have just a unique language.

Although each SPD is managed separately and independently, it must be compliant with the global data model, and the data model must be flexible to be easily adapted to the different needs of each smart place. This global data model is composed of the following three different object types to identify different spaces: "interest zones," "groups of interest points" and "interest points" as depicted in Fig. 8.3.

Hence, three possible ways for smart places to represent their spaces were created in order to have a more flexible prototype. These spaces can be represented through Interest Zones, groups of interest points and interest points. Those represent the most relevant information for the smartphone application users and can be displayed in a set of languages defined by each smart place. These spaces are made available in the map screen of the application. Each of these spaces must contain information

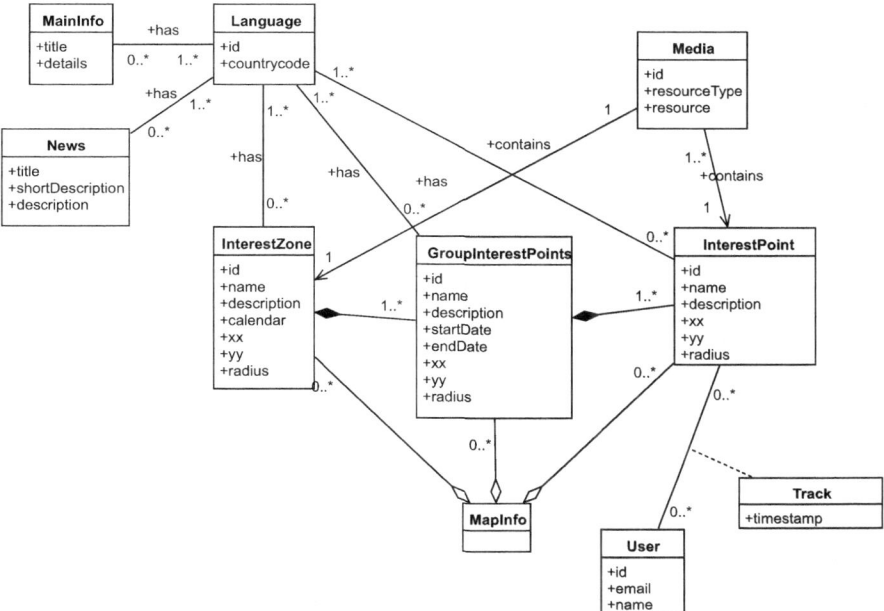

Fig. 8.3 Smart place data model (SPD)

about its location inside the building. Smart place managers must fill the mapping information ("MapInfo") for that specific space, detailing the pixel coordinates and radius which will be used to draw the point of interest on the map as depicted in Fig. 8.3. This information about the indoor location of each space can be either manually specified or imported into our prototype database using the information extracted from the BIM tools.

The "MainInfo" object contains the information that is displayed on the main screen of the application, and the "News" object is presented as a list with a title and short description with the possibility to view the entire news content as shown in Fig. 8.3.

The SPD model also includes a "Track" object. The purpose of this object is to record the different "InterestPoints," "GroupInterestPoints" or "InterestZones" visited by the "User." This object records the timestamp (date and time) of the visit of the user. The goal is to allow smart place managers to be able to learn and understand how visitors interact with the different interest points during their visit.

The Mobile Application section presents more details about the mobile application user interface that corresponds to each of the objects that are displayed to the end-user.

8.3.2 Building Information Modelling (BIM)

Building Information Modelling (BIM) is a collaborative process that consists of creating a 3D model of a building providing better building project management since it allows to have a "document management, coordination and simulation during the entire lifecycle of a project" [12]. In this process, it is possible to complement the model with additional information about the building, spaces of the building, such as rooms, and any other information.

The system provided to the building managers the possibility to load information extracted from a BIM tool directly into our prototype, since this modelling process is growing, and most modern buildings construction is based on it. This functionality results in a reduction of the time spent creating information about each interest zone, group of interest points and points of interest, since it is also necessary to define, for each of them, the position in the map for the prototype making it possible to the mobile users to see their location. In order to achieve these objectives, it is necessary to define the following information:

- spaceId – Identifier of the space.
- name – Name of the space that will appear in the mobile application,
- centerCoordinates – The coordinates allowing to draw in the map the visited spaces. This information must have the structure – (xx, yy, radius).
- datamodelObject – Identifies which object of the data model is. The allowed values are "interestZone," "interestGroup" and "interestPoint."
- childObjects – List of child objects taking into consideration the hierarchy defined in the data model.

In Fig. 8.4, an example of information that can be extracted from a BIM tool in a CSV file is presented.

Hence, using this model it is possible to define each prototype object information and its building location and also extract the building images, that can, in turn, be used in the mobile application on the map screen.

8.3.3 Content Management System (CMS)

The primary purpose of the developed solution was to offer a simple and open framework for smart place managers to create and manage digital content in

```
spaceId,name,centerCoordinates,datamodelObject,childObjects
dolphins,Dolphin Presentation,(231;307;127),interestZone,
mammals,Mammals,,interestGroup,[africanElephant,commonSeal]
africanElephant,African Elephant,(111;327;50),interestPoint,
commonSeal,Common Seal,(367;440;20),interestPoint,
```

Fig. 8.4 Extracted information from BIM tool

multiple formats and languages to offer to smart place visitors with geo-referenced context. Therefore, in order to offer an end-to-end solution to accomplish this goal, the framework involved the development of a content management system (CMS) component. The CMS that was developed for this prototype has the objective of providing smart place managers with a way to easily access and manipulate the data that is stored in their database.

The CMS also guarantees that all the data stored in the database has the correct format and structure to feed the mobile application. In order to ensure the prototype openness and affordability, the latest version of the Drupal (version 8) open-source CMS was selected, due to its customisability and adaptability to multiple scenarios as well as a large number of functionalities and broad community support. Selecting Drupal as our CMS, a specific Drupal module was developed that can be installed in any existing compatible Drupal web application. This module will create a new menu entry on the web application that will allow the staff to import the data from BIM solutions, configure the available languages, manage general information of the smart place, create and manage zones of interest, groups of interest points and each of the interest points and also manage the relevant news to be sent to the user.

For these kinds of smart places, one of the most important information is how the users are interacting, and it is here, in the CMS, that is possible to visualise some statistical information about this interaction, such as the number of users that entered a zone of interest, the most visited zones and points of interest, the total number of users that entered the smart place and much other detailed information.

Therefore, using the CMS, the entity responsible for the management of the content, in the new tab of the site, has access to a webpage where several options are displayed. One of them is "Manage Application Contents" that allows the manager to select the object and language of the desired information. Moreover, in turn, a displayed list of objects taking into account the options selected (Fig. 8.5) shows a list of interest points with English as the default selected language.

This provides a quick and easy way to access each object of the list. Simply clicking on the "View" operation on the list will open a new webpage with more details about the specific point of interest where "Edit" and "Delete" options are also available (as depicted on Fig. 8.6), and therefore the CMS contents can be easily accessed, edited and updated.

The CMS part of the prototype allows a reasonably natural manner for the smart place managers to continuously upgrade and update the data on the system that will

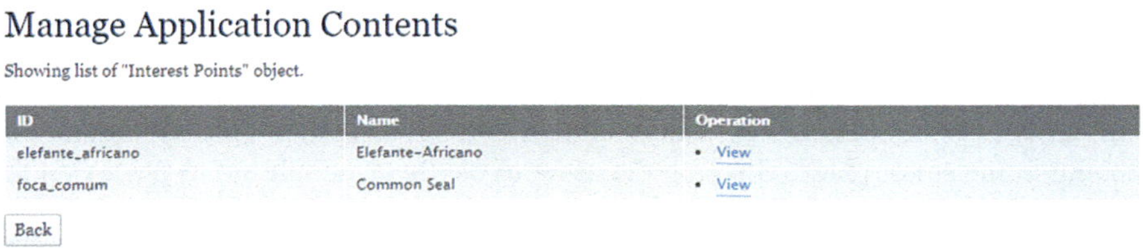

Manage Application Contents

Showing list of "Interest Points" object.

ID	Name	Operation
elefante_africano	Elefante–Africano	• View
foca_comum	Common Seal	• View

Back

Fig. 8.5 List of interest points

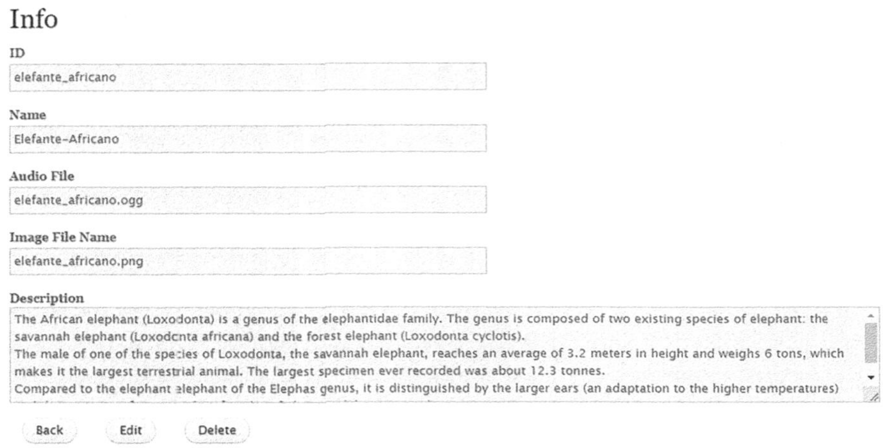

Info

ID

| elefante_africano |

Name

| Elefante-Africano |

Audio File

| elefante_africano.ogg |

Image File Name

| elefante_africano.png |

Description

The African elephant (Loxodonta) is a genus of the elephantidae family. The genus is composed of two existing species of elephant: the savannah elephant (Loxodonta africana) and the forest elephant (Loxodonta cyclotis).
The male of one of the species of Loxodonta, the savannah elephant, reaches an average of 3.2 meters in height and weighs 6 tons, which makes it the largest terrestrial animal. The largest specimen ever recorded was about 12.3 tonnes.
Compared to the elephant elephant of the Elephas genus, it is distinguished by the larger ears (an adaptation to the higher temperatures)

Back   Edit   Delete

Fig. 8.6 Interest point info

be presented to the smart place visitors. The solution will help reduce the burden and cost of smart place data maintenance.

8.3.4   Mobile Application

The smart places visitors access the contextual information provided about the place using a mobile smartphone application. The mobile application scans for existing nearby BLE devices signals in order to guarantee that the users will always have access to relevant information based on their location within the smart place. In order for this system to work, each user must grant the appropriate permissions and enable access to the device via Bluetooth connection and to location information on their mobile device. This will enable the application to be able to read the BLE signals, issue notifications and access the smart place information, obtained remotely from the CMS. In order to facilitate access to a more significant number of users, it was developed the MOG mobile application for the Android system.

The system is designed so that it allows the visitor to access information about a set of smart places in a single mobile application. The mobile application is split into two different views: Shared View that displays information managed in the MOG database and the Smart Place View that is managed by the staff of each of the existing smart places. The users can access the Shared View without the need of being in the smart place, allowing the users to list the available smart places on the application and to preview the content of a specific smart place before its visit.

The mobile application welcome screen (Fig. 8.7) displays the Shared View and is connected to the MOG database (MD). It has the general information about

Fig. 8.7 Welcome screen

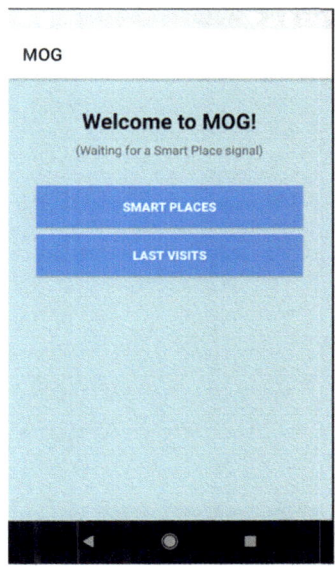

each smart place that is available in the system and the option to see a full list of the available smart places or the user's past visits. The mobile application offers the possibility for the user to select one available smart place from the list or automatically, based on the user location (if available), present contextual information about the smart place where the user is located.

If the user selects the "Smart Places" option, the mobile application shows a list of available smart places in the system with their schedule and street address that can be used to plan his route (from its current geolocation). Figure 8.8 shows a list of two example smart places used to demonstrate this prototype: one is the national natural history museum (MUNHAC), and the other is the city zoo (Jardim Zoológico de Lisboa).

When a specific smart place is selected, the application displays more information about the site, namely, the price (if any), schedule, address, public rating in the system and the personal rating that the user gave to this place, as depicted on Fig. 8.9. This screen includes the option to "See Location" that directs the visitor to the street address using Google Maps. Another option is to select the "App" button that directs the application to the Smart Place View (the specific app for the selected smart place).

The Smart Place View allows the user to access the smart place database of the chosen smart place. In this view, the user has access to all the information provided by the smart place managers through the CMS.

When a user enters for the first time in this view for a specific smart place, he will be redirected to a screen where he can choose from one of the available languages in that smart place (by default, the application will use the base language of the mobile user device). After the user defines the language, the application displays

Fig. 8.8 Smart place list

Fig. 8.9 Smart place info

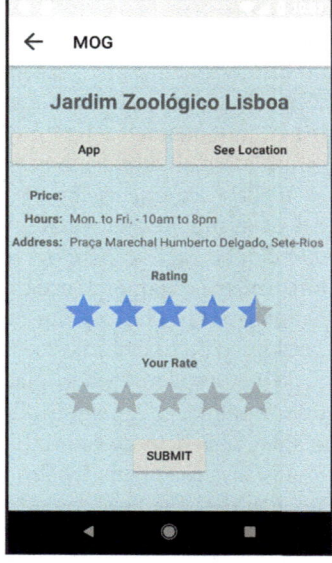

the primary information of that smart place that can be the history, some facts or any other information as shown in Fig. 8.10.

In this view, the user can also check the smart place map and the news about the smart place as depicted in Fig. 8.11. The news is listed containing the title and a short description, but if the user wishes to get more details, he can select specific news on the list, and all the detailed information will be displayed.

Fig. 8.10 Smart place main info

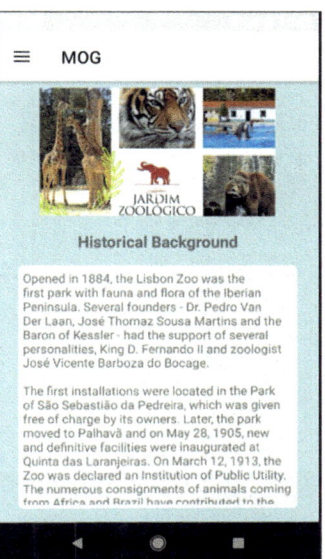

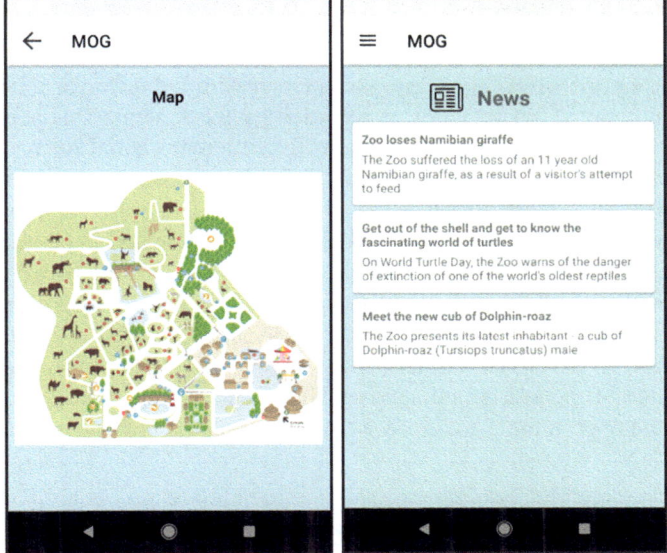

Fig. 8.11 Smart place map and news

The remaining information, such as the interest points, group of interest points and interest zones will only be available when the user intercepts a BLE signal. When this occurs, the user receives a notification, and after clicking on it, it will

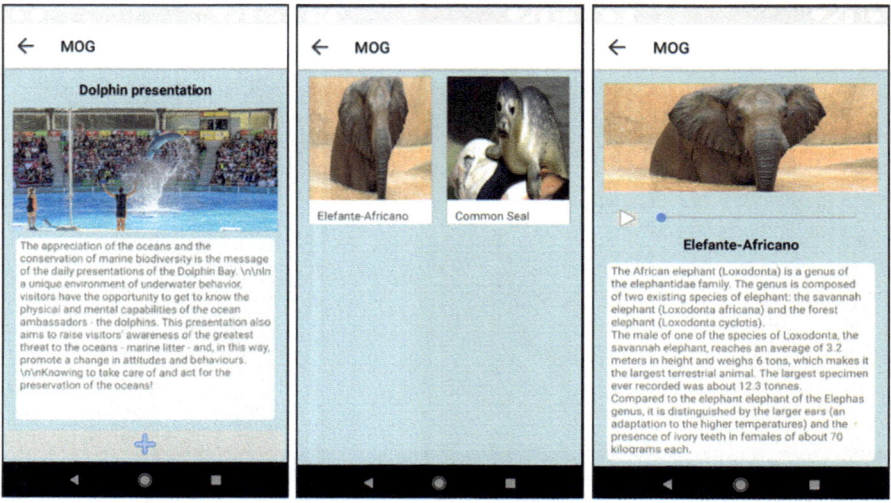

Fig. 8.12 Interest zone, group of interest points and interest point screens

open the mobile application in a screen showing the desired information as shown in Fig. 8.12.

While using the MOG application to interact with the different interest points, information about this interaction is recorded by the system. This action enables the collection of data from the user about the different visited InterestPoints and InterestZones as well as some additional information, such as the date and time of the visit, the visit duration and, in some cases, also the user opinion about the visited object or areas as well. The collected data is presented in an integrated and anonymised way to the smart place managers as well as some analytical information, such as smart place heat maps (indicating the most visited areas) and the most common routes the users follow inside the smart place.

This tracking information is useful for smart place managers to have a better understanding of the user's interaction with the smart place and identify potential problems and opportunities to improve their smart places management.

8.3.5 BLE Devices

Bluetooth Low Energy (BLE) devices [13] on the system will allow the users to receive push notifications and be redirected in the mobile application to the screen with relevant information considering his indoor location. This mechanism allows the creation of a more interactive and immersive environment that will enhance the visiting experience for the user.

The BLE devices used in this prototype are Proximity Beacons from Estimote [14]. These beacons take advantage of their own Proximity SDK [15] for the development of the mobile application. The Proximity Beacon supports Bluetooth 5.0, has a 5-year battery maximum time duration, a range of 100 meters and supports multiple programming languages such as Java or Swift. There are other multiple options for BLE beacons, but for this specific prototype, this specific beacon supplier was selected. The Proximity SDK allows the definition of multiple beacon attachments, which are represented in a "key-value" pair format, allowing us to get the values in the mobile application when an event is triggered. Besides that, the SDK provides an "onEnter" event that is triggered when the mobile device enters in range of a beacon signal, that we opted on using in order to provide relevant information based on the space that the end-user is entering.

As it was previously mentioned, in order to have a flexible system, three possible spaces were created: the interest zones, group of interest points and interest points. Therefore, each BLE device must have an attachment to identify how it is used by our prototype, thus avoiding reading information from other beacon networks that may already exist in the same space. Figure 8.13 depicts a set of multiple beacons in a smart place with several triggering actions.

The beacon signals are captured by the mobile application that accesses the MOG database and, based on the smart place identifier, gets the information needed to connect to the corresponding smart place database (SPD). After that, the mobile application uses it to connect and get the information of the specific location that the BLE device represents in order to display the relevant information to the user.

In the context of other types of smart places like museums, such as the natural history museum, the beacons should be distributed amongst the facilities according to the interest areas or interest points. In this case, the beacons can identify one specific part of an exhibition, a showroom or one interesting item.

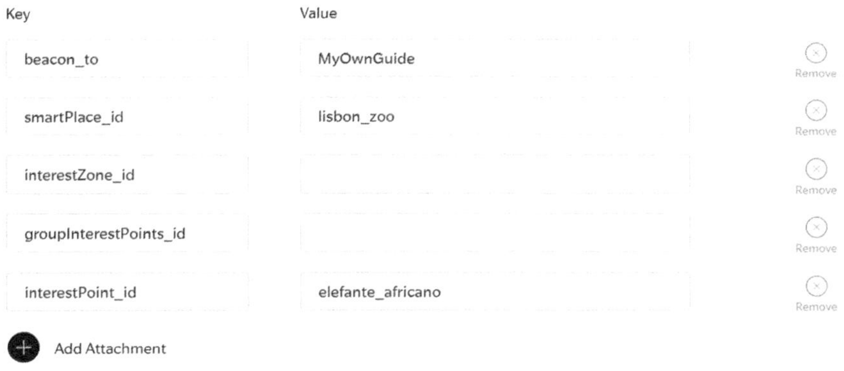

Fig. 8.13 Beacon attachments

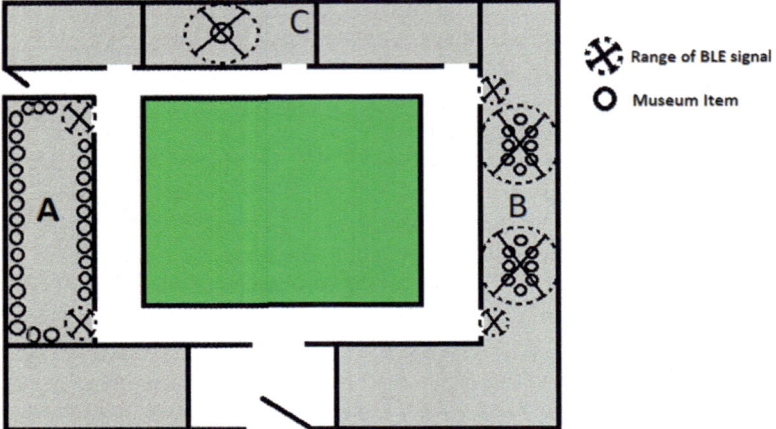

Fig. 8.14 Beacon placement example

Figure 8.14 shows an example of the indoor placement of beacons that allows the visitor to receive and click in notifications when entering rooms or simply see a list of items that are close to him.

8.4 System Comparison and Discussion

As mentioned, previously, it was possible to find some relevant approaches to respond to the needs of complex buildings, namely, those related to guidance and contextualised information for their users/visitors.

In this section, it is provided a comparison between some of these available approaches and the prototype described and implemented. First, in the related work section, we mentioned solution [3] that uses BIM to define emergency paths of a building, and then this information can be imported to a system and feed a mobile application that can be used by firefighters in rescue missions. This approach is not aimed at enhancing the guidance of building visitors or users, but the result is similar; this means, the resulting system has a mobile application that can guide users, based on BLE devices signal, taking into account information defined in a BIM.

The second and third works mentioned as [4, 5] are both aimed at enhancing the visiting experience of museum visitors. In [4], the approach has some functionalities, like communication to social networks in order to share their experience, that our approach does not. However, this solution is complex and can be too expensive for most museums, while our system was designed and developed aimed at being affordable and straightforward. The solution proposed in [5] is simpler, but the users

Table 8.1 Comparison between the different proposed solutions

	MOG	[3]	[4]	[5]	[6]
Centralised app	✓	–	–	–	✓
Multi-language	✓	–	–	–	?
Simple and cheap	✓	✓	–	✓	?
Indoor Location System	✓	✓	✓	✓	?

can only see the information in Italian which is a disadvantage, especially if the sites or buildings have foreign, non-native language-speaking visitors.

One of the main differences of our prototype is the use of a single centralised mobile application for different smart places; that can be sites, buildings or any other space. It is our understanding that this approach brings further benefits to the final users since they can plan and make the most of their visits without the need to install multiple different applications (one per smart place visited). This concept of centralisation was already mentioned in [6], but in this case, the authors proposed the development of a centralised system limited to a geographical area, which was not developed, and hence makes a comparison between the technologies impossible (Table 8.1).

In terms of costs, the proposed approach presents, at its core, serious cost reductions. First of all, it is mostly centred on open-source software, both in terms of the support infrastructure and also the developed components (the CMS is based on Drupal). The mobile application is developed in Android, and all of its configuration is made through the CMS. The back-end database for the prototype is currently based on Firebase, which is not free. However, there are two options: either support the payment of the Firebase account (after the free account expires) or use the internal API, that is currently being developed as an alternative to Firebase. The BLE beacons that we are using in out prototype are the Estimote Proximity Beacons that costs 99 USD per four beacons. Although, these beacons are used in our prototype, other less expensive beacons may be selected as well (currently there are other options that cost as low as 6 USD per beacon).

8.5 Conclusions and Future Work

Throughout this chapter, it was presented the design and development of an intelligent visiting system prototype that combines components from BIM systems with a content management system and a mobile application. All of those components are complemented with BLE devices to provide smart and interactive information to mobile application users, based on their location and visiting context. The system also provides valuable management information to the smart place managers allowing them to understand better and improve the users visiting experience.

This prototype is designed to offer complex buildings staff an appealing and interactive tool to provide information to their users/visitors while keeping it affordable and straightforward. Since different buildings have different needs, the prototype database has been designed to meet diverse requirements and to be easily adapted to each building or user profile.

The CMS based on a special-purpose developed Drupal module that can be installed in any Drupal web application allows the building staff to manage the data displayed to the users with the option to upload data extracted from a BIM tool. This module also provides vital analytical information about the interaction of the users with the smart place.

The prototype architecture was designed aimed to allow mobile application users to access information, in a standard interface for several buildings without the need to install multiple applications. The tracking capabilities of the system allow smart place managers to comprehend the way the visitors navigate through their spaces and capture relevant analytical data about visitor routes and most visited areas. This analytical data is absolutely crucial for better management decisions and space location improvements.

In order to test the developed system prototype, it was considered two specific use cases (the city zoo and a museum) that have different characteristics. The first one is a broader space, with a mix of open and closed spaces, while the second one has a smaller dimension and is entirely composed of indoor spaces. The heterogeneity of the selected use cases helped proof the openness and adaptability capabilities of the developed system.

The team is continuously working to improve the prototype and its functionalities. An area of improvement refers to the analysis of the user tracking information and the design of information dashboards that are presented to the smart place managers through the CMS. Another vital area of improvement is on the personalisation of the MOG smartphone app that will need to allow better specific customisation (mostly in terms of design) according to the smart place specificities.

References

1. 68% of the world population projected to live in urban areas by 2050, says UN | UN DESA | United Nations Department of Economic and Social Affairs. https://www.un.org/development/desa/en/news/population/2018-revision-of-world-urbanization-prospects.html. Accessed 12 June 2020.
2. Mobile devices a necessity in today's business world – TrackVia blog. https://trackvia.com/blog/infographics/mobile-devices-are-a-necessity-in-todays-business-world/. Accessed 12 June 2020.
3. Rueppel, U., & Stuebbe, K. M. (2008). BIM-based indoor-emergency-navigation-system for complex buildings. *Tsinghua Science and Technology, 13*(SUPPL. 1), 362–367. https://doi.org/10.1016/S1007-0214(08)70175-5.
4. Alletto, S., et al. (2016). An indoor location-aware system for an IoT-based smart museum. *IEEE Internet of Things Journal, 3*(2), 244–253. https://doi.org/10.1109/JIOT.2015.2506258.
5. Chianese, A., & Piccialli, F. (2014). Designing a smart museum: When cultural heritage joins IoT. In *Proceedings – 2014 8th International Conference on Next Generation Mobile Applications, Services and Technologies, NGMAST 2014*, pp. 300–306, https://doi.org/10.1109/NGMAST.2014.21.

6. Bae, E. S., Im, D. U., & Lee, S. Y. (2013). Smart museum based on regional unified app. *International Journal of Software Engineering and Its Applications, 7*(4), 157–166.
7. Ferreira, J., Resende, R., & Martinho, S. (2018). Beacons and BIM models for indoor guidance and location. *Sensors, 18*(12), 4374. https://doi.org/10.3390/s18124374.
8. Choi, M., Park, W. K., & Lee, I. (2015). Smart office energy management system using bluetooth low energy based beacons and a mobile app. In *2015 IEEE International Conference on Consumer Electronics, ICCE 2015*, pp. 501–502, https://doi.org/10.1109/ICCE.2015.7066499.
9. Corna, A., Fontana, L., Nacci, A. A., & Sciuto, D. (2015). Occupancy detection via iBeacon on Android devices for smart building management. *Proceedings -Design, Automation and Test in Europe, DATE, 2015-April*, 629–632. https://doi.org/10.7873/date.2015.0753.
10. Ishida, T., Shinotsuka, Y., Iyobe, M., Uchida, N., Sugita, K., & Shibata, Y. (2016). Development of a zoo walk navigation system using the positional measurement technology and the wireless communication technology. *Journal of Internet Services and Information Security, 6*(4), 65–84.
11. Firebase. https://firebase.google.com/. Accessed 12 June 2020.
12. Benefits of BIM | Building Information Modeling | Autodesk. https://www.autodesk.com/solutions/bim/benefits-of-bim. Accessed 12 June 2020.
13. What are beacons? – Kontakt.ioKontakt.io. https://kontakt.io/beacon-basics/what-is-a-beacon/. Accessed 12 June 2020.
14. Estimote – Experts in location and proximity solutions. https://estimote.com/. Accessed 12 June 2020.
15. Why should I use Proximity SDK? What are the benefits? – Estimote Community Portal. https://community.estimote.com/hc/en-us/articles/204100866-Why-should-I-use-Proximity-SDK-What-are-the-benefits-. Accessed 12 June 2020.

Chapter 9
Systematic Market and Asset Liquidity Risk Processes for Machine Learning: Robust Modeling Algorithms for Multiple-Assets Portfolios

Mazin A. M. Al Janabi

Abstract This chapter presents contemporary machine learning techniques for the computation of market and asset liquidity risk for multiple-assets portfolios. Furthermore, this research focuses on the theoretical aspects of asset liquidity risk and presents two critically robust machine learning processes to measuring the market liquidity risk for trading securities as well as for asset management objectives. To that end, this chapter extends research literature related to the computation of market and asset liquidity risks by providing generalized theoretical modeling algorithms that can assess both market and liquidity risks and integrate both risks into multiple-assets portfolio settings. The robust modeling algorithms can have practical applications for multiple-securities portfolios and can have many uses and application in financial markets, particularly in light of the 2007–2009 global financial meltdown in issues related to machine learning for the policymaking process and machine learning techniques for the Internet of Things (IoT) data analytics. In addition, risk assessment algorithms can aid in advancing risk management practices and have important applications for financial technology (FinTech), artificial intelligence, and machine learning in big data environments.

Keywords Artificial intelligence · Al Janabi model · Economic capital · Emerging markets · Financial engineering · Financial risk management · Financial markets · Internet of Things (IoT) · Liquidity risk · Machine learning · Portfolio management · Liquidity-Adjusted Value at Risk

M. A. M. Al Janabi (✉)
Tecnologico de Monterrey, EGADE Business School, Mexico City, Mexico
e-mail: mazin.aljanabi@tec.mx

© Springer Nature Switzerland AG 2021
F. P. García Márquez, B. Lev (eds.), *Internet of Things*, International Series in
Operations Research & Management Science 305,
https://doi.org/10.1007/978-3-030-70478-0_9

9.1 Introduction and Overview

The 2007–2009 global financial crunch has triggered additional industry demands for superior portfolio optimization algorithms besides contemporary risk management techniques and greater computational capabilities. To that end, machine learning technologies for the policymaking process and machine learning techniques for the Internet of Things (IoT) data analytics offer renewed prospects to address these challenges. As such, there is a rising weight of machine learning techniques in multi-assets portfolio optimization and modern risk management applications, with lots of key practical solutions currently put into operation and many more robust techniques being explored.

Machine learning for financial applications and the policymaking process sits at the crossroads of many growing and established disciplines. Since its earliest days, machine learning has taken advantage of robust optimization techniques and structured modeling algorithms for industrial applications in portfolio management and risk identification processes. Likewise, robust optimization techniques and risk management algorithms have earned importance in machine learning applications because of their large industrial applicability and useful theoretical characteristics, which includes machine learning uses for many industrial settings, such as machine learning for the policymaking process and the IoT.[1]

While a great deal has been written on the topic of risk management processes for credit and market (or price) risk, relatively little appears on the important issue of liquidity risk processes for large security positions in illiquid markets. Asset liquidity risk is a large and confusing subject, and indeed, the lack of liquidity in multiple-securities trading portfolios is perhaps one of the prevalent threats facing today's capital markets and has played a key role in major crises and losses during the last two decades [5, 6, 9].

Market liquidity refers to the ability to undertake financial securities transactions in such a way as to adjust trading portfolios and risk exposure profiles without significantly disturbing prevailing market condition and underlying prices. Market liquidity risk is a function of the depth[2] of the markets and their continuity, and it is influenced by trading strategies and by the type of hedge chosen, if the strategy involves hedging of exposure. Moreover, it is also a function of transaction size, product type, current market sentiment, and local trading patterns.

Market liquidity depends fundamentally on the existence of enough number of counterparties and their readiness to trade. The latter depends on investors' expectations vis-à-vis price level developments and also their risk aversion, as well as the available information at a given time. Underprivileged liquidity conditions

---

[1] For some of latest literature on machine learning, machine learning for the policymaking process, and expert systems in finance for modern portfolio optimization and regulatory risk management, we refer the readers to [4, 20, 29, 35].

[2] Depth is defined as the volume of possible trades without affecting prevailing market prices on order books.

thus indicate a relatively small number and size of daily transactions and give an indication of the size of a portfolio trading position that the market can absorb at a given level. An entirely liquid financial market would therefore pledge a single bid-ask price at all times and regardless of the asset quantities being traded. In fact, financial markets, even those viewed the most liquid, conform less than perfectly to this extreme pattern. As a result, asset liquidity risk is the risk of not being competent to quickly liquidate or hedge a trading position at existing market prices. Indeed, this market liquidity risk is unlike balance sheet liquidity risk, which arises from the incapability to raise liquid funds by offloading assets or liabilities from the balance sheet's books [6, 9]. The former asset liquidity risk is the focus of this chapter.

As it happens, changes in market operational conditions as well as the magnitude and nature of financial risk have demanded the writing down and structuring of Basel II and Basel III capital adequacy accords and basically revised and enlarged frameworks of Basel I.[3] These amendments leave the treatment of market risk largely unaltered from Basel I requirements and instead focus almost exclusively upon the formerly mistreated areas of credit and operational risks. Indeed, a key advancement of the Basel II and Basel III capital adequacy accords was the introduction of Value at Risk (VaR) as an internal risk measure to consolidate an institution's market risk into a single number expressed usually in monetary terms and the inclusion of liquidity risk. Whereas VaR is not a demanding quantity to evaluate in principle, assessing its key parameters and determining both their robustness and validity are non-trivial [7, 9].

Effectively, a large number of research articles are nowadays concerned in the examination of the intricacy of credit and operational risks, while market risk has received lesser attention, and as a result market risk research papers have lessened notably in number. Definitely, the VaR concept, however, has by no means been thoroughly looked into. One such ignored feature is asset liquidity risk which, because of its trend to compound other risks, is complex to detach and appraise effectively. In all but the simplest of situations, thorough market and asset liquidity risk metrics do not exist, and traditional VaR models typically disregard asset liquidity risk entirely [8, 9].

The existing attempts on the measurement of liquidity risk are poorly defined, and whether we agree or disagree upon it, VaR can at least be viewed as a starting point in contemplating the assessment of market risk. Unfortunately, there is no such standard point of departure for market liquidity risk measurement. Nonetheless, where liquidity risk is assessed at all, it is typically through deviations on two types of yardsticks. The first attempts to measure transaction cost risk and is based on the concept of bid-ask spreads, while the second endeavors to capture the risk of bearing down prevailing market prices by selling large quantities and is anchored in

---

[3]The Basel capital accord sets down the agreement among the G-10 central banks to apply common minimum capital standards to their banking institutions. The standards largely address the main risks incurred by banks such as credit, market, and operational. Currently, the Basel II and Basel III capital adequacy accords are embraced by other countries apart from the G-10 countries.

trade volume or outstanding positions. In most situations, however, market liquidity risk is measured in terms of a bid-ask spread and represents the costs to unwind the trading position; or alternatively it is assessed by adding an off-the-cuff liquidity risk multiplier[4] to the overall market risk exposure, usually measured by traditional VaR models. Therefore, traditional adjustments to VaR models are done on an ad hoc basis, and liquidity risk is factored loosely into VaR measures by assuring that the liquidation horizon is at least greater than an orderly unwinding period. By and large, the same horizon is applied to all asset classes, even though some trading assets may be more liquid than others [7, 9].

Despite some research into liquidity risk measurement, the financial services industry still finds it difficult to quantify and predict measurable attributes of market liquidity risk. In fact, most financial institutions have committed or are preparing to commit significant resources to managing liquidity risk. Nevertheless, there are no clear standards regarding the definition of the problem these entities' efforts are meant to solve, let alone the risk processes themselves. In the absence of accepted industry standards, risk professionals are faced with the challenge of defining an organization-specific internal approach that addresses market liquidity risk not only for a single trading security but also rather on an aggregate portfolio level. This is where this research comes in, as we strive to clarify the essence of the machine learning processes for market and asset liquidity risk, provide clear definition of the topic, and suggest methods for its mutual assessment at a portfolio level [5, 9].

In this chapter, we argue that market liquidity risk associated with the uncertainty of adverse price impact and the widening of the bid-ask spread, particularly for thinly traded or emerging market securities under adverse market conditions, is an important part of the overall market and asset liquidity risk and is therefore important components to model mutually. Next, we develop a clear-cut machine learning methodology for market liquidity risk processes that can be easily and flawlessly incorporated into standard VaR models and can be applied at a trading/investment portfolio level. Furthermore, we explain that ignoring any of the two components of liquidity effect can produce underestimates of market risk, particularly in emerging markets. Accordingly, we verify that the Basel II capital adequacy accord inadvertently is already monitoring liquidity risk and that by not modeling it unequivocally as part of the overall market liquidity uncertainty and therefore capitalizing against it, financial entities will be encountering despicably many violations of their capital requirements, particularly if their multiple-assets trading portfolios are clustered in emerging markets [7, 9].

In contrast to all existing published literatures pertaining to the application of machine learning (e.g., [20, 29, 35]), the use of machine learning techniques for the policymaking process and for the IoT data analytics to risk analysis and optimization of multiple-assets portfolios, our proposed robust market and liquidity risk algorithms differ in important ways from previous, however related research. To

---

[4]A multiplier that is incorrectly used quite frequently by researchers and practitioners is the square root of time since it overstates the overall market risk exposure.

that end, this chapter is an effort to describe and evaluate contemporary attempts in addressing market liquidity risk and to propose a concrete generalized theoretical market and asset liquidity modeling approach that can jointly tackle the measurement of these two risks for multiple-securities trading and asset management portfolios. It is anticipated in a second phase to apply the theoretical machine learning modeling algorithms developed herein to an emerging financial market, subject to obtaining a reliable and robust source of stratified market dataset. We aspire in the succeeding empirical paper to originate an empirical research paper by applying the theoretical machine learning modeling approach developed in this chapter to a particular case of an emerging market trading portfolio. Our aim would be to test the dataset empirically and to analyze the influence of both adverse price impact and transaction cost machine learning processes on the overall market liquidity risk profiles by enforcing meaningful financial and operational constraints [9].

The balance of the chapter proceeds as follows: Section 9.2 presents a review of current thinking and practices regarding liquidity risk measurement and thereafter highlights the main contributions of this research. Section 9.3 discusses the salient features of market and asset liquidity risks and derives the necessary quantitative foundations of two interrelated machine learning processes (models). First, we present our conceptual framework for understanding the machine learning process of market liquidity risk and their interaction and then show that Liquidity-Adjusted Value at Risk (L-VaR) algorithm, as a measure of adverse price impact market liquidity risk, can be derived for a single-asset portfolio assuming uniform liquidation over the holding period. We then broaden the analysis from one security to an entire multi-assets portfolio and derive a general robust machine learning model that incorporates the effects of holding multiple long- and short-sales illiquid assets on market and liquidity risk management, by simply scaling the multi-assets' L-VaR matrix. The discussion then turns to incorporate the impact of transaction costs and to develop a machine learning process that considers the time-varying volatility of the bid-ask spread. Finally, we integrate the various machine learning processes for the computation of the overall risk exposure, with an emphasis on the total market liquidity risk components and our proposed robust modeling approach. Section 9.4 includes detailed practical applications for contemporary portfolio optimization and selection and risk management objectives. This section includes as well a graphical flowchart that shows a concise outline of the overall market and liquidity objective risk-function and demonstrates the risk-engine's operational steps and their interrelationships. This flowchart highlights the required input parameters for risk management and portfolios optimization and selection and can aid in defining the processes for computer programming, artificial intelligence and machine learning for the policymaking process, and machine learning techniques for the IoT data analytics. Section 9.5 remarks on conclusions with further directions and recommendation for future research on the possible empirical uses of the robust machine learning modeling algorithms contained in this chapter.

9.2 Literature Review and Motivation of Present Research

A widespread number of contemporary literatures dealing with the microstructure of financial markets have been dedicated to categorize the determinants of market and liquidity risks and to model the nexus between both risks. Likewise, frequent studies on financial crises show that the shortage of liquidity is an element that is always present in times of major financial crises. Nevertheless, liquidity risk, a major component of market risk that is challenging to grasp, is still not sufficiently accounted for in modern risk assessment and management methods [6, 9].

Indeed, on one side methods for measuring market risk have been well developed and standardized in the academic as well as the banking world. Liquidity trading risk, on the other hand, has received less attention from researchers, perhaps because it is less significant in developed countries where most of the market risk methodologies were originated. In all but the simplest of circumstances, comprehensive metrics of liquidity trading risk management do not exist explicitly within modern portfolio theory [8, 9].

In effect, the conventional VaR approach to computing market (or trading) risk of a portfolio does not explicitly consider liquidity risk. Typical VaR models are based on modern portfolio management theory and assess the worst change in mark-to-market portfolio value over a given time horizon but do not account for the actual trading risk of liquidation. In general, customary fine-tunings are made on an ad hoc basis. At most, the holding period (or liquidation horizon) over which the VaR number is calculated is adjusted to ensure the inclusion of liquidity risk. As a result, liquidity trading risk can be imprecisely factored into VaR assessments by assuring that the liquidation horizon is as a minimum larger than an orderly liquidation interval Moreover, the same liquidation horizon is employed to all trading asset classes, albeit some assets may be more liquid than others may [7, 9].

Effectively, not only does this technique not differentiate between the various kinds of market and asset liquidity risks, but also it employs the square root of time multiplier, in which it is assumed that no autocorrelation exists between the rates of return on asset from one measurement period to another. The presumption of a lack of autocorrelation permits for simple addition of individual variances to produce the overall variance of the holding period. This postulation has been disputed over the past two decades by several authors [see, e.g., Danielsson and Zigrand [25]]. In addition, Al Janabi [10] recently reveals that the square root of time rule leads to a systematic overestimation of market risk. The author concludes that despite the widespread application and implementation of the square root of time multiplier in Basel II and Basel III regulatory accords, it nevertheless fails short to address the aim of Basel II and Basel III capital adequacy accords. It is clear that a comprehensive investigation into the nature of market and asset liquidity risk and its effect on distinct multiple-securities portfolios of both long- and short-sales illiquid assets is necessary [5, 9].

Without a doubt, neglecting liquidity risk can lead to an underestimation of the overall market risk and misapplication of capital cushion for the safety and soundness of financial institutions. In emerging financial markets, which are relatively well thought-out as illiquid, ignoring the liquidity risk can result in significant underestimation of the VaR estimate and especially under severe market conditions [10]. As a result, the increase tradability of assets in emerging markets necessitates a reexamination of current market and liquidity risk management techniques and specifically for multiple-securities trading or investment portfolios – of either long-only positions or a combination of long- and short-sales trading positions – and within short horizons of re-balancing and reporting focuses.

As such, the combination of the latest swift expansion of emerging markets' trading activities and the persistent turbulence in those markets has impelled liquidity trading risk to the vanguard of market risk management research and development. To that end, within the VaR framework, Jarrow and Subramanian [28] provide a market impact model of liquidity by considering the optimal liquidation of an investment portfolio over a fixed horizon. They derive the optimal execution strategy by determining the sales schedule that will maximize the expected total sales values, assuming that the period until liquidation is given as an exogenous factor. The correction to the lognormal VaR they derive depends on the mean and standard deviation of both: an execution lag function and a liquidation discount. Although the model is simple and intuitively appealing, it suffers from practical difficulties for its implementation. It requires the estimation of additional parameters such as the mean and the standard deviation of the discount factor and the period of execution – for which data are not readily available, none of which may be easy to estimate and may require subjective estimates such as a trader's intuition.

Bangia et al. [21] approach the liquidity risk from another angle and provide a model of VaR adjusted for what they call exogenous liquidity – defined as common to all market players and unaffected by the actions of any one participant. It comprises such execution costs as order processing costs and adverse selection costs resulting in a given bid-ask spread faced by investors in the market. On the contrary, endogenous liquidity is specific to one's position in the market, depends on one's actions, and varies across market participants. It is mainly driven by the size of the position: the larger the size, the greater the endogenous illiquidity. They propose splitting the uncertainty in market value of an asset into two parts: a pure market risk component arises from asset returns and uncertainty due to liquidity risk. Their model consists of measuring exogenous liquidity risk, computed using the distribution of observed bid-ask spreads and then integrating it into a standard VaR framework. Indeed, their argument is based on treating liquidity risk and market risk jointly, and thus they assume that in adverse market environments, extreme events in both returns and spreads arise concurrently. They argue that while the correlation between asset mid-price movements and bid-ask spreads is not perfect, it is strong enough during severe market conditions to persuade the handling of extreme movements in market and liquidity risk simultaneously.

In another research study, Angelidis and Benos [15] loosen the conventional, yet idealistic, postulation of perfect and frictionless financial markets (i.e., traders can either buy or sell any amount of securities without triggering major price changes). To that end, Angelidis and Benos [15] expand the earlier work of Madhavan et al.

[30] (who debated that traded volume can explicate security price movements) and exploit an L-VaR model based on bid-ask spread components, following the earlier work of Bangia et al. [21]. The authors argue that under this structure, asset liquidity risk is decomposed into its endogenous and exogenous components, thereby allowing an estimation of the liquidation risk of a specific trading position. The authors then apply L-VaR measures to the Athens Stock Exchange by incorporating bid-ask variation and the price effect of position liquidation. Their study focuses on the use of high-frequency transaction level data of stocks besides sorting out each stock according to their average transaction prices and capitalization. Furthermore, the results indicate that adverse selection increases with trade size while the cost component of the bid-ask spread decreases. Based on these findings, endogenous and exogenous liquidity risks are linked to spread components.

Almgren and Chriss [13] present a concrete framework for deriving the optimal execution strategy using a mean-variance approach and show a specific calculation method. Their approach has a high potential for practical application. They assume that price changes are caused by three factors: drift, volatility, and market impact. Their analysis leads to general insights into optimal portfolio trading, relating risk aversion to optimal trading strategy, and to several practical implications including the definition of L-VaR. Unlike Almgren and Chriss [13], Hisata and Yamai [27] turn the sales period into an endogenous variable and propose a practical framework for the quantification of L-VaR that incorporated the market liquidity of financial products. Their model incorporates the mechanism of the market impact caused by the investor's own dealings through adjusting VaR according to the level of market liquidity and the scale of the investor's position. In addition, Hisata and Yamai [27] propose a closed-form solution for calculating L-VaR as well as a method of estimating portfolio L-VaR.

On another front, Berkowitz [22] argues that unless the likely loss arising from liquidity risk is quantified, the models of VaR would lack the power to explicate the embedded risk. In practice, operational definitions vary from volume-related measures to bid-ask spreads and to the elasticity of demand. The author asserts that elasticity-based measures are of most relevance since they incorporate the impact of the seller actions on prices. Moreover, under certain conditions, the additional variance arising from seller impact can easily be quantified given observations on portfolio prices and net flows; and it is possible to estimate the entire distribution of portfolio risk through standard numerical methods.

Finally, in their research papers, Al Janabi [10], Al Janabi et al. [12], and Al Janabi, Ferrer, and Shahzad [11] establish novel frameworks for the modeling and computation of trading risk and for designing practical postmodern portfolio management techniques. The effects of illiquid assets that are dominant characteristics of emerging markets are also incorporated in the risk modeling algorithms. These literatures provide real-world risk management techniques and portfolio strategies that can be applied to structured multiple-securities portfolios in emerging, developed, and commodity markets. The intent is to propose a simple approach for including liquidation trading risk in standard VaR analysis and to capture the liquidity risk arising due to illiquid trading positions by obtaining an L-VaR estimate. The key methodological contribution is a different and less conservative liquidity scaling factor than the conventional root-time multiplier. The proposed machine learning add-on is a function of a predetermined liquidity threshold defined as the maximum position, which can be unwound without disturbing market prices during one trading day. In addition, the re-engineered Al Janabi model [10, 31] is quite simple to implement even by very large financial institutions with multiple assets and risk factors.[5]

Despite the increasing importance of trading risk management, published research in this specific risk management area is slow to emerge and specifically from the perspective of machine learning processes for market and asset liquidity risk. In particular, the main endeavor of this chapter is to fill a gap in the risk management and multiple-assets portfolios literature (especially from the perspectives of emerging and illiquid markets) and to bridge the disparity between the academic and professional finance communities.

As indicated above, asset prices are exposed to a variety of volatile market prices that can be and have been examined in a portfolio context. However, despite the rising interest in emerging markets, earlier research does not provide any broad methods for handling trading risk under illiquid and adverse market settings, particularly within emerging market trading portfolios. As such, the intent of this chapter is to present two robust machine learning techniques that aim to assess the risks incurred in the event of a deterioration in asset market liquidity and to probe to what extent these contemporary techniques may add to improving the overall market risk control in financial institutions and also to aid the pertinent authorities to improve their appraisals of financial stability using robust machine learning techniques for the policymaking process.

Considering the recent interest in market liquidity risk and the variability of the market risk factors of different emerging markets, the overall aim of this chapter is to explore the impact of both adverse price and transaction cost liquidity machine learning processes in the context of multiple-securities trading portfolios (of either long-only positions or a combination of long−/short-sales trading positions) and under the notion of different correlation factors (or other dependence measures) and liquidity horizons. In particular, this chapter develops L-VaR and bid-ask spread risk computational processes with the aid of different liquidation horizons and under a pre-determined confidence level. In contrast to all existing published literature pertaining to the application of L-VaR method to emerging markets, this chapter proposes new modeling algorithms for assessing a closed-form parametric L-VaR with explicit treatment of liquidity trading risk.

---

[5]For other relevant literature on liquidity, internal risk models, asset pricing, and portfolio choice and diversification, one can refer as well to Al Janabi [2]; Al Janabi [3]; Asadi and Al Janabi [19]; Arreola-Hernandez and Al Janabi [16]; Ruozi and Ferrari [37]; Grillini et al. [26]; Roch and Soner [36]; Al Janabi et al. [12]; Weiß and Supper [39]; Al Janabi et al. [11]; Madoroba and Kruger [31]; Madhavan et al. [30]; Amihud et al. [14]; Takahashi and Alexander [38]; Arreola-Hernandez, et al. [17]; Arreola-Hernandez, et al. [18]; Cochrane [23]; and Meucci [33], among others.

The principle adjustments that we present here consist essentially in adjusting traditional VaR method to take into consideration the liquidation of assets during the unwinding period along with incorporating the impact of the time-varying broadening of the bid-ask spread in times of stress conditions. As such, the key contribution of this chapter, to the fields of financial engineering and machine learning for the policymaking process and machine learning techniques for the IoT data analytics, is to extend VaR calculation to allow for a steady liquidation of the multiple-assets portfolio over the holding period and by showing that liquidity risk can be straightforwardly and intuitively integrated into the proposed L-VaR machine learning framework. Rather than modeling liquidity trading risk as such, the central focus of this work is to devise a wide-ranging and adaptable framework for handling market and asset liquidity risk.

The key methodological contribution is a different and more realistic liquidity-scaling factor than the conventional root-time multiplier. The proposed machine learning add-on is a function of a predetermined liquidity threshold defined as the maximum position, which can be unwound without disturbing market prices during 1 trading day. In addition, the re-engineered model is quite simple to implement even by very large financial institutions with multiple-assets and risk factors. In this chapter, we attempt to integrate and estimate the impact of liquidity trading risk into VaR models by explicitly incorporating the impact of both the time-volatility dimension of adverse asset prices and the dynamic movements in the bid-ask spread on market liquidity risk.

9.3   Modeling of Uncertainty with Robust Machine Learning Processes[6]

Market and asset liquidity risk in multiple-assets trading portfolios is the risk that the liquidation value of trading assets may differ significantly from their current mark-to-market values, and hence it is a function of the size of the trading positions (i.e., adverse price impact risk) and the price impact of trades (i.e., transaction cost liquidity risk). The first component arises when the trader is unable to quickly sell a security at a fair price, and this usually happens when few people normally trade the given security, or it could happen if the general market is in crisis and very few people are interested in buying more securities. In such a situation, the trader is assumed to be taking an extreme course of action by closing out the trading positions at the mid-price and refusing to give any price discount. The other extreme is to assume that the trader will sell out immediately by giving a discount that brings the price down to the bid price. This discount is an additional loss and crop up with the second component (i.e., the price impact of trades) and is characterized by an abrupt broadening of the bid-ask spread or even the complete vanishing of buy/sell flows

---

[6]Risk measures and modeling algorithms are drawn from Al Janabi [9] research paper.

and the incapability to trade. This widening in the bid-ask spread can often lead to an escalation in short-term volatility as well as the slump of financial markets as it contains the seeds of serious systemic turmoil. As a result, we can view these two possible loss mechanism components as two extreme manifestations of the same problem. In one extreme, the trader slowly sells at the current fair price but risks suffering additional losses. In the other extreme, the trader sells immediately at an unusually low price (in case he holds long-only position) or buys at high price in case he had short sold assets [9].

It is hence important to recognize the asset liquidity risk and its close relationship with market risk for trading position because it can add significant losses to the overall market risk exposure. Furthermore, if liquidity risk is not included in the risk measurements, it can give incentive to traders to buy illiquid securities since illiquid securities offer a higher expected return to compensate for their higher liquidity risk.

Since market and liquidity risks are interrelated and can simultaneously influence each other, it is then possible to define with reasonable accuracy that the overall market and liquidity risk of a trading position is the sum of two interrelated machine learning subcomponents, namely, (1) adverse price impact market liquidity risk component and (2) transaction cost market liquidity risk component [9]. In the following sections, we define each of these two risk components and then provide a rational explanation for the aggregation of both components for the sake of providing a generalized machine learning measure of both market and liquidity risks.

9.3.1 Machine Learning Process for the Modeling of Uncertainty Using a Closed-Form Parametric VaR Algorithms

One of the most significant advances in the past two decades in the field of measuring and managing financial risks is the development and the ever-growing use of VaR methodology. VaR has become a useful tool for monitoring risk, and its use is being encouraged by the Bank for International Settlements (BIS) and Basel II and Basel III committees on banking supervision. As a result, VaR has turned into the standard measure that financial analysts use to quantify financial risks including trading risk. VaR represents the potential loss in the market value of a portfolio of assets with a given probability over a certain time horizon. The main advantage of VaR over other risk measures is that it is theoretically simple and can be used to summarize the risk of an individual asset position or the risk of large portfolios of trading assets. Thus, VaR reduces the risk associated with any portfolio of trading assets to just one number – the expected loss associated with a given probability over a defined holding period [7, 9].

To compute VaR using the parametric method, the volatility of each risk factor is extracted from a pre-defined historical observation period. The potential effect of each component of the portfolio on the overall portfolio value is then worked out. These effects are then aggregated across the whole portfolio using the correlations between the risk factors (which are, again, extracted from the historical observation period) to give the overall VaR value of the portfolio with a given confidence level. A simplified computational process for the estimation of VaR risk factors (using a closed-form parametric method) for a single and multiple assets' positions is illustrated as follows [8, 9]:

We begin by defining 1-day asset return at time t, $R_{i,t}$ to be the log difference of mid-prices:

$$R_{i,t} = \ln \left(P_{i,t} \right) - \ln \left(P_{i,t-1} \right) = \ln \left[\left(P_{i,t} \right) / \left(P_{i,t-1} \right) \right] \tag{9.1}$$

where $R_{i,t}$ is the daily return of asset i, ln is the natural logarithm, $P_{i,t}$ is the current price level of asset i, and $P_{i,t-1}$ is the previous day asset price. Furthermore, from elementary statistics it is well known that for a Gaussian distribution, 68% of the observations will lie within 1σ (standard deviation) from the expected value, 95% within 2σ, and 99% within 3σ from the expected value. Accordingly, by taking a 1-day horizon over which the change in asset value is considered, and assuming that 1-day returns are Gaussian, the worst VaR of a single asset in monetary terms is:

$$\text{VaR}_i = \mid (\mu_i - \alpha * \sigma_i) \, (\text{MTM of Asset}_i * Fx_i) \mid \approx \mid (\alpha * \sigma_i) \, (\text{MTM of Asset}_i * Fx_i) \mid \tag{9.2}$$

where α is the confidence level (or, in other words, the standard normal variant at confidence level α) and σ_i is the standard deviation (volatility) of the asset that constitutes the single position. The MTM of Asset$_i$ (henceforth, A_i) indicates the amount of mark-to-market trading position in asset i. Without a loss of generality, we assume that the expected value of daily returns μ_i is zero. Though Eq. (9.2) includes some simplifying assumptions, researchers and practitioners in the financial markets for the estimation of VaR for a single trading position routinely use it [6, 9].

Trading risk in the presence of multiple risk factors is determined by the combined effect of individual risks. The extent of the total risk is determined not only by the magnitudes of the discrete risks but also by their correlation's parameters or any other dependence measures functions. Portfolio effects are crucial in risk management not only for large multiple-securities diversified portfolios but also for individual assets that depend on several risk factors. For multiple-assets portfolio, VaR is a function of each discrete asset's risk and the correlation factors (or any other dependence measures functions) between the returns on the individual assets and as follows [7, 9]:

$$\text{VaR}_P = \sqrt{|\text{VaR}|^T \mid \rho \mid \mid \text{VaR} \mid} \tag{9.3}$$

This formula is a general one for the computation of VaR$_P$ for any multiple-assets portfolio regardless of the number of assets, and it simply contains the VaRs for the constituent assets. It should be noted that this formula is presented in terms of matrix-algebra – a useful form to avoid mathematical complexity, as more and more securities are added. This approach can simplify the programming process and permits easy incorporation of short-sales positions in market risk management process. This means that in order to compute the VaR (of a portfolio of any number of assets), one needs first to create a vector $|$VaR$|$ of the individual VaR asset positions, explicitly n rows and one column ($n*1$) vector; a transpose vector $|$VaR$|^T$ of the individual VaR asset positions, an ($1*n$) vector, and hence the superscript "T" indicates transpose of the vector; and finally a matrix $|\rho|$ of all correlation factors between all assets (ρ), an ($n*n$) matrix [7, 9]. Consequently, as one multiplies the three matrices and then takes the square root of the result, one ends up with the VaR$_P$ of any portfolio with any n-number of assets. It should be noted that when reporting individual VaRs, these figures are always taken as positive, even though they represent a loss (which conventionally has a negative sign). In assessing the portfolio VaR$_P$, the sign of each trading asset "A_i" must be incorporated into the $|$VaR$|^T$ and $|$VaR$|$ vectors. That is, if the asset position is held long (i.e., you own it), then the $A_i > 0$, but if the asset has been sold short, then $A_i < 0$ [5, 9].

Worst-case VaR$_P$ (or undiversified VaR$_P$) can be deduced as a special case of Eq. (9.3) under the assumption that asset returns are perfectly positively correlated ($\rho = +1$) and that there are positive amounts of each asset. This indeed will give the worst-case scenario, since there are no benefits from diversification by holding multiple assets. Thus, the maximum value that the VaR$_P$ can take is given by setting $\rho = +1$ in Eq. (9.3), which gives:

$$\text{Worst-case VaR}_P = \text{VaR}_1 + \text{VaR}_2 + \ldots \cdots + \text{VaR}_n = \sum_{i=1}^{n} \text{VaR}_i \qquad (9.4)$$

Hence, in a worst-case scenario, the VaR$_P$ is simply the sum of the individual VaRs. In the real-world practices, it is unlikely that the correlation between the returns of the constituent assets is $\rho = +1$. However, under severe or crisis periods, it is often the case that correlation factors increase, and the worst-case VaR$_P$ provides a high figure that may be representative of these crisis periods. Indeed, in real-world risk management practices, risk managers usually look at both the diversified VaR$_P$ [Eq. (9.3)] and the worst-case VaR$_P$ [Eq. (9.4)]. This gives the risk managers a feel for what would happen if historical correlations did not stay the same but rather increased due to a crisis period. Moreover, it is worth noting that if $\rho = +1$ and one or more of the constituent trading assets is a short-sales position (i.e., $A_i < 0$), then there will be some risk offset and hence the worst-case scenario VaR$_P$ Eq. (9.4) cannot be hold as a representative of the maximum loss of the trading portfolio [5, 9].

9.3.2 Machine Learning Process for the Modeling of Adverse Price Impact Using Al Janabi Model

Trading asset liquidity is a key risk factor, which, until lately, has not been appropriately dealt with by risk models. Illiquid trading positions can add considerably to losses and can give negative signals to traders due to the higher expected returns they entail. The concept of liquidity trading risk is immensely important for using VaR accurately, and recent upheavals in financial markets confirm the need for laborious treatment and assimilation of liquidity trading risk into VaR models [6, 9].

In effect, traditional VaR models presume that the portfolio is stationary over the liquidation horizon and that market prices represent attainable transaction prices. This marking-to-market approach is adequate to quantify and control risk for an ongoing trading portfolio but may be more questionable if VaR is supposed to represent the worst loss over the unwinding period. As such, the question that may arise is how to adapt VaR to cope with asset liquidity consideration.

Market and asset liquidity risk arises when a forced liquidation of trading assets creates unfavorable price movements. Thus, liquidity considerations should be viewed in the context of both the asset and the liabilities of the financial entity. The simplest way to account for asset liquidity trading risk is to extend the holding period of illiquid positions to reflect a suitable liquidation period. An adjustment can be made by adding a multiplier to the VaR measure of each trading asset type, which at the end depends on the liquidity of each individual security. Nonetheless, the weakness of this method is that it allows for subjective estimation of the liquidation period. Furthermore, the typical assumption of a 1-day horizon (or any inflexible time horizon) within VaR framework neglects any calculation of trading risk related to liquidity effect (i.e., when and whether a trading position can be sold out and at what price). A broad VaR model should incorporate a liquidity premium (or liquidity risk factor). This can be worked out by formulating a method by which one can unwind a position, not at some ad hoc rate but at the rate that market conditions is optimal, so that one can effectively set a risk value for the liquidity effects. In general, this will raise significantly the VaR or the amount of economic capital[7] to support the trading position [8, 9].

In fact, if returns are independent and they can have any elliptical multivariate distribution, then it is possible to convert the VaR horizon parameter from daily to any t-day horizon. The variance of a t-day return should be t times the variance of

---

[7]Economic capital (risk capital) can be defined as the minimum amount of equity capital a financial entity needs to set aside to absorb worst losses over a certain time horizon with a certain confidence level. This is with the objectives of sustaining its trading operations activities and without subjecting itself to insolvency matters. Economic capital can be assessed with an internal method and modeling techniques such as L-VaR. Economic capital differs somehow from regulatory capital, which is necessary to comply with Basel II and Basel III requirements on capital adequacy. However, building an internal market risk modeling techniques to assess economic capital can significantly aid the financial entity in complying with Basel II and Basel III capital adequacy requirements.

a 1-day return or $\sigma^2 = f(t)$. Thus, in terms of standard deviation (or volatility), $S^2 = f(t)$, and the daily or overnight VaR number [VaR (1-day)] can be adjusted for any *t-day* horizon as:

$$\text{VaR }(t\text{-day}) = \text{VaR }(1\text{-day})\sqrt{t} \tag{9.5}$$

The above formula was proposed and used by *J.P. Morgan* in their earlier *RiskMetrics™* method [34]. This methodology implicitly assumes that liquidation occurs in one block sale at the end of the holding period and that there is one holding period for all assets, regardless of their inherent trading liquidity structure and ultimately leading to an overstatement of VaR. Unfortunately, the latter approach does not consider real-life trading situations, where traders can liquidate (or re-balance) small portions of their multiple-securities trading portfolios on a daily basis. The assumption of a given holding period for orderly liquidation inevitably implies that assets' liquidation occurs during the holding period. Accordingly, scaling the holding period to account for orderly liquidation can be justified if one allows the assets to be liquidated throughout the holding period [6, 9].

In this research work, we present a re-engineered and novel machine learning methodology, which is based on Al Janabi model [10, 31], for the computational process of a closed-form parametric L-VaR with direct assessment of market and asset liquidity trading risks. The proposed robust modeling algorithms and liquidity scaling factor are more realistic and less conservative than the conventional root-*t* multiplier. In essence, the suggested multiplier is a function of a predetermined liquidity threshold defined as the maximum position, which can be unwound without disturbing market prices during 1 trading day. The essence of the model relies on the assumption of a stochastic stationary process and some rules of thumb, which can be of crucial value for more accurate overall trading risk assessment during market stress periods when liquidity dries up. To that end, a practical framework of a robust machine learning methodology is proposed below with the purpose of incorporating and computing of illiquid assets' horizon L-VaR, detailed along these lines [7, 9]:

The market risk of an illiquid asset position is larger than the risk of an otherwise identical liquid position. This is because unwinding the illiquid position takes longer than unwinding the liquid position, and, as a result, the illiquid position is more exposed to the volatility of the market for a longer period of time. In this approach, a trading position will be well thought-out illiquid if its size surpasses a certain liquidity threshold. The threshold (which is determined by each trader) is defined as the maximum position which can be unwound, without disrupting market prices, in normal market conditions and during 1 trading day. Consequently, the size of the trading position relative to the threshold plays an important role in determining the number of days that are required to close the entire position. This effect can be translated into a liquidity increment (or an additional liquidity risk factor) that can be incorporated into VaR analysis. If, for instance, the par value of a position is $100,000,000 and the liquidity threshold is $50,000,000, then it will take 2 days to sell out the entire trading position. Therefore, the initial position will be exposed to market variation for 1 day, and the rest of the position (i.e., \$50,000,000) is subject to market variation for an additional day. If it assumed that daily changes of market values follow a stationary stochastic process, the risk exposure due to illiquidity effects is given by the following illustration, detailed as follows [7, 9]:

In order to take into account the full illiquidity of trading assets (i.e., the required unwinding period to liquidate an asset), we define the following [10]:

t = number of trading days for orderly liquidation of asset i position,
$\sigma_{adj}{}^2$ = variance of the illiquid trading asset i,
σ_{adj} = liquidity risk factor or standard deviation of the illiquid trading asset i.

The proposed machine learning approach assumes that the trading position is closed out linearly (liquidated in equal parts at the end of each day) over t-days, and hence it uses the logical assumption that the losses due to illiquid trading positions over t-days are the sum of losses over the individual trading days. Moreover, we can assume with reasonable accuracy that asset returns and losses due to illiquid trading positions are independent and identically distributed (*iid*) and serially uncorrelated day to day along the liquidation horizon and that the variance of losses due to liquidity risk over t-days is the sum of the variance (σ_i^2, for all $i = 1,2 \ldots,t$) of losses on the individual days, thus:

$$\sigma_{adj}{}^2 = \left(\sigma_1{}^2 + \sigma_2{}^2 + \sigma_3{}^2 + \cdots + \sigma_{t-2}{}^2 + \sigma_{t-1}{}^2 + \sigma_t{}^2\right) = \sum_{i=1}^{t} \sigma_i{}^2 \qquad (9.6)$$

In fact, the square root-t approach (Eq. [9.5]) is a simplified special case of Eq. (9.6) under the assumption that the daily variances of losses throughout the holding period are all the same as first day variance ($\sigma_1{}^2$); thus, $\sigma_{adj}{}^2 = (\sigma_1{}^2 + \sigma_1{}^2 + \sigma_1{}^2 + \cdots + \sigma_1{}^2) = t\sigma_1{}^2$. As discussed earlier the square root-t equation overestimates market and asset liquidity risk since it does not consider that traders can liquidate small portions of their multiple-securities trading portfolios on a daily basis and thus the whole asset trading position should be sold completely on the last trading day. However, this would be an overstatement of VaR; and the true VaR has to be between the 1-day position VaR and 1-day position VaR $\sqrt{t}$. Indeed, in real financial market operations, liquidation occurs during the holding period, and thus scaling the holding period to account for orderly liquidation can be justified if one allows the assets to be liquidated throughout the holding period. Certainly, for this special linear liquidation case and under the assumption that the variance of losses of the first trading day decreases linearly each day (as a function of t), we can derive from Eq. (9.6) the following [5, 9]:

$$\sigma_{adj}{}^2 = \left(\left(\frac{t}{t}\right)^2 \sigma_1{}^2 + \left(\frac{t-1}{t}\right)^2 \sigma_1{}^2 + \left(\frac{t-2}{t}\right)^2 \sigma_1{}^2 + \cdots \right.$$

$$\left. + \left(\frac{3}{t}\right)^2 \sigma_1{}^2 + \left(\frac{2}{t}\right)^2 \sigma_1{}^2 + \left(\frac{1}{t}\right)^2 \sigma_1{}^2\right) \qquad (9.7)$$

In this manner, if the asset position is liquidated in equal parts at the end of each trading day, the trader faces a 1-day holding period on the entire position, a 2-day holding period on a fraction $(t-1)/t$ of the position, a 3-day holding period on a fraction $(t-2)/t$ of the position, and so forth. Evidently, the additional liquidity risk factor depends only on the number of days needed to sell an illiquid trading position linearly. In the general case of t-days, the variance of the liquidity risk factor is given by the following mathematical functional expression of t:

$$\sigma_{\text{adj}}^2 = \sigma_1^2 \left(\left(\frac{t}{t}\right)^2 + \left(\frac{t-1}{t}\right)^2 + \left(\frac{t-2}{t}\right)^2 + \cdots + \left(\frac{3}{t}\right)^2 + \left(\frac{2}{t}\right)^2 + \left(\frac{1}{t}\right)^2 \right)$$

(9.8)

To compute the sum of the squares, it is convenient to use a short-cut approach. From mathematical finite-series, the following relationship can be obtained:

$$(t)^2 + (t-1)^2 + (t-2)^2 + \cdots + (3)^2 + (2)^2 + (1)^2 = \frac{t\,(t+1)\,(2t+1)}{6}$$

(9.9)

Hence, after substituting Eq. (9.9) into Eq. (9.8), the following can be achieved:

$$\sigma_{\text{adj}}^2 = \sigma_1^2 \left[\frac{1}{t^2} \left\{ (t)^2 + (t-1)^2 + (t-2)^2 + \cdots + (3)^2 + (2)^2 + (1)^2 \right\} \right] \text{ or }$$

$$\sigma_{\text{adj}}^2 = \sigma_1^2 \left(\frac{(2t+1)\,(t+1)}{6t} \right)$$

(9.10)

Accordingly, from Eq. (9.10) the adverse price liquidity risk factor can be expressed in terms of volatility (or standard deviation) as:

$$\sigma_{\text{adj}} = \sigma_1 \left\{ \sqrt{\frac{1}{t^2} \left[(t)^2 + (t-1)^2 + (t-2)^2 + \cdots + (3)^2 - (2)^2 + (1)^2 \right]} \right\} \text{ or }$$

$$\sigma_{\text{adj}} = \sigma_1 \left\{ \sqrt{\frac{(2t+1)\,(t+1)}{6t}} \right\}$$

(9.11)

The final result of Eq. (9.11) is of course a function of time and not the square root of time as employed by some financial market's participants based on the *RiskMetrics*™ methodologies. The above approach can also be used to compute L-VaR for any time horizon. Likewise, in order to perform the computation of L-VaR under illiquid market conditions, it is possible to use the adverse price liquidity factor of Eq. (9.11) and define the following single asset L-VaR:

$$\text{L-VaR}_{i_{\text{adj}}} = \text{VaR}_i \sqrt{\frac{(2t_i + 1)\ (t_i + 1)}{6t_i}} \tag{9.12}$$

where VaR_i is the Value at Risk of asset i under liquid market conditions; $\text{L-VaR}_{i_{\text{adj}}}$ is the Value at Risk of asset i under illiquid market conditions; and t_i is the number of trading days for orderly liquidation of the entire position of asset i fully.

The latter equation indicates that $\text{L-VaR}_{i_{\text{adj}}} > \text{VaR}_i$, and for the special case when the number of days to liquidate the entire asset is 1 trading day, then $\text{L-VaR}_{i_{\text{adj}}} = \text{VaR}_i$. Consequently, the difference between $\text{L-VaR}_{i_{\text{adj}}} - \text{VaR}_i$ should be equal to the residual asset market risk due to the illiquidity of asset i under illiquid market conditions. As a matter of fact, the number of liquidation days or closeout time (t_i) necessary to liquidate the entire position of asset i fully is related to the choice of the liquidity threshold; however the size of this threshold is likely to change under severe market conditions. Indeed, the choice of the liquidation horizon can be estimated from the total trading position size and the daily trading volume that can be unwound into the market without significantly disrupting market prices; and in actual practices it is generally estimated as [6, 9]:

$$t_i = |\ \text{Total Trading Position Size of Asset}_i / \text{Daily Trading Volume of Asset}_i\ |,$$

$$s.t. \quad t_i \geq 1.0 \tag{9.13}$$

As such, the closeout time (t_i) is the time required to bring the positions to a state where the financial entity can make no further loss from the trading positions. It is the time taken to either sell the long-only positions or alternatively the time required to buy securities in case of short-sales positions. In real practices the daily trading volume of any trading asset is estimated as the average volume over some period of time, generally a month of trading activities. In effect, the daily trading volume of assets can be regarded as the average daily volume or the volume that can be unwound under a severe crisis period. The trading volume in a crisis period can be roughly approximated as the average daily trading volume less a number of standard deviations. Albeit this alternative approach is quite simple, it is still relatively objective. Moreover, it is reasonably easy to gather the required data to perform the necessary liquidation scenarios.

In essence, the above liquidity scaling factor (or multiplier) is more realistic and less conservative than the conventional root-t multiplier and can aid financial entities in allocating reasonable and liquidity market-driven regulatory and economic capital requirements. Furthermore, the above robust machine learning algorithms can be applied for the computation of L-VaR for every trading position and for the entire portfolio of multiple assets. In order to compute the L-VaR for the full trading portfolio under illiquid market conditions ($\text{L-VaR}_{P_{\text{adj}}}$), the above modeling algorithms can be extended, with the aid of Eq. (9.3), into a matrix-algebra form to yield the following:

$$\text{L-VaR}_{P_{adj}} = \sqrt{\left|\text{L-VaR}_{adj}\right|^T \mid \rho \mid \mid \text{L-VaR}_{adj}\mid} \qquad (9.14)$$

The above mathematical structure (in the form of two vectors, $|\text{L-VaR}_{adj}|$ and $|\text{L-VaR}_{adj}|^T$, and a correlation matrix, $|\rho|$) can facilitate the mathematical modeling, machine learning iteration process, and the programming procedure so that the trading risk manager can specify different liquidation horizons for the whole portfolio and/or for each individual trading asset according to the necessary number of days to liquidate the entire asset completely. The latter can be achieved by specifying an overall benchmark liquidation period to liquidate the entire constituents of the portfolio fully.

9.3.3 Machine Learning Process for the Measurement of Transaction Costs

Another additional alternative to quantify the asset liquidity risk is to measure the average bid-ask spread relative to the mid-price. The bid price is the utmost price that the market-maker is disposed to pay at a given time to purchase a particular amount of assets. Likewise, the ask price is the lowest price at which the market-maker is willing to sell a given amount of assets, and the difference between the bid and ask prices (the bid-ask spread) reimburses the market-maker for the expediency of execution of orders offered to its counterparties. This spread measures the cost of a buy/sell or sell/buy cycle over a short period of time (i.e., two-way transaction). For this reason, only half-spread should therefore be attributed to a single transaction (sale or purchase) if one considers that the mid-price is the one that should be paid in a perfect liquid market [9].

This traditional view of asset liquidity risk in trading portfolios is based on the fact that there is a relationship between price and quantity. Thus, when the quantity of an asset that is traded is relatively small, the bid-ask spreads are low, and as the quantity increases, the price paid by the buyer of the asset increases and the price received by the seller of the asset decreases. That's why high liquid assets, such as major currencies or treasury bonds, are characterized by deep markets, where positions can be offset with very little price impact, while thin markets, such as over-the counter (OTC) derivative securities or some emerging markets equities, are those where any transaction can quickly affect prices.

Indeed, on one hand if the bid and ask prices are close to the mid-price, then this implies that there are many market participants who consent on the fair price of the security and are disposed to trade close to that price. On the other hand, if the bid-ask spread is wide, this means that few investors are keen to buy the security at the price the sellers think is fair. Thus, if a trader sought to sell the security instantly, the trader would have to lower the ask price to equal the bid rather than pass the time waiting for some investor to assent that the high ask price was fair. To that end, the first and most easily measurable attribute is the quoted percentage bid-ask spread for an asset which can be defined formally as [9]:

$$\text{Spread}_i \, (S_i) = \left[\text{ask price}_i - \text{ bid price}_i\right] / \left\{\left[\text{ask price}_i + \text{bid price}_i\right] /2\right\}$$
(9.15)

However since [ask price$_i$ + bid price$_i$]/2 = mid - price$_i$, we can write Eq. (9.15) as:

$$S_i = \left[\text{ask price}_i - \text{ bid price}_i\right] /\text{mid-price}_i$$
(9.16)

where the mid-price is halfway between the bid and the ask price and in liquidating a trading position the financial entity incurs a cost equal to $[A_i \, S_i] \, / \, 2$. Indeed, this reflects the fact that actual trades are not done at the mid-market prices, and a buy trade is done at a proportional amount $S_i \, / \, 2$ above the market price and a sell trade is done at a proportional amount $S_i \, / \, 2$ below the market price. Thus, it is possible to adjust for bid-ask spread by adding $[A_i \, S_i] \, / \, 2$ for each trading position in the portfolio. For a large trading portfolio with n-securities, the robust machine learning process of the total liquidity risk due to transaction cost can be defined formally as [9]:

$$\text{Transactions Cost Market Liquidity Risk (TCMLR)} = \sum_{i=1}^{n} \{\text{Abs}\,[A_i]\, S_i\} /2$$
(9.17)

where Abs indicates the absolute value of A_i since long-only and short-sales trading positions have the same impact on widening the bid-ask spread and thus no netting effect should be induced on transaction cost. In fact, this adjustment with transaction cost can be repeated for all assets in the trading portfolio, leading to a series of add-ons, and this sequence of positive terms increases linearly with the number of assets.

Nevertheless, the quoted spread in financial markets is not usually a precise reflection of transaction costs (for a buy/sell cycle) as some deals may be traded not at the bid or the ask price but rather at prices cited within or even outside the spread, yet for typical amounts. Particularly, the spread is cited for restricted amounts, and it ordinarily inclines to broaden in the existence of substantial order flows, which is what the notion of market depth refers to. Eventually, to realistically assess trading portfolios' risk exposure, it is indispensable to contemplate the transaction costs incurred during the liquidation period [9].

A trouble-free method would consist in adding the observed average of the half-spread to the traditional VaR methods as other researchers have done heretofore. This method does not however comprise the variability of the half-spread over time. Given that the spread is a measure of the liquidity available at a given time, this is why it would be wiser to try to extract from historical data series information on the statistical distribution of bid-ask prices and in particular on their volatility. With a view of an appropriate risk measurement, it is therefore important to encompass the bid-ask spread variability over time. Moreover, stress-testing and scenario analysis are also crucial to making the risk processes useful to financial institutions. Stress-testing will illustrate what the value of the trading portfolio will be in any given position. Furthermore, as volatility soars liquidity can dry out, hence, liquidity should also be stress-tested, as the bid-ask spread can reposition too by bounds and leaps in erratic markets. In what follows we present an improved model that considers the volatility of the spread and its variability over time until the last day of liquidating the whole trading position, detailed as follows [9]:

We define transaction cost market liquidity risk measurement in terms of a confidence interval (α) or a tail probability. Moreover, we define the machine learning process for transaction cost of market liquidity based on a certain average spread or an estimate of the expected or typical bid-ask spread, $\hat{S}_i$, plus a multiple of the spread volatility, σ_S, to cover most of the spread situations. Thus, Eq. (9.17) can be expressed in terms of average spread and volatility of the spread as:

$$\text{TCMLR} = \sum_{i=1}^{n} \left\{ \text{Abs} \, [A_i] \times \left(\hat{S}_i + \alpha \sigma_{Si} \right) \right\} / 2 \qquad (9.18)$$

Under the zero-mean normality hypothesis, we can set $\hat{S}_i = S_i$, the most recent observation on the relative spread. For at least some financial assets such as hard currencies, it may be preferable to set $\hat{S}_i$ conformably to a well-defined "typical level."

The above equation considers the average spread and its volatility but not the variability over time of the volatility factor; and hence an adjustment time factor is essential to reflect that volatility of spread is indeed also a function of time and it depends on the number of days left for full unwinding of the entire trading position. The essence of this assumption is based on the fact that the longer the number of days to liquidate fully the trading position, there is a superior likelihood that the spread volatility is not static but rather dynamic and thus one would expect the spread to diverge even further and overlooked as time of liquidation elapses. In order to take this effect into consideration, we proceed by defining that the trading position can be unwound in several days and for each trading day the remaining fraction(s) of the position will be the only remaining part(s) that can be influenced by the time variability of the spread volatility, detailed along these lines [9]:

In order to take into consideration the full illiquidity of assets (i.e., the required unwinding period to liquidate an asset and at which the bid-ask spread is likely to widen dynamically), we define the following:

$h_i =$ the number of liquidation days, necessary to liquidate the entire position of asset i fully, and that have direct influence on the movement in the bid-ask spread volatility,

$\sigma^2_{Si} =$ overnight (daily) variance of the bid-ask spread of asset i.

The proposed machine learning modeling algorithm assumes that the trading position is closed out linearly (liquidated in equal parts at the end of each day) over

h_i-days, and hence it uses the logical assumption that the losses due to the widening of the bid-ask spread over h_i -days are the sum of losses over the individual trading days. Moreover, we can assume with reasonable accuracy that asset returns and losses due to the widening of the bid-ask spread are independent and identically distributed (*iid*) and serially uncorrelated day to day along the widening horizon and that the variance of losses due to bid-ask spread over h_i -days is the sum of the variance ($\sigma_{Sin}{}^2$, for all $n = 1, 2\ldots, h_i$) of the bid-ask spread losses on each individual day, thus:

$$\sigma_{Si}{}^2 = \left(\sigma_{Si_1}{}^2 + \sigma_{Si_2}{}^2 + \sigma_{Si_3}{}^2 + \cdots + \sigma_{Si_h}{}^2 \right) = \sum_{n=1}^{h_i} \sigma_{Si_n}{}^2 \qquad (9.19)$$

A linear liquidation procedure of the asset is assumed, that is, the trader can proceed by selling equal fractions of each asset every day until the last trading day (h_i), where the entire asset is sold fully. Therefore, the remaining unsold fractions will be the only "left-over" amounts of the trading asset that can be influenced, during the next trading day, by the time-varying volatility of the bid-ask spread. Indeed, for the special linear liquidation case and under the assumption that the current variance of losses of the bid-ask spread ($\sigma_{Si_1}{}^2$) increases linearly each day (as a function of h), hence, the following can be deduced:

$$\sigma_{Si}{}^2 = \left(\left(\frac{1}{h_i}\right) \sigma_{Si_1}{}^2 + \left(\frac{2}{h_i}\right) \sigma_{Si_1}{}^2 + \left(\frac{3}{h_i}\right) \sigma_{Si_1}{}^2 + \cdots + \left(\frac{h_i}{h_i}\right) \sigma_{Si_1}{}^2 \right)$$
$$(9.20)$$

In this manner, if the asset position is liquidated in equal parts at the end of each trading day, the trader faces a widening of the bid-ask spread on a 1-day holding period by ($1/ h_i$) of the total position, a 2-day holding period on a fraction ($2/ h_i$) of the position, a 3-day holding period on a fraction ($3/ h_i$) of the position, and so forth. Evidently, the additional transaction cost liquidity risk factor depends only on the number of days needed to sell an illiquid trading position linearly. In the general case of h_i-days, the variance of the widening of bid-ask spread is given by the following mathematical functional expression of h_i:

$$\sigma_{Si}{}^2 = \sigma_{Si_1}{}^2 \left(\left(\frac{1}{h_i}\right) + \left(\frac{2}{h_i}\right) + \left(\frac{3}{h_i}\right) + \cdots + \left(\frac{h_i}{h_i}\right) \right)$$
$$(9.21)$$
$$\text{or} \qquad \sigma_{Si}{}^2 = \sigma_{Si_1}{}^2 \left(\frac{1}{h_i} (1 + 2 + 3 + \ldots\cdots + h_i) \right)$$

To compute the sum of the time fractions of the liquidation horizon, it is convenient to use a short-cut approach. From mathematical finite-series, the following relationship can be obtained:

$$(1 + 2 + 3 + \ldots \ldots \cdots + h_i) = \frac{h_i(h_i - 1)}{2} \tag{9.22}$$

Accordingly, Eq. (9.21) can be simplified to:

$$\sigma_{Si}{}^2 = \sigma_{Si_1}{}^2 \left[\frac{1}{h_i} (1 + 2 + 3 + \ldots \ldots \cdots + h_i) \right] \text{ or } \sigma_{Si}{}^2 = \sigma_{Si_1}{}^2 \left(\frac{h_i + 1}{2} \right) \tag{9.23}$$

Consequently, the volatility of the bid-ask spread as a function of bid-ask spread widening period h_i is:

$$\sigma_{Si} = \sigma_{Si_1} \left\{ \sqrt{\frac{1}{h_i} (1 + 2 + 3 + \ldots \ldots \cdots + h_i)} \right\} \text{ or } \sigma_{Si} = \sigma_{Si_1} \left\{ \sqrt{\frac{h_i + 1}{2}} \right\} \tag{9.24}$$

Substituting Eq. (9.24) into Eq. (9.18) yields the following time-varying bid-ask spread volatility relationship:

$$\text{TCMLR} = \sum_{i=1}^{n} \left\{ \text{Abs } [A_i] \times \left(\hat{S}_i + \alpha \, \sigma_{Si_1} \sqrt{\frac{h_i + 1}{2}} \right) \right\} / 2 \tag{9.25}$$

We will refer to the above equation as the percentile dynamic spread risk factor. Obviously, the dynamic spread risk factor is a function of time and reflects the stochastic nature of the bid-ask spread. Like so, the transaction cost market liquidity risk at a α confidence level is then measured by the current value of the spread risk factor or by the α percentile of the actual proportional daily changes in the half-spread over a given historical period, adjusted by a time function that denotes the necessary time to liquidate the asset fully. For all practical purposes, it is possible to assume that the bid-ask spread widening period (h_i) and the asset unwinding period (t_i) are equivalent, that is, $h_i = t_i$. Although this assumption may sound rather strong, in reality both h_i and t_i time periods are interrelated most of the time and can be considered equivalent for the sake of facilitating the programming process of both market and asset liquidity risk models [9].

9.3.4   Machine Learning Process for the Computation of the Overall Risk Exposure

Trading returns are typically measured from mid-market prices. Although this may be adequate for measuring daily profit and loss (P&L), it may not represent the actual fall in value if a large portfolio is to be liquidated. More specifically, the VaR method uses the mid-price or last price, ignoring the fact that liquidation occurs not at the bid-ask average price but at the bid-ask average less half the bid-ask spread, and this spread can fluctuate widely. Marking to market leads to an underestimation of the true risks because the realized value upon liquidation can deviate significantly from the market mid-price. Given the bid/offer spread that exists in the marketplace, and given that the bid/offer spread varies with how much one can unwind a trading position, the actual risk depends on the overall trading position size relative to the size that can be unwind. As discussed above, though VaR method in recent years has become a reference for market risk management, the model does not satisfactorily capture asset liquidity risk, which is an integral component of market risk and thus should not be treated or assessed in an isolated framework. The question that may arise is how to assess potential market/liquidity risk loss aggregates jointly under such conditions, which in turn can give insights into how to manage this risk.

Previous attempts were fulfilled by using standard VaR calculations and adjusting the result to the distribution of bid-ask spreads with the aim of computing the most unfavorable half-spread for a given time horizon and confidence threshold. The highest bid-ask spread liquidity cost is thus obtained and then added to the standard VaR defined for the same time horizon and the same confidence interval. Indeed, assessing the overall market liquidity risk of an asset by simply summing up its price risk cost (which is reflected by the traditional VaR model) and the bid-ask spread liquidity cost amounts to deducing that these two market and asset liquidity components are absolutely correlated (i.e., the high variability of the mid-price is associated with the high variability of the bid-ask spread). This presumption may on several occasion cause an underestimation of the overall market risk [9].

To that end, in this chapter we conceptually aspire not to split the uncertainty in market value of an asset, i.e., its overall market risk, into two parts, uncertainty that arises from asset returns, which can be thought of wrongly as a pure market risk component, and uncertainty due to liquidity risk component, as others researchers have done beforehand. In this way, we argue that market and liquidity risk components are correlated in most cases and can be integrated into one single market liquidity value that consists of two interconnected machine learning subcomponents. The first machine learning component of market and asset liquidity risk is attributed to the unwinding period or to the impact of adverse price movements. In contrast, the second machine learning component of the market liquidity risk processes focuses on the risk of variation in transaction costs due to bid-ask spreads, and it attempts to measure the likelihood that it will cost more than expected to liquidate the position and can be assessed as a percentile dynamic spread risk factor [9].

Certainly, both machine learning components play an important role in defining and quantifying market and asset liquidity risks, and these starting points allow us to define the overall market and asset liquidity risks as the sum of both components bearing in mind that in real-world financial operations, it is not feasible to distinguish clearly between market and liquidity risks and hence an assessment yardstick can be devised to appraise both market and liquidity risk simultaneously as one integrated component. Indeed, the first attribute already includes the impact of market risk and diversification benefits and can produce purely market risk exposure when the liquidation horizon (or unwinding period) is reset for 1 trading day. The second attribute can diminish in importance if the market is able to absorb order flows without provoking violent price adjustment that are unrelated to fundamental value [9]. Since the machine learning processes of both market and liquidity risk components are correlated in most cases, we can argue that:

$$\begin{aligned} &\text{Overall Asset Market Liquidity Risks (OAMLR)} \\ &= \text{Adverse Price Impact Market/Liquidity Risk} \\ &+ \text{Transactions Cost Market/Liquidity Risk} \end{aligned} \quad (9.26)$$

Equation (9.14) represents the total adverse price impact market liquidity risk on a portfolio level (L-VaR$_{P_{adj}}$), while Eq. (9.25) characterizes the aggregate transaction cost market liquidity risk for all trading assets, so that the following objective risk-function can be deduced[8]:

$$\begin{aligned} \text{OAMLR} = &\sqrt{\left|\text{L-VaR}_{adj}\right|^T \mid \rho \mid \mid \text{L-VaR}_{adj}\mid} \\ &+ \sum_{i=1}^{n}\left\{\text{Abs }[A_i] \times \left(\hat{S}_i + \alpha\, \sigma_{Si_1}\sqrt{\frac{h_i+1}{2}}\right)\right\}/2 \end{aligned} \quad (9.27)$$

As the number of long-only positive positions, n, increases, the first term L-VaR$_{P_{adj}}$ benefits from diversification effects, but the second transaction cost term does not. Thus, the relative importance of the second liquidity factor will be greater for large multiple-securities portfolios regardless if it is long-only or short-sales trading positions.[9] Indeed, ignoring any of the two components of market liquidity effect can produce underestimates of the overall market risk, particularly in emerging markets. Accordingly, the Basel II and Basel III capital adequacy accords by not modeling market and asset liquidity risk unambiguously as part of the overall market liquidity uncertainty and therefore capitalizing against it, financial entities will be encountering many violations of their capital requirements, particularly if their multiple-securities trading portfolios are located in emerging markets[10] [9].

---

[8]The overall market and asset liquidity risk-function can take into consideration the effects of nonlinearity and non-normality of asset returns on assets allocation by implementing Kendal's tau algorithm as a measure of nonlinear dependence or any other copula-based models to replace the linear correlation factors. Likewise, it can easily be adapted to resolve the issue of non-normality of asset returns using Cornish-Fisher expansion (as a measure of non-normality) or any other relevant non-normality modeling techniques.

[9]It is possible to compute from Eq. (9.27) the minimum amount of optimum economic capital, necessary to serve as a cushion to support current trading operation. This can be achieved by optimizing the overall nonlinear quadratic objective risk-function (i.e., Eq. (9.27)) subject to the application of certain operational and financial budget constraints as specified by the risk/portfolio manager.

[10]The issue of improving the precision of LVaR estimates, under the effects of non-normality and at extreme quantiles, can be tackled by using the Cornish-Fisher expansion [24]. In fact, the Cornish-Fisher expansion is a semi-parametric technique that estimates quantiles of non-normal

Admittedly, under ordinary situations, asset liquidity risk can be expected to be a diminutive part of financial-intermediaries' total market risk, and minimum certain aspects of it can be at least approximately assessed by some of the statistical processes described here. However, at times of financial tension, asset liquidity risk can become a far more important part of the overall market risk. Precisely at these upheaval times, standard market and asset liquidity risk processes are likely to be entirely deceptive. Assessing and monitoring market and asset liquidity risks should therefore be considered as an integral part of preparing for stress-testing and warning signals analysis. As such, market and asset liquidity risks should be treated as an essential part of managing the risk of extreme events, as during periods of market stress, time is of essence. Thus, early warning signals can be used by market participants to assess stress-tests, categorize vulnerabilities, and devise earlier liquidation and hedging of exposures decisions [9].

9.4   Practical Applications for Contemporary Portfolio Optimization and Selection and Risk Management

In this backdrop, the robust machine learning modeling techniques, algorithms, and expected empirical results are interesting in terms of theory as well as practical applications for multiple-assets portfolios and can have many uses and application in financial markets, particularly in light of the 2007–2009 global financial meltdown. In addition, the proposed novel techniques and risk assessment algorithms can aid in advancing risk management and portfolio optimization and selection practices in emerging, developed, and commodity markets, particularly in the wake of the 2007–2009 financial turmoil.

Furthermore, the proposed robust risk management techniques and algorithms can have important applications in machine learning and artificial intelligence, expert systems, smart financial functions, and financial technology (FinTech) in big data environments. Similarly, it can aid in the progress of regulatory technology (RegTech) for the global financial services industry and can be of interest to professionals, regulators, and researchers working in the fields of machine learn-

---

distributions as a function of standard normal quantiles and the sample skewness and excess kurtosis and can account properly for the strong negative skewness in equity returns at the time of a crash or event (crisis) market conditions [1]. In the context of a closed-form parametric LVaR, this technique allows extreme quantiles to be estimated from standard normal quantiles at high significance levels, given only the first four moments of the empirical return distribution. As such, distributions that are approximated using Cornish-Fisher expansion may offer significant improvement on backtesting results for a standard parametric LVaR model. Therefore, Cornish-Fisher approximation is quick and easy to use; however it is only accurate if the portfolio returns are not too highly skewed or leptokurtic. In such a case, Johnson's SU distribution and algorithm can provide better approximations to the parametric LVaR at extreme quantiles than the Cornish-Fisher LVaR.

ing for the policymaking process, machine learning techniques for the IoT data analytics, financial engineering, and FinTech and for those who want to advance their understanding of the impact of innovative risk computational techniques and reporting processes on regulatory challenges for the financial services industry and its effects on global financial stability. Furthermore, it provides key real-world implications for portfolio/risk managers, treasury directors, risk management executives, policymakers, and financial regulators to comply with the requirements of Basel III best practices on liquidly risk and capital adequacy requirements.

In a nutshell, the advantages of the theoretical and practical fundamentals of the contemporary machine learning techniques discussed in this chapter and its application to modern risk management and for the development of optimization algorithms for portfolios selection and assets management include:

1. The proposed machine learning modeling technique and algorithms are robust enhancements to the traditional Markowitz [32] mean-variance approach. The task for portfolio optimization can be performed by minimizing the objective risk-function of the overall risk exposure (i.e., Eq. (9.27)) while requiring a minimum expected return subject to imposing several meaningful financial and operational constraints under different market conditions. As such, the portfolio managers and risk officers can identify various closeout horizons, bid-ask spreads, and dependence measures and compute the overall risk exposure of both market and liquidity risks and the resulting investable portfolios. Moreover, portfolio managers and risk officers can associate the return/risk ratio and asset allocation of the obtained investable portfolios versus the classical Markowitz's [32] mean-variance method.

2. The risk-engine and its objective risk-function of the overall risk exposure (i.e., Eq. (9.27)) can be tweaked slightly to take into consideration the influence of nonlinearity and non-normality of asset returns by applying Kendal's tau algorithm as a measure of nonlinear dependence or any other copula-based models to replace the linear correlation factors. Likewise, it can easily be adapted to resolve the issue of non-normality of asset returns using Cornish-Fisher expansion (as a measure of non-normality) or any other relevant non-normality modeling techniques.

3. The proposed machine learning algorithms have the potential of producing realistic risk-return profiles and may improve real-world understanding of embedded risks and asymmetric microstructure patterns and could potentially create better investable portfolios for portfolio managers in developed and developing economies.

4. The proposed machine learning modeling algorithms can be implemented by portfolio managers and risk officers for the valuation of proper asset allocations of diverse investable portfolios under adverse and event market outlooks.

5. The robust risk algorithms and machine learning techniques can aid in solving some real-world dilemmas under stressed and adverse market conditions, such as the following: (1) the effect of liquidity when it dries up in financial markets; (2) the impact of correlation factors when there is a switching in their signs; and (3)

the integration of the influence of nonlinear and non-normal distribution of asset returns in portfolio optimization and management.

6. Finally, the machine learning modeling techniques and algorithms can provide an incentive for further research in the areas of portfolio optimization, asset allocation, and portfolio selection. Moreover, the techniques for the multivariate optimization of investable portfolios and asset allocation are widely applicable to any portfolio management end users, providing potential applications to practitioners and research ideas to academics.

In this background and to maximize its utility as a robust machine learning process for portfolio selection and risk management, we have constructed the operational and computational process of the overall risk management and portfolio management tool such that the proposed objective risk-function and robust scenario optimization algorithms can be used for the purposes of computer programming, artificial intelligence, machine learning for the policymaking process, and machine learning techniques for the IoT data analytics. For instance, it is possible as a practical application for risk management and portfolio selection to compute the minimum amount of optimum economic capital, necessary to serve as a cushion to support current trading operations. This can be realized by optimizing (i.e., minimizing) the overall nonlinear quadratic objective risk-function (i.e., Eq. (9.27)) subject to the application of certain operational and financial budget constraints as specified by the risk/portfolio manager [6, 9]. To that end, the below graphical flowchart shows a concise outline of the operational steps of the overall market and liquidity risk modeling algorithms and their interrelationships for computer programming, artificial intelligence, and machine learning objectives.

9.5   Concluding Remarks and Future Directions

The last few years have witnessed a rapid expansion of emerging market financial assets trading activities – with several turmoil in capital markets – and an increasing interest in the measurement and management of asset liquidity risk for portfolio management, asset allocation, and risk management purposes. It is thus essential, at this stage, to be able to adapt the definition of traditional tools of quantifying trading risk to the needs and the requirements of this new environment in which the asset liquidity factor plays a central role. Asset liquidity is a key factor in formalizing and measuring overall trading risk, and neglecting liquidity risk can lead to underestimation of overall trading risk and to undercapitalization of financial institutions, particularly if their multiple-securities portfolios are concentrated in emerging markets. This has assumed special significance as more and more financial entities, particularly in emerging markets, prepare themselves toward better internal modeling of liquidity trading risk within the context of Basel II and Basel III capital accord guidelines [7, 9].

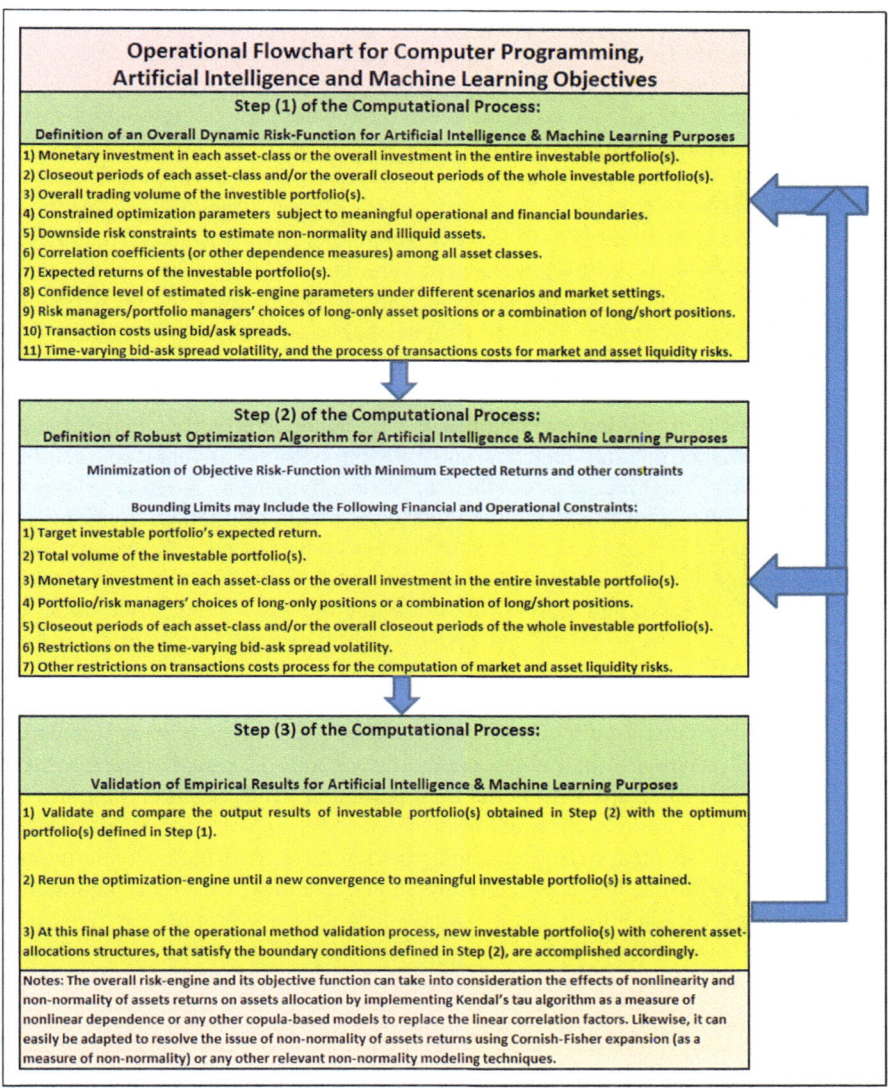

Source: Designed by the Author

Despite this, no standard technique for evaluating market and asset liquidity risk has surfaced. Definitely, Liquidity-Adjusted VaR (L-VaR) models do exist, and during the last two decades, L-VaR became one of the most popular tools for assessing trading risk across financial institutions. In fact, some L-VaR models are relatively sophisticated; however most of these models are related to single security VaR approaches, and their application to multiple-securities trading portfolios is inconsistent [6, 9]. Other unsophisticated methods such as those that rely on mainstream measures of leverage to appraise asset liquidity risk provide now and then worthless results.

In fact, the classical VaR computation is about the cost of liquidating traded portfolios in an adverse market and provides an estimate of the maximum potential loss that may be incurred on a position at a given time horizon and level of confidence; however it does not separate market risk from liquidity risk. Although in recent years it has become a reference for market risk management, the VaR model does not satisfactorily capture asset liquidity risk, which is a fundamental component of market risk. In computing VaR, it is generally assumed that the trading position can be liquidated or hedged within a fixed and reasonably short time frame. Moreover, it is assumed that the liquidation of asset positions has no effect on market prices and that the bid-ask spread remains stable irrespective of the size of the position [9]. Indeed, traditional VaR methods take for granted perfect markets, where an investor can buy and sell any amount of financial securities without causing a significant price change. Such a hypothesis is rarely confirmed in real financial market practices, particularly in emerging market environments, and as a result could lead to an underestimation of conventional VaR risk measures.

Additionally, the VaR method uses the mid-price or last known market price, ignoring the fact that liquidation occurs not at the bid-ask average price but at the bid-ask average less half the bid-ask spread, and this spread can fluctuate widely. However, as we have seen earlier, the quoted market price should not be used as a basis for reevaluating a portfolio that is to be sold on a less than perfectly liquid market, and in practical terms an account must be taken of its orderly liquidation value and the variation of its bid-ask spread throughout the liquidation period [9]. In conclusion, the standard VaR model is an unreliable guide because it ignores the risk to which a portfolio is exposed during its liquidation period. It is nonetheless doable to adapt VaR measures so as to integrate trading execution costs into the risk assessment framework. There are certainly ad hoc techniques for reevaluating VaR by artificially escalating the volatility of positions deemed illiquid or by enlarging the time horizon employed for calculating VaR. However, because they advocate subjective adjustments, these techniques do not deal straightforwardly with the issue of market and asset liquidity risks.

Given the rising need for measuring, managing, and controlling of financial risk, trading risk prediction under liquid and illiquid market conditions plays an increasing role in banking and finance sectors. To that end, this chapter focuses on contemporary practices and proposes novel machine learning internal modeling algorithms for the computational process of market and asset liquidity risks and within a multivariate context. In reality, one of the main challenges in the VaR concept is that the risk of a portfolio is measured independently from its size, which is equivalent to assuming constant market liquidity regardless of portfolio size. Indeed, this effect can be included in VaR assessments by adjusting the holding period to take size into account not at an ad hoc liquidity multiplier but rather with a liquidity risk factor that reflects real-world trading practices. That is why a range of low liquidity premium securities has to be identified, and then for each class, a quantification of the smallest and the largest amount of securities that can be unwound needs to be performed. When a position becomes too small or too large, a holding period of longer than 1 day must be applied [6, 9]. To that end, an attempt is made to remedy the above shortcomings by defining market and liquidity risks jointly as the sum of two interrelated components of robust machine learning processes. In view of that, this chapter looks at the dual and related dilemmas of:

1. Adjusting traditional VaR method at a portfolio level to reflect adverse price movements, during the unwinding period (t_i), on the liquidation of trading asset and without invoking the root-t rule.
2. Incorporation of a time-varying transaction cost into the overall assessment of market and asset liquidity risk during the bid-ask spread widening period (h_i).

Under this framework, the liquidation risk of a trading position will not only include the bid-ask spread as other researchers have done heretofore, but in addition a realistic liquidity risk factor that takes into consideration meaningful operational and financial circumstances. This mutual characterization of market and liquidity risks provides a robust and convenient machine learning modeling technique for including market and asset liquidity risks into VaR computations, which is now a standard in risk management procedures. Undeniably, the machine learning processes of the market liquidity modeling algorithms presented in this chapter do not incorporate all the microstructure aspects of liquidity trading risk management. However, it is effective as a tool for evaluating trading risk when the impact of illiquidity of certain financial products is significant.

The following step in this research is to select a particular emerging market or a region and strive to apply the proposed model to specific multiple-assets trading portfolios and then to compute empirically the impact of market and liquidity risks on the overall trading risk exposure.[11] We aspire in a second empirical research paper to apply the developed machine leaning modeling algorithms to the particular case of an emerging market multiple-securities trading portfolios and examine the influence of both adverse price impact and transaction cost on the overall market and liquidity risk profiles.

Finally, the machine learning modeling techniques, algorithms, and anticipated empirical results are interesting in terms of theory as well as practical applications for multiple-assets portfolios and can have many uses and application in financial markets, particularly in light of the 2007–2009 global financial meltdown. In addition, the proposed robust modeling techniques and risk assessment algorithms can aid in advancing quantitative risk management, portfolio optimization, and selection practices in emerging, developed, and commodity markets, particularly in light of the 2007–2009 financial turmoil. Furthermore, the offered risk management

---

[11] In addition, it is quite feasible to apply the novel modeling techniques and algorithms to the case of selected developed, emerging, and commodity markets. In this case, the proposed robust machine learning processes and modeling algorithms can be applied to multiple-securities trading and/or asset management portfolios to examine the effect of both adverse price impact and transactions cost on the overall market and asset liquidity risk exposures.

techniques and algorithms can have important applications in machine learning and artificial intelligence, expert systems, smart financial functions, and financial technology (FinTech) in big data environments. Similarly, it can aid in the progress of regulatory technology (RegTech) for the global financial services industry and can be of interest to professionals, regulators, and researchers working in the fields of machine learning for the policymaking process, machine learning techniques for the IoT data analytics, financial engineering, and FinTech and for those who want to advance their understanding of the impact of innovative risk computational techniques and reporting processes on regulatory challenges for the financial services industry and its effects on global financial stability. Furthermore, it provides key real-world implications for portfolio/risk managers, treasury directors, risk management executives, policymakers, and financial regulators to comply with the requirements of Basel III best practices on liquidly risk and capital adequacy.

Compliance with Ethical Standards

Funding: This study did not receive any funding from any entity or organization.

Conflict of Interest: The authors declare that they have no conflict of interest.

References

1. Alexander, C. (2008). *Market risk analysis volume IV, Value-at-Risk models*. Chichester/West Sussex/London: John Wiley & Sons, Ltd.
2. Al Janabi, M. A. M. (2020a). Is optimum always optimal? A revisit of the mean-variance method under nonlinear measures of dependence and non-Normal liquidity constraints. *Journal of Forecasting*. Early View Articles: https://doi.org/10.1002/for.2714
3. Al Janabi, M. A. M. (2020b). Multivariate portfolio optimization under illiquid market prospects: A review of theoretical algorithms and practical techniques for liquidity risk management. *Journal of Modelling in Management*. Early Cite Articles: https://doi.org/10.1108/JM2-07-2019-0178.
4. Al Janabi, M. A. M. (2019). Theoretical and practical foundations of liquidity-adjusted value-at-risk (LVaR): Optimization algorithms for portfolios selection and management. In N. Metawa, M. Elhoseny, A. E. Hassanien, & M. K. Hassan (Eds.), *Expert systems: Smart financial applications in big data environments*. Routledge/London: Taylor & Francis Group.
5. Al Janabi, M. A. M. (2015). Scenario optimization technique for the assessment of downside-risk and investable portfolios in post-financial crisis. *International Journal of Financial Engineering, 2*(3), 1550028.
6. Al Janabi, M. A. M. (2014). Optimal and investable portfolios: An empirical analysis with scenario optimization algorithms under crisis market prospects. *Economic Modelling, 40*, 369–381.
7. Al Janabi, M. A. M. (2013). Optimal and coherent economic-capital structures: Evidence from long and short-sales trading positions under illiquid market perspectives. *Annals of Operations Research, 205*, 109–139.
8. Al Janabi, M. A. M. (2012). Optimal commodity asset allocation with a coherent market risk modeling. *Review of Financial Economics, 21*, 131–140.

9. Al Janabi, M. A. M. (2011). A generalized theoretical modeling approach for the assessment of economic capital under asset market liquidity risk constraints. *The Service Industries Journal, 31*(13 & 14), 2193–2221.
10. Al Janabi, M. A. M. (2008). Integrating liquidity risk factor into a parametric value at risk method. *Journal of Trading,* (Summer), 76–87.
11. Al Janabi, M. A. M., Ferrer, R., & Shahzad, S. J. H. (2019). Liquidity-adjusted value-at-risk optimization of a multi-asset portfolio using a vine copula approach. *Physica A: Statistical Mechanics and its Applications, 536,* 122579.
12. Al Janabi, M. A. M., Arreola-Hernandez, J. A., Berger, T., & Nguyen, D. K. (2017). Multivariate dependence and portfolio optimization algorithms under illiquid market scenarios. *European Journal of Operational Research, 259*(3), 1121–1131.
13. Almgren, R., & Chriss, N. (1999). *Optimal execution of portfolio transaction.* Working Paper, Department of Mathematics, The University of Chicago.
14. Amihud, Y., Mendelson, H., & Pedersen, L. H. (2005). Liquidity and asset prices. *Foundations and Trends in Finance, 1*(4), 269–364.
15. Angelidis, T., & Benos, A. (2006). Liquidity adjusted value-at-risk based on the components of the bid-ask spread. *Applied Financial Economics, 16*(11), 835–851.
16. Arreola-Hernandez, J., & Al Janabi, M. A. M. (2020). Forecasting of dependence, market and investment risks of a global index portfolio. *Journal of Forecasting, 39*(3), 512–532.
17. Arreola-Hernandez, J., Hammoudeh, S., Khuong, N. D., Al Janabi, M. A. M., & Reboredo, J. C. (2017). Global financial crisis and dependence risk analysis of sector portfolios: A vine copula approach. *Applied Economics, 49*(25), 2409–2427.
18. Arreola-Hernandez, J., Al Janabi, M. A. M., Hammoudeh, S., & Nguyen, D. K. (2015). Time lag dependence, cross-correlation and risk analysis of U.S. energy and non-energy stock portfolios. *Journal of Asset Management, 16*(7), 467–483.
19. Asadi, S., & Al Janabi, M. A. M. (2020). Measuring market and credit risk under Solvency II: Evaluation of the standard technique versus internal models for stock and bond markets. *European Actuarial Journal.* Online First Articles: https://doi.org/10.1007/s13385-020- 00235-0.
20. Ban, G. Y., El Karoui, N., & Lim, A. E. B. (2018). Machine learning and portfolio optimization. *Management Science, 64,* 1136–1154.
21. Bangia, A., Diebold, F., Schuermann, T., & Stroughair, J. (1999). *Modeling liquidity risk with implications for traditional market risk measurement and management.* Working Paper, The Wharton School, University of Pennsylvania.
22. Berkowitz, J. (2000). *Incorporating liquidity risk into VAR models.* Working Paper, Graduate School of Management, University of California, Irvine.
23. Cochrane, J. H. (2005). *Asset Pricing,* Princeton University Press, Princeton, New Jersey.
24. Cornish, E. A., & Fisher, R. A. (1937). Moments and cumulants in the specification of distributions. *Review of the International Statistical Institute, 5,* 307–320.
25. Danielsson, J., & Zigrand, J.-P. (2006). On time-scaling of risk and the square-root-of-time rule. *Journal of Banking & Finance, 30*(10), 2701–2713.
26. Grillini, S., Sharma, A., Ozkan, A., & Al Janabi, M. A. M. (2019). Pricing of time-varying illiquidity within the Eurozone: Evidence using a Markov switching liquidity-adjusted capital asset pricing model. *International Review of Financial Analysis, 64,* 145–158.
27. Hisata, Y., & Yamai, Y. (2000). *Research toward the practical application of liquidity risk evaluation methods.* Discussion Paper, Institute for Monetary and Economic Studies, Bank of Japan.
28. Jarrow, R., & Subramanian, A. (1997). Mopping up liquidity. *Risk, 10*(12), 170–173.
29. Kalayci, C. B., Ertenlice, O., & Akbay, M. A. (2019). A comprehensive review of deterministic models and applications for mean-variance portfolio optimization. *Expert Systems with Applications, 125,* 345–368.
30. Madhavan, A., Richardson, M., & Roomans, M. (1997). Why do security prices change? A transaction-level analysis of NYSE stocks. *Review of Financial Studies, 10,* 1035–1064.
31. Madoroba, S. B. W., & Kruger, J. W. (2014). Liquidity effects on value-at-risk limits: Construction of a new VaR model. *Journal of Risk Model Validation, 8,* 19–46.

32. Markowitz, H. (1952). Portfolio selection. *Journal of Finance, 7*(1), 77–91.
33. Meucci, A. (2009). Managing diversification. *Risk, 22*(5), 74–79.
34. Morgan Guaranty Trust Company. (1994). *RiskMetrics-technical document*. New York: Morgan Guaranty Trust Company, Global Research.
35. Paiva, F. D., Cardoso, R. T. N., Hanaoka, G. P., & Duarte, W. M. (2019). Decision-making for financial trading: A fusion approach of machine learning and portfolio selection. *Expert Systems with Applications, 115*, 635–655.
36. Roch, A., & Soner, H. M. (2013). Resilient price impact of trading and the cost of illiquidity. *International Journal of Theoretical and Applied Finance, 16*(6), 1–27.
37. Ruozi, R., & Ferrari, P. (2013). Liquidity risk management in banks: Economic and regulatory issues. *Springer Briefs in Finance*. https://doi.org/10.1007/978-3-642-29581.
38. Takahashi, D., & Alexander, S. (2002). Illiquid alternative asset fund modeling. *Journal of Portfolio Management, 28*(2), 90–100.
39. Weiß, G. N. F., & Supper, H. (2013). Forecasting liquidity-adjusted intraday s with vine copulas. *Journal of Banking & Finance, 37*, 3334–3350.

Prof. Dr. Mazin A. M. Al Janabi is a full research-professor of finance and banking and financial engineering at EGADE Business School, Tecnologico de Monterrey, Santa Fe campus, Mexico City, Mexico. He holds a Ph.D. degree (1991) from the University of London, UK, and has more than 30 years of real-world experience in science and technology think tanks, engineering enterprises, financial markets, and academic institutions and in many different roles. He has worked for top international financial groups (e.g., ING-Barings and BBVA) where he held several senior management positions, such as Director of Global Market Risk Management, Head of Trading Risk Management, and Head of Derivative Products. Prof. Al Janabi has strong interest for research and developments within emerging economies and has several publications in international refereed journals, books, and chapters in books. Furthermore, his research and developments in quantitative finance have been formally classified in the academic literatures as "*Al Janabi Model*" for liquidity risk management (Liquidity-Adjusted Value at Risk, LVaR Model). Prof. Al Janabi has published top-tiered journals such as the following: *European Journal of Operational Research, Journal of Forecasting, International Review of Financial Analysis, Physica A: Statistical Mechanics and its Applications, European Actuarial Journal, Annals of Operations Research, Applied Economics, Economic Modelling, Review of Financial Economics, Journal of Asset Management, Service Industries Journal, Studies in Economics and Finance, Emerging Markets Finance and Trade, Journal of Risk Finance, Journal of Banking Regulation*, and *Annals of Nuclear Energy*, among others. He received several awards for excellence in teaching and research, and his biography is featured in Who's Who in the World (2013–Present) and in Who's Who in Science and Engineering (2016–Present).

Chapter 10
Context Modelling in Ambient Assisted Living: Trends and Lessons

Armel Ayimdji Tekemetieu, Corentin Haidon, Frédéric Bergeron, Hubert Kengfack Ngankam, Hélène Pigot, Charles Gouin-Vallerand, and Sylvain Giroux

Abstract The current Internet of Things (IoT) development involves ambient intelligence which ensures that IoT applications provide services that are sensitive, adaptive, autonomous, and personalized to the users' needs. A key issue of this adaptivity is context modelling and reasoning. Multiple proposals in the literature have tackled this problem according to various techniques and perspectives. This chapter provides a review of context modelling approaches, with a focus on services offered in Ambient Assisted Living (AAL) systems for persons in need of care. We present the characteristics of contextual information, services offered by AAL systems, as well as context and reasoning models that have been used to implement them. A discussion highlights the trends emerging from the scientific literature to select the most appropriate model to implement AAL systems according to the collected data and the services provided.

Keywords Ambient Assisted Living · Context awareness · Context modelling · Ambient Assisted Living Services · Internet of things

Glossary

AAL	Ambient Assisted Living
ADL	Activity of daily living
BN	Bayesian network
CBR	Case-based reasoning

A. A. Tekemetieu
Laboratoire DOMUS, Université de Sherbrooke, Sherbrooke, QC, Canada

Institut Universitaire de Technologie, Douala, Cameroon
e-mail: Armel.Ayimdji.Tekemetieu@USherbrooke.ca

C. Haidon · F. Bergeron · H. K. Ngankam · H. Pigot (✉) · C. Gouin-Vallerand · S. Giroux
Laboratoire DOMUS, Université de Sherbrooke, Sherbrooke, QC, Canada
e-mail: hubert.kenfack.ngankam@usherbrooke.ca

© Springer Nature Switzerland AG 2021
F. P. García Márquez, B. Lev (eds.), *Internet of Things*, International Series in Operations Research & Management Science 305,
https://doi.org/10.1007/978-3-030-70478-0_10

CNN   Convolutional neural network
ERT   Extremely randomized tree
GMM   Gaussian mixture model
HMM   Hidden Markov model
ICF   International Classification of Functioning
IoT   Internet of Things
k-NN   k-nearest neighbours
MCBS   Multi-cue background subtraction
MCI   Mild cognitive impairment
ML   Machine learning
MM   Markov model
NN   Neural network
QSR   Qualitative spatial representation and reasoning
RFID   Radio-frequency identification
RGB-D   Red Green Blue-Depth
RNN   Recurrent neural network
RTI   Radio tomographic imaging
SAT   Boolean SATisfiability problem
SMO   Sequential minimal optimization
SVM   Support vector machine

10.1 Introduction

The Internet of Things (IoT) has emerged as a field offering multiple devices and applications that fulfil the Ambient Assisted Living (AAL) purpose [1]. The IoT is widely used to provide a broad range of services including home automation and user monitoring. AAL and IoT are closely intertwined; IoT offers means to achieve AAL goals.

Providing services based on IoT supposed to react to events that are triggered in the environment. It is then essential for applications to perceive, understand and analyse the surrounding, which implies to be context-aware. Context-aware systems achieve their purpose by automatically considering the context they operate in without the user's explicit intervention [2]. Such systems improve usability by adjusting their services to the users and increase their efficiency with results that fit the context of use. They therefore hold significant potential to provide for adaptable services in ever-changing environments. AAL is a sub-discipline of context-aware systems which aims to improve the quality of life, especially for people experiencing difficulties in their everyday life. It particularly benefits from the adaptability of context-aware systems. In this chapter, we produce a literature review that focuses on AAL services that ensure health, autonomy and safety for people with special needs who desire to stay home, regardless of their age and physical and psychological conditions [3]. AAL systems need to be continually informed on the ongoing situation in order to counter risks, improve autonomy and cure and, so, without disturbing the inhabitants' habits. This implies that AAL systems are equipped with various sensors that collect information on the person with impairments evolving in his environment and actuators that modify the environment to adequately interact with him or her. Context-aware systems, by essence, must perceive the world of the inhabitant they intend to assist and reason on these perceptions. They are composed of organs that perceive, transmit, reason and communicate with the external world and deliver appropriate solutions that arise through several steps.

The first step is performed by sensors that collect contextual information from the environment. There are several types of sensors, and listing them quickly becomes irrelevant as new ones are continually being released in a rapidly growing market. To this day, no standard to represent data collected by sensors has been established, even from the same type of sensor. Often, values are graduated on different measurement units; on/off information may be expressed by the binary code 0/1 and vice versa.

In the second step, the data sensors collected is transmitted through different networks. There are various protocols for this process; some use Bluetooth, KNX or Zigbee, to name only a few. Gathering the various data coming from various sensors and protocol, communication is not trivial, and the use of middleware is recommended to tackle the convergence of context information. Among the frameworks that have appeared in recent years, CoCaMAAL presents a cloud-oriented middleware approach [4]. Its aim is to provide a unified way to generate context information and to send it to the cloud. A multi-agent approach has also been proposed where each sensor is monitored by an agent [5]. An agent is composed of a three-level architecture. The sensor, at the first level, communicates with its proprietary protocol to the second level, named sink. The sink is responsible for the generation of data stream that it then sends to the third level, the gateway. The gateway receives streams from all sinks and regroups all the agents. Other types of middleware can be found in the literature [6–9].

In the third step, the context-aware system reasons to elaborate actions that the actuators will carry out. Reasoning techniques, for the most part, are based on artificial intelligence to cope with constantly changing environments. This needs, on the one hand, to represent information that is dynamic, heterogeneous and sometimes inaccurate and, on the other hand, to adapt reasonings. Those are broadly classified into knowledge-based, data-driven and hybrid approaches. Each presupposes specific data modelling to perform the reasoning.

Finally, actions on the world are executed by actuators. Like sensors, the types of these devices have rapidly expanded regarding the effects, either visual, oral or under multiple modes, and the protocol they used. Context-aware systems must consider their impact on the environment and the inhabitant's reactions. This retroaction evaluation is part of the awareness of these systems. Creating new sensors and actuators and organizing them into various networks that allow for the establishment of complex and powerful data frameworks form the core of IoT research. For this chapter, we go one step further and examine how the data from the IoT can be used to build context-aware systems oriented towards AAL.

Several valuable surveys have been conducted on context-aware systems, IoT and AAL. Some focus on computational aspects, while others concern services offered. The survey conducted by [10] develops context representations, carried out by database and ontology modelling, and reasoning used to deal with the nature of context information. Reasoning is discussed according to the choice of sources, types of data and uncertainty of information. As well as [10], the surveys conducted by [11, 12] examine various models of representation, opening on architectures and AAL platforms. Criteria on interoperability, scalability, confidentiality, security and fault tolerance underlie the comparisons [13]. In a discussion includes situations where the models are applicable with respect to the nature of data and the types of sensors. A review of services offered by context-aware systems in smart homes is presented in [14] following by a discussion on the technical means, such as devices, protocols and algorithms, used to reason on context data. A more specific review focuses on AAL services, presenting tools, technologies and algorithms, as well as the applications in monitoring and the prevention of wandering and cognitive orthotics devices [3].

The goal of this chapter is to review recent context models in order to determine the most appropriate context modelling and reasoning approaches to consider for implementing specific AAL services based on IoT. Surveys conducted on the field tend to isolate services from context models. However, the type of service delivered may constrain not only the type of data collected by the IoT technology but also how these are represented and the type of reasoning. It is then important to build a bridge between AAL services and context models. We suggest that the choice of model and reasoning depends on the type of service delivered. To achieve this goal, we will present a review on context-aware systems for AAL covering the last decade (2010–2020) to identify last development trends. In this review, services, contextual representation and reasoning are described, and relations are established between them.

The chapter is organized as follows. An overview of the most frequently offered services in the AAL is presented in the first section. In the second section are presented the data used according to the context. The third section overviews the context models and reasoning that have been used during the last decade. In this section, we present each model extensively and give a detailed view of context modelling and reasoning developed to provide services. Doing this enables us to synthesize and derive trends in the discussion section before concluding the chapter.

10.2 Ambient Assisted Living Services

To address the impacts of the service choice on context representations and reasonings, we first define what is a service and more specifically an AAL service. We then present the services according to the beneficiaries, first the inhabitants and second the caregivers. We close this section by presenting the basic services that are needed to achieve the previous ones.

10.2.1 Definition of AAL Services

Reference [15] distinguishes care and assistance services, on the one hand, and software services on the other hand. The latter are defined in information technology as a set of functionalities performing actions. The focus is put on data, processing, control flow and interoperability between all the components. The former are derived from a business and customer perspective and are defined in terms of added value provided to customers. In this section, we adopt the perspective from the customer to present the various services related to AAL, where the customers are the beneficiaries of AAL, either inhabitants or caregivers.

AAL services for people with special needs are by nature medical and social. They shift the focus to helping frail people in their daily life, to compensate for the natural reduction in physical or cognitive capacities they encounter. The task to assist becomes then central, instead of the technology used to perform it.

It requires generally a collaboration between different actors and a user-centred approach to achieve the appropriate service that fulfils the collaborative assisted living ecosystem. Thus, an AAL service refers to a composite service or a set of services that combines several simpler services to meet customer needs. It usually aims to achieve some of these goals:

- Aid persons with specific needs in their activities of daily living (ADLs).
- Promote autonomy and social integration.
- Personalize assistance according to capacities, preferences and habits.
- Adapt the assistance according to the evolution of the persons.
- Integrate needs of caregivers to help providing care and reduce burden.
- Enhance coordination of care through efficient systems.

AAL services have been widely explored in ambient intelligence field, where technology is integrated seamlessly into everyday objects to empower people through sensitive and adaptive environments. Among the variety of AAL services offered, we mainly focus in this review on services delivered indoor as shown in Fig. 10.1. Outdoor assistance is covered in detail in the smart city literature. The indoor environment is generally restricted to smart homes [16, 17], but nursing homes and hospitals are also considered [18].

10.2.2 Services for Inhabitants

AAL services are dedicated generally to a wide set of inhabitants, most often elderly or frail people. For instance, [19] describes AAL services as providing intelligent and context-aware assistance for elderly people at home. Reference [20] states that most of AAL services are dedicated to seniors and people with special needs, disabilities or impairments. This is shared by [21] that points out the capacity of AAL services to assist frail persons anytime and anywhere in their ADLs. But some

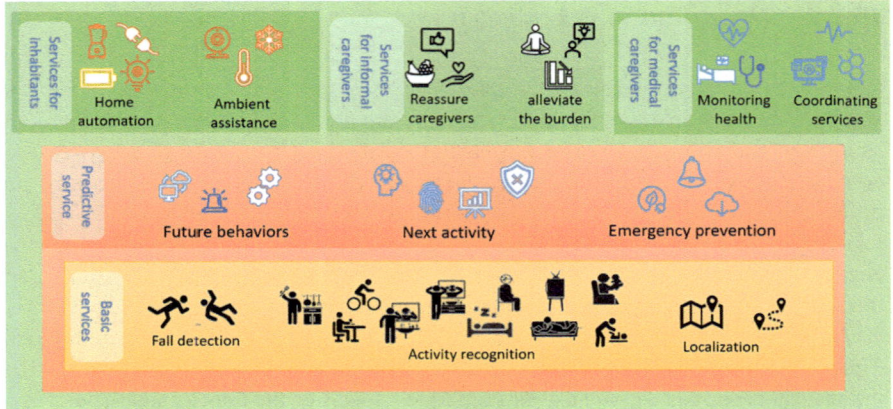

Fig. 10.1 Indoor ambient Assisted Living Services

services are dedicated for more specific categories of inhabitants including persons with loss of mobility [22], persons suffering from Alzheimer's disease [23] and other cognitive disabilities [4, 24], and persons experiencing a loss of perception or with chronic disease such as diabetics [25, 26].

There is a consensus among AAL designers that the off-the-shelf devices do not suit the inhabitant's needs and preferences. An adapted and personalized service is required to help inhabitants to stay home by assistive services, alert services and home automation.

Fostering autonomy is a major goal pursued by ambient assistance for inhabitants. Also called cognitive assistance when used to compensate cognitive deficits, the ambient assistance delivers appropriate prompts when the inhabitant forgets to carry out an ADL [27] or fails in performing it [16, 23, 24, 28]. Verbal and oral prompts are displayed to complete basic ADLs [16, 23], specific ADL such as taking medicine [26, 29] or more complex one, such as cooking [24]. Promptings are displayed in the smart home, on smart phones [30, 31] and through conversational agents [29, 32]. Some actions may even be physically carried out when the AAL system turns off electrical appliances [24, 30] or moves objects with robots [33].

In case of emergency, due to either abnormal physiological situation, lack of movements or abnormal body posture, AAL services alert the inhabitant or inform caregivers to resolve the situation [34]. In this case, it is important to quickly reach the inhabitant at the right moment in the right place [17, 31]. Feedback is also crucial to engage an efficient conversation between the inhabitant, AAL service and eventually caregivers to evaluate the dangerousness level [35].

Recent years have also seen the explosion of home automation services. Energy saving and lighting automation are often the targeted functionalities [1, 28]. The key principle is to personalize the service according to the on-going activity [36], the time of the day [23] and the inhabitant's perceptual capacities and preferences [28, 37].

10.2.3 Services for Caregiver

Caregivers benefit from AAL services, which help monitoring health, coordinating services and reducing burden. We use the term caregiver in a broad sense, meaning everyone who is giving care, including medical personnel and relatives with no medical training.

Relatives, also called informal caregivers, are often loved ones or neighbours, generally not living with the inhabitant. Few articles tackle the issue of an inhabitant living with his caregiver [38]. The area of expertise of the relatives is usually unknown and is not taken in account when deploying general services. Services dedicated for informal caregivers are aimed to reassure caregivers, alleviate the burden and help them prevent adverse situations [23].

Medical personnel, also called formal caregivers, are usually but not only nurses, beneficiary attendants, psychologists, occupational therapists and doctors. It is easier to define their expertise. Therefore, the language of interaction reflects the proper professional terms. In the hospital and in the nursing homes, the aim is to alert medical personnel as soon as a hazardous situation occurs [18, 39]. When the inhabitant lives at home, healthcare providers may be alerted remotely to intervene in the case of fall, fire risks and vital signs monitoring [30, 34, 35].

Recommendation systems are part of medical services to help making the right decision based on objective data coming from medical history and physiological and environmental sensors [5, 40]. Finally, coordination of the interventions between the multiple healthcare providers constitutes a service that requires context data [25].

10.2.4 Basic Services

Basic services are prerequisite for the elaborated services dedicated to inhabitants and caregivers that we have presented previously. They are intended to recognize what is going on in the smart home, either to identify the inhabitant's behaviour or to predict his next behaviour. Basic services concern mainly activity, body posture, location and identification of people.

10.2.4.1 Activity Recognition

Activity recognition is a popular service, and literature on this topic is abundant [29, 30, 41]. Activities are generally identified by a sequence of actions that may be sequential and a set of events occurring in the smart home. Context is helpful as most people reproduce habits leading to action repetition in the same order, at the same moment and the same place. Most often, authors discriminate activities among various ones from three [42] to five [43]. Activity recognition may occur in specific area of the smart home, like kitchen and bathroom [44].

The activity recognition helps diagnosing abnormal behaviours [1, 45], detecting change in the habits [4, 46] and predicting the next activity the inhabitant may perform [16].

10.2.4.2 Posture Recognition

Posture recognition consists most often to discriminate among three positions lying, sitting and standing. Associated with activity, it increases the likelihood of activity recognition [1, 27]. Posture recognition is intensively used to identify fall. A fall is detected when the posture changes abruptly from sitting or standing to lying at an unconventional place [27, 39].

10.2.4.3 Localization

Localization services aim to determine where persons or objects are within a given environment [47, 48]. While this service can be useful when someone gets lost, it is commonly used as a context information for other services, such as activity recognition or posture recognition.

A navigation service helps reaching a given destination. It combines a localization service with a cognitive assistance. This service usually involves a prediction of the next paths the inhabitant will follow to reach his goal [49]. The concept of destination is also extended to include completion of various tasks, as required by planification [31, 50].

10.2.4.4 Predictive Services

Even if predictive services are most often included in other basic services, some papers focus specifically on how to determine the next item, either activity, behaviour, medical status or room. They analyse the past and current situation to infer what might occur next.

Predicting next activities is part of some AAL services to determine the most likely activity to assist in the future [16]. Also, predicting the next place to go is the core of navigation services [48]. Prevention is by essence a predictive service, whose purpose is to avoid any dangerous situation, both medically and in the daily living [34]. In recent years, researchers pushed predictive services into the realm of psychological predictions. In [4, 46], the authors aim to detect long-term changes, predicting then future behaviours, future psychological states or future disease symptoms. This prediction relies heavily on context data as no sensor can measure directly a psychological state.

In this section, we presented a review of current services offered in a healthcare context. We have presented them as being independent services. However, many papers in the literature propose solutions that include more than one service. For instance, COOK [24] is a cooking assistant coupled with an autonomous security service for cooking. It combines a cognitive assistant, an emergency prediction service relying on a localization service for some safety rules.

10.3 Context Information and Context Awareness in AAL Systems

Understanding and defining the context are a prerequisite to its modelling. This section will describe sources and characteristics of context and context awareness and will emphasize its importance in AAL. We will present how the main challenges of context modelling are derived from the nature of context information, which is dynamic, heterogeneous and sometimes inaccurate.

Context is a concept used in several domains to generally describe all the information or circumstances related to a fact or an event and that can help to explain or understand it (definition adapted from the Oxford dictionary). For instance, in the field of education, the concept of learning context is centred toward a human and its learning resources: it is the "various circumstances in which learning might occur, where the learning context consists of students, culture, teachers, lesson plans, etc. In addition, learning context refers to the set of learning activities, including the space in which learning itself occurs, and students' perceptions of the ability of a particular space in providing rich learning experiences" [51]. In fact, some authors such as Bazire and Brézillon [52] found in the literature hundreds of definitions of the concept of context. Therefore, it is prerequisite to define the concept of context and context-aware computing applied to AAL systems for choosing the appropriate model.

In computer science and more specifically in ubiquitous computing, the Anind K. Dey definition of context is probably the most widely shared: "Context is any information that can be used to characterize the situation of an entity. An entity is a person, place, or object that is considered relevant to the interaction between a user and an application, including the user and applications themselves" [9]. The same author added that "a system is context-aware if it uses context to provide relevant information and/or services to the user, where relevancy depends on the user's task" [9]. Related to ambient systems, context-aware computing "describes the ability of the computer to sense and act upon information about its environment, such as location, time, temperature or user identity. This information can be used to enable selective responses such as triggering alarms or retrieving information relevant to the task at hand" [53]. From those three definitions, we can extract some findings:

The nature of information for describing a context is task dependent. In fact, the entity (user or system) tasks are central to the notion of context.

If we compared the context to a "space", the user, and more specifically the system/object with which the user is interacting to perform a task, is at the centre of this space.

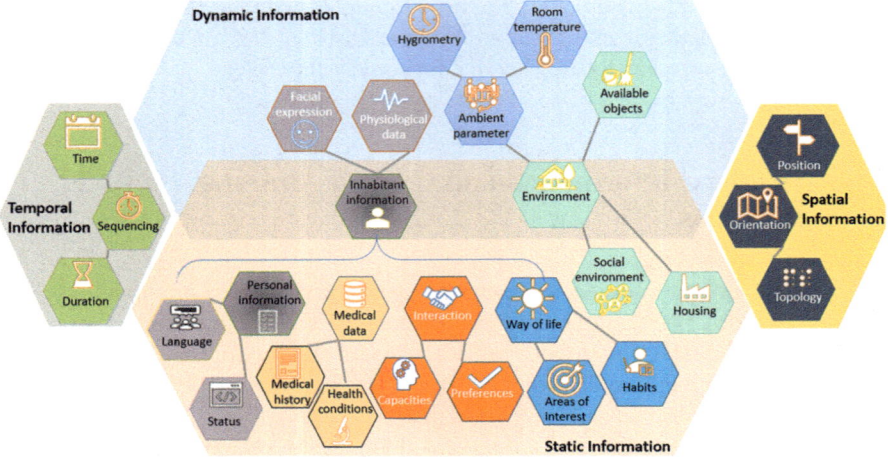

Fig. 10.2 Contextual information for AAL services

Information about the context (i.e. contextual information) can be divided into four categories: (i) information about the users; (ii) information about the environment/space surrounding the users; (iii) information about the spatial elements of that space; and (iv) information about time or temporal link between contextual information.

Based on these definitions and findings, we will, in the next lines, present and discuss about the concept of context and contextual information in AAL (Fig. 10.2).

10.3.1 Contextual Information on Inhabitants

Information about the users is part of contextual information. In AAL, final users who benefit from services include inhabitants as well as caregivers. We first focus on services for inhabitants. To deliver adequate information under suitable forms for assisting, alerting or preventing necessitates to know the capacities of the user to handle such information. Any contextual data regarding the user concern and ability to deal with the service when it is delivered is also relevant. We then divide the contextual information on inhabitants into two categories that correspond to the static and dynamic characteristics pointed out by [1]. The first category regards general information, including capacities and preference. This information is rather static or evolves slowly over time. The second information, dynamic in nature, regards the current situation of the inhabitant, especially his position or physiological data.

10.3.1.1 Static Information on Inhabitants

First, information of the status helps identify the inhabitant who will receive the service. Even if the status information is not always explicit, many authors determine name, age, gender and language as important information to hold [1, 27, 30, 46]. This information may be part of the medical history; some authors refer globally.

Second, as this literature review focuses on assistance, great emphasis is put on medical data such as diseases and symptoms. Some authors identify specific disease or health conditions, such as diabetes, pregnancy, diet and motor or cognitive diseases [25, 26, 29]. Most prefer to refer to a broad description of diseases they include in the medical history without specifying them. Especially they mention chronic diseases and medication and physiological data such as hypertension. Also, weight and size are indicators of health [46]. Some authors identify the medical model they rely on, either the international classification OMS [26] or a more local classification, hold by a shared medical record [18, 46, 54].

Third, some authors pay attention on how the service will be delivered. Besides the language, the interaction is determined by the sensorial capacities, for instance, failing eyesight [31, 55] and the preference such as the gender of the system voice [56]. The inhabitant profile is also determined by health conditions, such as head trauma that limits the number of stimuli [18]. Also, acceptation of messages is considered [56].

Fourth, the habits and areas of interest are taken in account, such as preferences in food or movies [29, 46]. Such habits may have an impact on health, such as smoking [54].

Finally, ethics consideration is part of the context due to the sensitive data handled. For instance, the level of confidentiality of the service delivered is determined by the situation and the persons who could be aware of the collected data [39].

10.3.1.2 Dynamic Information on Inhabitants

Delivering appropriate services needs to collect contextual data that allows to judge the severity of the situation. A plethora of vital signs are gathered to evaluate at each moment the health status. It includes heart rate, respiration rate, blood pressure, blood oxygen saturation, blood sugar level and body temperature [1, 18, 26, 27, 34, 46, 57]. It is gathered continuously through wearable devices or at specific moments with electronic devices such as finger pulse oximeter and blood sugar metre.

Recognizing emotion and facial expressions provides information on the pain felt and the confidence in the service [29, 56].

The location of the inhabitant and his position in space is also an important source of contextual data. It helps determine the service and its modality of delivering. Fire emergencies exemplify how the position data influences the service: where (in which room the message must be sent?); when (waiting for people coming back to the kitchen?); how (on the closer screen or by oral message?); and what (is the inhabitant not reachable requiring to turn off the stove automatically?) [24, 35]. Information on space and the influence of the position of the inhabitant will be more detailed in the Section Spatial Information.

10.3.2 Environmental Information

Environmental information is by nature contextual. It concerns everything that surrounds a person. In the International Classification of Functioning (ICF) model validated by the World Health Organization, the environment is a key component to explain the human being functioning [58]. Individuals characterized by their deficiencies and capacities interact with the environment to carry out activities. This interaction generates handicap if the individual with his capacities is unable to complete the desired activity in the specific environment. Among the physical, social and financial environmental aspects involved in ICF, context in AAL retains just the first two. Physical environment refers to all objects and physical structures that the person may be in contact with during his life. For the purpose of AAL, we restrict this physical environment to home. Social environment refers to the persons who surround the inhabitant and the ones he could meet to satisfy his goals and fulfil his activities. In both social and physical environments, static and dynamic features of the collected data are distinguished. We present first the data gathered to determine the physical environment and second the data to determine the social environment.

10.3.3 Physical Environmental Information

Physical environmental data describe on one hand how the inhabitant feels comfortable and on the other hand how he interacts with the environment to complete activities. The first set draws together data regarding ambient parameters [37, 40, 59]. Among multiple parameters some papers mention at least lightness [1, 28, 46], noise [34, 44, 46], temperature [17, 30], humidity [17, 59], and carbonic gas and smoke concentrations [32, 59]. The second set of data helps describe the current activity in process. Knowing the room where the inhabitant is or the seat he is sitting on points towards the activities to recognize. It supposes to locate the inhabitant and know the layout of space and furniture. Spatial reasoning will be described in the Section Spatial Information. We focus here on contextual data collected to help determining activities in progress. Spatial data are collected through infrared sensors, pression mats and contact on doors to locate the inhabitant. As almost all studies use such sensors, let us name just few [18, 23, 36, 43, 60, 61]. Some studies use specific information to determine the kind of activities in process as electrical power [35–37, 43, 59] or flow sensor [43]. Moreover, some activities are precisely targeted when a specific object is involved during its execution such as dry soil to water plant [32], phone when calling [56] and all radio-frequency identification (RFID) sensors placed on objects [26, 62]. Even more precisely, RGB-D (Red Green Blue-Depth) cameras inform about movements done by the inhabitant for recognizing current activities [39, 62–64]. Wearable sensors are generally used to collect physiological data, but accelerometer gives relevant information about the activity in process or the severity of the situation. It is the case when the inhabitant is falling [27, 34, 43, 62]. Finally, some authors pay attention to the state of the objects involved in the environment to ensure that they are available, such as battery level [59] and computer state [30].

10.3.4 Social Environment

Finally, the social environment is taken in account. It implies registering in the medical history the name and function of medical staff [25] and, in general, information on relatives [1, 25, 46, 48]. This information is necessary when caregivers need to be reached, either for informing of the evolution of the inhabitant's daily life or to alert when adverse events occur [36].

10.3.5 Temporal Information

On one hand, some context-aware systems are reacting to specific information at a specific time without any notions of historic or temporal logic. On the other hand, AAL services need, in most of the case, a history of the contextual information in order to adapt services or recognize series of human activities, for instance, knowing how much time a day a user is using the oven or if the oven was started before detecting someone in the shower. Such information is the premise of activity recognition.

Temporal information is essential to support activity recognition and error detection. Especially, determining if activities are executed in parallel or sequentially may lead to diverse inferences. It is then required to keep a trace of the time a contextual information has been collected. For that purpose, Allen [65] proposed a framework to support the temporal reasoning using the interval logic. His work is one of the cornerstones of the activity recognition. Since the work of Allen, the W3C proposed a draft recommendation for a definition of an OWL ontology to specify the time and the temporal relation between concepts [66]. It provides a framework for the use of the temporal concepts in ontologies that describe context, such as the model described in the next section.

Other projects propose to use machine learning (ML) approaches to manage temporal relation and, for instance, classify series of events into activities and thus generate higher level of contextual information, either decision trees [57], dynamic time warping [67], support vector machine (SVM) [57, 63], Bayesian networks (BNs) [16, 49], specialized probabilistic models such as Markov models (MMs) [36, 38, 46] or sequence mining [16, 50]. In [68], the authors are using a hybrid approach by extracting frequent episodes of events with the Apriori algorithm and using an MM to model the transition between the user's activities.

10.3.6 Spatial Information

Spatial information includes the structure of environment itself (i.e., the topology) and the position of the objects or users in the space. Combined with other contextual information, the movement of specific objects monitored over time helps inferring the activities the user is performing [41, 47]. It is required then at some extent to describe the space and its topology and know the positions of the entities (i.e., objects or users) in a Euclidean space.

Geometrical systems are used to describe spatial information. In [69], an ontology model includes a referential system where each physical entity received a three-dimensional cardinal position and a time stamp related to the last position when a user or an object was located. In [70], the authors extend the ontology model of [69] to describe an environment's topology. They include zones delimited by walls, cabinets and doors. Zones are described by a list of 2D positions, forming 2D geometrical structures, and entities (objects or users) are placed into zones. Finally, the users' field of view is also represented to determine which entities the user may perceive. This spatial information, added to other contextual information, allows reasoning over service provision on the most adapted devices for a specific user.

Most of the works use descriptive representations to reason on space, either using ontologies [7, 17] among other knowledge representations [49].

10.3.7 Delimiting the Context

One of the problems that come up regularly in the literature about context is to delimit its spatial and temporal boundaries. The definition proposed by [9], as the capacity for a computing system to perceive contextual information, does not stand anymore for distributed systems and IoT. In fact, context boundaries are constantly pushed by aggregating information for different nodes such as smart phones, sensor networks, etc. The context boundaries, instead of being delimited by the capacities of perception, may be defined by the goals of services offered. For instance, the context of cooking assistance [35] may be restricted to the preparation of meals, such as the culinary fence, the state of the meal in preparation and the state of the oven. However, in several systems that propose a framework for multiple services [16, 23], the context boundaries must then be extended until the upper one. But with web services, the boundaries need to be pushed even farther. Thus, the limits of context at the end must be ultimately specified by the developers and the different end users.

10.3.8 *Heterogeneity of Data*

The heterogeneity of the sensors that are producing data at different rhythms and in different formats raises the issue of context-aware standard. In one of the first context-aware system framework, the Context Toolkit [9], widgets are filtering and transforming data before sharing it to other services. In modern IoT sensor networks, such transformation can be performed directly in the nodes. However, in most AAL systems that implement context awareness, a certain level of context modelling is required to allow higher-level reasoning and inferences. In the next section, we are covering different approaches in modelling contextual information for AAL systems.

10.4 Approaches of Context Modelling in AAL Systems

As discussed in the preceding section, context is a complex but key aspect for AAL systems to provide adaptability to users' needs. This section focuses on studies that provide precise information on how authors approach context modelling and reasoning in their AAL systems. However, it is important to note that multiple studies in the literature do not explicit those concepts despite discussing context awareness [48] or support systems for AAL services [19, 38, 63, 64]. Hence, we could not include them inside our analysis. We describe several works done in the literature, focusing on their approaches of context modelling and reasoning. Approaches developed so far are either knowledge-based, a model is provided, holding semantical knowledge; or data-driven, data is the main source of reasoning; or sometimes both, what we will refer to as "hybrid approaches".

10.4.1 *Knowledge-Based Approaches*

Recent literature promotes logic-based and semantic models, where explicit description of domain knowledge and inference engines are used to derive implicit knowledge. Advantages of knowledge-based approaches include a shared understanding of data and their semantics, as well as reasoning mechanisms. Some of the recent works in this vein are summarized in the following.

Multiple works are dedicated to software architecture.

In 2010, [5] describes an architecture for IoT based on a multi-agent approach. The architecture handles low-level data stream of sensors and translates them into higher-level data, giving them a healthcare-related semantic, thanks to specialized ontologies and inference rules.

SAMURAI [7] is another architecture designed to tackle large-scale knowledge-based context. It relies on a semantic representation of the rooms and activities in OWL. Batch reasoning is performed using Apache Spark and simple RDF triples as rules. Complex event streams are handled by Esper and help provide higher-level interpretation of low-level events. Finally, GeoSPARQL's spatiotemporal reasoning data is used as an input for classification and clustering, opening the way to activity recognition.

The work in [33] describes a multi-agent robotic intelligence for user assistance in activities like moving objects. An event model is represented in an ontology when a SQL database stores agent's memory. Ontological reasoning is then performed to recognize the current situation, followed by the simulation of assistance in a virtual environment to ensure the feasibility of actions before doing them in the real world.

Finally, in 2018, [18] describes a cascading framework for healthcare support in hospitals and nursing homes. The framework rests on an ontology compiling medical domain and IoT knowledge to semantically annotate observations inside the environment. After filtering and aggregation, reasoning is performed on the observations locally and in the cloud using OWL 2 RL or DL, and the medical staff is prevented in case of emergency.

Medical staff can also benefit from recommendations to support their decisions especially using ontologies for contextual handling and rule-based inference.

In 2012, [25] proposes a tool to ease the coordination of professionals working with chronically ill patients. An OWL-DL ontology of the chronic illness domain has been built considering 19 diseases, 2 syndromes and 5 social issue specificities and adequate interventions. A personalized ontology is then built according to the patient diagnoses and symptoms, and probabilities of illness and effective interventions are computed based on the ontological properties and relations.

Reference [26] is a recommendation expert system for anti-diabetic drug selection built on top of an ontology (medicine name, composition and associated information), and a diabetic patient tests ontology in OWL with Protégé. Medical guidelines were used as criteria for SWRL rules about drug selection, which were then converted to JESS for reasoning. Recommendations are inferred by applying the rules to the patient test data, resulting in a list of recommended drugs and their descriptions.

On the patients' side, multiple instances of AAL systems are described.

COOK [24, 35] is a cognitive orthosis designed to help people with head trauma injury during meal preparation. The orthosis relies on an OWL ontology holding concepts such as home space, devices, assistance and activities. Data gathered from the sensors is fed to a "Preventive Assistance System" following hierarchical task network-inspired scenarios to detect hazardous situations, to alert the user and the caregiver and to stop the stove in case of emergency.

Reference [1] presents E-care@Home, an adapted house for older adults with special needs that can offer domestic automation and health e-monitoring (anomaly detection and emergency) based on activity recognition. In E-care@Home, context raw data streams from various environmental and body sensors are collected and stored into a database that feeds an ontology of sensors belonging to an ontology network that also contains ontologies on events, situations, time intervals and the physical environment. Activity recognition is then performed by a set of logic rules built on top of ontologies and non-monotonic reasoning using answer set programming for stream reasoning.

Reference [40] proposes Dem@Home, an ambient intelligence system for clinical support of people living with dementia. Ambient and wearable sensor observations and application domain specifics are captured in an OWL2 ontology that is aligned on DUL and integrates OWL Time[1] to capture temporal context. OWL2 reasoning enables activity recognition, while SPARQL rules are used to determine non-pharmaceutical interventions to improve care and to extract clinical problems.

Reference [28] proposes a home automation system that supports personalization for elderly persons and their caregivers. They use an ontology for devices and digital personality representation. The ontology integrates OWL Time for temporal aspects. Rules are added to determine automatic actions to perform and to check autonomously whether the intended actions are performed correctly.

Moreover, AAL solutions often rely on activity or situation recognition.

In [42] where raw data from pressure, contact and ultrasonic sensors are described in CoSSN (Cognitive SSN), an ontology that supports semantic detection of three activities (dressing up, watching TV, taking shower) by the means of SPARQL rules and queries.

Reference [60] provides some strong insights on how they use an ontology combined with a reasoner to perform real-time activity recognition despite focusing on time-window manipulation. The OWL-DL ontology holds representations of activities of daily living, house and sensors. Using pellet and their described algorithm, they achieve real-time activity recognition with high accuracy.

Reference [43] presents an ontology-based activity and body posture recognition for older adults with cognitive and physical impairments. An ontology is used to store data from wearable sensors, objects used and actions performed by users. OWL reasoning with HermiT reasoner enables to derive users' activities (cooking, having meal, taking medicine, washing dishes, watching TV, wandering in lounge, toileting) and body posture (standing, sitting, walking).

Reference [17] proposes an ontology-based situation-aware assistance for cognitively impaired people in smart homes. OWL reasoning using SPARQL is used for situation recognition (e.g. sleeping, making coffee, cooking, drinking, watching TV, location, events) and user prompting.

---

[1] https://www.w3.org/TR/owl-time/

Finally, for the recognition of complex kitchen and bathroom activities of ageing population in an AAL environment, [44] uses an ADL ontology enriched with rules to derive events from raw data of multiple sensors first and then activities from events.

Navigation and location are other topics discussed in the literature.

Reference [71] aims at minimizing the need in sensors by inferring the user's location and intention from their control logs, i.e. how they interact with the system and not with the environment. To do so, an ontology is built describing the user, devices, basic services, locations, effects and the AAL system itself. Relations link the user with doors, rooms, devices, services and their effect. SWRL rules are then used to infer the movement of the user and its intention and suggest adequate device or service activation.

Reference [48] presents one of the very few outdoor services considered in this review which is the assistive navigation system based on augmented reality for people with MCI. The system generates navigation based on the user's cognitive context (orientation needs) and well-known places to supply spatial orientation and cognitive facilitation. The user's context is represented by fuzzy sets that enable to dynamically generate routes due to the use of fuzzy logic.

Finally, some works cannot be labelled behind the previous categories.

Recently, Converness, a conversational assistance system that analyses verbal and nonverbal observations and provides speech-based information about basic care (e.g. injury treatment) to older adults with cognitive impairments (mild cognitive impairment (MCI), dementia), was proposed in [29]. Converness makes use of OWL2 ontologies to model sensor data, user profile (e.g. medical data, preferences), nonverbal data (e.g. gestures, facial expression) and conversation themes and topics. OWL2 reasoning and SPIN/SHACL rules are then used for topic understanding and conversational awareness when defeasible reasoning (non-monotonic rules) is used for user-centred conflict resolution (context disambiguation).

Concerning the management of a smart building, a comfort-compliant energy saving system is proposed in [59]. This work uses an OWL ontology to represent the smart building concepts, environmental parameters and devices, while rule-based agents and defeasible logics are used to enforce energy-saving policies in the automatic management of the smart infrastructure.

The works presented here show the importance of the integration of semantics in AAL systems. In fact, semantics provides a better understanding of the meaning of data collected by IoT devices and favours human and machine readability and easy interpretability. For example, [26], E-care@Home [1], Converness [29] and COOK [24, 35] go beyond sensor raw data and provide high-level descriptions of environments, users' needs and profiles, activities and their preconditions aligned with changes captured in raw data to provide health or safety assistance to users with special needs. However, capturing semantics requires a good understanding of the domain and procedures, a good trade-off between the expressivity of the chosen knowledge representation formalism and efficiency of reasoning and ideally a good mean to describe and reason on temporal relations between data or activities as in [1, 28]. In some cases, inaccurate or missing sensor readings, the availability of huge volume of data and the need for prediction of future behaviours can be hardly manage with knowledge-based techniques: here come into play data-driven approaches.

10.4.2 Data-Driven Approaches

Data-driven approaches use statistical and ML techniques on context datasets. The best strengths of these models are their independence from precise human description of knowledge and their ability to handle noise, uncertainty or incomplete sensor data. They have been widely used for some service provision in AAL systems.

A lot of works focus on activity or posture recognition as a baseline.

Reference [61] takes a brain-inspired approach for human activity recognition. Starting from the sensor values, a network of "neuro-symbolic" network, similar to a neural network (NN), is trained with online-available dataset. Additional knowledge and reasoning variables from external sources are supported such as time or presence. The current activity is then deducted by inputting the current situation to the network.

SCAN [62] is a framework for activity recognition which relies on three layers: recognizing artefacts with which the user interacts, inferring the user's activity and representing the user's activity. First, acquired data is compared to a threshold to extract the interactions between the user and his artefacts. Then, activity inference is performed by matching the duration, number of beats and artefacts with hard-coded criteria.

Reference [57] proposes a generic feature engineering approach. From a variety of wearable sensors, robust features are selected to generate reliable classification models for activity recognition. The aim is to reduce the costs by facilitating execution of algorithms on devices with limited resources and by using as few sensors as possible. In this study, SVM, random forest and extremely randomized trees (ERT) show better accuracy for all combinations of sensors among six classifiers.

Reference [63] presents novel methods and ideas to design automatic posture recognition systems using an RGB-D camera. Two supervised methods are introduced to learn and recognize human postures. The first method consists in training CNNs based on convolutional features extracted from 2D images to recognize human postures using transfer learning on RGB and depth images. The second method consists to model the posture using the body joint configuration in the 3D space and recognize posture through SVM classification of 3D skeleton-based features.

Reference [64] presents an activity recognition system based on skeleton data extracted from a depth camera that can be installed in an AAL environment. The system makes use of ML techniques to classify the actions that are described with a set of a few basic postures known as "key poses". The training phase creates several models related to the number of clustered postures by means of a multiclass SVM, trained with sequential minimal optimization (SMO). The classification phase adopts the X-means algorithm to find the optimal number of clusters dynamically for activity recognition.

Going further, some works tackle prediction or behaviour trends that may arise.

Reference [16], with MavHome project, aims "to create a home that acts as an intelligent agent" detecting actions of its inhabitants, predicting the next action and acting accordingly to assist [50]. Interactions between inhabitants and devices are stored inside a Markov chain of events; hence the next action is the action with the highest probability considering the current state and precedent known sequence of actions.

Reference [22] presents an AAL system that uses spatial and temporal context to recognize ADL and detect increasing or decreasing health conditions of elderly with diabetes and decreased mobility. Privacy-compliant low-resolution visual sensor data feeds a Hidden Markov Model (HMM) with k-nearest neighbours (k-NN) classifier for user's location. Mobility patterns and sleep duration estimates serve as the backbone of ADL recognition and problem detection.

To detect future anomalous behaviours of elderly suffering from dementia, [72] makes use of low-level wireless sensors (motion and door entry point) in an existing home, making it smart. The collected sensor observations are then represented either in time series or start time/duration parameters to enable an RNN to predict the future values of activities for each sensor and, then, the future behaviours of the resident.

Reference [32] designed a virtual butler which provides spatialized vocal interaction to the inhabitants. The state of all sensors within the home is stored inside a buffer and updated with new records to feed ML classification algorithm. Classification rules derived from a pre-trained multilayer perceptron neural network are used to predict whether a situation is normal or abnormal and to interact with the inhabitant accordingly.

Privacy is another important issue represented.

Reference [68] presents a pattern mining approach that does not necessarily involve highly intrusive sensors. Heterogenous sensor data are mined to detect frequent patterns, and activity recognition can then be deduced from the chain of events that is detected by the system.

Following this privacy trend, [39] proposes an intelligent risk detection and telecare assistant with a focus on privacy protection for long-term care of elderly or disabled people. The video-based system gives the opportunity to caregivers to assess the real risk and system interventions by visualizing the scene and the user at different levels of privacy including raw image, blur, silhouette or 3D avatar. The video stream is processed with Gaussian mixture model (GMM) and multi-cue background subtraction (MCBS) for object detection (e.g. faces, bodies) and situation recognition (events and activities).

Finally, some works deal with other concerns such as positioning or multi-occupancy.

Since many AAL services are based on location of objects of interest, [45] proposes a position-based AAL framework that combines a device-free localization system based on radio tomographic imaging (RTI) and an ADL monitoring system together, for ageing in place. In the monitoring system, the position-based marks offer the emergent representation of daily activities and are used with a convolutional neural network (CNN) to accomplish the tasks of recognizing ADLs and detecting anomalies.

Reference [38] explores the problem of multi-occupant context modelling through their data traces disambiguation. First, an accessibility graph of the binary sensors network is built. Then, sensor data is aggregated into user traces and used to train MMs of multiple occupants. Parameters are obtained by following a conditional least squares method combined with a distance-based assumption.

These approaches are very efficient for pattern recognition and prediction problems where some models are trained on raw data collected from various IoT devices to recognize actions/behaviours and/or predict next actions/behaviours. For instance, SCAN [62–64, 68] uses various sensors to classify activities, while systems like MavHome [16, 72] extend this scope with prediction. When privacy is a key, some systems make use of non-intrusive sensors [22, 68], or they change the way data are handled and presented accordingly [39, 63, 64]. It should be noted that data-driven approaches presented in the described works are appropriate when semantics is not a key and that there is enough annotated data and good processing power available. Furthermore, when IoT devices are subject to changes, the need for training data enforces to re-train data to adapt to changes in devices and can be a drawback of these approaches. Concerning data-driven algorithms, regardless of the theoretical model used (ad hoc models or mature models including MM, NN, BN), they are usually not reusable as they do not offer abstract reasoning mechanisms based on semantics. That's why hybrid approaches were developed to benefit from the strength of both knowledge-based and data-driven approaches and to mitigate their shortcomings.

10.4.3 Hybrid Approaches

A third category, hybrid approaches, has emerged to combine both strengths of knowledge-based and data-driven models. The last decade is also prominent in AAL services implemented this way.

Hybrid-approaches also rely on basic services such as activity recognition.

Reference [67] presents a system that recognizes ADLs using a kinect RGB-D camera. First, dynamic time warping algorithm learns and recognizes sub-activities (e.g. reaching, opening) that are used in a second time by a FuzzyDL reasoner to recognize high-level activities (e.g. making cereal, taking medicine). Activities are represented in a fuzzy ontology that includes the semantic interpretation of actions performed by users and handles vagueness and uncertainty.

Reference [49] proposes a hybrid approach based on computational narratives to interpret everyday activities. Various video and depth sources feed the author's qualitative spatial representation and reasoning (QSR) framework handling space, action and change representation, prediction or explanation. Activities are interpreted following Bayesian/Markov logic over the observation sequences.

Complete hybrid AAL systems are then built atop those basic services especially for medical purpose or user prompting.

In [34], pervasive healthcare monitoring is intended to offer a real-time interactive medical consultation, to predict risky situations and prompt the inhabitant in case of emergency. User's medical history and physiological and ambient data collected from various wearable and environmental sensors are represented in XML document. These data constitute the base for some case-based reasoning (CBR). A case-based reasoning approach is used where retrieval and adaptation are handled by hierarchical fuzzy rules. A k-NN function is then applied to determine the best solution.

Reference [36] proposes a context-aware decision-making under uncertainty for voice-based control of a smart home for people with reduced mobility, in emergency or in loss of autonomy. OWL2 ontologies are used to represent sensor and actuator raw data (e.g. microphones, infrared presence detectors, lights) at a low level and, at a reasoning level, concepts like activity, location and situations. The reasoning is performed in many ways: ontologies are enriched with SWRL rules for situation recognition (e.g. "main door open"), location is inferred using temporal dynamic networks for multisource fusion and spreading activation, and activity recognition and decision-making (e.g. "turn on the ceiling light") are based on ML.

iMessenger [27] is an activity monitoring and reminder delivery framework built on top of ontological modelling and context extraction. It utilizes an OWL ontology built in Protégé-OWL to describe activities as a series of events at specific locations over a period. Accelerometer data is translated into postures using SVM, and indoor location is determined using an RFID system. SWRL rules with temporal reasoning are used to provide feedback based on the consistency or inconsistency between the user's expected and observed behaviours.

Reference [30] presents a smart home system that can recognize 20 common ADL. The system predicts, reasons and interacts with the elderly through reminders and messages via a mobile phone and may also acts on the environment. Data from environmental sensors, RFID readers and user profile are represented in a taxonomy. To take in account vagueness and uncertainty of data collecting from diverse sources, a rough set theory helps building activity models as rule-based classification problems. Assistive actions are derived with CBR, followed by a rule-based reasoning that fine-tune the decision for a case.

Reference [23] designed an architecture for AAL applied to the night-time wandering scenario. An OWL ontology is used to represent the user scenarios of daily living inside the physical environment. Various reasoning approaches such as ontological reasoning, fuzzy logic, BNs or rules are used to determine activities and assist the resident.

Another notable mention is CoCaMAAL, with which Forkan et al. [4, 46] aim to detect long-term behavioural change and predict abnormality in an AAL. CoCaMAAL relies on user traces about presence, vital signs, activities and life patterns to detect changes in the daily living habits or health conditions. An ontology stores information about persons, places, environment and devices, which is then translated into XML to train an HMM. Pushing the current context into this HMM allows the system to detect if an abnormal behaviour or long-term change is happening.

BDCaM [54] is an extension of CoCaMAAL dedicated for people with limited mobility, regarding situations of loss of autonomy and emergency. They propose a context-aware decision-making under uncertainty and based on big data. OWL2 ontologies are used to represent sensor and actuator raw data at a low level. Reasoning, based on concepts like activity, location and situations, is performed in various ways. Ontologies are enriched with SWRL rules when a specific situation is recognized (e.g. "main door open"). Location is inferred using temporal dynamic networks for multisource fusion and spreading activation. Activity recognition and decision-making are based on ML.

Finally, optimal service delivery is discussed in [37] with a context-aware application that provides services according to a predefined preference of a user. The system collects raw sensor data into a database and uses an ontology to draw high-level context. Based on context data here called service-triggering information, a k-NN classifier combined with an ontology-based context modelling infers the predefined service that will maximize user's satisfaction.

An overview of the presented hybrid works points out that the integration of knowledge-based and data-driven techniques could help build systems that are capable of semantic interpretation and logic reasoning while taking advantage on historicized and sometimes imprecise data collected over time to recognize habits and predict the future. In this way, systems like iMessenger [23, 27, 30, 67] make use of data-driven models to derive low-level context information in real time (opening, moving, reaching, etc.) that are then used by ontology-based rule reasoning mechanisms to derive upper-level context knowledge (activities, posture, location, etc.) and provide feedback adapted to situations. On the contrary, systems like [36, 37, 54] do the inverse by rather using ontologies for situation recognition and data-driven models for decision-making. No matter the way you go, hybrid systems can become cumbersome if not well managed and should be implemented carefully to not fall into unnecessary big, complicated and costly systems that function poorly.

10.4.4 Comparison Between Approaches

Tables 10.1, 10.2, 10.3, 10.4, 10.5 and 10.6 resume the links between services and reasoning approaches. The tables list all the reviewed articles, grouped according to the service they deliver. Each table is dispatched between data-driven, knowledge-

Table 10.1 Basic service – activity recognition

Data	Context modelling	Context reasoning	Ref.
Data-driven approach			
Camera image (low level included) and depth image	GMM, MCBS for object interaction/activity recognition		[39]
	HMM based on mobility patterns and sleep duration	k-NN	[22]
	SVM trained with SMO	X-means	[64]
Wearable sensor data	Classifier (logistic regression, random forest, ERT, SVM, k-NN, BN)		[57]
Any sensor data, time, presence	NN alike		[61]
Radio devices	CNN over RTI		[45]
Any sensor data	User interaction with objects as a series of beats	Custom rules	[62]
	Frequent pattern mining with presented algorithm and mapping function		[68]
Knowledge-driven approach: Ontology			
Any sensor data	Sensors, physical environment, activities	Pellet reasoner, time-window algorithm	[60]
		Rules	[44]
	User personality, devices, OWL time		[28]
	Physical environment, ADLs	ML, RDF batch reasoning, spatiotemporal reasoning (GeoSPARQL)	[7]
Pressure, contact, ultrasonic sensor data	(CoSSN): Activities, observation, features of interest, cognitive stimulus	SPARQL rules	[42]
Environmental and body sensor data	Sensors, events, situations, time intervals, physical environment	Logic rules and non-monotonic reasoning (answer set programming)	[1]
	Sensors, events, time, dementia related (DUL)	OWL2 reasoning	[40]
Hybrid approach			
Environmental and body sensor data	XML: Medical data, wearable and ambient sensors	CBR: Fuzzy rules for retrieval and adaptation, k-NN selection	[34]
Accelerometer data, RFID tags	Ontology: Physical environment places linked to RFID, activities as events linked to posture and places	Kalman filters and SVM classification of activities. Activity consistency validation through SWRL and SQWRL rules	[27]

(continued)

Table 10.1 (continued)

Data	Context modelling	Context reasoning	Ref.
Camera image (low level included) and depth image	Fuzzy ontology: Activities as sequential execution of sub-activities	k-NN for sub-activity recognition on the posture. Fuzzy rules for high-level activity recognition	[67]
	CLP (QSR), Bayesian/Markov model		[49]
Any sensor data	Ontology: Physical environment, devices, appliances, activities	Ontological reasoning, fuzzy logic, BNs, rules	[23]

Table 10.2 Basic service – posture recognition

Data	Context modelling	Context reasoning	Ref.
Data-driven approach			
Any sensor data	CNN from 2D images, transferred to RGB-D images; and SVM over skeleton model		[63]
Knowledge-driven approach: Ontology			
Environment and body sensor data	Sensors, objects, events (interactions), actions performed	Activity recognition and body posture through OWL reasoning with HermiT	[43]
Hybrid approach			
Accelerometer data, RFID tags	Ontology: Physical environment (RFID), activities (events with posture and place)	Kalman filters and SVM classification of activities. Activity consistency validation through SWRL and SQWRL rules	[27]

Table 10.3 Basic service – fall detection

Data	Context modelling	Context reasoning	Ref.
Data -driven approach			
Camera and depth	GMM, multi-cue background subtraction for object interaction/activity recognition		[39]
Hybrid approach			
Accelerometer data, RFID tags	Ontology: Physical environment (RFID), activities (events with posture and place)	Kalman filters and SVM classification of activity. Consistency validation through SWRL and SQWRL rules	[27]

driven and hybrid approach. The reference number identifies the article and the type of gathered data, and the context modelling and context reasoning are mentioned when available.

Table 10.4 Predictive services

Service	Data	Context modelling	Context reasoning	Ref.
Data-driven approach				
Next activity	Sequence of actions	Markov chain of events	Current state highest probability	[16, 50]
Future behaviours	Motion and door entry point	Time series, start time/duration parameters	Recurrent NN	[72]
Knowledge-driven approach				
Navigation	User well-known places, position (GPS)	Fuzzy sets	Fuzzy logic	[48]
Emergency prevention	Environmental and body sensor	Ontology: Sensors, events, situations, time intervals, physical environment	Logic rules and non-monotonic reasoning (answer set programming)	[1]
	Environmental and body sensor, physiological and medical status, Bluetooth bracelet presence	Ontology: ACCIO-based (physical space, sensors, medical observations, nurses, patients, etc.) plus medical symptoms, diagnoses, faults	Semantic annotation at the reception, C-SPARQL/custom rules	[18]
Hybrid approach				
Future behaviours	User traces about presence, physiological data, activities, life patterns	Ontology: Persons (profile, habits), physical space (places), devices	HMM classifier trained with XML representation of the ontology	[4, 46]
			Above plus supervised learning to improve user and general rules	[54]
Emergency prevention	Environmental and body sensor data	XML: Medical data, wearable and ambient sensors	CBR: Fuzzy rules for case retrieval and adaptation, k-NN for selection	[34]

The first three tables present the basic services. Most of the basic services concern activity recognition (Table 10.1). No knowledge-driven approach is used for fall detection (Table 10.3). At the reverse, recommendation systems, which are dedicated to medical caregivers, are only based on knowledge-driven approaches (Table 10.6).

Predictive services use basic services to predict next activities, behaviours or position. They are part of emergency services in order to prevent hazardous situations. Table 10.4 lists the articles that focus on predictive services even if other ones mention to make prediction.

Most AAL systems for inhabitants combine various services offering ambient assistance as well as alert in case of emergency. Home automation services are

Table 10.5 Services for inhabitants

Data	Context modelling	Context reasoning	Ref.
Data-driven approach			
Binary sensor data	Markov chain with CLS and presented assumption		[38]
Any sensor data	Multilayer perceptron neural network, classification algorithms		[32]
User traces	Markov chain of user traces and interactions with the system		[16, 50]
Knowledge-driven approach: Ontology			
Any sensor data, user profile, service requests	Physical environment, sensors, user profile	Fuzzy rules	[70]
User control logs	User, devices and their effects, basic services, locations, AAL system	Adequate device/service activation through SWRL rules	[71]
Low-level sensor data stream	Patient physiological metrics, physical environment actions, sensor events	Inferring healthcare-related high-level data through inference rules	[5]
Sensor data, interaction context	Meta-concepts, events, queries and facts, scenarios or knowledge. SQL database for agent memory	Situation recognition and assistance through ontological reasoning and virtual reality simulation	[33]
Sensor data as events	User personality, devices, time (OWL time)	Rules	[28]
Wireless sensor, actuator and smart meter data	Smart building, environment parameters and devices	Rules, defeasible logic	[59]
Any sensor data	Seven ontologies: (1) sensors, actuators, medical devices, appliances; (2) actions, activities; (3) physical space; (4) actors; (5) medical information; (6) services/applications; (7) time	SPARQL rules	[17]
Speech	Ontology: Sensor data, medical data, user preferences, nonverbal data (gestures, face), conversation themes and topics	SPIN/SHACL rules, non-monotonic rules for context disambiguation	[29]
Environmental kitchen sensor data		Ontological reasoning over hierarchical task network-inspired scenarios	[24, 35]

(continued)

Table 10.5 (continued)

Data	Context modelling	Context reasoning	Ref.
Hybrid approach			
Speech, infrared presence detectors, lights	Ontology: Sensors (microphone, infrared presence detectors, lights), activities, physical environment places, situations	SWRL rules for situation recognition, temporal dynamic networks for location inference, ML activity recognition and decision-making	[36, 54]
Environmental sensors data, RFID readers, body sensors, camera image	Contextual labels: User profile (name, sex, age, preferences), tasks, social situation, temporality, environment	SPARQL rules, CBR	[30]
Any sensor data, user preferences	Ontology: Person and relations, time frames, locations, activities	k-NN to select the service that will maximize user's satisfaction	[37]
Environment and body sensor data	XML: Medical data, wearable and ambient sensors	CBR: Fuzzy rules for case retrieval and adaptation, k-NN for selection	[34]
Any sensor data	Ontology: Physical environment, devices, appliances, activities	Ontological reasoning, fuzzy logic, Bayesian networks, rules	[23]
Accelerometer data (smartphone), RFID tags	Ontology: Physical environment places linked to RFID, activities as events linked to posture and places	Kalman filters and SVM classification of activities. Activity consistency validation through SWRL and SQWRL rules	[27]

also included in ambient assistance when the AAL service modifies the physical environment to offer a comfortable ambiance personalized according to time of the day and activities. Table 10.5 resumes all the services for inhabitants.

Among the services for caregivers, the articles reviewed refer on services to formal caregivers (Table 10.6). They concern most often medical services.

10.5   Discussion

The last decade works on context-aware AAL have been extensively presented to derive a trend among context modelling and reasoning. Some findings from previous reviews are still accurate [12, 73]. Key-value [4] and markup language like XML [34] are still used to store context data for data-driven reasoning. However,

Table 10.6 Services for caregivers

Data	Context modelling	Context reasoning	Ref.
Knowledge-driven approach: Ontology			
Patient tests (discrete physiological data)	Anti-diabetic drugs (medicine, composition, contraindication, HbA1c%), patient tests	SWRL rules, JESS reasoning	[26]
	Chronic illness signs, symptoms, interventions, assessments, syndromes. Tailored to the patient	Inference/counting properties	[25]
Any sensor data	Sensors, events, time, dementia related (DUL)	Activity recognition with OWL2 reasoning, non-pharmaceutical interventions through SPARQL rules	[40]

other approaches like key-value, markup and object-oriented modelling, which have been widely used 10 years ago to capture domain knowledge, tend to disappear in knowledge-based systems to be replaced by ontologies.

In the following, we explore what influences the choice of context modelling and reasoning. Starting with the context data, specifically its nature and the sensors used to collect data, we then show how some services induce the type of modelling.

Considering the recent literature, when it comes to choose convenient context modelling and reasoning approach for service implementation, some other issues have been raised up beyond the service itself: nature of data and types of sensors.

10.5.1   Nature of Data

Nature of data is important for decision-making. In fact, inaccurate data lead to poor decisions and then to irrelevant services. Sometimes it happens that sensors stop working or worse give non-sense data. These device failures generate uncertain or incomplete data. In addition, inhabitants themselves can be source of uncertainty. For instance, they may leave home for a long time to go on holidays or to hospital. If they forgot to turn off the AAL system, data are still collected leading to errors in decision. At the reverse, inhabitants who usually live alone may invite guests who introduce confusion in the data collected. To deal with this uncertainty and vagueness in data, some context models include fuzzy sets [48] and fuzzy ontologies [74], while reasoning is performed with fuzzy logics [48], fuzzy rules [34, 46], BNs [23, 49] and Markov logics [36, 49, 50].

10.5.2 Visual Sensors

Either low-resolution visual sensors [22] or high-resolution RGB-D cameras [63, 67] require computer vision algorithms for data-driven analysis and exploitation. In this way, k-NN [22, 67], GMM [39], MM [22, 49], SVM [27, 63, 64], NN [61], dynamic time warping [67] and CBR [30, 34] are used to classify user activities, body postures and falls in AAL systems.

10.5.3 Biosensors

The wide adoption of wearable biosensors among people leads to increase the amount of collected data and the number of advanced pervasive healthcare systems. It was expected that this increase of digital data would promote data-driven approaches for health monitoring. However, ontologies are the most used context model, combined with rule reasoning (either classic, fuzzy or non-monotonic) for prompt and alert propagation, emergency and recommendations in health monitoring systems [1, 5, 18, 25, 30, 75]. These systems can turn hybrid when data-driven reasoning is added to achieve more accurate results or to extend the services with anomaly detection and the prediction of future behaviours. It is the case with k-NN [34], MM [4, 46] or supervised learning [54] which is added to achieve more accurate results or to extend the services with anomaly detection and the prediction of future behaviours.

10.5.4 Activity, Body Posture and Fall Recognition Services

As previously stated, data-driven classification models are the most used when the environment is equipped with visual sensors. However, visual sensors are not always appropriate due to the high cost of high-resolution cameras, the need for a performing machine processing and privacy issues. To avoid such inconvenience, several AAL systems make use of other types of sensors, more affordable and privacy compliant. Wearable sensors and non-visual ambient sensors include, among others, accelerometers, passive infrared, contact and mobile phones. Therefore, data-driven models are used only occasionally, such as SVM [57] and CNN [45]. The reasoning approach is more likely knowledge based. Ontologies with rule reasoning are largely prominent [1, 7, 28, 40, 42, 44, 60]. They are sometimes coupled with SVM [27] and BN [23].

10.5.5 Predictive Services

Predictive services are most often based on historical context data. The significant amount of available data collected from multiple sensors collected over time suggests the prevalence of data-driven models. In fact, the review shows that MM has been used for predicting the next activity [50, 76] and inhabitants' future behaviours [46, 54]. NN also appears to be a useful model to improve reasoning on temporal for sequential or parallel activities. NN is also used to predict future anomalous behaviours [72]. The prediction of future health state and prevention of health emergency rely most often on physiological data that are gathered by biosensors. These predictions are widely handled by ontologies and rule reasoning [1, 18]. They can be extended with data-driven reasoning to efficiently take advantage on historical data like k-NN to refine CBR [34].

10.5.6 Temporal Reasoning

Managing time-stamped data and representing temporal relationships are essential in AAL systems, whether to detect or predict activity, body posture or fall; to offer ambient assistance, home automation and navigation services; or in case of emergency. The most obvious finding of this review is the wide use of ontologies to implement various types of AAL services. Decision-making is then provided with OWL or SPARQL rules. This is a bit surprising while weaknesses of ontologies have been widely reported, especially regarding the difficulty to deal with temporal data [77, 78]. On the opposite, the efficiency of MM and NN has been established [72, 79]. This preponderant use of ontologies can be explained by many efforts that have been done to overcome this weakness. For instance, the development of Time Ontology[2] (OWL Time) as a W3C recommendation helps describing temporal properties of resources in ontologies. OWL Time is used in some of the reviewed works [17, 28, 40]. In the same vein, ontologies are also coupled with data-driven models to enhance time management [7, 37, 46, 67].

10.5.7 Services for Inhabitants

Services for inhabitants provide direct assistance, either for comfort, for daily task execution or in case of emergency. The review shows that a pure data-driven approach like in [32] is rare. Most of the time, a knowledge-based approach, such as an ontology, represents information, and rules are triggered for decision-making,

---

[2]https://www.w3.org/TR/owl-time/

such as SWRL and SPARQL rules. SPIN, fuzzy rules and defeasible rules often appear to derive adapted and personalized services to the user or to give alert in case of emergency. Hybrid approaches are also common for the provision of services to inhabitants. In fact, ontological reasoning is enhanced by associating data-driven approaches like BN [23], Markov logics [36] and k-NN [37] to ontologies.

This intensive use of ontologies to describe services for inhabitants can be explained by the fact that these services rely on the knowledge the system has on environment and the inhabitant. It means to be able to describe the home and the installed devices, including those for user-home communication. It also implies to be able to specify the capacities, the deficits and the preferences of inhabitants. In addition, the structure and the shareable nature of ontologies favour their integration with other models like data-driven ones.

10.6 Conclusion

Many context and reasoning models have been proposed in the last decade to capture context data and extract relevant knowledge for decision-making in ever-changing environments. AAL systems, which make use intensively of IoT devices and algorithms, aim to offer comfort, safety, assistance and monitoring. In this review of literature, we have adopted two guidelines, first to review more specifically the context-aware AAL systems dedicated for people with specific needs and second to present the review from a service-oriented perspective. Our hypothesis was that the nature of services and the types of collected data impact the choice of modelling and reasoning on context.

To this end, several AAL systems of different types developed in the last decade have been investigated. We classify them in three groups: basic services, which are usually prerequisite for more elaborated ones, services usually provided to improving the lifestyle of inhabitants and the services that enable caregivers to monitor inhabitant's actions in the AAL environment. We then clarify context awareness terminologies and the data mainly gathered in AAL. An extensive and comprehensive review of selected works has been carried out to derive technical development trends in terms of context modelling and reasoning for AAL service provision. To resume the reasoning approaches, it is worth pointing out they are separated into two broad schools of thought: knowledge-driven approaches where ontologies enriched by logical rules are preponderant and data-driven approaches where supervised and unsupervised classification techniques among others are prevailing. A third approach aims to benefit from the strengths of the two previous ones by combining them into a hybrid approach.

Some trends in choosing context modelling have emerged from this review. First, the types of sensors influence data modelling and reasoning. Numerous digital data collected by cameras imply the use of data-driven models for activity, body posture and fall classification. When other ambient sensors are used, ontologies are favoured for those services and sometimes are combined with data-driven models. Biosensors used in health monitoring produce data more often handled in ontologies or hybrid systems. This approach is completed by various data-driven models to deliver more accurately prompts, alerts and recommendations. Whatever the delivered service, uncertainty and vagueness coming from data force to complete the initial approaches. Fuzzy sets, fuzzy ontologies and fuzzy rules are added in knowledge-based approach; BN and MM are widely used in data-driven approaches.

No trend is emerging from services to caregivers. However, regarding the implementation of services to inhabitants, research efforts are converging towards knowledge representation in ontologies and rule reasoning. Data-driven reasoning completes occasionally this approach. When it comes to predict the future, data-driven models like MM and NN take advantage on historical data collected over time to provide relevant insights on the events more likely to occur.

In the future, it is expected that the IoT market diversify its products. AAL systems tend also to become more complex, offering more than one service. It appears then that in the future AAL system will mix different approaches, by using the most convenient one to implement a specific service or group of services. The challenge will be in an optimal combination, to take advantage of them instead of getting lost in a myriad of models. We do not pretend to have covered all the services available in AAL systems, even less to predict the next years. We neither intend to make a critical review of the works presented. However, this work has tried to give an insight of the most suitable modelling and reasoning technique to select for a given AAL service.

References

1. Alirezaie, M., Renoux, J., Köckemann, U., et al. (2017). An ontology-based context-aware system for smart homes: E-care@home. *Sensors, 17*, 1586. https://doi.org/10.3390/s17071586.
2. Baldauf, M., Dustdar, S., & Rosenberg, F. (2007). A survey on context-aware systems. *International Journal of Ad Hoc and Ubiquitous Computing, 2*, 263–277.
3. Rashidi, P., & Mihailidis, A. (2013). A survey on ambient-assisted living tools for older adults. *IEEE Journal of Biomedical and Health Informatics, 17*, 579–590. https://doi.org/10.1109/JBHI.2012.2234129.
4. Forkan, A., Khalil, I., & Tari, Z. (2014). CoCaMAAL: A cloud-oriented context-aware middleware in ambient assisted living. *Future Generation Computer Systems, 35*, 114–127. https://doi.org/10.1016/j.future.2013.07.009.
5. Aritoni, O., & Negru, V. (2010). Sensors data-stream processing middleware based on multi-agent model. *Scalable Computing: Practice and Experience, 11*, 19–32. https://doi.org/10.12694/scpe.v11i1.636.
6. Klimek, R. (2018). Exploration of human activities using message streaming brokers and automated logical reasoning for ambient-assisted services. *IEEE Access, 6*, 27127–27155. https://doi.org/10.1109/ACCESS.2018.2834532.
7. Preuveneers, D., Berbers, Y., & Joosen, W. (2016). SAMURAI: A batch and streaming context architecture for large-scale intelligent applications and environments. *Journal of Ambient Intelligence and Smart Environments, 8*, 63–78. https://doi.org/10.3233/AIS-150357.
8. Magableh, B., & Albeiruti, N. (2012). Detecting the onset of dementia using context-oriented architecture. In *Proceedings - 6th international conference on next generation mobile applications, services, and technologies, NGMAST 2012* (pp. 24–30).

9. Dey, A. K., Abowd, G. D., & Salber, D. (2000). A context-based infrastructure for smart environments. In *Managing interactions in smart environments* (pp. 114–128). London: Springer.
10. Bettini, C., Brdiczka, O., Henricksen, K., et al. (2010). A survey of context modelling and reasoning techniques. *Pervasive and Mobile Computing, 6*, 161–180. https://doi.org/10.1016/j.pmcj.2009.06.002.
11. El murabet, A., Abtoy, A., Touhafi, A., & Tahiri, A. (2018). Ambient assisted living system's models and architectures: A survey of the state of the art. *Journal of King Saud University - Computer and Information Sciences, 32*, 1–10.
12. Li, X., Eckert, M., Martinez, J. F., & Rubio, G. (2015). Context aware middleware architectures: Survey and challenges. *Sensors (Switzerland), 15*, 20570–20607. https://doi.org/10.3390/s150820570.
13. Perera, C., Zaslavsky, A., Christen, P., & Georgakopoulos, D. (2014). Context aware computing for the internet of things: A survey. *IEEE Communication Surveys and Tutorials, 16*, 414–454. https://doi.org/10.1109/SURV.2013.042313.00197.
14. Alam, M. R., Reaz, M. B. I., & Ali, M. A. M. (2012). A review of smart homes - past, present, and future. *IEEE Transactions on Systems, Man, and Cybernetics Part C: Applications and Reviews, 42*, 1190–1203. https://doi.org/10.1109/TSMCC.2012.2189204.
15. Camarinha-Matos, L. M., Ferrada, F., Oliveira, A. I., et al. (2014). Care services provision in ambient assisted living. *IRBM, 35*, 286–298. https://doi.org/10.1016/j.irbm.2014.08.001.
16. Cook, D. J., Youngblood, M., Heierman, E. O., et al. (2003). MavHome: An agent-based smart home. In *Proceedings of the 1st IEEE international conference on pervasive computing and communications, PerCom 2003* (pp. 521–524).
17. Chen, L., & Nugent, C. (2010). Situation aware cognitive assistance in smart homes. *Journal of Mobile Multimedia, 6*, 263–280.
18. De Brouwer, M., Ongenae, F., Bonte, P., & De Turck, F. (2018). Towards a cascading reasoning framework to support responsive ambient-intelligent healthcare interventions. *Sensors (Switzerland), 18*. https://doi.org/10.3390/s18103514.
19. Wojciechowski, M. (2010). End user context modeling in ambient assisted living. *International Journal of Advanced Pervasive and Ubiquitous Computing, 1*, 61–80. https://doi.org/10.4018/japuc.2009090804.
20. Mocholí, J. B., Sala, P., & Naranjo, J. C. (2010). Ontology for Modeling interaction in ambient assisted living environments. In *XII Mediterranean conference on medical and biological engineering and computing 2010*.
21. Ayari, N., Chibani, A., Amirat, Y., & Matson, E. (2016). A semantic approach for enhancing assistive services in ubiquitous robotics. *Robotics and Autonomous Systems, 75*, 17–27. https://doi.org/10.1016/j.robot.2014.10.022.
22. Eldib, M., Deboeverie, F., Philips, W., & Aghajan, H. (2016). Behavior analysis for elderly care using a network of low-resolution visual sensors. *Journal of Electronic Imaging, 25*. https://doi.org/10.1117/1.jei.25.4.041003.
23. Kenfack Ngankam, H., Pigot, H., Lorrain, D., et al. (2020). Context awareness architecture for ambient-assisted living applications: Case study of nighttime wandering. *Journal of Rehabilitation and Assistive Technologies Engineering, 7*. https://doi.org/10.1177/2055668319887864.
24. Pinard, S., Bottari, C., Laliberté, C., et al. (2019). Design and usability evaluation of COOK, an assistive technology for meal preparation for persons with severe TBI. *Disability and Rehabilitation. Assistive Technology*, 1–15. https://doi.org/10.1080/17483107.2019.1696898.
25. Riaño, D., Real, F., López-Vallverdú, J. A., et al. (2012). An ontology-based personalization of health-care knowledge to support clinical decisions for chronically ill patients. *Journal of Biomedical Informatics, 45*, 429–446. https://doi.org/10.1016/j.jbi.2011.12.008.
26. Chen, R. C., Huang, Y. H., Bau, C. T., & Chen, S. M. (2012). A recommendation system based on domain ontology and SWRL for anti-diabetic drugs selection. *Expert Systems with Applications, 39*, 3995–4006. https://doi.org/10.1016/j.eswa.2011.09.061.
27. Zhang, S., McCullagh, P., Nugent, C., et al. (2013). An ontological framework for activity monitoring and reminder reasoning in an assisted environment. *Journal of Ambient Intelligence and Humanized Computing, 4*, 157–168. https://doi.org/10.1007/s12652-011-0063-1.

28. Jacquet, C., Mateos, M., Bretault, P., et al. (2012). An ambient assisted living framework supporting personalization based on ontologies. In *In AMBIENT 2012, the second international conference on ambient computing, applications, services and technologies*. IARIA.
29. Meditskos, G., Kontopoulos, E., Vrochidis, S., & Kompatsiaris, I. (2019). Converness: Ontology-driven conversational awareness and context understanding in multimodal dialogue systems. In *Expert Systems*. Hoboken: Blackwell Publishing Ltd.
30. Zhou, F., Jiao, J., Chen, S., & Zhang, D. (2011). A case-driven ambient intelligence system for elderly in-home assistance applications. *IEEE Transactions on Systems, Man, and Cybernetics Part C: Applications and Reviews, 41*, 179–189. https://doi.org/10.1109/TSMCC.2010.2052456.
31. Skillen, K.-L., Chen, L., Nugent, C. D., et al. (2014). Ontological user modelling and semantic rule-based reasoning for personalisation of help-on-demand services in pervasive environments. *Future Generation Computer Systems, 34*, 97–109. https://doi.org/10.1016/J.FUTURE.2013.10.027.
32. Costa, N., Domingues, P., Fdez-Riverola, F., & Pereira, A. (2014). A mobile virtual butler to bridge the gap between users and ambient assisted living: A smart home case study. *Sensors (Switzerland), 14*, 14302–14329. https://doi.org/10.3390/s140814302.
33. Adjali, O., Hina, M. D., Dourlens, S., & Ramdane-Cherif, A. (2015). Multimodal fusion, fission and virtual reality simulation for an ambient robotic intelligence. In *Procedia computer science* (pp. 218–225). Amsterdam: Elsevier B.V.
34. Yuan, B., & Herbert, J. (2014). Context-aware hybrid reasoning framework for pervasive healthcare. *Personal and Ubiquitous Computing, 18*, 865–881. https://doi.org/10.1007/s00779-013-0696-5.
35. Olivares, M., Giroux, S., De Loor, P., et al. (2016). An ontology model for a context-aware preventive assistance system: Reducing exposition of individuals with traumatic brain injury to dangerous situations during meal preparation. In *2nd IET international conference on Technologies for Active and Assisted Living (TechAAL 2016). Institution of Engineering and Technology*. pp 3 (8.)-3 (8.).
36. Chahuara, P., Portet, F., & Vacher, M. (2017). Context-aware decision making under uncertainty for voice-based control of smart home. *Expert Systems with Applications, 75*, 63–79. https://doi.org/10.1016/j.eswa.2017.01.014.
37. Humayun Kabir, M., Robiul Hoque, M., & Yang, S. H. (2015). Development of a smart home context-aware application: A machine learning based approach. *International Journal of Smart Home, 9*, 217–226. https://doi.org/10.14257/ijsh.2015.9.1.23.
38. Ghasemi, V., & Pouyan, A. A. (2017). Modeling users' data traces in multi-resident ambient assisted living environments. *International Journal of Computational Intelligence Systems, 10*, 1289. https://doi.org/10.2991/ijcis.10.1.88.
39. Padilla-López, J. R., Chaaraoui, A. A., Gu, F., & Flórez-Revuelta, F. (2015). Visual privacy by context: Proposal and evaluation of a level-based visualisation scheme. *Sensors (Switzerland), 15*, 12959–12982. https://doi.org/10.3390/s150612959.
40. Andreadis, S., Stavropoulos, T. G., Meditskos, G., & Kompatsiaris, I. (2016). Dem@home: Ambient intelligence for clinical support of people living with dementia. In *CEUR workshop proceedings*.
41. Bergeron, F., Giroux, S., Bouchard, K., & Gaboury, S. (2017). RFID based activities of daily living recognition. In *2017 IEEE SmartWorld Ubiquitous Intelligence and Computing, Advanced and Trusted Computed, Scalable Computing and Communications, Cloud and Big Data Computing, Internet of People and Smart City Innovation, SmartWorld/SCALCOM/UIC/ATC/CBDCom/IOP/SCI 2017* (pp. 1–5). IEEE.
42. Zgheib, R., De, N. A., Villani, M. L., et al. (2017). A flexible architecture for cognitive sensing of activities in ambient assisted living. In *Proceedings – 2017 IEEE 26th international conference on enabling technologies: Infrastructure for collaborative enterprises, WETICE 2017* (pp. 284–289). Institute of Electrical and Electronics Engineers.
43. Noor, M. H. M., Salcic, Z., & Wang, K. I. K. (2018). Ontology-based sensor fusion activity recognition. *Journal of Ambient Intelligence and Humanized Computing*, 1–15. https://doi.org/10.1007/s12652-017-0668-0.

44. Bennasar, M., Price, B. A., Stuart, A., et al. (2019). Knowledge-based architecture for recognising activities of older people. In *Procedia computer science* (pp. 590–599). Amsterdam: Elsevier B.V.
45. Tan, Z., Xu, L., Zhong, W., et al. (2018). Online activity recognition and daily habit modeling for solitary elderly through indoor position-based stigmergy. *Engineering Applications of Artificial Intelligence, 76*, 214–225. https://doi.org/10.1016/j.engappai.2018.08.009.
46. Forkan, A. R. M., Khalil, I., Tari, Z., et al. (2015). A context-aware approach for long-term behavioural change detection and abnormality prediction in ambient assisted living. *Pattern Recognition, 48*, 628–641. https://doi.org/10.1016/j.patcog.2014.07.007.
47. Bergeron, F., Bouchard, K., Gaboury, S., & Giroux, S. (2018). Tracking objects within a smart home. *Expert Systems with Applications, 113*, 428–442. https://doi.org/10.1016/j.eswa.2018.07.009.
48. Hervás, R., Bravo, J., & Fontecha, J. (2014). An assistive navigation system based on augmented reality and context awareness for people with mild cognitive impairments. *IEEE Journal of Biomedical and Health Informatics, 18*, 368–374. https://doi.org/10.1109/JBHI.2013.2266480.
49. Bhatt, M., Suchan, J., & Schultz, C. (2013). Cognitive interpretation of everyday activities - toward perceptual narrative based visuo-spatial scene interpretation. In *OpenAccess series in informatics* (pp. 24–29).
50. Das, S. K., Cook, J., Bhattacharya, A., et al. (2002). The role of prediction algorithms in the MavHome smart home architecture. *IEEE Wireless Communications, 9*, 77–84. https://doi.org/10.1109/MWC.2002.1160085.
51. Psyché, V., Daniel, B., & Bourdeau, J. (2019). Adaptive learning spaces with context-awareness. In A. Coy, Y. Hayashi, & M. Chang (Eds.), *Intelligent tutoring systems* (pp. 7–13). Cham: Springer International Publishing.
52. Bazire Maryand Brézillon, P. (2005). Understanding context before using it. In D. Anindand, B. Kokinov, D. Leake, & R. Turne (Eds.), *Modeling and using context* (pp. 29–40). Berlin/Heidelberg: Springer.
53. Ryan, N. S., Pascoe, J., & Morse, D. R. (1998). Enhanced reality fieldwork: the context-aware archaeological assistant. in *Computer Applications in Archaeology*, Oxford:Tempus Reparatum.
54. Forkan, A. R. M., Khalil, I., Ibaida, A., & Tari, Z. (2015). BDCaM: Big data for context-aware monitoring—A personalized knowledge discovery framework for assisted healthcare. *IEEE Transactions on Cloud Computing, 5*, 628–641. https://doi.org/10.1109/tcc.2015.2440269.
55. Zerawa, S.-A., Pollhammer, K., & Turek, T. (2011). Simplifying routine task using contactless smartcards. In *IEEE AFRICON conference*.
56. López-Cózar, R., & Callejas, Z. (2010). Multimodal dialogue for ambient intelligence and smart environments. In *Handbook of ambient intelligence and smart environments* (pp. 559–579). New York: Springer.
57. Zdravevski, E., Lameski, P., Trajkovik, V., et al. (2017). Improving activity recognition accuracy in ambient-assisted living systems by automated feature engineering. *IEEE Access, 5*, 5262–5280. https://doi.org/10.1109/ACCESS.2017.2684913.
58. Stucki, G. (2005). International classification of functioning, disability, and health (ICF). *American Journal of Physical Medicine & Rehabilitation, 84*, 733–740. https://doi.org/10.1097/01.phm.0000179521.70639.83.
59. Stavropoulos, T. G., Kontopoulos, E., Bassiliades, N., et al. (2015). Rule-based approaches for energy savings in an ambient intelligence environment. *Pervasive and Mobile Computing, 19*, 1–23. https://doi.org/10.1016/j.pmcj.2014.05.001.
60. Okeyo, G., Chen, L., Wang, H., & Sterritt, R. (2014). Dynamic sensor data segmentation for real-time knowledge-driven activity recognition. *Pervasive and Mobile Computing, 10*, 155–172. https://doi.org/10.1016/j.pmcj.2012.11.004.
61. Velik, R. (2014). A brain-inspired multimodal data mining approach for human activity recognition in elderly homes. *Journal of Ambient Intelligence and Smart Environments, 6*, 447–468. https://doi.org/10.3233/AIS-140266.

62. Martínez-Pérez, F. E., González-Fraga, J. Á., Cuevas-Tello, J. C., & Rodríguez, M. D. (2012). Activity inference for ambient intelligence through handling artifacts in a healthcare environment. *Sensors, 12*, 1072–1099. https://doi.org/10.3390/s120101072.
63. El Amine Elforaici, M., Chaaraoui, I., Bouachir, W., et al. (2018). Posture recognition using an rgb-d camera: Exploring 3d body modeling and deep learning approaches. In *2018 IEEE life sciences conference, LSC 2018* (pp. 69–72).
64. Manzi, A., Dario, P., & Cavallo, F. (2017). A human activity recognition system based on dynamic clustering of skeleton data. *Sensors (Switzerland), 17*. https://doi.org/10.3390/s17051100.
65. Allen, J. F. (1983). Maintaining knowledge about temporal intervals. *Communications of the ACM, 26*, 832–843. https://doi.org/10.1145/182.358434.
66. Hobbs, J. R., & Pan, F. (2017). Time ontology in OWL: Candidate recommendation. In *W3C Consort*. https://www.w3.org/TR/owl-time/.
67. Díaz-Rodríguez, N., Cadahía, O. L., Cuéllar, M. P., et al. (2014). Handling real-world context awareness, uncertainty and vagueness in real-time human activity tracking and recognition with a fuzzy ontology-based hybrid method. *Sensors (Switzerland), 14*, 18131–18171. https://doi.org/10.3390/s141018131.
68. Chikhaoui, B., Wang, S., & Pigot, H. (2011). A frequent pattern mining approach for ADLs recognition in smart environments. In *Proceedings of the 25th international conference on advanced information networking and applications* (pp. 248–255).
69. Abdulrazak, B., Chikhaoui, B., Gouin-Vallerand, C., & Fraikin, B. (2010). A standard ontology for smart spaces. *IJWGS, 6*, 244–268.
70. Gouin-Vallerand, C., Abdulrazak, B., Giroux, S., & Dey, A. K. (2013). A context-aware service provision system for smart environments based on the user interaction modalities. *Journal of Ambient Intelligence and Smart Environments, 5*, 47–64. https://doi.org/10.3233/AIS-120190.
71. Allègre, W., Burger, T., Antoine, J. Y., et al. (2013). A non-intrusive context-aware system for ambient assisted living in smart home. *Health and Technology, 3*, 129–138.
72. Lotfi, A., Langensiepen, C., Mahmoud, S. M., & Akhlaghinia, M. J. (2012). Smart homes for the elderly dementia sufferers: Identification and prediction of abnormal behaviour. *Journal of Ambient Intelligence and Humanized Computing, 3*, 205–218. https://doi.org/10.1007/s12652-010-0043-x.
73. Castillejo, E., Almeida, A., López-De-Ipiña, D., & Chen, L. (2014). Modeling users, context and devices for ambient assisted living environments. *Sensors (Switzerland), 14*, 5354–5391.
74. Rodríguez, N. D., Cuéllar, M. P., Lilius, J., & Calvo-Flores, M. D. (2014). A survey on ontologies for human behavior recognition. *ACM Computing Surveys, 46*, 1–33.
75. Chen, L., Nugent, C. D., & Wang, H. (2012). A knowledge-driven approach to activity recognition in smart homes. *IEEE Transactions on Knowledge and Data Engineering, 24*, 961–974. https://doi.org/10.1109/TKDE.2011.51.
76. Cook, D. J., Youngblood, M., Heierman, E. O., et al. (2003). MavHome: An agent-based smart home. In *Proceedings of the first IEEE international conference on pervasive computing and communications, 2003. (PerCom 2003)* (pp. 521–524). Fort Worth, TX: IEEE Comput. Soc.
77. O'Connor, M. J., Hernandez, G., & Das, A. (2011). A rule-based method for specifying and querying temporal abstractions. In M. Peleg, N. Lavrač, & C. Combi (Eds.), *Artificial intelligence in medicine* (pp. 255–259). Berlin/Heidelberg: Springer.
78. Weichert, F., Mertens, C., Walczak, L., et al. (2013). A novel approach for connecting temporal-ontologies with blood flow simulations. *Journal of Biomedical Informatics, 46*, 470–479. https://doi.org/10.1016/j.jbi.2013.03.004.
79. Lotte, F., Bougrain, L., Cichocki, A., et al. (2018). A review of classification algorithms for EEG-based brain-computer interfaces: A 10 year update. *Journal of Neural Engineering, 15*, 031005.

Chapter 11
Design of Algorithm for IoT-Based Application: Case Study on Intelligent Transport Systems

Jayanthi Ganapathy

Abstract Internet of Things (IoT) is a platform governed by information and communication technologies that facilitates affordable data communication among heterogeneous devices in large scale. However, computation-rich applications running on IoT need specific considerations as user response plays key role in critical situations particularly in transportation, health care, and smart cities. In this view, this chapter explains in detail characteristics of various software components that are in use in IoT over existing communication networks and presents various problem-solving techniques for IoT applications in intelligent transport systems. Further, the role of algorithms and computational structures for development of efficient IoT application is illustrated in detail with three real-time case studies in transportation domain.

Keywords Machine learning · Spatial · Temporal · Time series forecasting · Transportation · Traffic engineering · Intelligent systems

11.1 Introduction

The physical objects in real world can be interconnected, and information can be digitized over communication network using suitable software applications and services. Things in IoT consist of sensing elements, embedded computing systems, and actuators. These objects need to communicate in real time for data store, transfer, computing, etc., thus enabling machine to machine communication. Massive IoT devices are involved in a variety of day-to-day applications, and hence the cost of device needs to be reduced. Heterogeneous devices connected via Internet exhibit diverse compatibility issues for which middleware are required.

J. Ganapathy (✉)
Faculty of Information and Communication Engineering, Anna University, Chennai, India

© Springer Nature Switzerland AG 2021
F. P. García Márquez, B. Lev (eds.), *Internet of Things*, International Series in Operations Research & Management Science 305,
https://doi.org/10.1007/978-3-030-70478-0_11

227

The functional requirement of middleware: "In IoT, middleware are required to compute with any device, anytime within any context, with anyone, on any service, in any path on communication network, in any place (environment) anywhere" [1, 2]. To meet these requirements, there have been a number of research proposals originated to address the issues in core elements of IoT.

The core elements that form IoT from handheld devices to high-end servers are sensor networks, radio-frequency identification, machine to machine communication, vehicle to vehicle communication in case of transportation, data acquisition, control, and monitoring [1, 2, 23, 36, 45]. The rest of this chapter is organized as follows: Sect. 11.2 discusses application of IoT. Section 11.3 presents machine learning and IoT in transportation research. Section 11.4 explains in detail the problem-solving techniques in IoT-based transportation. Sections 11.5, 11.6, and 11.7 present case study on algorithmic design for IoT-based transportation. Finally, Sect. 11.8 discusses the advantages of each algorithm, and Sect. 11.9 concludes the chapter with summary.

11.2 IoT Applications

Middleware application and services for IoT are emerging day by day to address diverse application in real time. The key application areas are discussed as follows:

Health care: The well-being of patient could be developed remotely using wireless sensors. The state of infection can be monitored by doctor remotely without the physical presence of the patient. Other wearable devices can help in monitoring health by measuring blood sugar, cholesterol, pressure, or temperature [3]. The types of facilities available in mobile health-care system are listed in Table 11.1.

Intelligent home automation systems: Home appliances like air conditioner, telecommunication devices, refrigerators, and other household machineries could be connected via Internet for optimizing energy consumption, and efficient use of these appliances could be monitored anywhere remotely. Automated home security

Table 11.1 IoT-based mobile health care

Sl. no	Mobile health care
1	Fertility and pregnancy tracking
2	Pharma medical delivery
3	Pill tracking
4	Appointment scheduling
5	Doctor discovery
6	On-demand health-care unit
7	Diabetes management
8	Pharmacy delivery
9	Telemedicine
10	Remote doctors and health assistance

systems such as door lock, authentication of family members, and robots for home assistance are some of the examples for IoT based applications.

Logistics management: Smart tags using RFID technology significantly help in tracking goods from time of placing the order for goods up to its delivery. These technologies help in recommendation and personalization of client.

Surveillance systems: Video object recognition systems help in identifying suspicious cases, dislocation of hazardous elements using cameras installed on road side units, infrastructure, etc.

Intelligent transport systems: IoT-based application development on sensor embedded in vehicles, mobile units, and road side infrastructure units can offer route guidance with traffic information, helps in preventing accidents with warning messages and directions, and also helps in driverless car. Emerging IoT technology has expanded the capabilities of transport infrastructure. Machine to machine communication-based V2V infrastructure helps in locating vehicle and exchanges data like vehicle speed, mobility, and other locations near to them and transfers data to the server [2]. This way sudden accidents and vehicle crash could be avoided while proving better navigation. Bus fleet monitoring system was developed using RFID tags. Infrared sensor counts the passengers boarding the buses. Hardware module named TI-CC3200 is connected with LCD for information display to passenger [4]. The example of fleet management system is shown in Fig. 11.1.

Real-time Transport Information System is the hot topic of transportation researches, the outcome of which is that it renovates metropolitan transport for the public in all major cities of nation. Technology-driven traffic management is one among the key processes in developing the nation worldwide. Presently, intelligent transport systems (ITS) have developed in all nations, wide across the globe to provide transport infrastructure that disseminates sophisticated information services along with operational services such as electronic toll collection systems (ETCS), automatic vehicle detection systems (AVDS), traffic surveillance systems, etc. [5].

In recent years, most of the transportation research works highly focus on short-term traffic forecasting considering the traffic parameters, namely, speed, volume, flow, and occupancy. Implementations of intelligent transport systems (ITS), Advanced Traveller Information Systems (ATIS), and traffic information systems (TIS) have rendered data communication and information service to commuters

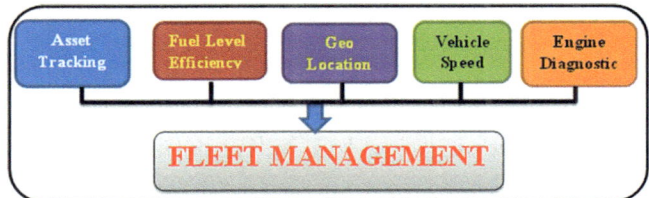

Fig. 11.1 IoT-based fleet management

all over the nation. This has facilitated enormous traffic data management and analysis by advanced data management systems (ADMS) [6]. Dynamic strategies in the development of traffic predictors result in successful traffic operations with solution to real-time challenges in daily traffic operations such as mitigation of congestion, identification of measures to control dynamic variations of traffic flow, and analyzing spatial and temporal distribution of traffic data that influences congestion.

Conventional methods like historical averages with time series traffic data were used with urban traffic control system (UTCS). Despite the advances in the development of transport infrastructure and availability of traffic data, information processing on such datasets to convert into software service so as to enable location-based query on software systems in transportation was highly challenging.

Transportation planning infrastructure with software-enabled ITS relies on real-time traffic data archived by ADMS for efficient storage and retrieval of historical and current traffic data. The advancements in transportation infrastructure have reported challenges to transportation researcher with a conclusion that the operation of ITS is not complete unless it anticipates traffic conditions in the near future, i.e., less than 30 min in future [7, 8].

In this view, most of the research studies on forecasting methods have shown directions toward proactive traffic operations through computationally intensive predictive modeling, subsequently providing precise Traveler's Information Service (TIS). Freeways, arterials, expressways, and highways contribute significant traffic data for trend analysis, pattern matching, outlier detection, clustering, and forecasting [7, 9]. However, reduction of transportation congestion for the benefit of commuters is still active in demanding computationally efficient and accurate methods.

With reference to enormous work carried out in the transportation research worldwide, this chapter highlights the problem-solving techniques in general for IoT-based transportation and illustrates the significance of sequential pattern mining algorithm [41] in forecasting near future traffic condition with real-time case study. Recent research works aimed at identifying extreme traffic conditions in a highly fluctuating traffic flow. However, the results achieved earlier are not reliable as the computational system reacts differently in various traffic conditions [38]. Therefore, this chapter presents the use of non-parametric instance-based learning techniques in identifying extreme traffic conditions. Finally, the use of spatial and temporal relations in routing vehicular traffic is explained with dynamic vehicle routing algorithm as a problem-solving approach in IoT-based traffic congestion management.

11.3   Machine Learning and IoT in Transportation Research

Road network connecting major arterial junctions in a metropolitan city demands technology-driven traffic operation such as monitoring of traffic flow and allocation of route, thus facilitating transportation infrastructure to the public. Such operation goes adverse, when vehicle flow through network monotonically increases in periodic intervals. This may occur due to yearly increase or unprecedented traffic flow over such network during peak hours. In addition, traffic flow over the road segments linked by the network may appear or disappear. As a result, road segment remains linked or separated because of dynamic increase in vehicle flow in spatial locations during the travel. Thus, traffic on road network is robust (highly fluctuating) and unprecedented (irregular structure) and has extremeness (unusual behavior) with sudden rise and fall in congestion at arterial junction.

Today's transportation systems play an essential role in the development of a nation. It is necessary that travel information has to be made available in the view of delayed travel experienced by commuters. The advancement in information technology and travel information service has made the services easy to commuters to avoid unexpected delay in their travel. In this view, various research works reported the use of traffic data and its applications in forecasting dynamic traffic conditions.

Traffic time series with univariate and multivariate approaches was well established using time series models such as autoregressive integrated moving average (ARIMA), seasonal ARIMA (SARIMA), and vector autoregressive moving average (VARMA). In addition, historical averages, linear regression, and Kalman filters too showed competitive results. In contrast, non-parametric regression which is another broad category of data-driven computation method has potential influence in traffic operations as it learns the near future state of traffic condition from traffic states available at the past [10, 11]. Thus, non-parametric methods are not limited by estimation of parameters unlike the time series models where selection and estimation of model parameters are done based on assumptions of past traffic states. Therefore, non-parametric k-NN applies well to traffic datasets that are nonlinear as well as possess deterministic structure [12]. The formulation of autoregressive model is based on the assumption that current value of time series Z_t can be defined in terms of linear expression of its past observances Z_{t-1}, Z_{t-2}, Z_{t-3}, $\ldots$, Z_{t-p}, and random error ε. Autoregressive process $AR(p)$ of order p is defined as $Z_t = \psi_1 Z_{t-1} + \psi_2 Z_{t-2} + \cdots + \psi_p Z_{t-p} + c_t$ where $\psi_1, \psi_2, \psi_3, \ldots, \psi_p$ are coefficients of univariate random process.

Technology developments in ITS have devised a spectrum of computation methods in traffic operations. Prediction horizon was reported as the key issue in ITS-based transportation planning. Traffic conditions exhibit distinct spatial behavior and tend to evolve over time. Time series analysis of such variations would help researchers to identify the intrinsic temporal and spatial relationships in traffic operations [10].

The outcome of transportation research done over the past three decades is ADMS enabled software service-based Traveller Information System. The following section explains the applications of different computational methods in IoT-based transportation applications.

11.4 Problem-Solving Techniques for IoT-Based Transportation

11.4.1 Time Series Analysis

Traffic volume, speed, occupancy and flow are fundamental variables involved in prediction of traffic flow in the near future say 5 min to less than 60 min, hence termed as short-term traffic forecasting which helps in operational planning. Traffic flow is time varying (dynamic), continuous, and stochastic where random events such as shocks and fluctuations are intrinsically present in physical traffic flow. Time series of traffic volume data is an ordered set of traffic data measured in consecutive time points. The characteristics of these datasets can be analyzed in both time and frequency domain. Relationships between time lags are investigated in time domain analysis [13] using autocorrelation analysis, a specific tool for analyzing time-lagged relationship. Consider the traffic volume of a day shown in Fig. Fig. 11.2. Cyclic variations are investigated using frequency domain analysis. Spectral and wavelet transformations [14] are used for analyzing cyclic variations. The intrinsic components present in time series of traffic data are as follows:

(i) *Trend analysis*: Traffic data is dynamic and tends to change over time. For example, the fall and rise in vehicle flow on a lane are dependent on time [15].
(ii) *Seasonality behavior*: Traffic flow is seasonal where it exhibits daily, weekly, and monthly patterns in a calendar year with or without fluctuations [16].
(iii) *Randomness*: Traffic flow is affected by external interferences that are neither predictable, nor do they repeatedly occur in specific pattern. These variations occur randomly in time series of traffic data.
(iv) *Cyclic variations*: Traffic flow exhibits short-term fluctuations that cyclically repeat, where the duration of the cycle varies with respect to time [17].

The advancement in ITS has made the application of intensive computational methods possible in anticipating traffic conditions due to the availability of vast historical data. In early 1991, non-parametric regression has proven solution against parametric methods like ARIMA in analysis of unprecedented traffic conditions. Application of non-parametric methods was found to be significant in analyzing the extremeness in traffic flow characteristics say congested state to uncongested state of traffic behavior. However, it has been reported by various researchers that non-parametric approaches have replaced the computational complexity, yet the performance is not better than conventional time series analysis that is based on statistical techniques [18].

Time series model ARIMA and its variants do not rely on historic data, whereas non-parametric methods learn the system from vast historical data. The computational difficulty in estimation of parameters with time series models was replaced by simple machine learning approach with simple distance metric. These systems learn by instances which are experiences collected at the past. Thus, k-NN method does not possess complex structures, whereas estimation of model

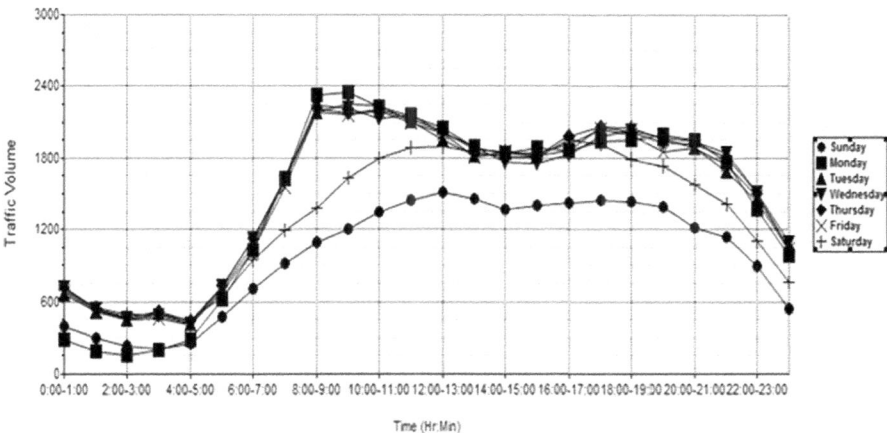

Fig. 11.2 Traffic volume of a day

parameters with ARIMA and its variants relies on complex mathematical structures [19]. Computational overhead with highly fluctuating traffic was experienced even with kernel-based machine learning techniques like neural networks and support vector machine (SVM) [20, 21].

Dynamic traffic condition is well anticipated by non-parametric regression techniques compared to time series analysis. This method was found to be effective even with missing data [22]. Moreover, k-NN method has its significance in analyzing nonlinear traffic behavior. Temporal and spatial dependencies of traffic were considered to enhance direct k-NN as a method of predicting traffic condition at successive time steps [20]. Although historical averages, linear regression, and Kalman filters are found to be competitive, they do not provide intended results. In addition, Box Jenkin's time series models such as ARIMA, SARIMA, and VARMA apply well based on assumption of traffic data, whereas non-parametric regression predicts near-future traffic without any assumption about data; instead they learn from past experiences.

Extremeness in traffic conditions is a dynamic phenomenon where rise and fall in traffic volume occur randomly. This deviation from regular traffic structure with reference to time, apart from free flow and peak hour traffic flow, needs attention in analyzing the near-future traffic state. Moreover, researchers have given prime importance to fluctuating traffic flow, whereas extreme traffic characteristics and its impact over congested traffic flow had been of less interest. This has highly motivated to apply a non-parametric regression analysis to identify extreme traffic. A regression method coupled with k-NN is proposed, in which global neighbor at multistep identifies unusual traffic structure when a candidate traffic data which is a local instance at single step is updated to search dataset. The various problem-solving techniques are shown in Table 11.2.

Table 11.2 Problem-solving techniques in traffic management

Techniquesc	Methodology	Models and algorithms	Real-time traffic operation
Time series Traffic analysis	Trend analysis	ARIMA	Daily traffic profile
	Seasonality behavior	SARIMA	
	Randomness	Auto-correlation analysis	
	Cyclic variations	Spectral analysis	
Machine learning	Supervised	Ensemble methods, decision trees, support vector regression, k-NN	Outlier and extreme traffic condition
	Unsupervised	k-means, fuzzy C-means	Route navigation, optimization of vehicle routing
	Reinforcement	CNN Auto-encoders Recurrent attention model Non-linear autoregressive exogenous model (NARX)	Short-term traffic forecasting

11.4.2   Machine Learning Techniques

11.4.2.1   Supervised Learning

Ensemble method is a framework consisting of different collection of classifiers using which weak classifiers are boosted to become strong in classifying features [26]. This technique was proposed in [27]; Adaptive boosting method named AdaBoost was developed to track eye contact and head movement in detecting driver's consciousness [26, 27, 29, 32, 39]. Another well-known ensemble method is using series of decision trees as weak learners from which mean value is obtained as output. This method is reluctant to the effect of over-fit compared to single decision trees. This method was enhanced in [27]; the author ensembles four models in prediction of traffic flow both in shorter and longer horizon.

The classification problem deals with computation on input features to produce several possible outcomes. Decision trees are candidate methods used in classifying objects based on different features. Similarly, regression trees are used in which response variable is regressed using independent variable where the out-come is a numeric value instead of binary class in decision tree. The applications of decision tree and regression tree classifiers are widely addressed in traffic incident detection. This is achieved using ensemble of these algorithmic techniques. They are specifically used in tracking the behavior of drivers especially in tracking eye contact and head movement [26, 27]. Logistic regression [26] approach is used for binary classification.

Traffic flow prediction based on joint probability using Bayesian networks is proposed in [28]. Further, the performance of Bayesian approach is enhanced by combining seasonal factors in ARIMA time series model named SARIMA. Thus, probabilistic classifiers performed equally well with time series models and methods. Another supervised learning technique is instance-based learning. In non-parametric regression method k-NN, k-nearest neighbors are identified from the training datasets, and average of neighbors is computed to evaluate neighbor in test dataset [38–40]. Other linear classifiers without probabilistic reasoning were also proved results in traffic prediction. One such candidate method widely used in transportation is SVR [23, 24, 35]. Support vectors are evaluated using minimal structural risk optimization techniques. Regression of support vectors helps in predicting traffic flow in next successive time instance [14, 37, 38].

Artificial neural network uses non-linear function in hidden layer to extract features based on linear combination of input variables. Computation is performed in hidden layer. The neurons in hidden layers are updated based on residual error using feedback mechanism. Feed forward NN consist of single hidden layer and trained with back-propagation technique using non-linear gradient descent function [28]. This formulation is much applied in prediction of real-time accidents where historical information such as traffic volume, lane occupancy, and travel time are being used. The result of model is compared with k-NN and regression tree [29] and feed forward neural network [18, 23, 27–30].

11.4.2.2 Unsupervised Learning

Grouping of elements based on similarities and patterns is termed as clustering, an unsupervised learning technique widely applied on dense datasets. Clustering is performed without labels and training methods. In contrast, classification is performed with labels [22].

The most widely used k-means algorithm separates data into k clusters such that mean value of clusters has minimal residual error [33, 34]. In [12] k-means is applied to optimize the cost of travel between supplier and delivery centers. In fuzzy C-means [26], each instance belonging to a class is examined using membership function to predict traffic on real road network. The results are compared with k-NN method. Layer-wise greedy training strategy is being adopted to improve traffic control and monitoring [14, 31].

11.4.2.3 Reinforcement Learning

Deep learning enforces computing capabilities over unstructured data using principles of reinforcement learning strategy. Convolution neural network (CNN) is widely used in transportation using datasets captured from cameras installed on roadside units [24, 31, 35]. CNN has a collection of fully connected layers in addition to pooling layer and convolution layer [40]. Real-time traffic network assignments are performed using deep belief network [38, 43–45]. Auto-encoders are used in traffic flow prediction; stacked models were widely used [35, 42]. Deep recurrent attention model (DRAM) [25] is a variant of recurrent neural net used for sequential manipulation over large datasets. These models are found to be competitive with non-linear autoregressive exogenous model (NARX) [28].

Route optimization is essential for reducing travel time and emission of environmental pollutants as well [13]. Reliable path computing is part of route guidance system which uses various machine learning techniques using IoT infrastructure. V2V technology is used to perform group routing [36]. Optimal traffic network is configured using combined K-means and DB scan techniques [12]. Multiple approaches like SARIMA, FF-NN, and NARX models were developed in [25–28] for traffic prediction in shorter and longer horizons.

When physical objects in real world are connected to coordinate a process, algorithmic problem-solving approach is highly demanded as data manipulation is essential in the form of data wrangling, store, extraction, and transformation. Moreover, real-time data processing layer is essential in IoT-based transportation as travel time at each instance can be sequenced in predicting traffic information in next time instance [41]. The case study in Sect. 11.5 presents data mining framework for traffic prediction. When traffic condition is adverse, temporal structure of extreme traffic conditions provide useful information in travel time estimates. Section 11.6 illustrates problem-solving technique with case study on transportation traffic behavior. Section 11.7 explains a methodology for routing vehicular traffic using spatial and temporal relations.

11.5 Traffic Sequence Mining Framework for Prediction of Traffic Volume on Highways

11.5.1 Problem Description

Road traffic datasets such as volume, speed, and travel time in time series may have generalized, redundant and/or non-redundant, periodic, and episodic occurrences of sequence patterns. Various sequential pattern mining algorithms are in use in these application areas. Although numerous algorithms were in use, enhanced further by researchers computationally efficient mining algorithm is in high demand, particularly in traffic congestion analysis of transportation network. Traffic data preparation by pre-processing, dimensionality reduction by symbolic representation, mining of traffic sequence patterns and rules, and prediction of traffic volume are the functional components involved in the proposed traffic sequence mining framework, and it is shown in Fig. 11.3. The input phase comprises of data collection and pre-processing.

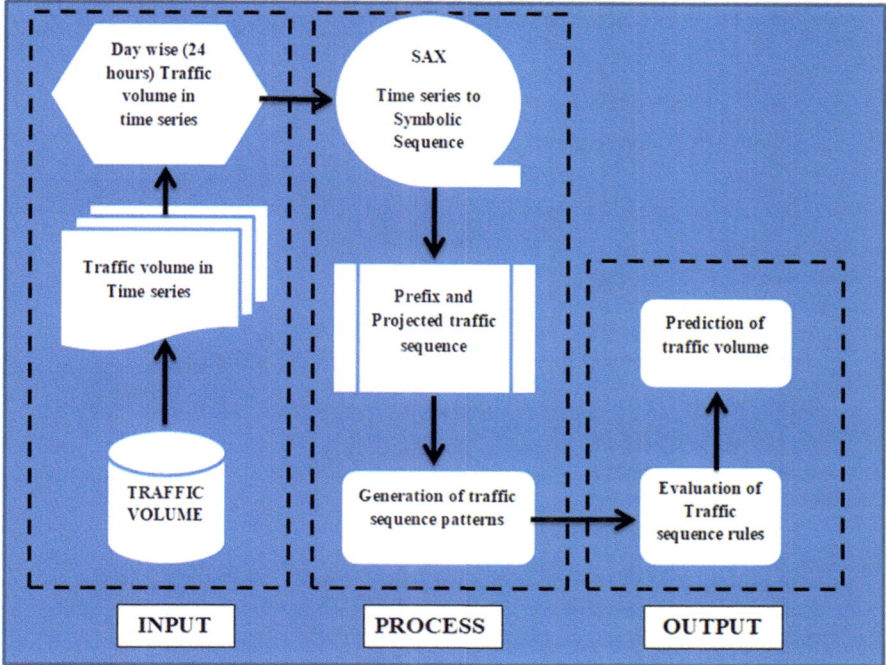

Fig. 11.3 Traffic sequence mining framework

The real traffic volume data collected is pre-processed into time series. This time series is converted into symbolic sequence using symbolic aggregate approximation method.

11.5.2   Methodology

PrefixSpan is pattern growth mining method. This approach recursively scans the sequence datasets to discover larger patterns. Compared to candidate generation of a priori based algorithms, pattern growth shows its efficiency by adopting the principle of FP growth technique. Thus, candidate generation is effectively reduced by replacing *join and prune step* with temporary memory structure called projected datasets. However, this approach has its limitation in the creation of this temporary storage, read, and write input-output operations in terms of memory scans at the time of execution. PrefixSpan approach employs depth first search on projected database to generate the frequent sequence patterns.

Algorithm 11.1 PrefixSpan $(\lambda, L, S_\lambda, t_k)$
Input:

λ : Frequent traffic sequence initially set to null,

L   : Length of traffic sequence,

S_λ : Traffic sequence database,

t_k : Time of day in minutes,

σ_{min} : user defined support to evaluate frequent traffic sequence in S_λ,

Output: Traffic sequence pattern.

Method:

01: Scan traffic sequence database S_λ.

02: **FOR** each t_k **DO**

03: Determine the traffic volume V.

04: Evaluate traffic prefix ρ at t_k .

05: Evaluate each frequent symbolic sequence.

06: **END FOR**

07: **FOR** each frequent symbol representing traffic volume **DO**

08: Append frequent symbol to λ.

09: **ENDFOR**
10: **FOR** each λ **DO**

11: Construct $S_{\lambda'}$ which is projected traffic sequence database.

12: **ENDFOR**

13: Call PrefixSpan(λ',L+1,$S_{\lambda'}$, t_k).

The adverse rise and fall of traffic in urban transportation during peak hours of day cause significant delay in travel especially during peak hours. Although PrefixSpan is capable of mining sequences in general, application specific to transportation requires improvement in PrefixSpan considering traffic during peak hour and its impact in travel time. Travel time in urban transport is characterized by traffic volume as the vehicles need to wait in queue during its travel. The advances in ITS have made the availability of traffic information easy so as to support travel decisions. PrefixSpan runs in pseudo polynomial time as execution time is function of input sequence length. Therefore, the algorithm is scalable.

The source of input to traffic pattern analysis is the symbolic sequence. In the processing phase, PrefixSpan algorithm is used to identify frequent traffic sequence patterns. Every pattern mining algorithm uses data structure to store intermediate results. Projected database is used in Prefixspan to store prefix and sequences. The frequent sequences are evaluated for various minimum support values. The generated frequent sequences are source of input for evaluating traffic sequence rules. Frequent traffic sequential rule common to more than one traffic sequence is evaluated for various minimum support and confidence levels; a procedure similar to a priori based association rule mining is used. The prediction of traffic volume is thus effected from the evaluated traffic sequence rules.

TT-PrefixSpan algorithm [41] is proposed for prediction of traffic flow on highway by mining travel time-based traffic sequences. Traffic sequences representing traffic volume in range of travel time are generated, and traffic volume is predicted by evaluating traffic sequence rules from the generated frequent traffic sequences [41].

PrefixSpan algorithm is presented in Algorithm 11.1 for mining traffic sequences from given set of sequences, where each sequence represents traffic volume for give time of day in minutes. Real-time traffic conditions can be captured by mining traffic sequences using data-driven sequential pattern mining (SPAM) technique. When traffic information is provided, PrefixSpan algorithm which is an SPAM technique helps in analyzing traffic flow throughout the day.

11.5.3 Mining Frequent Traffic Sequence Rules

The steps for mining frequent traffic sequence rules are given in Algorithm 11.2. Frequent traffic sequence pattern is scanned as shown in line 01. A sequential rule is evaluated when support value of rule is greater than or equal to user-defined minimum support count value as shown in line 02. Confidence of a rule is evaluated when rule confidence is greater than or equal to minimum confidence level as shown in line 04. Those rules whose support and confidence are greater than minimum value is stored in frequent rule set as shown in line 05.

Algorithm 11.2: Mining Frequent Traffic Sequence Rules
Input:

λ : Frequent traffic sequences,

t_k : Time of peak traffic,

$\sigma_{min}, conf_{min}$: minimum support and confidence to evaluate frequent traffic sequence rule in S_λ

Output: Traffic sequence rule S_{RC} initially set to null.

Method:

01: Scan frequent traffic sequences λ.

02: Evaluate sequential rule $\lambda_x \Rightarrow \lambda_y$ such that its sequential support is

$$(\sigma_{seqrule}) = \frac{\sigma(\lambda_x \Rightarrow \lambda_y)}{|S|} \geq \sigma_{min}$$

03: **FOR** every pair of sequence $\lambda_x, and \lambda_y$ AND $\sigma_{seqrule} \geq \sigma_{min}$ **DO**

04: Evaluate $confidence(\lambda_x \Rightarrow \lambda_y) = \dfrac{\sigma_s(\lambda_x \Rightarrow \lambda_y)}{\sigma_s(\lambda_x)}$

05: **IF** $confidence(\lambda_x \Rightarrow \lambda_y) > conf_{min}$ **THEN** $S_{RC} = S_{RC} \cup (\lambda_x \Rightarrow \lambda_y)$

06: **ENDIF**

07: **ENDFOR**

Prediction of traffic volume is done using frequent traffic sequence rule as shown in Algorithm 11.3. The rule set is scanned as shown in line 01. For a given time instance, the consequent of a rule in the set is the predicted traffic volume for the antecedent in the previous time instance as shown in line 02 and 03. The prediction of traffic volume by mining traffic sequence is extended to check the reliability of the IoT-based traffic management in real time.

Algorithm 11.3: Prediction of Traffic Volume
Input:

$S_{R \mathcal{L}}$: Traffic sequence rules

t_k : Time of peak traffic,

Output: Traffic volume in next sequence

Method:

01: Scan the traffic sequence rules $S_{R \mathcal{L}}$.

02: **FOR** each rule $\mathcal{R} \mathcal{L} \in S_{R \mathcal{L}}$ **DO**

03: $V_k = \lambda_y$, when λ_y is the consequent traffic sequence for the traffic sequence λ_x in the antecedent

04: **ENDFOR**

06: **FOR** every symbol in sequence vector V_k , **DO**

07: Extract the symbolic traffic volume.

08: **END FOR**

11.6   Learning Extreme Transportation Traffic Conditions Using Local and Global Instance-Based Regression

11.6.1   Problem Description

Urban transportation experiences delayed travel due to lack of services on road, unbound capacity of lanes, temporary non-availability of services, etc. In addition, increase in volume of vehicle over time, along the major roads connecting the city, also contributes a significant amount to traffic congestion especially during peak hours. The interest of this work is to present a data-driven approach to analyze the extremeness of traffic, which is unusual traffic either a very low or high that is distinct from regular traffic flow. The extreme traffic condition is analyzed using combined local and global k-NN regression method in a highly fluctuating traffic. A global neighbor at multi-step identifies unusual behavior in traffic structure. The local instances in direct k-NN at single step are updated to identify global neighbors. The following definitions are used in formulation of Algorithm 11.4.

Algorithm 11.4 Combined Local_Global Regression
Subroutine Global_Neighbor (Training dataset X, Time T)

Input: Local neighbor instance initially null.

Output: The predicted traffic volume for given time t.

Method

Step 1: Initialize global neighbor instance Y'[i].

Step 2: For each x_i in training vector X[t]

   Step 2a: Compute Global Neighbor Y' [i] = call Local_Neighbor(X,T)

   Step 2b: Update the training dataset with the local neighbor instances.

$$X'[i] = X[i] \cup Y'[i]$$

   Step 2c. Increment the time step.

Method

Step 1: Initialize the number of neighbors k such that k>1.

Step 2: Initialize the local neighbor instances X'[t].

 Step 2: Define X[t] as volume of traffic collected at past (training dataset).

 Step 3: For each x in the training dataset X[t] at T_i, $n \le i < n\text{-}k\text{+}1$ where n is maximum time step

  Step 3a: Compute Euclidean Distance (D) = $\sqrt{(T_i - T_{i-1})^2}$

  Step 3b: The local neighbor X'[t] is the traffic volume at the smallest

   distance D.

  Step 3c: The predicted traffic volume is

   For local instance I_i and the desired number of local neighbor k_j, $j > 1$

  Step 3c.1: $I[i] = 1 / k_j \sum_{t=1}^{m} X'[t]$

   Step 3c.2: Increment each neighbor.

   Step 4: Increment time step.

   Step 4: Return (Y).

   End

Definition 11.1 Time Step (T)
T_i is the observed traffic volume of the day and T_{i+1} is the time step in days for which the traffic volume is to be predicted such that $0 \le i < n$, where n is maximum time step in days to be considered such that $X(T) = \{x_1, x_2, x_3, \ldots, x_n\}$ denotes the number of vehicle flow in 24 h of day T_i and $X'(T) = \{x'_1, x'_2, x'_3, \ldots, x'_n\}$ is the number of vehicle flow predicted in 24 h for the day T_{i+1}.

Definition 11.2 Distance Metric (*D*)
The local neighbor instance is evaluated based on Euclidean distance measure between *i*th day T_i and $(i-1)$th day T_i as shown in Eq. 11.1.

$$\text{Euclidean distance } (D) = \sqrt{(Ti - Ti - 1)^2} \tag{11.1}$$

Definition 11.3 Input Vector

$$X[t] = [x_1, x_2, x_3, x_4, \ldots, x_m] \tag{11.2}$$

The input vector $X[t]$ defined in Eq. (11.2) is the historic dataset representing number of vehicle flow in 24 h time "*m*" of the day T_i where "*t*" varies from $1 \leq t \leq m$.

Definition 11.4 Output Vector

$$X'[t] = \left[x_1', x_2', x_3', \ldots, x_m'\right] \tag{11.3}$$

The output vector $X'[t]$ defined in Eq. (11.3) be the estimated traffic volume at time step in days based on historic dataset $X[t]$ and distance measure D.

Definition 11.5 Local Neighbor
The local neighbor is an instance evaluated based on distance metric D from traffic dataset collected at past. This process is repeated for desired number of time steps. Let k_i be the number of neighbors for $i = 1, 2, 3, \ldots, n$ defined by the user. A local neighbor is the instance $I = I_1, I_2, I_3, \ldots, I_n$ obtained by averaging the number of nearest neighbor for each k in the training dataset D using distance metric such that $I_i \in k_i$.

Definition 11.6 Global Neighbor
The instances identified repeatedly by updating the local neighbors to the training dataset X and same distance metric are used to evaluate global neighbors.

11.7 Dynamic Vehicle Routing

11.7.1 Problem Description

Urban transport system is a time-varying network. Traffic information in preceding time instances contributes in analyzing traffic in succeeding instances, and spatial information of traffic is required to re-route the path when there is congestion. The objective of this study is to manage congestion by re-routing the path at every time instance. It is dynamic re-routing by finding alternate path to congested route by augmenting time-varying network considering the temporal and spatial relations.

The method spatial temporal re-route given in Algorithm 11.5 STAR explains reliable path computation.

Algorithm 11.5 Method Spatio-Temporal Re-route (G, u, v)

Declare Check_Connect(G, u, v, t_i)

Declare Detect (u, v, t_i) as Boolean

u   : Source vertex

v : Destination vertex

R_j : Vector consisting of road segments between u and v

R_{corr} : Road segments with highly correlated traffic flow

J_x : Vector consisting of arterial junctions between u and v

G : Road network consisting of road segments R_j connecting arterial junctions J_x

Input: G is the graph representing the road network with spatial relations, temporal relations and edge cost initialized using cost adjacency matrix.

Method

01: For every time instance t_i where i ranges from 1 to 24 for a source 'u' and destination 'v'.
    // Check the spatial connection

02: G' = Call Check_Connect (G, u, v, t_i);
    //Re-routing the congested path with reduced number of vertices

03: At each time instance t_i get list of arterial junction J_i connected between source and destination from spatially extracted road network.
04: At time instance t_i, mark the distance d at arterial junction as zero and all other junction as infinity.
05: For each road segments in R_j connecting arterial junction evaluate $Corr(R_1, R_2, ..., R_j)$ 1<j<m, where m is number of road segments connecting the arterial junction R_j
06: $R_j' = R_j - R_{corr}$

07: Identify the next adjacent arterial junction J in J_x connecting R_j' and mark the distance d as current junction J_c.
08: For each junction in J_i from n^{th} arterial junction in the list J_x.
09: Update the distance d as d_{update} = distance J_d + distance (J_c-J_n).
    //Add the current distance of arterial junction J_c with distance connecting J_c - J_n.

10: If distance d found smaller than current distance of J_x.
11: Set d_{update} as current distance of J_x.

12: Mark the nth arterial junction in J_x as visited.

13: Repeat step 5 until all arterial junctions J in J_x are visited.

     Function Detect (u, v, t_i)

     Begin

At time instance t_{i-1} such that t_{i-1} before t_i holds find TTI (u, v) where

          TTI(u,v)=(travel_time-freeflow_time)/(freeflow_time);

          if (TTI(u, v)>1)

          return TRUE;

End

Function Check_Connect (G, u, v, t_i)

Begin

For all R_j between 'u' and 'v'

          {   if(Detect (u, v. t_i))

          set cost (u, v) as infinity;

          else

          set cost (u, v) with actual distance in G   }

G=G - {set of edges with cost infinity};

return G;

End

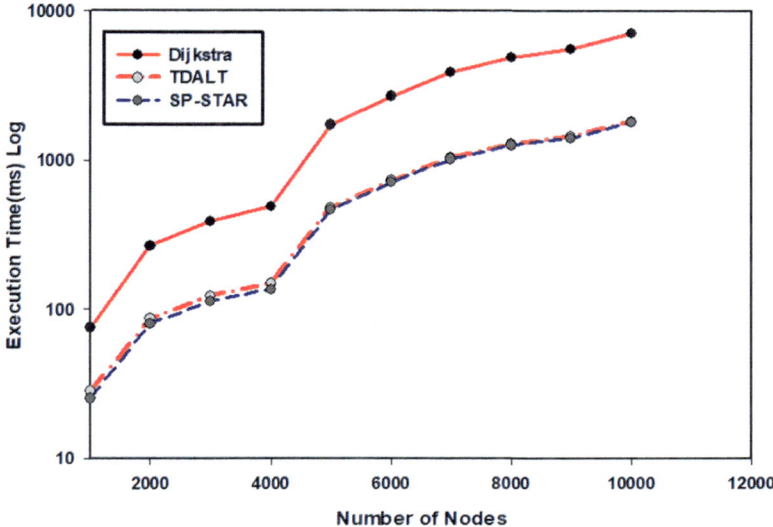

Fig. 11.4 Execution time of STAR for different number of nodes: comparison of methods

Recurring and non-recurring traffic congestion of physical traffic flow exhibits temporal variations. Moreover, temporal traffic information alone is insufficient when there is need for reliable path. In a spatially connected road network, a reliable path is identified based on traffic flow rate in successive time instances. However, a fully automated traffic management system is not feasible. Temporal and spatial information essentially contributes to path reliability in travel decisions. Thus, road network could be modeled as spatial-temporal network whose edge weight is augmented with temporal traffic information. Arterial junctions in the road network need to be connected based on spatial and temporal characteristics of traffic on adjacent links. The spatial temporal re-route algorithm given below describes path identification based on dynamic traffic conditions using Check_Connect() and Detect() routines. These routines identify congestion-free road segments that are connected to arterial junctions. These routines are called to identify the path connecting a source to destination. The execution time of algorithm is very minimal compared to Dijkstra and better than TDALT routing algorithm as shown in Fig. 11.4.

11.8   Discussion

In a connected environment, real-time travel data is heterogeneous by storage forms and voluminous for computation. One problem-solving approach that can enable online travel time prediction is traffic mining framework, an essential framework for IoT-based traffic management. The mining framework extracts useful traffic sequence patterns and rules for predicting travel time in next time instance. The case study on data mining technique shows the significance of traffic sequence mining approach for short-term traffic prediction.

Sequencing travel information at each time instance helps in predicting travel time, whereas traffic outlier detection is useful in analyzing extreme traffic conditions. An unusual traffic behavior can be detected in a daily traffic profile when traffic state at local neighbor is updated at each time instance to extract global neighbor. The case study on instance-based learning approach shows the significance of non-parametric regression technique in identifying extreme traffic conditions in a daily traffic profile.

Routing algorithm plays an essential role in travel time decisions. When travel information is known, spatial-temporal re-route algorithm dynamically routes the vehicle using temporal and spatial relations. The methodology is presented to show the significance of temporal and spatial relations in dynamic vehicle routing applications.

11.9 Conclusion

This chapter highlighted the need for computation technique in emerging technologies. Problem-solving techniques for IoT-based transportation problem are presented. Machine learning algorithms for IoT-based applications are explained. The significance of algorithmic problem-solving approach is illustrated with three case studies.

The first case study describes prediction of traffic volume using pattern mining technique. Traffic sequence mining framework for prediction of traffic volume on highways involves pre-processing of raw traffic facts such as traffic volume, speed, and travel time by converting time series of traffic volume to symbolic representation. Traffic sequence patterns are extracted using PrefixSpan algorithm, a fundamental sequential pattern mining technique. The generated patterns are evaluated for frequent traffic sequences. These sequences are further manipulated to identify frequent traffic sequence rules. The outcome of this algorithm is prediction of traffic volume by extracting traffic sequence rules. Hence, sequential pattern mining approach predicts traffic volume in next time instance by sequence travel time at each previous time instances.

The second case study describes algorithm for learning adverse or extreme transportation traffic conditions using instance-based regression. The fundamental machine learning technique k-NN is applied to local database to evaluate the instances. These local instances are updated in the training dataset to evaluate global instance. Regression technique is applied to evaluate the outlier. Identifying outlier traffic condition by updating traffic state of each time instance using regression technique is the outcome of local and global instance-based regression method. This problem-solving approach helps in travel decision as extreme traffic condition in a daily traffic profile is made known earlier especially during peak hour travel.

The third case study describes vehicle routing problem on time-varying network. Temporal and spatial traffic information in preceding time instances contributes in analyzing traffic in succeeding instances. Dynamic re-routing is performed using spatial temporal re-route algorithm. Reliable path is computed based on spatial and temporal characteristics of traffic on adjacent road links connecting the arterial junctions. Steps to optimize spatial temporal re-route algorithm for better performance and reliable routing are left to work in future considering traffic information at each arterial junction between source and destination.

References

1. Razzaque, M. A., Jevric, M. M., et al. (2016). Middleware for internet of things: A survey. *IEEE Internet of Things Journal, 3*(1), 70–95.
2. Al Mamun, M. A., Puspo, J. A., & Das, A. K. (2017). An intelligent smartphone based approach using IoT for ensuring safe driving. In *Proceedings of the 2017 IEEE International Conference on Electrical Engineering and Computer Science (ICECOS)*, Palembang, Indonesia, 22–23 August 2017, pp. 217–223.
3. Bandyopadhyay, S., Sengupta, M., Maiti, S., & Dutta, S. (2011). A survey of middleware for internet of things. In A. Ozcan, J. Zizka, & D. Nagamalai (Eds.), *Recent trends in wireless and mobile networks. CoNeCo 2011, WiMo 2011. Communications in Computer and Information Science* (Vol. 162). Berlin/Heidelberg: Springer.
4. Chowdhury, D. N., Agarwal, N., Laha, A. B., & Mukherjee, A. A. (2018). Vehicle-to-vehicle communication system using IoT approach. In *Proceedings of the 2018 IEEE second international conference on Electronics, Communication and Aerospace Technology (ICECA)*, Coimbatore, India, 29–31 March 2018, pp. 915–919.
5. Al-Deek, H. M., Radwan, E. A., Mohammed, A. A., & Klodzinski, J. G. (1996). Evaluating the improvements in traffic operations at a real-life toll plaza with electronic toll collection. *Intelligent Transportation System Journal of Technology Planning and Operation Research, 3*(2), 37–41.
6. Turochy, R. E., & Smith, B. L. (2002). Measuring variability in traffic conditions by using archived traffic data. *Transportation Research Record, 1804*(2), 168–172.
7. Smith, B. L., & Demetsky, M. J. (2004). Investigation of extraction transformation and loading techniques for traffic data. *Transportation Research Record, 1879*, 9–16.
8. Vlahogianni, E. I., Golias, J. C., & Karlaftis, M. G. (2004). Short-term traffic forecasting: Overview of objectives and methods. *Transport Reviews, 24*(5), 533–557.
9. Vlahogianni, E. I., Geroliminis, N., & Skabardonis, A. (2008). Empirical and analytical investigation of traffic flow regimes and transitions in signalized arterials. *Journal of Transportation Engineering, 134*(12), 512–522.
10. Zhang, J., Wang, F. Y., Wang, K., Lin, W. H., et al. (2011). Data-driven intelligent transportation systems: A survey. *IEEE Transaction on Intelligent Transport Systems, 12*(4), 1624–1639.
11. Oh, S., Byon, Y. J., Jang, C., & Yeo, H. (2018). Short-term travel-time prediction on highway: A review on model-based approach. *ASCE Journal of Civil Engineering, 22*, 298–310.
12. Chang, H., Lee, H., & Yoon, B. (2012). Dynamic near-term traffic flow prediction: Systemoriented approach based on past experiences. *IET Intelligent Transport Systems, 6*(3), 292–305.
13. Thomas, T., Weijermars, W., & Van Berkum, E. (2010). Predictions of urban volumes in single time series. *IEEE Transaction on Intelligent Transport System, 11*(1), 71–80.

14. Ghosh, B., Basu, B., & Mahony, M. O. (2010). Random process model for urban traffic flow using a wavelet-Bayesian hierarchical technique. *Computer Aided Civil and Infrastructure Engineering, 25*(8), 613–624.
15. Ermagun, A., Chatterjee, S., & Levinson, D. (2017). Using temporal detrending to observe the spatial correlation of traffic. *PLoS One, 12*(5), 1–21.
16. Guardiola, I., Leon, T., & Mallor, F. (2014). A functional approach to monitor and recognize patterns of daily traffic profiles. *Transportation Research Part B: Methodological, 65*(7), 119–136.
17. Kamarianakis, Y., Gao, H. O., & Prastacos, P. (2010). Characterizing regimes in daily cycles of urban traffic using smooth-transition regressions. *Transportation Research-Part C, 18*(5), 821–840.
18. Gary, A. D. (1991). Non parametric regression and short term freeway traffic forecasting. *Journal of Transportation Engineering, 117*(2), 178–188.
19. Rajabzadeh, Y., Amir, H. R., & Hamidreza, A. (2017). Short-term traffic flow prediction using time-varying Vasicek model. *Transportation Research Part C, 74*(11), 168–181.
20. Yu, B., Song, X., Guan, F., Yang, Z., et al. (2016). k-Nearest neighbour model for multiple-time-step prediction of short-term traffic condition. *Journal of Transportation Engineering, 142*(6), 04016018.
21. Almeida, P. R. D., Oliveira, L. S., Britto, A. S., Silva, E. J., & Koerich, A. L. (2015). PKLot—A robust dataset for parking lot classification. *Expert System Application, 42*, 4937–4949.
22. Yu, J., Chang, G. L., Ho, H. W., & Liu, Y. (2008). Variation based online travel time prediction using clustered neural networks. In *Proceedings of the 11th International IEEE Conference on Intelligent Transportation Systems*, Beijing, China, 12–15 October 2008, pp. 85–90.
23. Geetha, S., & Cicilia, D. (2017). IoT enabled intelligent bus transportation system. In *Proceedings of the 2017 2nd International Conference on Communication and Electronics Systems (ICCES)*, Coimbatore, India, 19–20 October.
24. Amato, G., Carrara, F., Falchi, F., Gennaro, C., Meghini, C., & Vairo, C. (2017). Deep learning for decentralized parking lot occupancy detection. *Expert Systems Application, 72*, 327–334.
25. Ba, J., Mnih, V., & Kavukcuoglu, K. (2014). Multiple object recognition with visual attention. *arXiv, arXiv:1412.7755.*
26. Devi, S., & Neetha, T. (2017). Machine learning based traffic congestion prediction in a IoT based smart city. *International Research Journal of Engineering and Technology, 4*, 3442–3445.
27. Dogru, N., & Subasi, A. (2018). Traffic accident detection using random forest classifier. In *Proceedings of the 2018 15th Learning and Technology Conference (L&T)*, Jeddah, Saudi Arabia, 25–26 February 2018, pp. 40–45.
28. Fusco, G., Colombaroni, C., Comelli, L., & Isaenko, N. (2015). Short-term traffic predictions on large urban traffic networks: Applications of network-based machine learning models and dynamic traffic assignment models. In *Proceedings of the 2015 IEEE International Conference on Models and Technologies for Intelligent Transportation Systems (MT-ITS)*, Budapest, Hungary, 3–5 June 2015, pp. 93–101.
29. Ghadge, M., Pandey, D., & Kalbande, D. (2015). Machine learning approach for predicting bumps on road. In *Proceedings of the 2015 IEEE International Conference on Applied and Theoretical Computing and Communication Technology (iCATccT)*, Davangere, India, 29–31 October 2015, pp. 481–485.
30. Ghosh, A., Chatterjee, T., Samanta, S., Aich, J., & Roy, S. (2017). Distracted driving: A novel approach towards accident prevention. *Journal of Advanced Computer Science & Technology, 10*(8), 2693–2705.
31. Gopalakrishnan, K. (2018). Deep learning in data-driven pavement image analysis and automated distress detection: A review. *Data, 3*(3), 28.
32. Hou, Y., Edara, P., & Sun, C. (2015). Traffic flow forecasting for urban work zones. *IEEE Intelligent Transportation Systems Society, 16*, 1761–1770.

33. Kanoh, H., Furukawa, T., Tsukahara, S., Hara, K., Nishi, H., & Kurokawa, H. (2005). Short-term traffic prediction using fuzzy c-means and cellular automata in a wide-area road network. In *Proceedings of the 2005 IEEE Intelligent Transportation Systems*, Vienna, Austria, 16 September 2005, pp. 381–385.
34. Kulkarni, A., Mhalgi, N., Gurnani, S., & Giri, N. (2014). Pothole detection system using machine learning on Android. *International Journal of Emerging Technology and Advanced Engineering, 4*, 360–364.
35. Kwon, D., Park, S., Baek, S., Malaiya, R. K., Yoon, G., & Ryu, J. T. (2018). A study on development of the blind spot detection system for the IoT-based smart connected car. In *Proceedings of the 2018 IEEE International Conference on Consumer Electronics (ICCE)*, Las Vegas, NV, USA, 12–14 January 2018, pp. 1–4.
36. Liu, W., Kim, S. W., Marczuk, K., & Ang, M. H. (2014). Vehicle motion intention reasoning using cooperative perception on urban road. In *Proceedings of the 2014 IEEE 17th International Conference on Intelligent Transportation Systems (ITSC)*, Qingdao, China, 8–11 October 2014, pp. 424–430.
37. Lv, Y., Duan, Y., Kang, W., Li, Z., & Wang, F. Y. (2014). Traffic flow prediction with big data: A deep learning approach. *IEEE Intelligent Transportation Systems Society, 16*, 865–873.
38. Munoz-Organero, M., Ruiz-Blaquez, R., & Sánchez-Fernández, L. (2018). Automatic detection of traffic lights, street crossings and urban roundabouts combining outlier detection and deep learning classification techniques based on GPS traces while driving. *Computers, Environment and Urban Systems, 68*, 1–8.
39. Ng, J. R., Wong, J. S., Goh, V. T., Yap, W. J., Yap, T. T. V., & Ng, H. (2019). Identification of road surface conditions using IoT sensors and machine learning. In *Computational science and technology* (pp. 259–268). Singapore: Springer.
40. Ozbayoglu, M., Kucukayan, G., & Dogdu, E. (2016). A real-time autonomous highway accident detection model based on big data processing and computational intelligence. In *Proceedings of the 2016 IEEE international conference on Big Data (Big Data)*, Washington, DC, USA, 5–8 December 2016, pp. 1807–1813.
41. Jayanthi, G., & Jothilakshmi, P. (2019). Prediction of traffic volume by mining traffic sequences using travel time based PrefixSpan.IET. *Intelligent Transport Systems, 13*(7), 1990–2004. https://doi.org/10.1049/iet-its.2018.5165.
42. Ryder, B., & Wortmann, F. (2017). Autonomously detecting and classifying traffic accident hotspots. In *Proceedings of the 2017 ACM International Joint Conference on Pervasive and Ubiquitous Computing and 2017 ACM International Symposium on Wearable Computers*, Maui, HI, USA, 11–15 September 2017, pp. 365–370.
43. Sang, K. S., Zhou, B., Yang, P., & Yang, Z. (2017). Study of group route optimization for IoT enabled urban transportation network. In *Proceedings of the 2017 IEEE International Conference on Internet of Things (iThings) and IEEE Green Computing and Communications (GreenCom) and IEEE Cyber, Physical and Social Computing (CPSCom) and IEEE Smart Data (SmartData)*, Exeter, UK, 21–23 June 2017, pp. 888–893.
44. Wu, Q., Huang, C., Wang, S. Y., Chiu, W. C., & Chen, T. (2007). Robust parking space detection considering inter-space correlation. In *Proceedings of the 2007 IEEE International Conference on Multimedia and Expo*, Beijing, China, 2–5 July 2007.
45. Yang, J., Han, Y., Wang, Y., Jiang, B., Lv, Z., & Song, H. (2017). Optimization of real-time traffic network assignment based on IoT data using DBN and clustering model in smart city. *Future Generation Computer Systems, 108*, 976–986.

Chapter 12
Examining Spatial Movement Patterns of Travelers: Cases in Tourist Destinations

Masahide Yamamoto, Mitsuru Sato, and Tatsuo Kamitani

Abstract This chapter uses "Mobile Kukan Toukei™" (mobile spatial statistics) to examine people's characteristics and spatial movement patterns in specific tourist destinations in Nagoya City. This chapter also attempts to estimate visitor volume and flow using movement data acquired by Wi-Fi tracking sensors installed widely in tourism destinations. A Wi-Fi tracking sensor is a device that acquires a media access control (MAC) address unique to communication devices such as smartphones. By installing sensors in a tourism area, the same MAC address is acquired between them, and a visitor's movement information can be collected. This chapter examined wide-area travel routes of visitors in the northern part of the Kyoto Prefecture and combined data obtained through sensors with other survey data to clarify movement patterns of visitors for each attribute within the area.

Keywords Wi-Fi tracking sensor · Mobile Kukan Toukei™ · Tourism · Statistical population data · Mobile phone

12.1 Introduction

In recent years, Japan's tourism industry has been enjoying an increasing number of incoming international tourists. According to the Japan National Tourism Organization [1], Japan had approximately 31.9 million international tourists in 2019.

However, tourism sharply decreased in 2020 due to the worldwide spread of the coronavirus disease (COVID-19). The JNTO [1] claimed that the number dropped by 93.0% in March 2020 (from 2.76 million in March 2019 to 194,000 in March

M. Yamamoto (✉)
Faculty of Foreign Studies, Nagoya Gakuin University, Nagoya, Japan
e-mail: myama@ngu.ac.jp

M. Sato · T. Kamitani
Department of Regional Management, The University of Fukuchiyama, Kyoto, Japan
e-mail: sato-mitsuru@fukuchiyama.ac.jp

© Springer Nature Switzerland AG 2021
F. P. García Márquez, B. Lev (eds.), *Internet of Things*, International Series in
Operations Research & Management Science 305,
https://doi.org/10.1007/978-3-030-70478-0_12

2020). The pandemic poses a challenge not only to the tourism industry but also to society as a whole. Moreover, it has forced the international community to alter its mannerisms, particularly in the way people work, interact, and live. Therefore, adapting to the new circumstances should be a key element to survive the tough new era.

A serious impact on the world economy is expected[1] due to restrictions to the movement of people to prevent the disease from further spreading. In other words, the movement has been one of the principal driving forces of the economy.[2] Thus, it is important to examine and understand it.

Currently, IoT has come into use in various aspects of human lives in order to improve their efficiency. This chapter attempts to propose alternatives to more accurately grasp people's movements by utilizing the IoT. In this chapter, the application of "Mobile Kukan Toukei" (mobile spatial statistics[3]) provided by NTT DOCOMO, Inc. and DOCOMO Insight Marketing, Inc. is introduced to infer the number of travelers in specific tourist destinations and examine their characteristics. Mobile Kukan Toukei is statistical population data created by operational data from mobile phone networks. It is possible to estimate the population structure of a region by gender, age, and residential area using this service (Fig. 12.1). Statistical population data obtained herein are derived through a non-identification process, aggregation processing, and concealment processing. Therefore, it is impossible to identify specific individuals.

12.2   Attempts to Utilize IoT in Tourism

So far, the IoT has been mainly used to understand the operation status of public transportation systems, including congestion, in tourism-related fields. For example, it is possible to see where buses are running in many cities in real time. A similar attempt is observed in Esashi Town in Hokkaido, which provides tourists with location information about floats during its traditional festival.

Kontogianni and Alepis [4] outlined previous research on "smart tourism" including tourism studies on IoT (Table 12.1). In terms of tourism, IoT can enable the creation of smart technological environments that connect physical and digital infrastructures. This allows smart tourism systems to identify tourists' context in a pervasive but not intrusive way and attend to their needs [4].

---

[1] The British Broadcasting Corporation (BBC) [2] reported that, according to Asian Development Bank, the coronavirus pandemic could cost the global economy between \$5.8 and \$8.8 tn (£4.7–£7.1 tn).

[2] The coronavirus lockdown, which severely restricted people's movement, has forced several countries' economies to shrink. For example, *The Wall Street Journal* [3] reported that the UK economy shrank 20.4% in April compared with March, and gross domestic product was 24.5% lower than the same month of the previous year.

[3] "Mobile spatial statistics" is the translation of "Mobile Kukan Toukei."

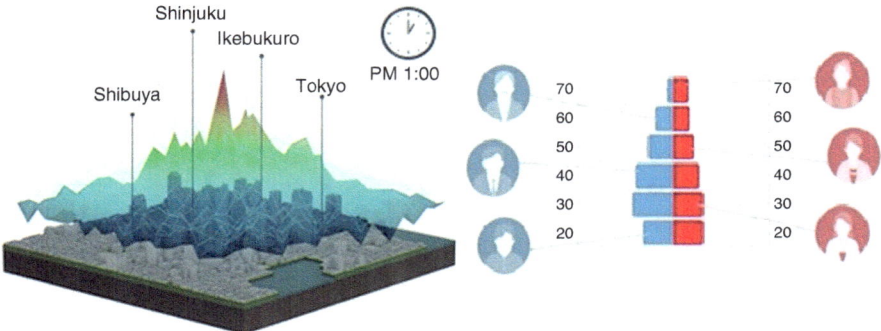

Fig. 12.1 The statistical population data collected from Mobile Kukan Toukei.
Note: Retrieved July 2, 2019, from https://www.nttdocomo.co.jp/corporate/disclosure/mobile_spatial_statistics/#p01

This chapter focuses on location data mainly extracted from individual digital devices such as mobile phones. Location data provides a considerable amount of useful information not only to the tourism industry but to society in general.[4]

12.2.1   Extracting Location Data of People Through IoT

Attempts to extract the location data have been principally conducted in research field. Studies using mobile phone location data for tourism surveys can be traced back to 2008. Ahas et al. [13] introduced the applicability of passive mobile positioning data. They used a database derived from roaming location (foreign phones) and call activities in network cells: the database included location, time, random identification, and country of origin of each called phone. Using examples from Estonia, their study described the peculiarities of the data, data gathering, sampling, handling of the spatial database, and various analytical methods to demonstrate that mobile positioning data have valuable applications for geographic studies. The Japan Tourism Agency [14] also conducted a similar study using international roaming service in December 2014.

Since the survey of Ahas et al. [13], several studies employing location data have emerged. Liu et al. [15] investigated the extent to which behavioral routines could reveal the activities being performed at mobile phone call locations at the time when users initiate or receive voice calls or messages. Using data collected

---

[4]Location data has been used to analyze people's movements when natural disaster or infectious disease (COVID-19) occurs. In addition, the data can be utilized to provide better services. For example, understanding consumers' characteristics through the location data can enable tourism businesses to optimize goods and services, which could influence customer satisfaction.

Table 12.1 Smart tourism approaches related to IoT

Author	Context awareness	Recommender system	Real time	Augmented reality	Big data	Cultural heritage	Privacy preserving
Tripathy et al. [5]	✓		✓				
Tussyadiah et al. [6]				✓			
Nitti et al. [7]	✓	✓	✓				
Sun et al. [8]	✓	✓	✓		✓	✓	
Atembe et al. [9]							✓
Khallouki et al. [10]	✓	✓	✓				
Lin et al. [11]					✓		
Gretzel et al. [12]							

Source: Compiled by the author based on Kontogianni and Alepis [4]

from the natural mobile phone communication patterns of 80 users over more than a year, they assessed the approach via a set of extensive experiments. Based on the ensemble of models, they achieved prediction accuracy of 69.7%. The experiment results demonstrated the potential of annotating mobile phone locations based on the integration of data mining techniques with the characteristics of underlying activity-travel behavior.

A variety of related studies have also been conducted. Gao et al. [16] attempted to examine the methods used to estimate traffic measures using information from mobile phones, taking into account the fact that each vehicle likely contains more than one phone because of the popularity of mobile phones. Steenbruggen et al. [17] used mobile phone data to provide new spatio-temporal tools for improving urban planning and reducing inefficiencies in current urban systems. They addressed the applicability of such digital data to develop innovative applications to improve urban management.

Another attempt needs to be mentioned here. The Project Report that Okinawa Prefecture published (2013) is of a study that used location data obtained from a domestic mobile phone network. The aim of the project was to survey the characteristics and behavior of tourists who were visiting Okinawa Prefecture. Okinawa pref. conducted the survey in order to grasp the trends and needs of repeat customers. The survey revealed the composition of tourists to Okinawa Prefecture by residence, gender, and age. They examined how the number of travelers changes depending on the month (October 2012 and January 2013) and the day of the week.

The above approaches are quite effective when analyzing extensive areas. However, to obtain data in a narrow area such as a specific tourist facility, it is impossible to exclude unnecessary data. This study also demonstrates an alternative method to extract data in such areas.

12.2.2   Tourism Research on Wi-Fi Tracking Sensors

The rapid spread of information and communication technology and the IoT has produced a variety of big data that is being used in research in the tourism field. Tourism-related big data can be broadly categorized into three types of data: user-generated content (UGC), device, and transactional data [18]. Large amounts of data in both structured and unstructured formats are generated, recorded, stored, and accumulated by the relevant entities in tourism, such as tourists, destination management organizations (DMOs), online travel agencies, accommodation providers, local governments, etc. Such big data is providing a new analytical perspective on research issues such as tourism demand, tourist behavior, and tourist satisfaction [18].

In particular, through the development of technologies that support the IoT, digital tracking data on tourist movement has been collected via devices that can then be used for tourism research. It is the collection and accumulation of large, high-quality data to track tourists' spatio-temporal behavior through devices such as

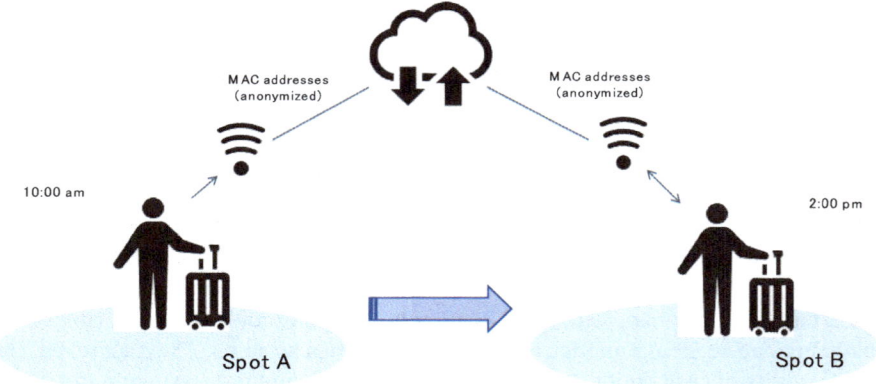

Fig. 12.2 Using Wi-Fi packet sensors to understand the movement of tourists

global positioning systems (GPS), smartphones, and Bluetooth and Wi-Fi tracking sensors [18, 19]. There are clear advantages to digital tracking data [18, 19]. The data is temporally and spatially accurate, and the geographic and temporal scope of the dataset is wide [18]. In addition, tracking data can be supplemented using surveys, sensors, and other sources [19].

Wi-Fi tracking sensors are one of the most effective devices to collect and record data on the movements of tourists. Through a Wi-Fi interface, it detects a device— usually at the location where the sensor is installed—and collects and records anonymized MAC addresses [20]. The data acquired by Wi-Fi tracking sensors is not the movement of the device itself, as provided by GPS; by using a timestamp of detection in individual sensors and estimating transitions between sensors, tourists' movements are understood [18]. This method allows continuous data collection over a long period at a low cost [19, 20]. Data are collected without direct contact with tourists [19]. No direct request or pre-registration for tourists is required, and no active work such as having an application installed on a smartphone is required [18, 20]. More to the point, it is possible to track without notifying tourists (Fig. 12.2), as those who are tracked are unaware [18]. In addition, Wi-Fi tracking sensors can be used in congested indoor areas or near tall structures where GPS connectivity is not warranted [18].

On the other hand, the Wi-Fi tracking sensor has a few weaknesses. First, unlike GPS data, there is a limited range in which the sensor can detect the device, which limits the geographical scope of data that can be collected [18]. Second, the data acquired by the sensors is anonymized MAC addresses sent by devices with Wi-Fi interfaces, which only provide a small amount of information about the tourists [19]. The third and biggest issue is the impact on tourists' privacy in the survey and concern over revealing the exact location of tourists without notice or consent [21, 18]. In this regard, technology to conceal the actual MAC address has been introduced to protect privacy. However, new techniques have been proposed to disable such concealment techniques, and the current privacy protection is not sufficient [22, 23].

There are fewer tourism studies using data acquired by Wi-Fi tracking sensors than studies using digital tracking data from other devices [18]. Most tourism studies using digital tracking data have analyzed GPS, mobile location, Bluetooth tracking, and geocoded social media [19]. Thus far, Bonné et al. [21] collected Wi-Fi tracking data at a popular international music festival in Belgium that attracted 100,000 people, simultaneously tracking the spatial spread of thousands of visitors during the 3-day music festival. Chilipirea et al. [24] installed 27 Wi-Fi tracking sensors at a festival that attracted nearly 130,000 people in a city center in the north of the Netherlands and examined the cleaning methods of the datasets the sensors acquired. Nunes et al. [22] examined the possibility of using Wi-Fi tracking sensors to provide information regarding the spatio-temporal patterns of visitor movements to stakeholders in the tourism sector at well-known European tourist destination, Madeira Island.

In the future, the field of tourism research using Wi-Fi tracking data is expected to expand as devices with Wi-Fi interfaces, such as smartphones, become more widespread [18]. For example, given the strength of Wi-Fi tracking sensors, there are research questions to be asked, such as tourist behavior at tourist events, recommendations to tourists, and emergency management [18]. On the other hand, because of the sensor's characteristics, the data range is narrow. Therefore, studies indoors or in dense areas of the facility are more appropriate. However, by adding a twist to the sensor locations, it is possible to understand the widespread flow of tourists, as in the research of Nunes et al. [22]. The analysis of this study visualizes the flow of tourists in a tourist area across multiple municipalities. It is also essential to protect the privacy of the tourists who are surveyed for Wi-Fi tracking. In the data collection, notification about the sensor is required. In addition, it is desirable to avoid the analysis of privacy-related information, such as the location of individual tourists, using only sensor data. Therefore, to respect the privacy of the individuals from whom the data are collected, the procedure of interpretation combined with other log and survey data—such as that presented in the analysis of this study— would be one alternative.

12.3 Utilizing Mobile Kukan Toukei to Examine the Movement Patterns of Travelers

The survey was conducted between April 2015 and October 2019. The sites studied in this survey are mainly tourist destinations in Nagoya City, which became temporarily popular when a theme park opened in 2017. Moreover, the locations and characteristics of individuals obtained herein are derived through a non-identification process, aggregation processing, and concealment processing. Therefore, it is impossible to identify specific individuals.

Table 12.2 The survey areas and the regional mesh codes

Survey area	Mesh code	Type of codes
① Nagoya Station	5236-6700	Tertiary
② Nagoya Castle	5236-6721-2, 5236-6722-1	1/2
③ Port of Nagoya Public Aquarium	5236-5700-3, 5236-5710-1	1/2
④ Atsuta Shrine	5236-5752-2	1/2
⑤ Kinjo Wharf	5236-4667-1, 5236-4667-2	1/2
⑥ Kanayama Station	5236-5772-1	1/2
⑦ Sakae	5236-6702	Tertiary
⑧ Osu Shopping Street	5236-5792-1	1/2

Note: A regional mesh code is a code for identifying the regional mesh, which is substantially divided into the same size of a square (mesh) based on the latitude and longitude in order to use it for statistics. The length of one side of a primary mesh is about 80 km, and those of secondary and tertiary meshes are about 10 km and 1 km, respectively

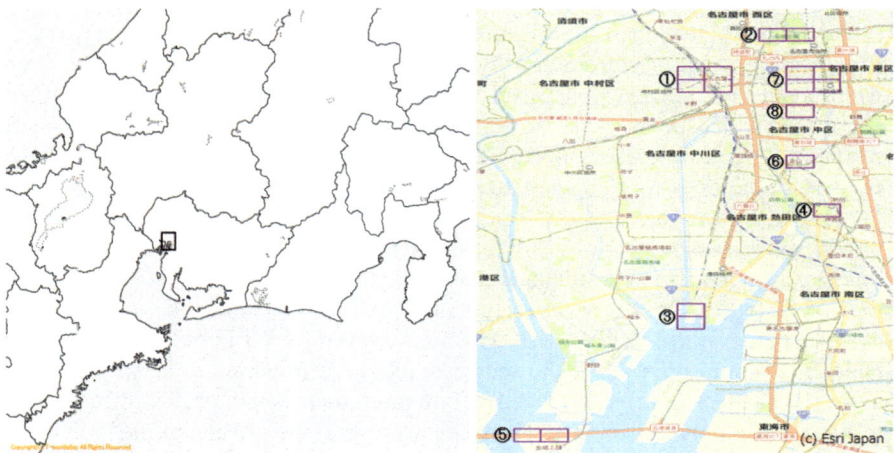

Fig. 12.3 Survey areas in Nagoya City

12.3.1 Identifying the Number of Travelers and Their Characteristics in Tourist Destinations in Nagoya City

The survey areas are presented in Table 12.2 and Fig. 12.3. A regional mesh code is a code for identifying the regional mesh. It stands for an encoded area that is substantially divided into the same size of a square (mesh) based on the latitude and longitude in order to use it for statistics. With regard to regional mesh, there are three types of meshes: primary, secondary, and tertiary. The length of one side of a primary mesh is about 80 km, and those of secondary and tertiary meshes are about 10 km and 1 km, respectively.

In addition, split regional meshes also exist, which are a more detailed regional division. A half-regional mesh is a tertiary mesh that is divided into two equal pieces in the vertical and horizontal directions. The length of one side is about 500 m. Furthermore, the length of one side of a quarter and 1/8 regional meshes is about 250 m and 125 m, respectively.

12.3.2 The Results of the Survey Conducted in Nagoya City

Figure 12.4 compares two major downtown areas in Nagoya. It is likely that the so-called "Meieki" (i.e., Nagoya Station) area has succeeded in attracting more visitors possibly due to its redevelopment schemes, whereas Sakae showed a slight decline. Similar trends are observed with Kanayama and Osu (see Fig. 12.5).

Nagoya Castle also enjoyed an increase in tourist population because of the redevelopment of its neighboring area (Fig. 12.6). Kinshachi Yokocho shopping

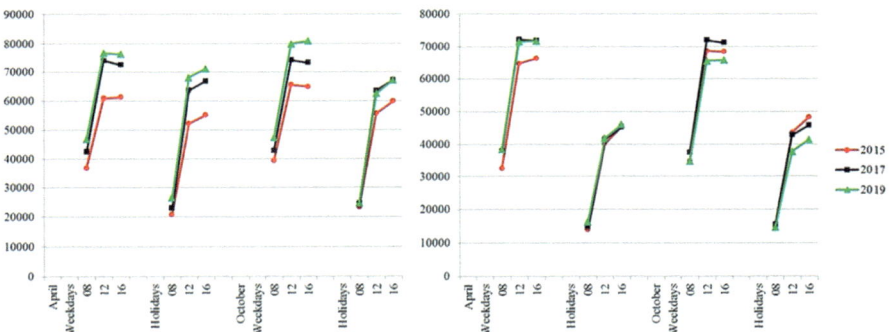

Fig. 12.4 Regional population trends (left, Nagoya Station; right, Sakae)

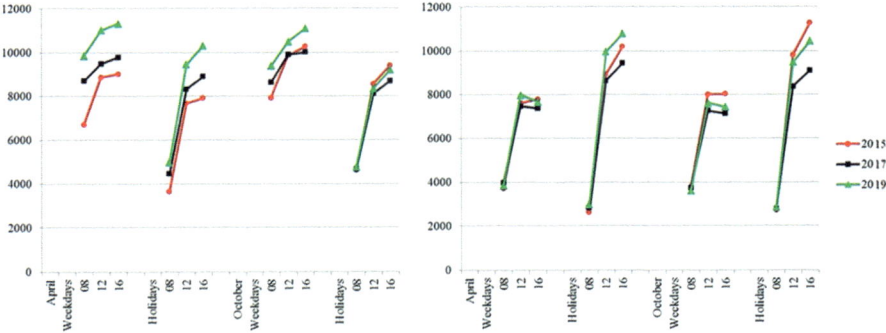

Fig. 12.5 Regional population trends (left, Kanayama Station; right, Osu)

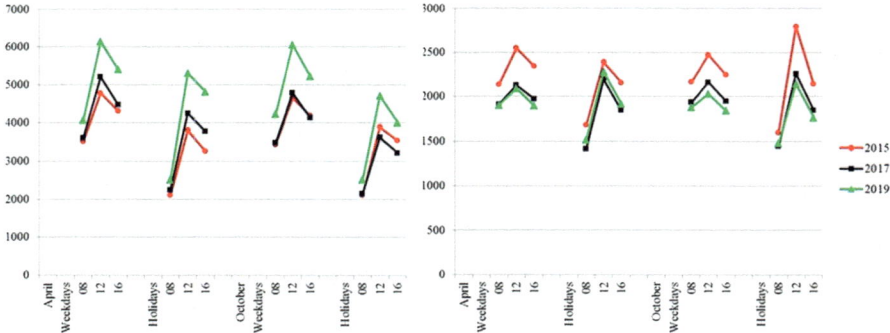

Fig. 12.6 Regional population trends (left, Nagoya Castle; right, Atsuta Shrine)

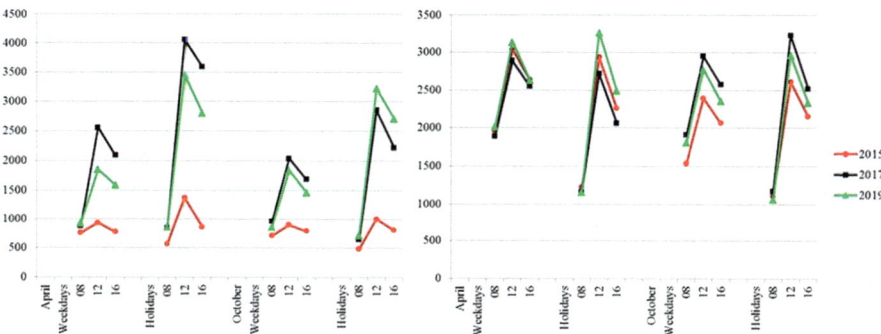

Fig. 12.7 Regional population trends (left, Kinjo Warf; right, Nagoya Port)

street opened to revitalize the area in March 2018. Conversely, the population at Atsuta Shrine has been declining.

Kinjo Warf houses a Lego theme park (based on the toy construction system) as its main attraction. Comparisons before and after the opening of the theme park (Fig. 12.7) revealed that it had a remarkable impact (especially on the holidays during April 2017, immediately after the opening). However, the effect can be seen only around that facility; similar transitions in population cannot be observed at other sites. Originally, Nagoya Port Aquarium was expected to become a major competitor to the facility, but no particular effect was observed there.

When focusing on the demographic attributes of the population in each area, Nagoya Station and the Sakae area attracted visitors of a relatively wider range of age (Fig. 12.8). While women in their 20s were expected to crowd these areas, it was actually men in their 40s that were predominantly found in the Osu shopping street (see Fig. 12.9).

Moreover, it was seen that Atsuta Shrine's (Fig. 12.10) population structure houses a higher elderly population than other areas. On the other hand, there were many people in their 30s and 40s in Kinjo Wharf (Fig. 12.11). Therefore, it could

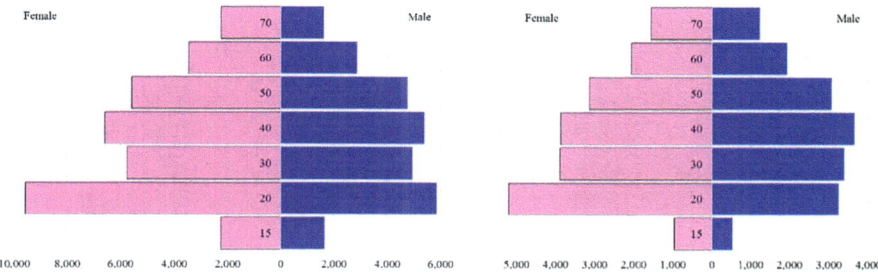

Fig. 12.8 Attributes of population in the area (left, Nagoya Station; right, Sakae) (12:00 a.m.–1:00 p.m. on holidays in October 2019)

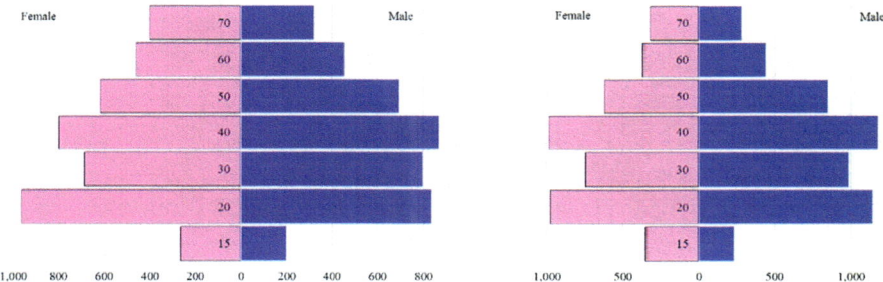

Fig. 12.9 Attributes of population in the area (left, Kanayama Station; right, Osu) (12:00 a.m.–1:00 p.m. on holidays in October 2019)

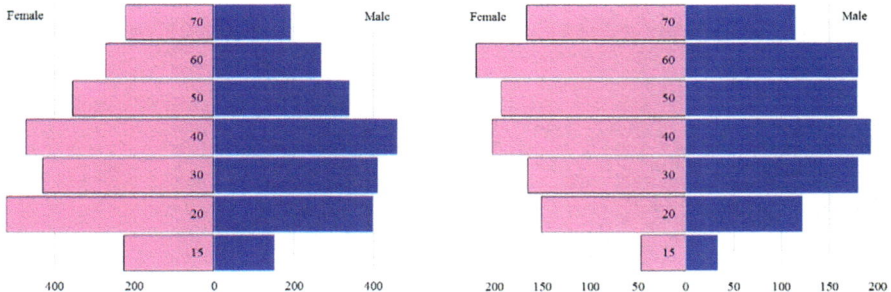

Fig. 12.10 Attributes of population in the area (left, Nagoya Castle; right, Atsuta Shrine) (12:00 a.m.–1:00 p.m. on holidays in October 2019)

be concluded that families occupied a large proportion of the population structure. A similar tendency was observed at the Port of Nagoya Public Aquarium.

Examining the statistical data of the residential area, Nagoya Station, Sakae, and Osu have attracted visitors from a variety of distant regions (Figs. 12.12 and 12.13), while visitors of Atsuta Shrine (Fig. 12.14) were mostly from Aichi Prefecture, where the shrine is located. Kinjo Wharf (Fig. 12.15) mainly attracted visitors from

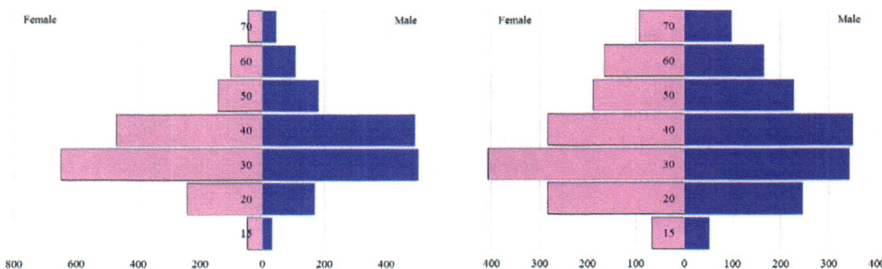

Fig. 12.11 Attributes of population in the area (left, Kinjo Warf; right, Nagoya Port) (12:00 a.m.–1:00 p.m. on holidays in October 2019)

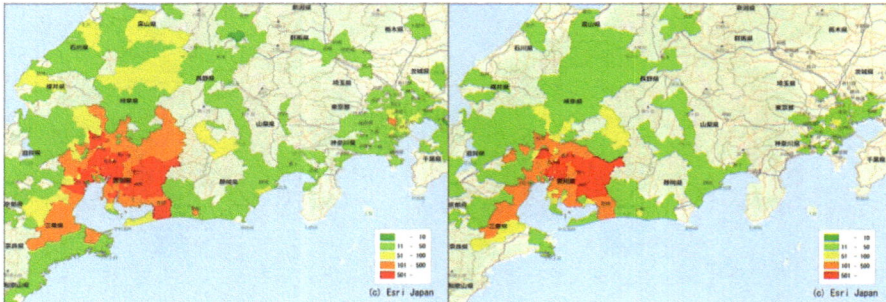

Fig. 12.12 Residential area of population in the area (left, Nagoya Station; right, Sakae) (12:00 a.m.–1:00 p.m. on holidays in October 2019)

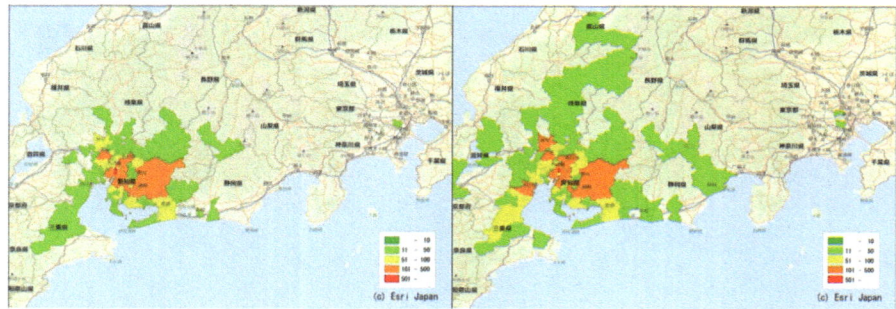

Fig. 12.13 Residential area of population in the area (left, Kanayama Station; right, Osu) (12:00 a.m.–1:00 p.m. on holidays in October 2019)

the Chubu region (i.e., central Japan), especially the Tokai area and the Port of Nagoya Public Aquarium.

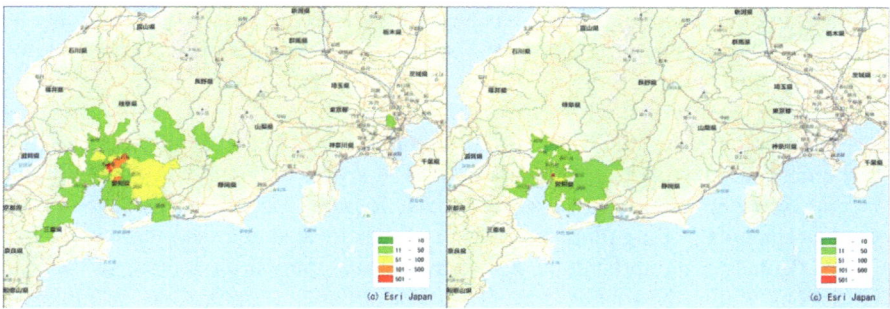

Fig. 12.14 Residential area of population in the area (left, Nagoya Castle; right, Atsuta Shrine) (12:00 a.m.–1:00 p.m. on holidays in October 2019)

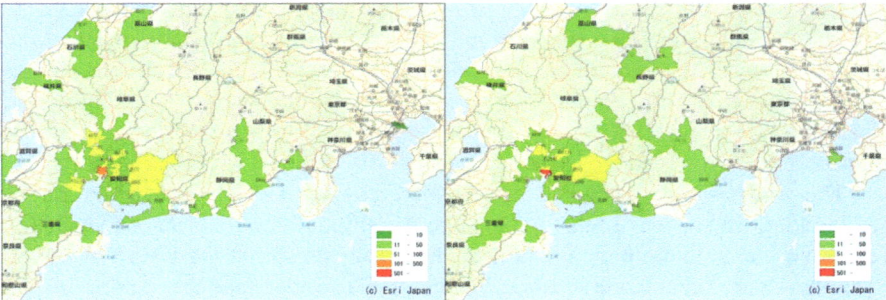

Fig. 12.15 Residential area of population in the area (left, Kinjo Warf; right, Nagoya Port) (12:00 a.m.–1:00 p.m. on holidays in October 2019)

12.4 Analyzing the Wi-Fi Tracking Sensor Data with Other Survey Data to Clarify Travelers' Movement Patterns

12.4.1 Analysis Overview

In this analysis, to understand tourists' travel routes over a wide area, we used data obtained from tourists' communication devices using Wi-Fi tracking sensors[5] installed in a tourist zone in the northern part of Kyoto Prefecture. About 60 tracking sensors have been established at major tourist facilities and tourist information centers across the zone's municipality. We also combined the data obtained by the sensor with the data on parking lot use and the questionnaire data to analyze the movement patterns of visiting tourists who visited Ine town, located within the tourist zone. The questionnaire was conducted between July 2017 and June 2018

---

[5]When the tracking sensor obtains a unique MAC address for a communication device such as a smartphone, it processes the true MAC address to conceal it.

as the Ine Town Tourism Survey. Japanese travelers responded to the questionnaire. The questionnaire included questions on age, gender, place of residence, number of days visited, location visited, satisfaction with the location visited, and amount spent at the location visited.

The tourism zone, called "the Kyoto by the Sea Tourism Zone," is composed of five cities and two towns in the northern part of Kyoto Prefecture. Amanohashidate is one of Japan's three most scenic spots, located about 2 h from Kyoto and Osaka—Japan's leading tourist cities. Ine town is located at the northern part of the Tango Peninsula, comprising the Kyoto by the Sea Tourism Zone. One of the main attractions within the tourist zone, it has boat houses designated as an important traditional building preservation area. In recent years, there has been an increase in the number of domestic and foreign tourists owing to the scenic beauty of the area.

For the analysis, data were borrowed from the DMO of the Kyoto by the Sea Tourism Zone and Ine town. The data are (1) Wi-Fi packet sensor log data, (2) usage data of the Ine town parking lot,[6] and (3) the answer data of the Ine town tourist survey. The period of analysis was fiscal year 2017, specifically the summer season from July 1 to September 30. Yearly, the summer season is the highest and busiest time for Ine town compared to other periods. The target of the analysis was Japanese tourists.

The analysis was conducted as follows. First, the data obtained from the Wi-Fi tracking sensor was used to count the transitions between sensor installations and then illustrate the flow and movement of tourists within the Kyoto by the Sea Tourism Zone. Second, the sensor data were used to understand the regional outflow and inflow routes of visitors to Ine town and identify the movement between the four sensor locations[7] in Ine town. Third, we analyzed the parking in Ine town trends of each parking lot and the time spent by parking users. Fourth, using the data from the Ine town tourist survey of Japanese tourists, we categorized sightseeing spots and tourists by using visitation data and organized the characteristics of each. We then combined the findings from these analyses to estimate the characteristics of Japanese tourists in Ine town and their travel routes (see Table 12.3).

---

[6]Ine town operates three pay parking lots: Ineura Park (capacity, 22 cars), Shichimensan (67 cars), and Onishi (37 cars). Of these, the Ineura Park and Shichimensan parking lots are close to the main tourist attraction, Ineura Park. Each parking lot has an automated parking system that records the number of cars used and fees charged.

[7]Ine town has installed Wi-Fi tracking sensors at four major tourist spots: Roadside Station Ine, Ferry Terminal, Ineura Park, and Urashima Park.

Table 12.3 Process of analysis

	Content	Data
Step 1	Illustrate the flow and movement of tourists within the Kyoto by the sea tourism zone	Wi-fi tracking sensor data
Step 2	Identify the regional outflow and inflow routes of visitors to Ine town and the movement in the town	Wi-fi tracking sensor data
Step 3	Analyze the parking trends of each parking lot in Ine town and the time spent by parking users	Parking lot data
Step 4	Categorize sightseeing spots and Japanese tourists in Ine town	Questionnaire data

Fig. 12.16 Movement patterns of tourists (using the GSI map and adding the status of transitions between two locations (GSI maps are electronic maps provided by the Geospatial Information Authority of Japan (GSI), one of the government agencies. It contains topographic maps, photographs, elevations, topographic classifications, and disaster information. In this study, we downloaded the GSI map and loaded the data of the number of transitions between two points to describe the movement patterns.))

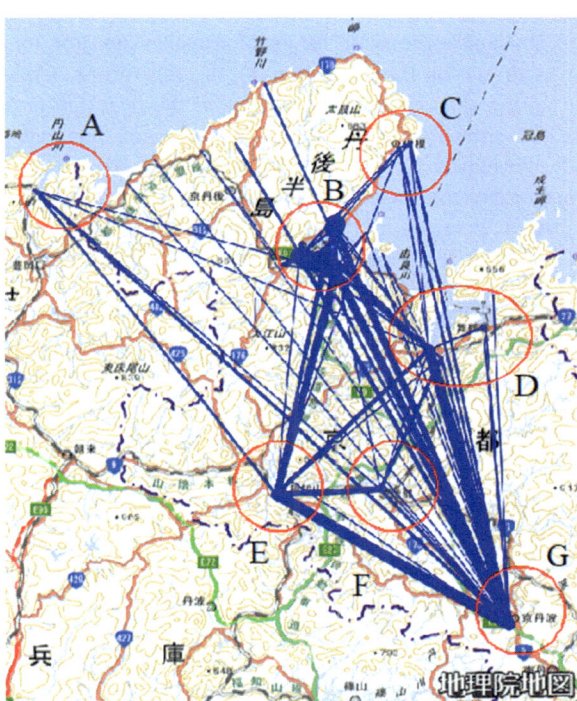

12.4.2 Widespread Travel Routes for Tourists within the Kyoto by the Sea Tourism Zone

Figure 12.16 shows the results of counting the two locations where devices with the same MAC address have moved and then connecting the lines from the count results. The period was FY 2017, and the number of records in the data was 137,117,226. The line in the figure is set to 10,000 cases as one dot, so if there are many moves, the transition line is thicker. In addition, the figure does not show any movement patterns of less than 10,000.

The area in the figure indicated by the circles denotes a hub for tourist travel routes. In particular, the transition lines were concentrated in Areas B and G. Area B was located at Amanohashidate, a major tourist spot, and was visited by many visitors. Area G was a roadside station[8] attached to the Kyotanba parking area on the Kyoto Jukan Expressway, and it can be inferred that many people traveled by car. Area C is Ine town, the area that was the subject of the following analysis.

12.4.3 Flow of Tourists Visiting Ine Town

To visualize the wide range of travel routes for tourists visiting Ine town, a line was drawn on the map showing the transitions between the locations where Wi-Fi tracking sensors were installed and the installation points within Ine town. Figure 12.17 shows the movement between each installation point within Ine town and those outside of it from July to September 2017. One dot represents 2500 transitions, and travel routes with less than 2500 transitions are not shown. Many tourists who visited Ine town had outflows and inflows between Areas B (Amanohashidate), D (Roadside Station Maizuru), E (Fukuchiyama Tourist Information Center), and G (Roadside Station Kyotanba).

Figure 12.18 shows the amount of outflow and inflow between points in Ine town on the map. The numbers in the figure show the amount of people who have moved. The thickness of the arrows in the figure is set to 1000 people as one point. Of the points in Ine town, the roadside station Ine and the Ferry Terminal were the nexus to outside of town. In addition, the highest number of tourist movements within Ine town was between the roadside station Ine and the Ferry Terminal. It was found that travel between the three points, including Inenura Park, is the main route for tourists in Ine town.

The correlation coefficients for the number of sensor logs by day at each point in Ine town during the period under analysis showed a strong positive correlation ($r = 0.81$) between Roadside Station Ine and the Ferry Terminal at a statistically significant level ($p < 0.001$). A strong positive correlation ($r = 0.74$) was also found between the roadside station Ine and Ineura Park at a statistically significant level ($p < 0.001$). It can be inferred that the roadside station Ine has become an important point in the flow of tourists in Ine town.

---

[8]There are more than 1100 roadside stations in Japan, which are public services that combine rest, commercial, and accommodation facilities.

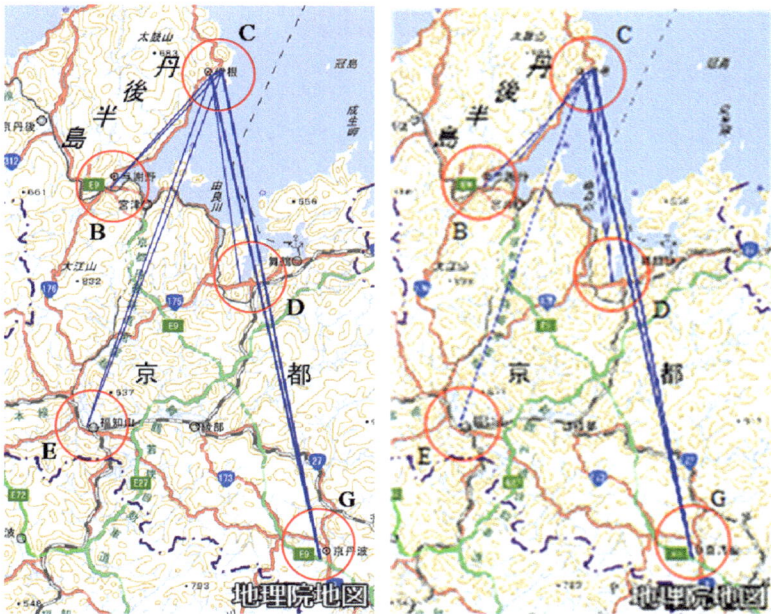

Fig. 12.17 Inflow into Ine town (*left*) and outflow from Ine town (*right*) (using the GSI map "GSI," adding the status of the transition between the two locations)

12.4.4   Trends in the Use of Ine Town Parking Lot

According to data from the Ine Town Tourist Survey, the majority of Japanese visitors to Ine Town travel by car. Therefore, we used data on the use of the parking lots operated by Ine town to understand the parking situation of each parking lot and the time spent by parking users. Correlation analysis was then performed on the parking use data and tracking sensor data.

When the turnover rate[9] of each parking lot in the period under analysis was calculated, the turnover rate for the entire period was higher for the Ineura Park parking lot (2.77) and Shichimensan parking lot (1.18). In particular, on holidays, the turnover rate at the Ineura Park parking lot had risen to 4.55, while the turnover rate at the Shichimensan parking lot had also risen to 2.09. In addition, when calculating the average length of stay of one car per day for each parking lot over the entire period, the Ineura Park parking lot had the highest number of days with less than 80 min, while the Shichimensan parking lot had the highest number of days with less than 80 and 130 min. Ineura Park and Shichimensan parking lots were

---

[9]The turnover rate is the average daily use of each parking lot divided by the number of available parking spaces each has.

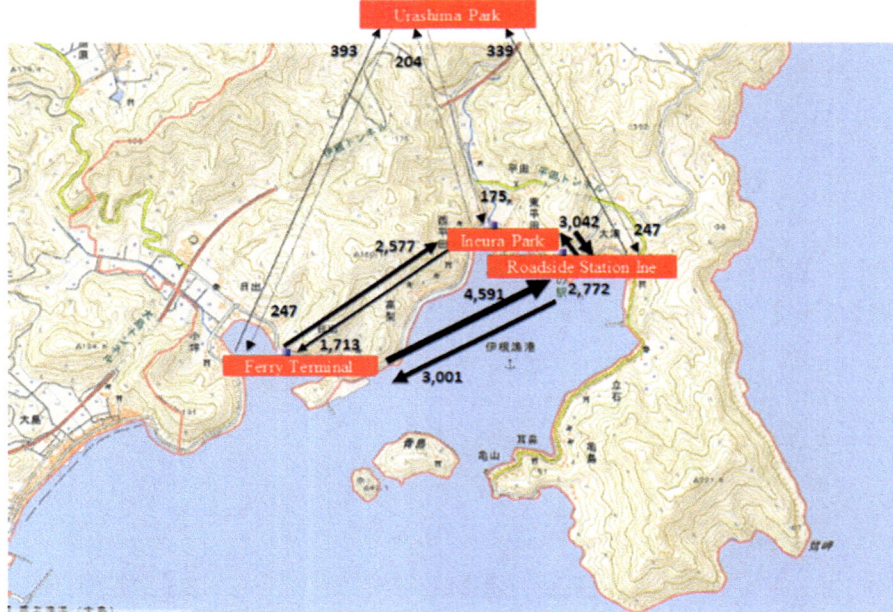

Fig. 12.18 Amount of movement between points in Ine town. (Created using jSTAT-MAP (STAT-MAP is a geographic information system provided by the Ministry of Internal Affairs and Communications, which is one of the government agencies. It contains statistical survey data for Japan and allows you to create a statistical map on the Web))

used more often, and the length of stay for those using the Shichimensan parking lot was longer than the users of Ineura Park parking lot.

Correlation coefficients were also obtained for the number of sensor logs at each location in the town and the turnover rate at each parking lot. Strong positive correlations ($p < 0.001$) were found at statistically significant levels ($p < 0.001$) for the number of sensor logs in the roadside station Ine, between the turnover of the Ineura Park parking lot and the turnover of the Shichimensan parking lot, located in the Important Traditional Building Preservation District. The increase in the number of tourists visiting the Roadside Station Ine has tended to increase the use of both the Inenura Park and Shichimensan parking lots.

12.4.5 Categorization of Tourism Based on Survey Response Data

For the analysis of the Ine town tourist survey, we used respondent data of tourists ($n = 626$) who visited between July and September 2017. In the analysis,

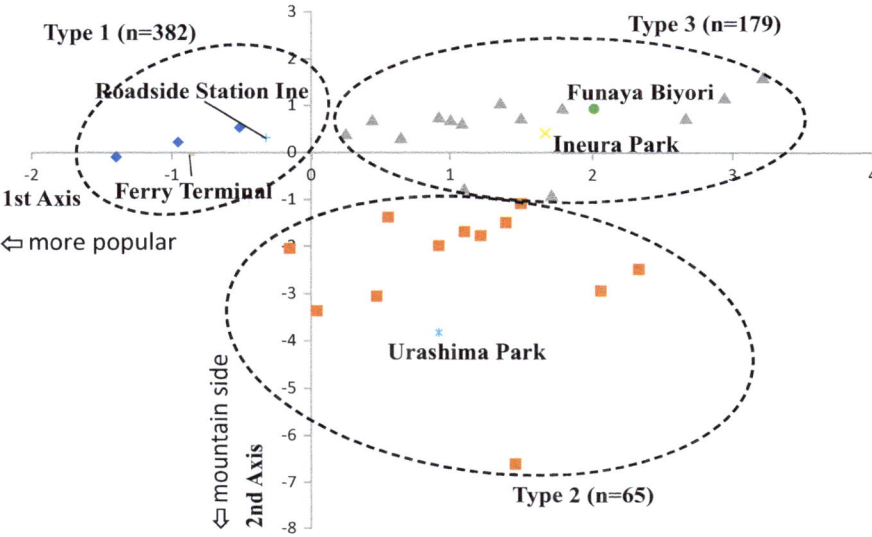

Fig. 12.19 Typology of Japanese tourists visiting Ine town (By Quantification method III, related categories are grouped together, and respondents who show similar response patterns also are grouped together. Then, it can summarize the information on similarities among samples and response categories on axes to produce a clear locational correspondence between respondents and categories.) ($n = 626$)

quantification method III[10] was used to analyze the categorical data that answered the sites visited. Then, a non-hierarchical cluster analysis (K-means method) was performed using the sample scores obtained by the quantification theory III analysis.

Figure 12.19 shows a visualization of the typology of tourists based on the points visited. Using the category and sample scores obtained from the quantification theory III analysis, we plotted the main tourist sites[11] in Ine town and each respondent on the same coordinate axis. We then categorized the tourists with close sample scores, i.e., those with similar visit behavior to each of the sites, into three categories using non-hierarchical cluster analysis. The type was considered a movement pattern within Ine town and was divided based on the points that the respondents visited.

---

[10]Quantification method III is used to explore the data structure in cases where the type of data is qualitative such as patterns of responses to questionnaire [26, 27]. It is similar to "correspondence analysis" and called "quantification method III" in Japan [27]. The method quantifies the categories and samples and reveals the interrelationships between the categories and samples [26, 27].

[11]There are five major sightseeing spots: Roadside Station Ine, Ferry Terminal, Ineura Park, Urashima Park, and Funaya Biyori. Funaya Biyori is a tourist exchange facility, built by Ine town, where restaurants are located. There is no Wi-Fi tracking sensor installed at this spot.

When organizing each type, characteristics were found regarding age, place visited, and length of stay. Firstly, Type 1 is tended to visit Ine's main attractions—the Roadside Station Ine and the Ferry Terminal—and there were many middle-aged and older couples. The time spent in the town was short, as there was not much travel to other tourist attractions in the town. Secondly, Type 2 was more likely to visit Urashima Park, which is a less visited spot in Ine town, than the other types. This tourist type was mostly in their 60s, and their stay was relatively long. Thirdly, Type 3 had a high percentage of visits to Ineura Park and its surrounding attractions, with a high number of young and middle-aged tourists. This type also had the longest stay in the town.

12.4.6   Understanding Tourist Movements Through a Combination of Wi-Fi Tracking Data and Other Data

The combination of the previous analysis' findings provides a more concrete interpretation of the movement patterns of Japanese tourists visiting Ine town during the summer season. Over 85% visitors to Ine town often stopped at the Roadside Station Ine and the Ferry Terminal, by car from the Roadside Station Kyotanba on the Kyoto Jukan Expressway. It was found that they had only visited the Roadside Station Ine and the Ferry Terminal and had moved on to other tourist attractions outside of Ine town. In addition, there was a difference in turnover and length of stay between the Inenura Park parking lot and the Shichimensan parking lot, which has strong ties to the Roadside Station Ine. At minimum, it could be deduced that the main users of the Shichimensan parking lot are Type 3 tourists who spend the most time in the town.

12.5   Conclusion

Comparing the population structures of tourist spots in Nagoya City in 2015, 2017, and 2019, it was observed that Nagoya Station and Sakae were most successful in attracting visitors of a relatively wider age range, especially women in their 20s. These areas could also have attracted visitors from a variety of distant regions. On the other hand, there were many men and women in their 30s and 40s near prefectures in Kinjo Wharf and the Port of Nagoya Public Aquarium.

   In this analysis, the data obtained from the Wi-Fi tracking sensor was used to understand the wide area travel routes of tourists with communication devices in the zone. We also combined data obtained from sensors in a town with parking lot usage data and survey data to reveal the movement patterns of different types of visitors. The analysis using tracking sensor data in combination with other data was useful. There is not much information to be acquired from the sensor. Therefore, the insight from the data on tourists and the surrounding environment was important to gain a concrete understanding of tourists' movement patterns. On the other hand, regarding protecting privacy—which is the biggest concern in the use of sensor data—analysis that directly conflicts with tourists' personal information should be avoided. From this perspective, we believe an analytical method that combines sensor data with other data is worthwhile.

This chapter first captured the number of visitors in tourist destinations and analyzed their attributes based on the statistical population data of mobile phones. Understanding visitors' characteristics will enable tourism businesses to optimize their services, which will in turn influence customer satisfaction.

However, it is difficult to obtain data in a narrow area such as a specific tourist facility because unnecessary data cannot be excluded. This study also demonstrated an alternative method to extract data in such areas and suggested using the Mobile Kukan Toukei and Wi-Fi tracking sensors depending on the situation.

12.6 Future Research

In the future, to examine the usefulness of sensor data, we would like to use data mining methods and analyze a combination of various data, such as tourists' comments on social media, tourism operators' sales data, and weather data.

It is also conceivable to use these mobile spatial statistics along with ICT services such as Google Trends to predict the number of new event customers. By using these with website access analysis, it is now possible to accurately predict the number of customers and attributes of travelers, which were previously difficult.

Yamamoto [25] demonstrated a regression analysis by connecting the Mobile Kukan Toukei and keyword search volume. The various interests of the tourists influence their keyword search before or during travel and ultimately emerge as some kind of trend in a specific keyword's search volume. The study also attempted cross-correlation analyses among them. As a result, a linear equation could be derived. These findings could lead to a model to forecast tourism demand in a destination.

A similar method can be adopted using the Wi-Fi tracking sensor. By performing statistical processing by associating changes in the keyword search volume in the search engine with data on the number of visitors and number of guests at the sightseeing spot, it will be possible to construct a more sophisticated tourism demand forecasting system.

Numerous events have recently been held to attract visitors to revitalize the economy in some areas in Japan where typhoons and regional heavy rains frequently occur. More accurate demand forecasting will make it possible to optimize the quantity of goods and number of non-regular employees necessary for holding events in advance.

Acknowledgments This work was supported by the Private University Research Branding Project.

The "Mobile Kukan Toukei™" and logo are trademarks of NTT DOCOMO, Inc.

References

1. Japan National Tourism Organization. (2020). *Statistics since 2003 visitor arrivals*. https://www.jnto.go.jp/jpn/statistics/since2003_visitor_arrivals.pdf. Accessed 5 July 2020.
2. The British Broadcasting Corporation. (2020). *Coronavirus 'could cost global economy $8.8tn' says ADB*. https://www.bbc.com/news/business-52671992. Accessed 5 July 2020.
3. The Wall Street Journal. (2020). *U.K. Economy shrank 20% in April as lockdown hit*. https://www.wsj.com/articles/u-k-economy-shrank-20-in-april-as-lockdown-hit-11591945270. Accessed 5 July 2020.
4. Kontogianni, A., & Alepis, E. (2020). Smart tourism: State of the art and literature review for the last six years. *Array, 6*, 100020. https://doi.org/10.1016/j.array.2020.100020.
5. Tripathy, A. K., Tripathy, P. K., Ray, N. K., & Mohanty, S. P. (2018). iTour: The future of smart tourism: An IoT framework for the independent mobility of tourists in smart cities. *IEEE Consumer Electronics Magazine, 7*(3), 32–37.
6. Tussyadiah, I. P., Jung, T. H., & tom Dieck, M. C. (2018). Embodiment of wearable augmented reality technology in tourism experiences. *Journal of Travel Research, 57*(5), 597–611.
7. Nitti, M., Pilloni, V., Giusto, D. D., & Popescu, V. (2017). IoT architecture for a sustainable tourism application in a smart city environment. *Mobile Information Systems*. https://doi.org/10.1155/2017/9201640.
8. Sun, Y., Song, H., Jara, A. J., & Bie, R. (2016). Internet of things and big data analytics for smart and connected communities. *IEEE*. https://doi.org/10.1109/ACCESS.2016.2529723.
9. Atembe, R. (2016). The use of smart technology in tourism: Evidence from wearable devices. *Journal of Tourism and Hospital Management*. https://doi.org/10.17265/2328-2169/2015.12.002.
10. Khallouki, H., Abatal, A., & Bahaj, M. (2018). An ontology-based context awareness for smart tourism recommendation system. May 2–5, 2018. In *Proceedings of the International Conference on Learning and Optimization Algorithms: Theory and Applications*, LOPAL, Rabat, Morocco, May 2018.
11. Lin, C., Liu, W., & Lu, Y. (2019). Three-dimensional internet-of-things deployment with optimal management service benefits for smart tourism services in forest recreation parks. *IEEE*. https://doi.org/10.1109/ACCESS.2019.2960212.
12. Gretzel, U., Sigala, M., Xiang, Z., & Koo, C. (2015). Smart tourism: Foundations and developments. *Electronic Markets, 25*(3), 179–188.
13. Ahas, R., Aasa, A., Roose, A., Mark, Ü., & Silm, S. (2008). Evaluating passive mobile positioning data for tourism surveys: An Estonian case study. *Tourism Management, 29*(3), 469–485.
14. Japan Tourism Agency. (2014). *Keitaidenwa Kara Erareru Ichijouhou Touwo Katuyoushita Hounichi Gaikokujin Doutaichousa Houkokusho* [Foreign visitors' dynamics research report utilizing mobile phone location information]. http://www.mlit.go.jp/common/001080545.pdf. Accessed 5 July 2020.
15. Liu, F., Janssens, D., Wets, G., & Cools, M. (2013). Annotating mobile phone location data with activity purposes using machine learning algorithms. *Expert Systems with Applications, 40*(8), 3299–3311.
16. Gao, H., & Liu, F. (2013). Estimating freeway traffic measures from mobile phone location data. *European Journal of Operational Research, 229*(1), 252–260.
17. Steenbruggen, J., Tranos, E., & Nijkamp, P. (2015). Data from mobile phone operators: A tool for smarter cities? *Telecommunications Policy, 39*(3–4), 335–346.

18. Li, J., Xu, L., Tang, L., et al. (2018). Big data in tourism research: A literature review. *Tourism Management, 68*, 301–323.
19. Shoval, N., & Ahas, R. (2016). The use of tracking technologies in tourism research: The first decade. *Tourism Geographies, 18*(5), 587–606.
20. Andión, J., Navarro, J., López, M., et al. (2018). *Smart behavioral analytics over a low-cost IoT Wi-Fi tracking real deployment.* https://doi.org/10.1155/2018/3136471. Accessed 24 Apr 2020.
21. Bonné, B., Barzan, A., Quax, P., et al. (2013). WiFiPi: Involuntary tracking of visitors at mass events. In *2013 IEEE 14th International Symposium on a World of Wireless*, Madrid, Spain, 4–7 June 2013.
22. Nunes, N., Ribeiro, M., Prandi, C., et al. (2017). *Beanstalk: A community based passive Wi-Fi tracking system for analysing tourism dynamics.* https://doi.org/10.1145/3102113.3102142. Accessed 24 Apr 2020.
23. Vanhoef, M., Matte, C., Cunche, M., et al. (2016). Why MAC address randomization is not enough: An analysis of Wi-Fi network discovery mechanisms. In *Proceedings of the 11th ACM on Asia Conference on Computer and Communications Security*, Xi'an, China, 30 May–3 June 2016.
24. Chilipirea, C., Petre, A. C., Dobre, C., et al. (2016, June). Presumably simple: Monitoring crowds using WiFi. In *2016 17th IEEE International Conference on Mobile Data Management*, Porto, Portugal, 13–16 June 2016.
25. Yamamoto, M. (2019). A regression analysis of trends in population changes in tourist destinations: Using keyword search volume and statistical population data. *Journal of Global Tourism Research, 4*(2), 99–109.
26. Hayashi, C. (1952). Prediction of phenomena from qualitative data and quantification of qualitative data. *Annals of the institute of statistical mathematics, 3*, 69–98.
27. Hayashi, C. (1992). Quantification method III or correspondence analysis in medical science. *Annals of Cancer Research and Therapy, 1*(1), 17–21.

Chapter 13
Use of UAVS, Computer Vision, and IOT for Traffic Analysis

**Paloma Peiro, Carlos Quiterio Gómez Muñoz,
and Fausto Pedro García Márquez**

Abstract One of the greatest needs today in road safety and its conservation work is to obtain traffic data in real time to predict traffic and increase safety of people. In this work, a camera embedded in an Unmanned Automatic Vehicle in static flight has been used to get information about traffic in a roundabout. These infrastructures are key since they are considered conflictive points in the circulation flow, and it is complex to analyze. A system has been developed to analyze images online and that obtains vehicle behavior data in real time. The system offers information such as vehicle count, their instantaneous speed at each moment, average speed of each one, individual trajectory, traffic density, lane changes, trouble spots, etc. The information provided by this system allows a better decision-making, increased security, improved traffic flow, and how to schedule maintenance tasks carried out by conservatives.

Keywords Internet of things · Traffic information · UAV · Drone · Computer vision · Roundabout

13.1 Introduction

Roads have a great impact on societies and economies. Many country policies consider the road safety as one of their main concerns. It influences social and economic aspects, because they allow connecting places and people, daily movements, transporting goods, etc. However, reducing traffic accidents in these infrastructures continues to be the main objective to be achieved. The World Health

P. Peiro · C. Q. Gómez Muñoz (✉)
Universidad Europea de Madrid, Villaviciosa de Odón, Spain
e-mail: CarlosQuiterio.Gomez@universidadeuropea.es

F. P. García Márquez
Ingenium Research Group, Castilla-La Mancha University, Ciudad Real, Spain
e-mail: FaustoPedro.Garcia@uclm.es

© Springer Nature Switzerland AG 2021
F. P. García Márquez, B. Lev (eds.), *Internet of Things*, International Series in
Operations Research & Management Science 305,
https://doi.org/10.1007/978-3-030-70478-0_13

Organization estimates that road crashes kill 1.25 million people yearly and 3400 road accidents per day [1, 2]. The increase in the road network and the number of vehicles (very diverse), the state of preservation of vehicles, the use of roads by very diverse users, and economic impositions are some of the factors that contribute to a potential increase in traffic accidents. Traffic accidents can happen for many reasons, but they usually occur when at least one of these factors fails: the human factor, the vehicle, and the road. In relation to the road, the objective of road safety is to improve them, increasing the protection of users, and try to eliminate accidents or at least reduce their severity [3–5]. In the last years, from the organisms in charge of road safety, computer vision research has been used together with the Internet of Things [6–8]. This field grows exponentially due to the multiple applications of implantation and the increase in processing capacity and power of current microprocessors. Machine learning is becoming an effective tool for identifying objects after proper training [9–15]. The use of classifiers and neural networks [16–23] allows to detect pre-established events such as accidents, sudden maneuvers, inadequate speeds, detection of infractions, etc.

Although the hardware for computer vision processes has come a long way in recent years and has lowered its costs, the current trend is to perform the heaviest processing in the cloud, so that latest technology hardware is not needed in the acquisition devices [24, 25]. This allows IoT devices to be simplified in sensors, basic pre-processing, power, and high-speed connection to the Internet. For example, in a self-contained car connected to the Internet using 5G, images from different cameras can be transmitted in real time, and a server (i.e., MEC, Multi-Access Edge Computing) analyzes those images at high speed. From these images, it could be determined if there is an obstacle on the road, if there are cyclists nearby, or to reduce human failure by detecting signs on the road. This technology is closely linked to the autonomous car, which can connect with other vehicles and obtain information from the structures through IoT.

13.1.1 Road Safety in the Roundabouts

The most important maneuver in the roundabouts is the insertion into the ring road. A vehicle must find a gap between the traffic of the ring road, which circulates at low speed, and then it must leave the same way without risking the safety of others. Of all possible intersections, roundabouts are the safest. These infrastructures allow the intersection of different roads while reducing the dangerous situations that can occur in other types of intersections. The severity of accidents that take place in roundabouts is lower compared to other accidents that occur in other types of intersections. However, the number of roundabout accidents has increased in recent years, with 8.2% of accidents with victims and 2.7% of fatalities [26]. Comparatively, motorcycles are the vehicles with the most accidents [27, 28]. In intercity roundabouts, where traffic speeds are higher than in urban roundabouts, the most common factor in an accident is loss of vehicle control at and within ring road access. This is generally due to driving at an inappropriate speed for road conditions (insufficient speed or, normally, excessive speed) [29]. Reasons that can lead to driving at this speed may be poor design of the roundabout and its accesses, poor visibility of the roundabout, or the behavior of the driver [30].

13.1.2 Accidents in Roundabouts

The most common types of accidents in roundabouts are [31]:

- The collision on the access road.
- The frontal-lateral collision between the vehicle that is incorporated and the one that is circulating on the ring road.
- The frontal-lateral collision between the vehicle that wants to exit the roundabout and the one that is circulating on the ring road.
- The side collision at accesses with more than one lane and on the circular lane derived from braiding movements (lane changes), which can be sudden, to locate in the lane most appropriate to the needs of each one.
- The departure of the track that may be due to excessive speed, sudden maneuvers, or the need to avoid an accident.
- The frontal collisions in the branches, between the vehicle that accesses the roundabout, and the one that leaves it.
- The fall on the road of two-wheeled vehicles.

13.1.3 Objectives with IoT for Traffic Analysis

In this chapter it is proposed a system that combines three technologies: UAV to obtain images of different infrastructures [32, 33], IoT with 5G connectivity to transmit data obtained by the UAV camera and telemetry, and computer vision to be performed on a cloud server that allow real-time processing [34–36].

In one hand, this would allow real-time information to be obtained from those infrastructures being inspected and to act quickly in case of detecting any anomaly on the road or accident. On the other hand, the behavior of drivers can be studied in real time, to improve decision-making, for example, anticipating traffic jams, enabling new lanes, or improving infrastructure and signaling. For this, the drone should be equipped with a video capture device, which, through IoT, sends the captured images to a server [37, 38]. It will be the server who is responsible for performing computer vision processing to extract useful information.

Artificial vision systems have evolved rapidly in recent years, reducing the cost of sensors and increasing their processing power. It is common to use recording cameras with image analysis and interpretation software for traffic control, toll management, knowledge of vehicle density in certain areas, or analysis of driver behavior in high-risk areas.

The objective of this work is to develop a system which allows, through the acquisition of images with Unmanned Automatic Vehicles (UAVs) and the use of computer vision techniques, to obtain traffic information in real time, helping decision-making to improve traffic. The system obtains the following information:

- **Vehicle tracking.**

  The system uses images taken with the camera of a UAV, and its algorithms allow to detect the vehicles and elements of interest, as well as the place they occupy at any time on the road. The main advantage is automatically having information of interest and being able to alert those responsible for traffic in certain situations if required.
- **Data of the trajectories followed by the vehicles with the lane changes.**

  The possibility of observing the trajectories of the vehicles with precision, in real time or afterward, offers multiple study possibilities. When a vehicle makes a strange path in a specific area, such as at an intersection or roundabout, it may be due to problems with the layout, signage, or existing speed limits.
- **Study of traffic density.**

  In order to determine the best traffic alternatives, it is essential to know the usual routes of drivers and when they take them. The objective is to perform an automated treatment of the images obtained from the camera of the UAV, controlling the vehicles that have passed by each road, the flow of routes, the most followed routes, and the most committed traffic violations.
- **Vehicle capacity.**

  The system replaces the manual counts carried out by field operators with very slow data processing and electromagnetic loops or loops located on the pavement that over time are expensive to maintain and do not end up giving accurate results. This system guarantees the recognition of moving vehicles and their real-time count.
- **Instantaneous speed and average speed of each vehicle.**

  The instantaneous speed of the vehicle is always indicated since it appears on the image. This data allows the study of the type of traffic in a roundabout. It is necessary to know the access, interior circulation, and exit speeds of the vehicles to make decisions about possible changes in layout or marking to increase safety. The average speed is collected and linked to the trajectory of each vehicle.
- **Obtaining visual data on vehicle behavior in different situations.**

  The system allows the generation of reports with graphs of statistical data. This allows to detect possible inefficiencies in the intersection roads, offering information on the fluidity of the intersection in real time.

13.2 Case Study and Experimental Setup

13.2.1 Description

A roundabout with the following characteristics has been chosen to carry out the study:

Dimensions
The roundabout has an internal diameter of 40 m (diameter of its central island) and an external diameter of 60 m. In roundabout design, if these distances are high, they can result in increased speed along the ring road. In this roundabout, the above values are adequate from the point of view of road safety.

Branch Lines
The number of branches is 4, being relatively equidistant from each other and with a good design: their axes pass approximately through the geometric center of the central island. Three of the branches allow entry and exit to the roundabout. The fourth branch only allows the roundabout exit. In addition, only one of the entrances has two lanes, and the other two entrances only have one lane (Fig. 13.1).

Number of Lanes
The ring road in the roundabout has two lanes, which is adequate since one of the access branches has two lanes. If all the branches had a single lane, the arrangement of two lanes on the ring road would be the source of possible conflicts in traffic.

Fig. 13.1 Direction of movement in the branches of the roundabout

13.2.2   Speed Control

The factors that determine the speed of circulation in a roundabout are the following:

- The geometry of the infrastructure.
- Dimensions and available space.
- Traffic density.
- Access speeds to the roundabout.
- Signage at the roundabout (traffic lights, etc.)

The goal of speed control is to facilitate drivers to enter through one branch and exit through another safely. In relation to the access speeds to the roundabout, a good design of the accesses to the ring road is very important. Furthermore, the angle between the trajectory of the vehicles entering the road and that of those driving on the ring road is important. For example, if the trajectory of the vehicles that access the ring road is tangent to the path through that ring road, access to high speeds is favored without respecting the priority of those who are already driving on the ring road. On the contrary, if it is very small, the insertion of vehicles into the ring road is difficult (Fig. 13.2).

On the other hand, the separating islands of the different direction of the branches improve the access path to the ring road of the roundabout. In this way, the speed of access to the roundabout is reduced, adapting to the new situation in which it is going to circulate.

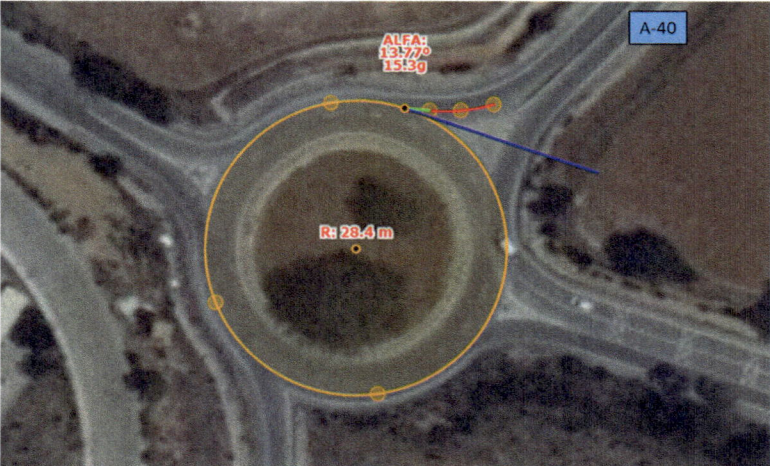

Fig. 13.2 Access angle from the branch

13.2.3   Hardware

The system hardware is divided into the ground system and the air system.

13.2.3.1   The Air System

The air system consists of a UAV that takes images and videos of the selected infrastructure at a suitable height for vehicle analysis according to the characteristics of the camera.

In this case, a Phantom 4 Advance UAV has been used. The Phantom 4 is a quadcopter of reduced dimensions, included in the weight category of less than 2 kg (Fig. 13.3). It has a high-definition camera with recording in 4 K format and transmission of images to the ground in HD. The camera is stabilized in three axes and is controllable by the pilot through the transmitter, aided by a screen or mobile device that shows the pilot images and telemetry in real time.

13.2.3.2   The Ground System

The ground system consists of a computer, which is responsible for performing image processing tasks. The computer is connected to the UAV to receive the HD images in real time and the telemetry. Furthermore, with the implementation of 5G, the system will be able to directly broadcast the HD image to a server and carry out the processing in the cloud. In this way, the end user could receive the results of each inspection directly on a computer or mobile device.

Other option that will be implemented in the future in this system is that the device connected to IoT is mounted on the drone, directly sending the images obtained by the camera of the UAV to the server using 5G, which would eliminate the need to transmit video to the ground, and it would send image with higher quality and less latency, something crucial in real-time processing.

Fig. 13.3 UAV Phantom 4 type

13.3   Methodology

The information obtained from the camera of the UAV can be divided into two groups: the information obtained from the infrastructure being studied and the information regarding the vehicles that are circulating through it.

13.3.1   Infrastructure Information

Images are acquired for several seconds, and an image software stabilization is carried out for the identification of the infrastructure parameters. Then, the median of the values of each pixel of each image is performed to obtain the background of the image without any vehicle appearing. Through the detection of circular shapes and prediction of missing contours, it is proceeded to search for circular or oval shapes. The inner contour of the roundabout is detected first. The external contour is detected by obtaining a concentric circumference whose radius is greater than the previous one and whose points coincide with the outer contours of the roundabout. Finally, dashed lines are searched between both perimeters to identify if there is more than one lane and determine it (Fig. 13.4).

Once the size in pixels of the diameters of each circumference is obtained, the size in pixels of the width of each lane is obtained. This distance in pixels is then transformed to meters by trigonometry using information from the height of the UAV, focal distance, and field of view. Knowing the size of each lane, the number of lanes each branch has is obtained.

Fig. 13.4 Lane detection inside the roundabout

13.3.2   Information of Moving Vehicles

Several methods are combined for the detection of vehicles:

- Subtract each frame from the previous one to detect the contours of moving objects.
- Subtract each frame of the image from the background of the infrastructure previously obtained.
- A Gaussian filter is used to eliminate noise, which are small pixels or objects whose area is less than a predetermined number of pixels.
- Blob analysis is performed to calculate statistics of detected objects (Fig. 13.5). That is, from the groups of pixels with a value of 1 (white) of the binary image, it is obtained the data (stored in matrices) of the centroid of the detected object, the bounding box, and the area [39].

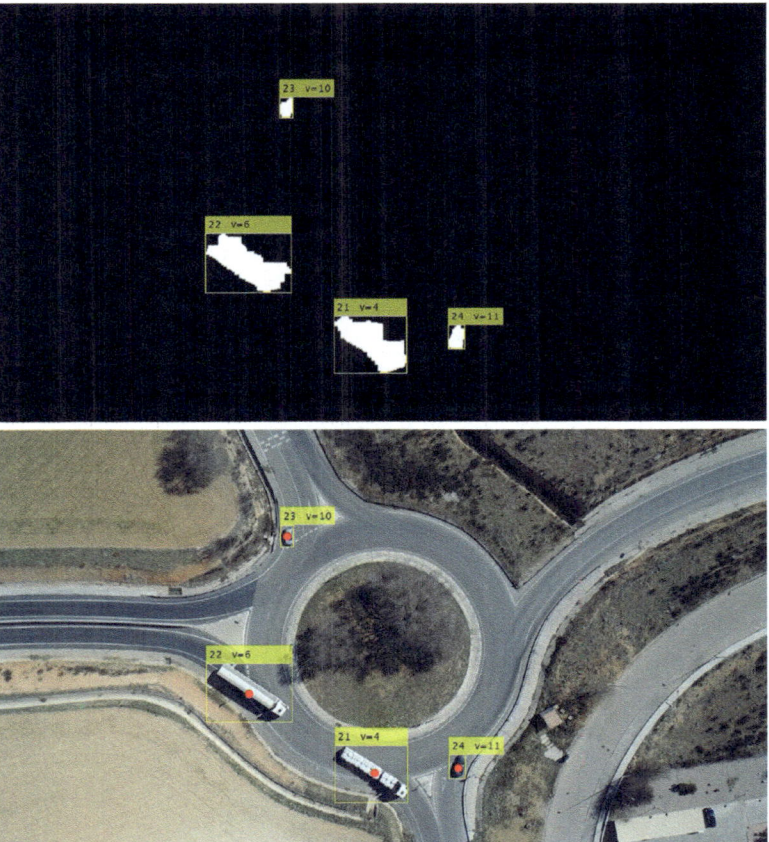

Fig. 13.5 Segmentation of vehicles moving in the roundabout

Once the moving objects are detected, the following information can be obtained:

- **Trajectory of each vehicle.**

    The centroid of each object is studied, and its displacement along the image is obtained using the Kalman filter to obtain the trajectory of each vehicle. The algorithm studies each detected object in a frame, evaluating the distance to all other objects in the previous frame. If the distance of any of the combinations is small enough, the points are connected and, therefore, form part of the path of the same object.

- **Instantaneous speed and average speed.**

    Information is available on all the centroids of each object and their displacement between different frames. With this information, the instantaneous speed of each object can be calculated. In this case, the distance in meters of each pixel has been calculated, which is 0.1718 m, and since the video has a rate of 30 frames per second, the speed of each vehicle can be calculated in real time, since it is detected until it exits the screen. Furthermore, by averaging this instantaneous speed with the instantaneous speeds of previous frames of this same object, the average speed of each vehicle can be obtained.

- **Vehicle size.**

    The system can differentiate between the sizes of several vehicles. It has been dimensioned to distinguish between heavy vehicles, passenger cars, and motorcycles. To make this differentiation, the area (in number of pixels) of the detected object is analyzed and classified according to limits. Since the number of pixels varies in each frame and in some cases the object could change category, the accumulated mean of the area is used for each object.

- **Vehicle count.**

    The vehicle count is performed after checking that the detected object corresponds to a moving vehicle. A new vehicle number is assigned to each object that appears new on the screen and meets the requirements to be detected as a new vehicle. The vehicle number is indicated next to the drawing of its trajectory and its bounding box.

- **Study of traffic density.**

    To study the traffic density, all the paths obtained during the analysis are superimposed, and the areas with a greater number of overlapping paths are detected. It is indicated below which is the entrance and the exit that correspond to that trajectory with more overlaps to obtain relevant traffic indications. The superposition of the paths as a function of time is studied and provides an objective information of the traffic density in each segment of the roundabout.

Fig. 13.6   Tracing of the trajectory 1 analysis of sections that cross the lines

13.4   Results

The initial step to improve the road safety is to obtain relevant information on the habits of drivers in traffic and the influx of traffic in certain time zones. This information about traffic in roundabout is shown below, and it allows, after analysis, to make decisions and improve circulation by implementing measures such as improving infrastructure or add new signs. After data collection and image processing, the system can output the following information related to traffic status.

13.4.1   Analysis of Trajectories

13.4.1.1   Trajectory 1

The trajectory of each vehicle through the displacement of its centroid is obtained and compared with the information obtained from the infrastructure. In the first case study, the trajectory was carried out correctly, both at the entrance and at the exit of the roundabout (Fig. 13.6).

There are two areas where the path cuts the lane lines. This happens because the centroid of the vehicle moves when considering the shadow of the vehicle as an object of the same vehicle. It can be seen in Fig. 13.7.

Fig. 13.7 Centroid of object is deviated due to inclusion of its shadow in segmentation

Fig. 13.8 Tracing of the trajectory 2 (*blue*) and correct path (*green*)

13.4.1.2 Trajectory 2

The path would be incorrect because the path of the vehicle (blue line) crosses the outer lane immediately upon entering the roundabout. And it leaves the roundabout from the inside lane without first moving outside long enough before departure. With these abrupt lane changes in case of coinciding with more vehicles, it would cut off all vehicles that circulate in the outer lane. The correct path would be the green one (Fig. 13.8).

Fig. 13.9 Tracing of the trajectory 3 and sudden exit of the roundabout analysis

13.4.1.3 Trajectory 3

Correct trajectory at the beginning, but the change of lane from the interior to the exterior does not take place sufficiently before departure (Fig. 13.9).

13.4.1.4 Trajectory 4

Correct trajectory regarding the use of the lanes. When the vehicle enters in the roundabout, it leaves the limits of the lane. When studying the video, it is observed that the vehicle is a truck, so it is possible that this maneuver is to adjust the necessary entry angle due to its length. In the case of heavy vehicles, it has been chosen to include a 25% tolerance to compensate for their openings in the maneuvers (Fig. 13.10).

13.4.1.5 Trajectory 5

Incorrect path. The vehicle joins the inner lane of the roundabout to exit at the first exit. In a short space of time, it interrupts the traffic of the outer lane of the roundabout twice without the anticipation necessary to maintain security (Fig. 13.11). The shape of this layout is due to the high speed that the vehicle takes both on the approach to the roundabout and on the exit. Considering that the speed limit is 40 km/h, it is calculated that the instantaneous speed of the vehicle has always been higher, obtaining an average speed of 51 km/h.

Fig. 13.10 Tracing of the trajectory 4

Fig. 13.11 Tracing of the trajectory 5

13.4.2 Analysis of Average Speeds

The average speeds of each vehicle are indicated with the trajectory, next to the track number and the vehicle number. This average speed is calculated from the appearance of the vehicle on the screen until its departure. The speed limit of the roundabout and the three sections of road leading to it is 40 km/h. This information can vary greatly if the vehicle stops for yielding the passage with respect to another that does not stop. The roundabout has four legs. Three of them enter and exit and a fourth only exit. Due to the location of this roundabout, the intersecting roads have

Table 13.1 Average speed for each branch of the roundabout and type of vehicle

	Average speed		Access from A-40		Access from A-3		Access from NIIIa	
Type	(m/s)	(km/h)	(m/s)	(km/h)	(m/s)	(km/h)	(m/s)	(km/h)
Passenger cars	9.46	34.06	6.00	21.6	10.40	37.44	10.45	37.62
Heavy vehicles	6.52	23.49	7.10	25.56	6.00	21.60	5.90	21.24

Fig. 13.12 Trajectory and instantaneous speed of the vehicles detected on the screen

very different traffic, but with the security measures in place to reduce the speed of vehicles from all roads, enter the roundabout and drive for it with similar speeds. Table 13.1 shows the average speed for each type of vehicle and branch.

13.4.3 Analysis of Instantaneous Speeds

Moving vehicles are detected, showing in real time their instantaneous speed in meters per second. For them, the displacement in pixels between the same object in two consecutive frames is studied and is divided by the elapsed time between frames (Fig. 13.12).

This instantaneous speed data reflects the type of actual driving that is taking place in the roundabout. The speed of access to a roundabout, the speed inside it, and the exit speed of the roundabout can be calculated and analyzed. To obtain this instantaneous speed and not obtain data on when the vehicle is stationary, two zones have been distinguished. The first is that of the three entrances and the second is inside the roundabout. Table 13.2 shows the vehicle speeds in the access area to the roundabout.

Table 13.2 Vehicle speeds in the access areas to the roundabout

Type	Access from A-40		Access from A-3		Access from NIIIa	
	(m/s)	(km/h)	(m/s)	(km/h)	(m/s)	(km/h)
Passenger cars	15.00	54.00	11.00	39.60	8.50	30.6
Heavy vehicles	12.30	44.40	4.00	14.40	3.00	10.80

Table 13.3 Vehicle speeds in the ring lane of the roundabout

	Speed inside the roundabout	
	(m/s)	(km/h)
Passenger cars	9.20	33.12
Heavy vehicles	6.25	22.50

The highest speeds are collected by access from the A-40 since this motorway ends at the roundabout without previous bifurcations or route variations that require slowing down. The circulation through the access from the A-3 meets the maximum speed limits. The exit of the A-3 has a long deceleration lane and a curved path that requires compliance with the required speed. Access from the N-III also complies with the speed limit, being a two-way highway with slower traffic due to heavy vehicle traffic from an industrial estate. In addition, the analysis of the speed through the interior of the roundabout has been studied by dividing the mobile fleet into passenger cars and heavy vehicles (Table 13.3).

The results correspond to what was expected in both cases. It has been detected that the average speed of circulation inside the roundabout is below the maximum speed limit of 40 km/h. Few cases are detected that exceed this limit in the recording time of test videos.

13.4.4 Vehicle Counting and Classification

The vehicle count is performed after verifying that the detected object corresponds to a moving vehicle and the vehicle track is created with the collected information (Fig. 13.13).

To classify the vehicles, the area in pixels of the segmented objects is determined, due to the difference in area between motorcycles, cars, and trucks. This method only works for a specific flight height. This approach will be enhanced by implementing deep learning and object recognition techniques to increase the robustness of the system.

The traffic map data indicates that less than 3023 vehicles/day/lane should enter the roundabout on the A-40, of which 8% are heavy vehicles. Extrapolating the data obtained throughout the duration of the video, 3421 vehicles/day/lane would be obtained, of which 20% are heavy vehicles [40].

Fig. 13.13 Count of the number of vehicles that appear in the image in a period

Fig. 13.14 Overlapping of different trajectories over time

13.4.5 Traffic Density Analysis

Uniting all the trajectories obtained in a certain time, the traffic density or intensity is displayed, and it is possible to detect which sections have the highest traffic intensity. If this process is applied in a period of time in which traffic increases or retentions are created, it can be observed where the flow of vehicles is heading, thus being able to implement additional traffic management measures to improve those intensity peaks (Fig. 13.14).

Fig. 13.15 Marking of areas where drivers often cross the continuous lines

Figure 13.15 shows the trajectories of ten vehicles. It is possible to differentiate the zones and lanes of more affluence. The behavior of drivers is also reflected in these images, detecting a tendency in all vehicles to cut the angle of entry to the roundabout from the A-40 and to cut back on the exit by the N-III. The preservation of roads in this area should increase containment measures to increase traffic safety at this access and at this exit.

13.4.6 Trouble Spots Inside the Roundabout

In the roundabouts the main trouble spots are produced by the crossing of paths. Figure 13.16 shows the critical points of the roundabout. Although not all possible trajectories appear, all of them have been considered.

Once the analysis of the data thrown by the system has been carried out, it is concluded that:

- Drivers tend to perform the maneuver poorly when there is little traffic at the roundabout, and they tend to travel at higher speeds, passing from one lane to another without signaling early enough.
- Access to the roundabout from motorways occurs at a higher speed, causing more sudden decelerations or more pronounced lane crossings. This could be solved with better signaling and the implementation of sound bumps near the roundabout.

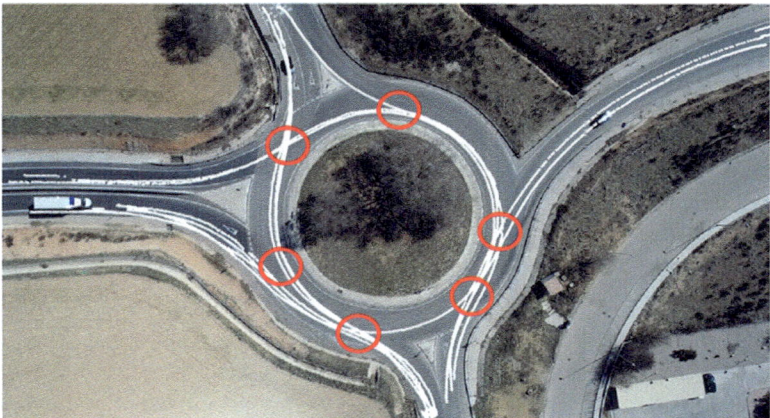

Fig. 13.16 Detection of confluences and bifurcations in the paths that indicate points where the risk of accident increases

13.5 Conclusions

The objective of this work has been to develop a system based on the Internet of Things that allows through UAV recordings to improve the circulation and safety of road traffic, offering different easy and intuitive tools:

- Vehicle tracking.
- Data of the paths followed by the vehicles with the braiding movements made.
- Study of the traffic density that allows its characterization.
- Vehicle capacity.
- Instantaneous speed and average speed of each vehicle.
- Obtaining visual data on vehicle behavior in different situations.

With the implementation of 5G, it is expected that the UAV can transmit the images and telemetry directly to a server in the cloud, where all the processing will take place. Recordings of the traffic that circulates in the roundabout under study have been made with a UAV in static flight from 120 m located on the vertical axis of the central ring of the ring road.

The tracking of objects from the application is carried out mainly in three very different stages:

- Object detection, frame by frame, differentiating them through a binary mask. Elimination of noise and failed detections with a Gaussian filter. Data storage of detections with a Blob analysis.
- Adjustment of detection sensitivity. Identification of the different detections through the frames of the same object with a Kalman filter.
- Repeat through all frames assigning new detections and showing results.

After data collection and execution of the videos obtained, a basic road safety analysis has been carried out that immediately and visually allows us to deduce the type of traffic and the behavior of users on the ring road as well as on the accesses to the same. The critical points of the roundabout have been identified, the common paths and errors have been analyzed, the braiding movements have been identified, the access speeds and interior circulation have been compiled, and the traffic intensities in the different lanes, both access and exit, have been studied., interiors to the roundabout.

The work has been concluded with results to be considered in view of possible improvements focused on the security of the roundabout:

- Of the trajectories 70% are partially correct. Access and movement in lanes inside are adequate, but there are usually errors in the path at the entrances or exits, as well as short notice in changing lanes from inside to outside the circular ring. Only 28% of the trajectories can be considered completely correct.
- The maximum speed limit for traffic inside the roundabout is met almost in all vehicles. However, the speed limit is not met in the areas near the accesses to the roundabout.
- The vehicle capacity corresponds to the total "average daily intensity" expected for 2019 in the access of the A-40, not meeting the balance of heavy vehicles.

The results obtained have been validated with the current traffic and layout regulations in order to guarantee their validity and validity. It has been validated that the system created constitutes a quick and intuitive tool that allows obtaining specific data for the road analysis of traffic. This information can be very useful for road maintenance companies and to obtain statistical studies. One of the future lines is to create a fleet of autonomous UAVs that inspect different critical points. In this way, it will be possible to analyze traffic data from different conflict points of the road network and improve decision-making work for its maintenance or increase in security and containment elements.

References

1. Wegman, F. (2017). The future of road safety: A worldwide perspective. *IATSS Research, 40,* 66–71.
2. Peden, M., Scurfield, R., Sleet, D., Mohan, D., Hyder, A. A., Jarawan, E., & Mathers, C. D. (2004). *World report on road traffic injury prevention.* Geneva: World Health Organization.
3. Pliego Marugán, A., Garcia Marquez, F. P., & Lev, B. (2017). Optimal decision-making via binary decision diagrams for investments under a risky environment. *International Journal of Production Research, 55,* 5271–5286.
4. Pliego Marugan, A., & Garcia Marquez, F. P. (2016). A novel approach to diagnostic and prognostic evaluations applied to railways: A real case study. *Proceedings of the Institution of Mechanical Engineers, Part F: Journal of Rail and Rapid Transit, 230,* 1440–1456.
5. García Márquez, F. P., Segovia Ramírez, I., & Pliego Marugán, A. (2019). Decision making using logical decision tree and binary decision diagrams: A real case study of wind turbine manufacturing. *Energies, 12,* 1753.

6. Meidan, Y., Bohadana, M., Shabtai, A., Guarnizo, J. D., Ochoa, M., Tippenhauer, N. O., & Elovici, Y. (2017). Profiliot: A machine learning approach for IoT device identification based on network traffic analysis. In *Proceedings of the symposium on applied computing*, pp. 506–509.
7. Sadeghian, O., Moradzadeh, A., Mohammadi-Ivatloo, B., Abapour, M., & Garcia Marquez, F. P. (2020). Generation units maintenance in combined heat and power integrated systems using the mixed integer quadratic programming approach. *Energies, 13*, 2840.
8. García Márquez, F. P., Segovia Ramírez, I., Mohammadi-Ivatloo, B., & Marugán, A. P. (2020). Reliability dynamic analysis by fault trees and binary decision diagrams. *Information, 11*, 324.
9. Arcos Jiménez, A., Gómez Muñoz, C. Q., & García Márquez, F. P. (2018). Machine learning for wind turbine blades maintenance management. *Energies, 11*, 13.
10. Gómez, C., García, F., Arcos, A., Cheng, L., Kogia, M., Mohimi, A., & Papaelias, M. (2017). A heuristic method for detecting and locating faults employing electromagnetic acoustic transducers. *Eksploatacja i Niezawodność, 19*, 493.
11. Gómez, C. Q., Villegas, M. A., García, F. P., & Pedregal, D. J. (2016). Big data and web intelligence for condition monitoring: A case study on wind turbines. In *Big data: Concepts, methodologies, tools, and applications* (pp. 1295–1308). Hershey: IGI Global.
12. Gómez Muñoz, C. Q., Arcos Jiménez, A., García Márquez, F. P., Kogia, M., Cheng, L., Mohimi, A., & Papaelias, M. (2018). Cracks and welds detection approach in solar receiver tubes employing electromagnetic acoustic transducers. *Structural Health Monitoring, 17*, 1046–1055.
13. Jiménez, A. A., Márquez, F. P. G., Moraleda, V. B., & Muñoz, C. Q. G. (2019). Linear and nonlinear features and machine learning for wind turbine blade ice detection and diagnosis. *Renewable Energy, 132*, 1034–1048.
14. Jiménez, A. A., Muñoz, C. Q. G., & Márquez, F. P. G. (2019). Dirt and mud detection and diagnosis on a wind turbine blade employing guided waves and supervised learning classifiers. *Reliability Engineering & System Safety, 184*, 2–12.
15. Gómez Muñoz, C. Q., García Marquez, F. P., Hernandez Crespo, B., & Makaya, K. (2019). Structural health monitoring for delamination detection and location in wind turbine blades employing guided waves. *Wind Energy, 22*, 698–711.
16. Jiménez, A. A., Muñoz, C. Q. G., Marquez, F. P. G., & Zhang, L. (2017). Artificial intelligence for concentrated solar plant maintenance management. In *Proceedings of the tenth international conference on management science and engineering management* (pp. 125–134). Springer.
17. Muñoz, C. Q. G., Marquez, F. P. G., Lev, B., & Arcos, A. (2017). New pipe notch detection and location method for short distances employing ultrasonic guided waves. *Acta Acustica United with Acustica, 103*, 772–781.
18. Muñoz, C. Q. G., Marquez, F. P. G., Liang, C., Maria, K., Abbas, M., & Mayorkinos, P. (2015). A new condition monitoring approach for maintenance management in concentrate solar plants. In *Proceedings of the ninth international conference on management science and engineering management* (pp. 999–1008). Springer.
19. Muñoz, C. Q. G., Márquez, F. P. G., & Tomás, J. M. S. (2016). Ice detection using thermal infrared radiometry on wind turbine blades. *Measurement, 93*, 157–163.
20. Ramirez, I. S., Muñoz, C. Q. G., & Marquez, F. P. G. (2017). A condition monitoring system for blades of wind turbine maintenance management. In *Proceedings of the tenth international conference on management science and engineering management* (pp. 3–11). Springer.
21. García Marquez, F. P., & Gómez Muñoz, C. Q. (2020). A new approach for fault detection, location and diagnosis by ultrasonic testing. *Energies, 13*, 1192.
22. Jiménez, A. A., Zhang, L., Muñoz, C. Q. G., & Márquez, F. P. G. (2020). Maintenance management based on machine learning and nonlinear features in wind turbines. *Renewable Energy, 146*, 316–328.
23. Pliego Marugán, A., & García Márquez, F. P. (2019). Advanced analytics for detection and diagnosis of false alarms and faults: A real case study. *Wind Energy, 22*, 1622–1635.

24. Garcia Marquez, F. P., Pliego Marugan, A., Pinar Perez, J. M., Hillmansen, S., & Papaelias, M. (2017). Optimal dynamic analysis of electrical/electronic components in wind turbines. *Energies, 10*, 1111.
25. Gomez, C. Q., Garcia, F. P., Arcos, A., Cheng, L., Kogia, M., & Papelias, M. (2017). Calculus of the defect severity with EMATs by analysing the attenuation curves of the guided waves. *Smart Structures and Systems, 19*, 195–202.
26. LA ASOCIACIÓN, T.D.C.Y.; LAS INFRAESTRUCTURAS, V.E. Monográfico n°.
27. Arndt, O., & Troutbeck, R. J. (1998). Relationship between roundabout geometry and accident rates. *Transportation Research Circular, 28*, 21–16.
28. Kamla, J., Parry, T., & Dawson, A. (2016). Roundabout accident prediction model: Random-parameter negative binomial approach. *Transportation Research Record, 2585*, 11–19.
29. Martínez-Falero, V. V. (2013). Conservación y gestión. *Rutas: Revista de la Asociación Técnica de Carreteras, 46*–55. http://www.tpfingenieria.com/images/pdfs/MONOGRAFICO2013.pdf
30. Chen, Y., Persaud, B., Sacchi, E., & Bassani, M. (2013). Investigation of models for relating roundabout safety to predicted speed. *Accident Analysis & Prevention, 50*, 196–203.
31. Xiqués Triquell, J. (2016). *Variables definitorias de las glorietas y su incorporación a las especialidades científicas* (Doctoral thesis). Universitat Politècnica de Catalunya.
32. Gonzalo, A. P., Marugán, A. P., & Márquez, F. P. G. (2020). Survey of maintenance management for photovoltaic power systems. *Renewable and Sustainable Energy Reviews, 134*, 110347.
33. Márquez, F. P. G., & Chacón, A. M. P. (2020). A review of non-destructive testing on wind turbines blades. *Renewable Energy, 161*, 998–1010.
34. Márquez, F. P. G., & Ramírez, I. S. (2019). Condition monitoring system for solar power plants with radiometric and thermographic sensors embedded in unmanned aerial vehicles. *Measurement, 139*, 152–162.
35. Marugán, A. P., Chacón, A. M. P., & Márquez, F. P. G. (2019). Reliability analysis of detecting false alarms that employ neural networks: A real case study on wind turbines. *Reliability Engineering & System Safety, 191*, 106574.
36. Herraiz, Á. H., Marugán, A. P., & Márquez, F. P. G. (2020). Photovoltaic plant condition monitoring using thermal images analysis by convolutional neural network-based structure. *Renewable Energy, 153*, 334–348.
37. Marquez, F. G. (2006). An approach to remote condition monitoring systems management. In *2006 IET international conference on railway condition monitoring* (pp. 156–160). IET.
38. Márquez, F. P. G. (2010). A new method for maintenance management employing principal component analysis. *Structural Durability & Health Monitoring, 6*, 89.
39. Chen, T.-H., Lin, Y.-F., & Chen, T.-Y. (2007). Intelligent vehicle counting method based on blob analysis in traffic surveillance. In *Second international conference on innovative computing, information and control (ICICIC 2007)* (p. 238). IEEE.
40. Transportes, M.d.F.S.d.E.d.I.y. (2017). *Mapa de tráfico*. Madrid, Spain: Red de Carreteras del Estado.

Index

A

Activity recognition, 195–196
Activity-travel behavior, 255
Advanced data management systems (ADMS), 230
Advanced Traveller Information Systems (ATIS), 229
Al Janabi model
  illiquid market conditions, 172
  liquidity scaling factor, 172
  L-VaR, 169
  machine learning iteration process, 173
  market and asset liquidity risks, 168
  proposed machine learning, 170
  re-engineered and novel machine learning, 169
  robust modeling algorithms, 169
  short-cut approach, 171
  square root-*t* approach, 170
  threshold, 169
  VaR models, 168
Alzheimer's disease, 123
Amanohashidate, 264
Ambient Assisted Living (AAL) services
  activity, 218
  activity recognition, 212–213
  basic services
    activity recognition, 195–196
    localization, 196
    posture recognition, 196
    predictive services, 196–197
  biosensors, 218
  body posture, 218
  caregivers, 195, 217
  context awareness, 197–198
  definition, 202–203
  environmental information, 200
  heterogeneity, 203
  information (*see* Contextual information)
  physical environmental data, 200–201
  social environment, 201
  spatial information, 202
  temporal information, 201–202
  context modelling
    comparison, 211, 214, 216
    data-driven, 207–209
    hybrid, 209–211
    knowledge, 203–207
  definition, 193
  fall detection, 213
  fall recognition, 218
  goals, 193
  indoor, 194
  inhabitants, 193–194, 215–216, 219–220
  nature of data, 217
  posture recognition, 213
  predictive services, 214, 219
  temporal reasoning, 219
  visual sensors, 218
Analytic machine learning, 50
ARIMA, *see* Autoregressive integrated moving average (ARIMA)
Asset liquidity modeling approach, 159
ATIS, *see* Advanced Traveller Information Systems (ATIS)
Automatic vehicle detection systems (AVDS), 229

Printed by Printforce, the Netherlands